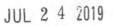

P9-DCW-774

Get Updates and More on Nolo.com

Go to this book's companion page at:

www.nolo.com/back-of-book/RET.html

When there's an important change to the law affecting this book, we'll post updates. You'll also find articles and other related materials.

More Resources from Nolo.com

Legal Forms, Books, & Software
Hundreds of do-it-yourself products—all written in plain English, approved, and updated by our in-house legal editors.

Legal Articles
Get informed with thousands of free articles on everyday legal topics. Our articles are accurate, up to date, and reader friendly.

Find a Lawyer
Want to talk to a lawyer? Use Nolo to find a lawyer who can help you with your case.

⚖ NOLO **The Trusted Name**
(but don't take our word for it)

"In Nolo you can trust."
THE NEW YORK TIMES

"Nolo is always there in a jam as the nation's premier publisher of do-it-yourself legal books."
NEWSWEEK

"Nolo publications…guide people simply through the how, when, where and why of the law."
THE WASHINGTON POST

"[Nolo's]…material is developed by experienced attorneys who have a knack for making complicated material accessible."
LIBRARY JOURNAL

"When it comes to self-help legal stuff, nobody does a better job than Nolo…"
USA TODAY

"The most prominent U.S. publisher of self-help legal aids."
TIME MAGAZINE

"Nolo is a pioneer in both consumer and business self-help books and software."
LOS ANGELES TIMES

14th Edition

IRAs, 401(k)s & Other Retirement Plans

Strategies for Taking Your Money Out

Twila Slesnick, PhD, Enrolled Agent
& Attorney John C. Suttle, CPA

FOURTEENTH EDITION	JUNE 2019
Editor	BETH LAURENCE
Cover Design	SUSAN PUTNEY
Production	SUSAN PUTNEY
Proofreading	ROBERT WELLS
Index	ACCESS POINTS INDEXING
Printing	BANG PRINTING

ISSN 2377-2441 (print)
ISSN 2377-2492 (online)

ISBN 978-1-4133-2637-6 (pbk)
ISBN 978-1-4133-2638-3 (ebook)

This book covers only United States law, unless it specifically states otherwise.

Please note

We believe accurate, plain-English legal information should help you solve many of your own legal problems. But this text is not a substitute for personalized advice from a knowledgeable lawyer. If you want the help of a trained professional—and we'll always point out situations in which we think that's a good idea—consult an attorney licensed to practice in your state.

Acknowledgments

Thanks to Nolo editor Robin Leonard for her intelligent and skillful editing of the first edition—and for adding a dose of levity to the entire process. For multitudes of subsequent editions, thanks to Nolo editor Amy DelPo for her keen eye and clear thinking. She smoothed the way for editors to come and permanently endeared herself to the authors. Most recently, the arduous task of editing a book about retirement plans has fallen to JinAh Lee, Lisa Guerin, and Beth Laurence, all of whom have proved themselves more than capable of assuming the mantle.

About the Authors

Twila Slesnick, PhD, Enrolled Agent

Twila specializes in tax and investment planning for retirees and prospective retirees. She also provides pension plan consulting to individuals and small businesses. She has conducted numerous seminars throughout the United States in the areas of retirement and tax planning. Twila has been featured on television and radio programs across the country and in publications including *Money Magazine, U.S. News & World Report, The Wall Street Journal, Kiplinger's, Newsweek*, and *Consumer Reports*. Twila has a Bachelor's, Master's, and PhD, all from the University of California, Berkeley. She lives in Colorado.

John C. Suttle, CPA, Attorney

John has been practicing law since 1980. His law practice, Suttle, Goh & Barber, LLP, consists of estate and trust planning, probate administration, tax and business counseling, retirement planning under ERISA, and representing clients before the IRS and other taxing authorities. He has been a tax practitioner since 1974. John is a graduate of Stanford University (BA), University of California's Haas School of Business (MBA), and Hastings College of the Law (JD). He lives in Atherton, California.

Table of Contents

Appendixes

Your Retirement Companion

L et's start with the basics. There are many kinds of retirement plans and many possible sources for owning one. This book is about how to take money out of your retirement plans.

You might have a retirement plan at work, an IRA that you set up yourself, or a plan or an IRA you've inherited. Or you might have all three. You might still be contributing to a plan, or you may be retired. No matter what your situation, you will find information in this book to help you through the minefield of rules.

There are many reasons to take money out of a retirement plan. You might want to borrow the money for an emergency and pay it back (or not). Maybe you quit your job and you want to take your share of the company's plan. Perhaps you're required by law to withdraw some of your retirement funds because you've reached a certain age.

Whatever your situation, you probably have a lot of questions about your plan and how to take money out of it. This book can answer:

- How do I know what kind of retirement plan I have? (See Chapter 1.)
- Do I have to wait until I retire to get money out of my plan or my IRA? (See Chapter 3.)
- Can I borrow money from my 401(k) plan to buy a house? (See Chapters 3, 4, and 5.)
- What should I do with my retirement plan when I leave my company or retire? (See Chapter 2.)
- When do I have to start taking money out of my IRA? (See Chapter 5.)
- How do I calculate how much I have to take? (See Chapter 6.)
- Can I take more than the required amount? (See Chapter 6.)
- What happens to my retirement plan when I die? (See Chapters 7 and 8.)

- Can my spouse roll over my IRA when I die? (See Chapters 7 and 8.)
- What about my children? Can they put my IRA in their names after I die? Do they have to take all the money out of the account right away? (See Chapters 7 and 8.)
- If I inherit a retirement plan, can I add my own money to it? Can I save it for my own children, if I don't need the money? (See Chapters 7 and 8.)
- Am I allowed to set up a Roth IRA? Should I? (See Chapter 9.)
- Can I convert my regular IRA to a Roth IRA? Should I? (See Chapter 9.)
- How is a Roth 401(k) plan different from a Roth IRA? (See Chapter 10.)

To help you answer these and other questions, we include many examples to guide you through the decision-making process and take you through calculations. You will also find sample tax forms that the IRS requires, along with instructions for how to complete them.

This book contains tables to help you calculate distributions. It also contains sample letters and worksheets you can use to communicate with the IRS or with the custodian of your IRA or retirement plan. We've even included some important IRS notices so you can read firsthand how the IRS thinks about certain critical issues.

The tax rules for pensions, IRAs, 401(k)s, and other types of retirement plans are notoriously complex, which can be all the more frustrating because they are important to so many people. The good news is that help is here: This book makes the rules clear and accessible.

Get Updates and More Online

When there are important changes to the information in this book, we'll post updates online, on a page dedicated to this book:

www.nolo.com/back-of-book/RET.html

You'll find other useful information there, too, including author blogs, podcasts, and videos.

Types of Retirement Plans

Who Should Read Chapter 1

Read this chapter if you aren't certain which types of retirement plans you have, either through your employer or as a self-employed person. Also read this chapter if you have an IRA but aren't sure which type.

How many people have warned you that you'll never see a penny of the hard-earned money you've poured into the Social Security system and that you'd better have your own retirement nest egg tucked away somewhere? Perhaps those doomsayers are overstating the case, but even if you eventually do collect Social Security, it is likely to provide only a fraction of the income you will need during retirement.

Congress responded to this problem several decades ago by creating a variety of tax-favored plans to help working people save for retirement. One such plan is set up by you, the individual taxpayer, and is appropriately called an individual retirement account or IRA. Another, which can be established by your employer or by you if you are self-employed, is referred to by the nondescript phrase "a qualified plan." A qualified plan is one that qualifies to receive certain tax benefits as described in Section 401 of the U.S. tax code.

There are other types of retirement plans, too, which enjoy some of the same tax benefits as qualified plans but are not technically qualified because they are defined in a different section of the tax code. Many of these other plans closely follow the qualified plan rules, however. The most common of these almost-qualified plans are tax-deferred annuities (TDAs) and qualified annuity plans. (Don't be thrown by the name. Even though it may be called a qualified annuity plan, it is not defined in Section 401 and, therefore, is not a qualified plan in the purest sense.) Both of these plans are defined in Section 403 of the tax code. Because many of the rules in Section 403 are similar to those in Section 401, TDAs and qualified annuity plans are often mentioned in the same breath with qualified plans.

All qualified plans, TDAs, and qualified annuity plans have been sweetened with breaks for taxpayers to encourage them to save for retirement.

Helpful Terms

Adjusted gross income (AGI). Total taxable income reduced by certain expenses, such as qualified plan contributions, IRA contributions, and alimony payments.

Beneficiary. The person or entity entitled to receive the benefits from an insurance policy or from trust property, such as a retirement plan or an IRA.

Deductible contribution. A contribution to a retirement plan that an employer may claim as a business expense to offset income on the employer's tax return. You may know it as simply the employer's contribution. In the case of an IRA, a deductible contribution is one that an individual taxpayer may use to offset income on the individual's tax return.

Distribution. A payout of property (such as shares of stock) or cash from a retirement plan or an IRA to the participant or a beneficiary.

Earned income. Income received for providing goods or services. Earned income might be wages or salary or net profit from a business.

Eligible employee. An employee who qualifies to participate in the employer's plan because he or she has met the eligibility requirements (such as having worked for the employer for a specified number of years).

Nondeductible contribution. A contribution to a retirement plan or an IRA that may not be claimed as a business expense or used as an adjustment to offset taxable income on an income tax return.

Nondiscrimination rules. The provisions in the U.S. tax code that prohibit certain retirement plans from providing greater benefits to highly compensated employees than to other employees.

Participant or active participant. An employee for whom the employer makes a contribution to the employer's retirement plan.

Tax-deductible expense. An item of expense that may be used to offset income on a tax return.

Tax deferral. The postponement of tax payments until a future year.

Vested benefit. The portion of a participant's retirement plan accumulation that a participant may keep after leaving the employer who sponsors the plan; or the portion that goes to a participant's beneficiary if the participant dies.

And working people have saved, often stretching as far as they can to put money into their retirement plans. But saving is only half the equation. The government also wants you to take money out of the plan and spend it chiefly on your retirement. For that reason, the government has enacted a series of rules on how and when you can—or, sometimes, must—take money out of your retirement plan. (Taking money out is called a distribution.)

What does this mean for you? If you or your employer has ever put money into a retirement plan and received tax benefits as a result, then you cannot simply take the money out whenever you want. Nor can you leave it in the plan indefinitely, hoping, for example, to pass all of the funds on to your children.

Instead, you must follow a complex set of rules for withdrawing money from the plan during your lifetime, and your beneficiaries must follow these rules after your death. These rules are called distribution rules, and if you or your beneficiaries don't follow them, the government will impose penalties, sometimes substantial ones.

This chapter identifies and briefly describes the types of retirement plans to which these distribution rules apply. If you have a retirement plan at work or if you have established one through your own business, you should find your plan listed below. Also, if you have an IRA, you will find your particular type among those described below.

There is also an entire category of plans known as nonqualified plans to which distribution rules do not apply. Such plans are used by employers primarily to provide incentives or rewards for particular—usually upper management—employees. These plans do not enjoy the tax benefits that IRAs and qualified plans (including TDAs and qualified annuities) do, and they consequently are not subject to the same distribution restrictions. Although this chapter helps you identify nonqualified plans, such plans have their own distribution rules, which fall outside the scope of this book.

Identifying your particular retirement plan probably won't be as difficult as you think. This is because every plan fits into one of four broad categories:

- qualified plan
- IRA

- plan that is neither an IRA nor a qualified plan, but has many of the characteristics of a qualified plan, or
- plan that is neither an IRA nor a qualified plan, and does not have the characteristics of a qualified plan.

Qualified Plans

A qualified plan is a type of retirement savings plan that an employer establishes for its employees and that conforms to the requirements of Section 401 of the U.S. tax code. Why is it called "qualified"? Because if the plan meets all of the requirements of Section 401, then it qualifies for special tax rules, the most significant of which is that contributions the employer makes to the plan on behalf of employees are tax deductible. Probably the best-known qualified plan is the 401(k) plan, discussed below.

The advantages to you, the employee, working for an employer with a qualified plan, are not only the opportunity to accumulate a retirement nest egg, but also to postpone paying income taxes on money contributed to the plan. Neither the contributions you make nor any of the investment returns are taxable to you until you take money out of the plan. In tax jargon, the income tax is deferred until the money is distributed and available for spending (usually during retirement).

Congress also built in some safeguards to help ensure that your plan assets are around when you finally do retire. For example, the assets must be held in trust and are generally protected from the claims of creditors.

In return for these tax benefits, the plan must comply with a number of procedural rules. First, the plan must not discriminate in favor of the company's highly compensated employees. For example, the employer may not contribute disproportionately large amounts to the accounts of the company honchos. Also, the employer may not arbitrarily prevent employees from participating in the plan or from taking their retirement money with them when they leave the company. Finally, the plan must comply with an extremely complex set of distribution rules, which is the focus of this book.

Seven of the most common types of qualified plans are described below.

Those plans are:

- profit-sharing plans, which include 401(k) plans and Roth 401(k) plans
- stock bonus plans
- money purchase pension plans
- employee stock ownership plans
- defined benefit plans
- target benefit plans, and
- plans for self-employed people, called Keogh plans.

Profit-Sharing Plans

A profit-sharing plan is a type of qualified plan that allows employees to share in the profits of the company and to use those profits to help fund their retirement. Despite the plan's title and description, an employer doesn't have to make a profit in order to contribute to a profit-sharing plan. Similarly, even if the employer makes a profit, it does not have to contribute to the plan. Each year, the employer has discretion over whether or not to make a contribution, regardless of profitability.

When the employer contributes money to the plan on behalf of its employees, the contributions are generally computed as a percentage of all participants' compensation. The annual contribution to all accounts can be as little as zero or as much as 25% of the total combined compensation of all participants. For the purposes of making this calculation, the maximum compensation for any individual participant is capped at $280,000. (The $280,000 increases from time to time for inflation.) No individual participant's account can receive more than $56,000 in a single year. (The $56,000 cap also increases from time to time for inflation.)

> **EXAMPLE:** Joe and Martha participate in their company's profit-sharing plan. Last year, the company contributed 25% of their respective salaries to the plan. Joe's salary was $120,000 and Martha's was $310,000. The company contributed $30,000 for Joe (25% × $120,000). The company's contribution for Martha was limited to the $56,000 ceiling, however, because 25% of Martha's salary was actually $77,500, which is above the limit.

This year, the company's profits tumbled, so the company decided not to make any contributions to the profit-sharing plan. Thus, the company will not contribute any money to the plan on Joe or Martha's behalf.

There is an exception to the $56,000 limit for individuals who are older than 50 and who contribute to a 401(k) plan. For those individuals, the limit is increased by $6,000.

401(k) Plans

A special type of profit-sharing plan, called a 401(k) plan, is named imaginatively after the subsection of the tax code that describes it. A traditional 401(k) plan allows you to direct some of your compensation into the plan, and you do not have to pay income taxes on the portion of your salary you direct into the plan until you withdraw it.

The plan may or may not provide for employer contributions. Some employers make matching contributions, depositing a certain amount for each dollar a participant contributes.

> **EXAMPLE:** Fred participates in his company's 401(k) plan. His company has promised to contribute 25¢ for each dollar of Fred's salary that he directs into the plan. Fred's salary is $40,000. He directs 5% of his salary, which is $2,000, into the plan. The company matches with a $500 contribution (which is 25¢ × $2,000).

Other employers contribute a fixed percentage of compensation for each eligible employee, whether or not the employee chooses to contribute to the plan.

> **EXAMPLE:** Marilyn's salary for the current year is $60,000. Her company has a 401(k) plan that does not match employee contributions. Instead, the company contributes a flat 3% of each eligible employee's salary to the plan. Marilyn is saving to buy a house, so she is not currently directing any of her salary into the 401(k) plan. Nonetheless, the company will contribute $1,800 (which is 3% × $60,000) to the plan for Marilyn.

The $56,000 limit applies to 401(k) plans, meaning the combined employer and employee contributions can't exceed $56,000 per year.

Roth 401(k) Plans

Although so-called Roth 401(k) plans are hot right now, the shocking truth is that there is no such thing as a Roth 401(k) plan. However, employers are permitted to add to a traditional 401(k) plan a special Roth feature, called a "qualified Roth contribution program." This feature allows employees to defer some of their salary into a "designated Roth account" instead of into the traditional 401(k) plan account.

The difference between the two types of accounts is in the tax treatment. Whereas contributions to traditional 401(k) plan accounts are tax deductible, contributions to designated Roth accounts are not. Instead, the tax benefits for designated Roth accounts come when you take distributions, which will be tax free as long as you meet certain requirements. (See Chapter 10 for a complete discussion of Roth 401(k) plans or designated Roth accounts.)

Stock Bonus Plans

A stock bonus plan is like a profit-sharing plan, except that the employer must pay the plan benefits to employees in the form of shares of company stock.

> **EXAMPLE:** Frankie worked for Warp Corp. all her working life. During her employment, she participated in the company's stock bonus plan, accumulating $90,000 by retirement. When she retired, Warp Corp. stock was worth $100 per share. When the company distributed her retirement benefits to her, it gave her 900 shares of Warp Corp. stock.

Money Purchase Pension Plans

A money purchase pension plan is similar to a profit-sharing plan in the sense that employer contributions are allocated to each participant's individual account. The difference is that the employer's contributions are mandatory, not discretionary. Under such a plan, the employer promises to pay a definite amount (such as 10% of compensation) into each participant's account every year. In that sense, money purchase pension plans are less flexible for employers than are profit-sharing plans.

As with a profit-sharing plan, the maximum amount that an employer can contribute to the plan for all participants combined is 25% of the total combined compensation of all participants (although each participant's compensation is limited to $280,000 for purposes of making this calculation).

The maximum that the employer can contribute to any given participant's account in a year is either $56,000 or the agreed-to amount of the participant's compensation—whichever is less. (The $280,000 and $56,000 caps increase from time to time for inflation.)

> **EXAMPLE:** Sand Corp. has a money purchase plan that promises to contribute 25% of compensation to each eligible employee's account. Jenna made $45,000 last year and was eligible to participate in the plan, so the company contributed $11,250 (25% × $45,000) to her account for that year. This year, the company is losing money. Nonetheless, the company is still obligated to contribute 25% of Jenna's salary to her money purchase plan account for the current year.

Employee Stock Ownership Plans (ESOPs)

An employee stock ownership plan, or ESOP, is a type of stock bonus plan that may have some features of a money purchase pension plan. ESOPs are designed to be funded primarily or even exclusively with employer stock. An ESOP can allow cash distributions, however, as long as an employee has the right to demand that benefits be paid in employer stock.

Because an ESOP is a stock bonus plan, the employer cannot contribute more than 25% of the total compensation of all participants and no more than $56,000 into any one participant's account.

Defined Benefit Plans

A defined benefit plan promises to pay each participant a set amount of money as an annuity beginning at retirement. The promised payment is usually based on a combination of factors, such as the employee's final compensation and the length of time the employee worked for the company. If the employee retires early, the benefit is reduced.

> **EXAMPLE:** Damien is a participant in his company's defined benefit plan. The plan guarantees that if Damien works until the company's retirement age, he will receive a retirement benefit equal to 1% of his final pay times the number of years he worked for the company. Damien will reach the company's retirement age in 20 years. If Damien is making $50,000 when he retires in 20 years, his retirement benefit will be $10,000 per year (which is 1% × $50,000 × 20 years). If he retires early, he will receive less.

Once the retirement benefit is determined, the company must compute how much to contribute each year in order to meet that goal. The computation is not simple. In fact, it requires the services of an actuary, who uses projections of salary increases and investment returns to determine the annual contribution amount. The computation must be repeated every year to take into account variations in investment returns and other factors and then to adjust the amount of the contribution to ensure the goal will be reached.

Even though, under certain circumstances, defined benefit plans permit much higher contributions than other qualified plans, they are used infrequently (especially by small companies) because they are so complex and expensive to administer.

Target Benefit Plans

A target benefit plan is a special type of money purchase pension plan that incorporates some of the attributes of a defined benefit plan. As with a money purchase plan, each participant in a target benefit plan has a separate account. But instead of contributing a fixed percentage of pay to every account, the employer projects a retirement benefit for each employee, as with a defined benefit plan. In fact, the contribution for the first year is computed in the same way a defined benefit plan contribution would be computed, with the help of an actuary. The difference, though, is that after the first year, the contribution formula is fixed. While a defined benefit plan guarantees a certain retirement annuity, a target benefit plan just shoots for it by estimating the required annual contribution in the employee's first participation year and then freezing the formula. The formula might be a specific dollar amount every year or perhaps a percentage of pay.

If any of the original assumptions turn out to be wrong—for example, the investment return is less than expected—the retirement target won't be reached. The employer is under no obligation to adjust the level of the contribution to reach the original target if there is a shortfall. Conversely, if investments do better than expected, the employee's retirement benefit will exceed the target, and the increased amount must be paid to the employee.

> **EXAMPLE:** Jack is 35 when he becomes eligible to participate in his company's target benefit plan. Jack's target retirement benefit is 60% of his final pay. Assuming Jack will receive wage increases of 5% each year and will retire at 65 after 30 years of service, Jack's final pay is projected to be $80,000. His target retirement benefit, then, is $48,000 (60% of $80,000). In order to pay Jack $48,000 a year for the rest of his life beginning at age 65, the actuaries estimate that the company must contribute $4,523 to Jack's account every year. The company will contribute that amount, even if Jack doesn't receive 5% raises some years, or if other assumptions turn out to be wrong. Thus, Jack may or may not receive his targeted $48,000 during his retirement years. It might be more or it might be less.

Plans for Self-Employed People (Keoghs)

Qualified plans for self-employed individuals are often called Keogh plans, named after the author of a 1962 bill that established a separate set of rules for such plans. In the ensuing years, Keoghs have come to look very much like corporate plans. In fact, the rules governing self-employed plans are no longer segregated, but have been placed under the umbrella of the qualified plan rules for corporations. Nonetheless, the Keogh moniker lingers, a burr in the side of phonetic spellers.

If you work for yourself, you may have a Keogh plan that is a profit-sharing plan, money purchase pension plan, or defined benefit plan. If so, it will generally have to follow the same rules as its corporate counterpart, with some exceptions.

Individual Retirement Accounts

Most people are surprised to learn that individual retirement accounts, or IRAs, exist in many forms. Most common is the individual retirement account or individual retirement annuity to which any person with earnings from employment may contribute. These are called contributory IRAs. Some types of IRAs are used to receive assets distributed from other retirement plans. These are called rollover IRAs. Still others, such as SEPs and SIMPLE IRAs, are technically IRAs even though some of their rules are quite similar to those of qualified plans. Finally, Roth IRAs combine the features of a regular IRA and a savings plan to produce a hybrid that adheres to its own set of rules. You can learn more about each type of IRA in the following sections.

Traditional Contributory IRAs

If you have income from working for yourself or someone else, you may set up and contribute to an IRA. The IRA can be a special depository account that you set up with a bank, a brokerage firm, or another institutional custodian. Or it can be an individual retirement annuity that you purchase from an insurance company.

You may contribute a maximum of $6,000 each year, or $7,000 if you will reach age 50 by the end of the year. If you are not covered by an employer's retirement plan, you may take a deduction on your tax return for your contribution. If you are covered by an employer's plan, your IRA might be fully deductible, partly deductible, or not deductible at all depending on how much gross income you have.

In 2019, if you are single and covered by an employer's plan, your contribution is fully deductible if your adjusted gross income, or AGI, is less than $64,000 and not deductible at all when your AGI reaches $74,000. Between $64,000 and $74,000, the deduction is gradually phased out. For married individuals, the phaseout range is from $103,000 to $123,000 if the IRA participant is covered by an employer plan. For an IRA participant who is not covered by a plan but whose spouse is covered, the phaseout range is $193,000 to $203,000.

> **EXAMPLE 1:** Jamie, who is single and age 32, works for Sage Corp. and participates in the company's 401(k) plan. This year he will make $40,000. Eager to save for retirement, Jamie decides to contribute $6,000 to an IRA. Since his income is less than $64,000, Jamie will be able to take a $6,000 deduction on his tax return for the IRA contribution, even though he also participated in his employer's retirement plan.

> **EXAMPLE 2:** Assume the same facts as in Example 1 except that Jamie's salary is $80,000. Although Jamie is permitted to make an IRA contribution, he may not claim a deduction for it on his tax return because his income is more than $74,000.

> **EXAMPLE 3:** Assume Jamie made $80,000, but Sage Corp. does not have a retirement plan for its employees. Because Jamie is not covered by an employer's retirement plan, his $6,000 IRA contribution will be fully deductible even though he made more than $74,000.

Rollover IRAs

If you receive a distribution from a qualified plan, you might decide to put some or all of it into an IRA. (See Chapter 2 for information about how and why you might do this.) The IRA that receives the qualified plan distribution is called a rollover IRA.

Although rollover IRAs used to have some special features, the 2001 pension law eradicated most of the differences between contributory and rollover IRAs.

Simplified Employee Pensions

A simplified employee pension, or SEP, is a special type of IRA that can be established by your employer or by you, if you are self-employed. Designed for small businesses, SEPs have many of the characteristics of qualified plans but are much simpler to set up and administer.

Under a SEP, each participant has his or her own individual retirement account to which the employer contributes. The contributions are excluded from the participant's pay and are not taxable until they are distributed from the plan. If you are self-employed, you may set up a SEP for yourself, even if you have no employees.

The advantage of a SEP over a regular IRA is that the contribution limits are higher. The contribution can be as much as 25% of your annual compensation, up to a maximum contribution of $56,000.

The disadvantage of a SEP, from an employer's perspective, is that the participation and vesting rules for SEPs are less favorable than those for qualified plans. Participation rules determine which employees must be covered by the plan and must receive contributions to their plan accounts. Vesting rules determine how much an employee is entitled to if the employee leaves the job or dies. An employer who establishes a SEP is required to make contributions on behalf of virtually all employees. Furthermore, the employees must be 100% vested at all times, which means that they must be allowed to take 100% of their plan account with them when they leave the company, no matter how long they have been employed there. Those can be costly requirements for small employers whose staff often includes many short-term, part-time employees. By contrast, 401(k) plans (and other qualified plans) can stretch the period before an employee is fully vested to as long as six years.

SIMPLE IRAs

A Simplified Incentive Match Plan for Employees, or SIMPLE IRA, is yet another type of IRA designed specifically to make it easier for small employers (those with 100 or fewer employees) to establish a retirement plan. A SIMPLE IRA is a salary reduction plan that, like a 401(k) profit-sharing plan, allows employees to divert some compensation into retirement savings.

As with a SEP, contributions to a SIMPLE IRA are deposited into a separate IRA for each participating employee. The participant may select any percentage of compensation to defer into the plan—even zero—but the total dollar amount cannot exceed $13,000 per year ($16,000 if you are at least age 50 by the end of the year).

⊙ **TIP**

Dollar amounts change. From time to time, the dollar amounts are increased for inflation. Each year, usually in October, the IRS publishes the contribution levels for the following year. You can find the new numbers on the IRS website at www.irs.gov. Search for "Pension Plan Limitations" to find out what the numbers will be for the upcoming year.

Unlike the employee, the employer is absolutely required to make a contribution to a SIMPLE IRA. The employer has two options:

- It can match the employee's contribution up to 3% of the employee's compensation. (Under certain circumstances, the employer may match less than 3%, but never more.)
- As an alternative to matching, the employer may contribute a flat 2% of compensation (up to a maximum compensation of $280,000) to the accounts of all eligible employees, whether or not the employee directs any salary into the plan.

EXAMPLE 1: Tabor Corp. has four employees, who earned the following salaries:

Jane	$25,000
Jake	$20,000
Bree	$35,000
Holly	$50,000

Tabor's SIMPLE IRA offers to match employees' contributions up to 3% of compensation. All four employees are eligible to participate. Jane and Jake each direct $9,000 of their salaries into the plan, while Bree and Holly direct none of their salaries into the plan. Tabor Corp. contributes $750 (which is 3% × $25,000) for Jane and $600 (3% × $20,000) for Jake. It contributes nothing for Bree or Holly.

EXAMPLE 2: Assume the same facts as in Example 1 except that instead of matching contributions, Tabor's plan requires a contribution of 2% of compensation to the accounts of all eligible employees. So, Tabor contributes $500 for Jane (which is 2% of $25,000) and $400 (2% of $20,000) for Jake. It also contributes $700 (2% of $35,000) for Bree and $1,000 (2% of $50,000) for Holly, even though Bree and Holly did not direct any of their salaries into the plan.

Roth IRAs

At first glance, a Roth IRA looks a lot like a traditional contributory IRA because annual contribution limits are the same. Beyond that, though, the similarities are more difficult to see. For one thing, none of your contributions to a Roth IRA are ever deductible on your tax return. Furthermore, your ability to make a Roth IRA contribution begins to phase out when your AGI exceeds $193,000 (for joint filers) or $122,000 (for single filers). And you are not permitted a contribution at all when your AGI exceeds $203,000 (for joint filers) or $137,000 (for single filers). (Recall that with a traditional IRA, you may make a contribution even if your income is high and you are covered by an employer's plan. You might not be able to deduct the contribution on your tax return, however.)

The big advantage of a Roth IRA is that if you qualify to make contributions, all distributions from the IRA are tax free—even the investment returns—as long as the distribution satisfies certain requirements. Furthermore, unlike traditional IRAs, you may contribute to a Roth IRA for as long as you continue to have earned income. (In the case of traditional IRAs, you can't make any contributions after you reach age 70½.)

Although Roth IRAs belong to the IRA family and are subject to many of the IRA rules, the abundant exceptions and variations in treatment make it difficult to rely on what you know about traditional IRAs when trying to figure out what to do with a Roth IRA. Consequently, we devote all of Chapter 9 to Roth IRAs. In that chapter, we point out the distinguishing characteristics of the Roth IRA and identify which of the distribution rules in this book apply to it and which do not. Before you take any action on a Roth IRA based on what you know about the traditional IRA rules, be sure to read Chapter 9.

Almost-Qualified Plans

Tucked into the voluminous tax code are a number of hybrid plans that are not strictly qualified plans, but that share many of the benefits and restrictions of qualified plans. The two most common, and the two that most closely mirror the qualified plan rules, are qualified annuity plans and tax-deferred annuities.

Qualified Annuity Plans

The rules for a qualified plan require that the assets of the plan be held by an administrator in a trust. Congress carved out an exception to this rule by adding Section 403(a) to the tax code. Section 403(a) allows employers to use contributions to purchase annuities for employees directly from an insurance company—under what are called qualified annuity plans. This alternative to holding the contributions in a trust can simplify administration. In almost every other respect, the rules and regulations that apply to qualified plans also apply to qualified annuity plans.

Tax-Deferred Annuities

If you are a university professor or an employee of a public school or nonprofit organization, odds are that you are covered by an annuity plan of a public charity or public school, more commonly referred to as a tax-deferred annuity, or TDA. TDAs, defined in Section 403(b) of the tax code, are typically funded with individual annuity contracts purchased from an insurance company. When you retire, your benefits are usually paid to you as a monthly annuity for the rest of your life, although some TDAs offer other distribution options, such as a lump-sum payment.

TDAs, like 401(k) plans, are permitted to offer a participant an option to contribute to a designated Roth account in lieu of or in combination with contributions to the traditional TDA account. (See Chapter 10 for more information about designated Roth accounts.)

TDAs are not qualified plans and do not track the qualified plan rules as closely as qualified annuity plans do. For example, distributions from TDAs are not eligible for special tax options, such as averaging and capital gains treatment. (See Chapter 2 for more information about tax options.) However, the vast majority of the distribution rules that apply to qualified plans also apply to TDAs. The exceptions are noted where relevant in the chapters that follow.

Nonqualified Plans

Big business being what it is—subject to the sometimes wise and sometimes questionable judgment of bosses—many companies offer special incentives and compensation packages to key employees. The incentives might come in the form of deferred cash bonuses, stock certificates, or stock options. Very often, the boss doesn't offer the same deal to everyone.

Because the incentives are not available to everyone, such plans generally do not satisfy the nondiscrimination requirements of qualified plans and are, therefore, called nonqualified plans. Because they are nonqualified, they are not subject to the same rigorous vesting, participation, and distribution requirements.

Nonqualified plans have some additional distinctive features: An employer may not deduct contributions to the plan, assets of the plan are not required to be held in trust, and the assets of the individual participants are not protected from the claims of creditors. Because nonqualified plans are not subject to the same distribution rules as IRAs, qualified plans, qualified annuities, and TDAs, they are not covered in this book.

Creditor and Bankruptcy Protection

Corporate retirement plans have long been safe from creditors, thanks to the Employee Retirement Income Security Act of 1974, commonly known as ERISA. However, that law does not protect retirement plans for self-employed individuals, nor does it protect IRAs of any kind.

Protection for those plans came in 2005 through a new law titled the Bankruptcy Abuse Prevention and Consumer Protection Act. That law provides debtors in bankruptcy with an exemption for retirement assets in qualified plans, qualified annuities, tax-sheltered annuities, and self-employed plans.

In addition, the law exempts all assets in an IRA that are attributable to rollovers from a retirement plan described above. If you happen to have a traditional IRA or Roth IRA containing assets that are not attributable to a rollover from some other type of retirement plan (for example, the assets are from amounts you contributed directly to the IRA), then you will also be allowed an exemption of up to $1,362,800 total for the assets in those contributory IRAs. The exemption amount is increased every three years for inflation. Note, however, that the Supreme Court ruled in 2014 that this protection does not extend to inherited IRAs. An inherited IRA is one that passes to a nonspouse beneficiary, or to a spouse who elects to leave the IRA in the name of the deceased.

Key Tax Code Sections

§ 401(a)

Qualified Plans in General (including Keoghs): Profit-sharing, stock bonus, money purchase pension, and defined benefit plans.

§ 401(k)

Cash or Salary Deferral Plan: A special type of qualified plan. Can be profit-sharing or stock bonus plan.

§ 402A

Optional Treatment of Elective Deferrals as Roth Contributions: Feature added to a 401(k) plan or 403(b) plan (TDA) that allows employees to contribute to a Roth account. Funded by employee's salary deferral.

§ 403(a)

Qualified Annuity Plan: Plan established by employer that is not a public charity or public school. Funded by the employer with purchased annuities.

§ 403(b)

Annuity Plan of Public Charity or Public School: Commonly called tax-deferred annuity, or TDA. Usually funded with purchased annuities owned by the employee.

§ 408

IRAs: Contributory, rollover, SEP, and SIMPLE.

§ 408A

Roth IRAs.

An Overview of Tax Rules

Our tax laws provide both incentive and opportunity to sock away significant sums for retirement. The combination of an up-front tax deduction for contributions to retirement plans, years of tax-deferred growth, and eventual taxation at relatively low rates (such as during retirement) can produce dramatic returns on retirement savings.

Taxation Fundamentals

To reap maximum benefit from your retirement plan, you must contribute as much as you can through the years, and you must adhere to certain guidelines when you draw money out. Keep in mind that your financial goal should be to maximize your after-tax wealth. It won't do you much good to accumulate a comfortable nest egg if you lose the bulk of it to taxes. To minimize your tax bill, follow these basic strategies:

- Defer the payment of tax.
- Pay tax at the lowest rate.
- Avoid tax penalties.

Defer the Payment of Tax

When you have a choice, it is usually best to delay or defer the payment of income tax for as long as possible. During the deferral period, you will have the use of money that would otherwise have gone to taxes; if you invest it, that money will help generate more tax-deferred income. The easiest way to defer the payment of tax is by deferring the receipt of income. For example, if you have the option of taking a distribution from

Helpful Terms

After-tax dollars. The amount of income left after all income taxes have been withheld or paid.

Amortization. The reduction of a debt through periodic payments of principal and interest.

Basis. An amount treated as the purchase price or cost of an asset for purposes of determining the taxable gain or loss when the asset is sold.

Custodian. A person or an entity that is in possession of property belonging to another. For example, the custodian of an IRA is the institution that holds the stocks, bonds, cash, or other property of the IRA, even though the assets actually belong to the individual who established and funded the IRA.

Distribution. A payout of property (such as shares of stock) or cash from a retirement plan or an IRA to the participant or a beneficiary.

Fair market value (FMV). The price at which an item could be sold at retail by a willing seller to a willing buyer.

Net unrealized appreciation. The amount by which an asset has increased in value before it is sold.

Nondeductible contribution. A contribution to a retirement plan or an IRA that may not be used as a business expense or an adjustment to offset taxable income on an income tax return.

Pretax dollars. Total taxable income before income taxes have been paid.

Pro rata. Proportionately. For example, an amount distributed pro rata over four years is distributed evenly over those four years. Property that is distributed pro rata to its owners is distributed according to the percentage of each owner's interest.

Tax bracket or marginal tax bracket. The rate at which each additional dollar of income will be taxed. Under the Internal Revenue Code, a certain amount of income is taxed at one rate, and additional income is taxed at another. Therefore, it is possible that if you have one more dollar of income it will be taxed at a different rate than the previous dollar. Your marginal rate is the rate at which your next dollar of income will be taxed.

Trustee. A person or an entity that holds legal title to the property in a trust. For example, a qualified retirement plan is a trust that is administered by a trustee who manages the trust property for the plan participant.

your retirement plan this year or next, it is often better to wait. As the tables below show, even a one-year delay can be beneficial. Your money grows while the tax man waits.

Many people vastly underestimate the benefits of tax-deferred compounding of investment returns inside a retirement plan account. Take a look at Tables I and II below. Both cases assume a simple 8% return on your investment and a flat 24% tax rate. Table I shows what happens if you take $10,000 out of your IRA, pay tax on it, and invest the remainder for 15 years. Because the investment is outside your IRA, each year you will pay tax on your interest, dividends, and capital gains.

Now look at Table II, which shows what happens if you leave the $10,000 inside the IRA. The table projects the value of your investment after one year, two years, or more. After 15 years, the total value of your IRA will be $31,722, which is $13,301 more than the balance shown in Table I after 15 years. If you take the money out and pay the tax on the distribution, your balance will be $24,108, which is still $5,687 more than you would have if you had paid the tax in Year One and invested the money outside the IRA. This is true even though you start with the same amount of money, earn the same investment return, and are subject to the same tax rate in both situations.

Occasionally, it may be better not to defer distributions (if you expect to be in a permanently higher tax bracket in the future, for example). Or perhaps the income you earn outside the IRA will be taxed at a capital gains rate that is lower than your ordinary income tax rate. Bear in mind, however, that a slightly higher tax bracket or a temporary spike in your tax rate is not usually enough justification to accelerate distributions. Your tax rate would have to increase significantly to offset the enormous benefits of compounded growth.

Pay Tax at the Lowest Rate

Generally, your goal should be to pay tax on all of your retirement income at the lowest possible rate. But how will you know when the time is right to take the money out? Most people will be in a lower tax bracket after retirement, which provides yet another reason to defer distributions as long as possible.

Table I

Withdraw from IRA:	$10,000		
Pay income tax:	$2,400		
Invest remainder:	$7,600		
Investment return:	8%		
Tax Rate:	24%		

Year	Initial Investment Beginning of Year	Interest Earned	Current Year Tax on Interest	Total Investment Year End
1	$ 7,600	$ 608	$ 146	$ 8,062
2	8,062	645	155	8,552
3	8,552	684	164	9,072
4	9,072	726	174	9,624
5	9,624	770	185	10,209
6	10,209	817	196	10,830
7	10,830	866	208	11,488
8	11,488	919	221	12,187
9	12,187	975	234	12,928
10	12,928	1,034	248	13,714
11	13,714	1,097	263	14,547
12	14,547	1,164	279	15,432
13	15,432	1,235	296	16,370
14	16,370	1,310	314	17,365
15	17,365	1,389	333	18,421

Table II

Leave inside IRA: $10,000
Investment return: 8%
Tax Rate: 24%

Year	Initial Investment Beginning of Year	Interest Earned	Current Year Tax on Interest	Total Investment Year End	Tax If Distributed	Net If Distributed*
1	$ 10,000	$ 800	$ 0	$ 10,800	$ 2,592	$ 8,208
2	10,800	864	0	11,664	2,799	8,865
3	11,664	933	0	12,597	3,023	9,574
4	12,597	1,008	0	13,605	3,265	10,340
5	13,605	1,088	0	14,693	3,526	11,167
6	14,693	1,175	0	15,869	3,808	12,060
7	15,869	1,269	0	17,138	4,113	13,025
8	17,138	1,371	0	18,509	4,442	14,067
9	18,509	1,481	0	19,990	4,798	15,192
10	19,990	1,599	0	21,589	5,181	16,408
11	21,589	1,727	0	23,316	5,596	17,720
12	23,316	1,865	0	25,182	6,044	19,138
13	25,182	2,015	0	27,196	6,527	20,669
14	27,196	2,176	0	29,372	7,049	22,323
15	29,372	2,350	0	31,722	7,613	24,108

*Compare last column with last column of Table I.

Avoid Tax Penalties

A raft of penalty taxes awaits you if you fail to comply with the myriad distribution laws. Some penalties are designed to discourage you from withdrawing money before you retire. Others target people who want to leave their retirement funds to their heirs. Penalties are discussed at length in subsequent chapters, but be advised: It is rarely wise to take a distribution and pay a tax penalty, even if it seems like a small amount to you. Not only will you have to pay the penalty when you file your next tax return, but you will also have to report the distribution as income and pay regular income tax on it. When you factor in the loss of tax-deferred compounded growth, you might even be better off borrowing the money you need, rather than dipping into your retirement plan.

At some point, though, you certainly will take money out of your retirement plan, whether it is because your employer distributes it to you when you leave your job, because you need the money, or because the law requires you to withdraw it. When that time comes, you must understand how retirement plans are taxed and know your options. You will also need to be aware of potential penalties in order to stay out of harm's way.

General Income Tax Rules for Retirement Plans

When you take money out of a retirement plan, whether it is an IRA, a qualified plan, a qualified annuity, or a TDA, some basic income tax rules apply. They are:

- Distributions are taxable immediately.
- Your basis is not taxable.
- You don't have to withdraw cash.
- You may not claim losses.
- Divorce or inheritance does not change the basic tax rules.

Although each rule has exceptions, expect the rule to apply in most situations. Read more about each rule in the sections below.

Distributions Are Taxable Immediately

First and most basic: All distributions will be taxed in the year they come out of the plan. Exceptions to this rule occur when you roll over your distribution into another retirement plan or a traditional IRA within 60 days, or when your employer transfers the distribution directly into another plan or traditional IRA. In these cases, you do not pay income tax until the money is eventually distributed from the new plan or IRA. (See "Income Tax on Qualified Plans and Qualified Annuities," below, for more about rollovers.)

If you ask your employer to transfer your retirement plan into a Roth IRA (as opposed to a traditional IRA), the transaction will be treated as a conversion to a Roth IRA. Assuming you are eligible to make the conversion, you will be required to pay income tax in the year of the conversion on any pretax amounts that are transferred from your employer's plan to your Roth IRA. For more information about conversions, see Chapter 9.

> **CAUTION**
>
> **Some money might be withheld!** Beware of rules that require your plan administrator to withhold money to cover income taxes you may owe when you take money out of your retirement plan—even if you plan to roll it over. You can avoid the withholding by having your employer transfer the retirement funds directly into another retirement plan or IRA. (See "Income Tax on Qualified Plans and Qualified Annuities," below, for more about these withholding rules.)

Your Basis Is Not Taxable

If you made contributions to a retirement plan or an IRA for which you were not permitted to take a tax deduction on your tax return, then you have what is called "basis" in the plan. In other words, you have contributed money to a plan or an IRA that you have already reported as income on your tax return. You will not have to pay taxes on those amounts a second time when you take the money out of your plan, but unfortunately, you usually don't have the luxury of deciding when to withdraw the portion of the money attributable to the basis.

If you have a regular IRA or a Keogh (see Chapter 1 for a description of these plans), your basis generally comes out pro rata, which means that every time you take a distribution, part of it is taxable and part is not. You compute the taxable and nontaxable portions of each distribution on IRS Form 8606 and submit it with the rest of your tax return at tax time. (A copy of Form 8606 is in Appendix A.)

> EXAMPLE 1: Over the years, you contributed a total of $10,000 to your IRA. You were not permitted to claim a tax deduction on your tax return for any of those contributions. Thus the $10,000 is all after-tax money, or basis. On December 31, the fair market value of the IRA was $45,000. During the year, you withdrew $5,000 to help cover living expenses. Part of the $5,000 is taxable, and part is not. To determine the tax-free portion, use the following method:
>
> Step One: Add the distributions you took during the year to the fair market value of the IRA on December 31.
> $5,000 + $45,000 = $50,000
>
> Step Two: Divide your total basis in the IRA by the amount from Step One.
> $10,000 ÷ $50,000 = 0.2 or 20%
>
> Step Three: Multiply the result in Step Two by the amount of the year's distribution.
> 20% × $5,000 = $1,000

You will not have to pay taxes on $1,000 of the $5,000 distribution, but the remaining $4,000 will be subject to income tax.

CAUTION

Multiple IRAs. If you have more than one IRA, all of your IRAs (including traditional IRAs, SEPs, and SIMPLE IRAs, but not Roth IRAs) are combined and treated as one for purposes of computing the tax-free portion of each distribution.

EXAMPLE 2: You have two IRAs. Over the years, you made nondeductible contributions of $8,000 to IRA #1. All of your contributions to IRA #2 were deductible. Consequently, your total basis for both IRAs is $8,000. On July 19 of this year, you withdrew $5,000 from IRA #1. On December 31, the fair market value of IRA #1 was $45,000 and IRA #2 was $30,000. To determine the tax-free portion of the distribution, you must follow these steps:

Step One: Determine the total fair market value of all of your IRAs as of December 31.
$45,000 + $30,000 = $75,000

Step Two: Add the distributions you took during the year to the total from Step One.
$5,000 + $75,000 = $80,000

Step Three: Determine the total basis (nondeductible contributions) for all IRAs.
$8,000 + $0 = $8,000

Step Four: Divide the total basis from Step Three by the amount from Step Two.
$8,000 ÷ $80,000 = 0.1 or 10%

Step Five: Multiply the result in Step Four by the amount of your distribution.
10% × $5,000 = $500

You will not have to pay tax on $500 of the $5,000 distribution, but you will on the remaining $4,500.

Roth IRAs and Roth 401(k) plans are different; they have special basis rules. (See Chapters 9 and 10, respectively, for more information.) In the case of an employer plan, the contributions you made with dollars on which you already paid taxes are usually distributed as a lump sum when you retire, unless you elect to take your retirement benefits as an annuity. If so, you may have to take your basis out pro rata, a little bit with each annuity payment.

You Don't Have to Withdraw Cash

Generally, when you take a distribution from an IRA, you may choose the assets you want to withdraw; you are not required to take cash. For example, suppose you want to withdraw $20,000. Your portfolio consists of $10,000 in cash and the remainder in stocks and bonds. You may take your $20,000 in any combination of cash and property you choose. You may take part of your distribution in cash and part in stocks and bonds, or even all of it in stock.

If you take a distribution in property other than cash, the amount of the distribution is the fair market value of the property (such as the stock) on the day it comes out of the IRA. Also, the fair market value of the property (on the day it's distributed) becomes the tax basis of the property.

> **EXAMPLE:** You decide to take a distribution from your retirement account on June 1. On that day, the total value of your account is $50,000, of which $10,000 is in cash and the remainder in 1,000 shares of MacBlue stock valued at $40 per share. The stock was purchased in the IRA for $10 per share. You decide to withdraw all of the cash and 250 shares of MacBlue stock. The total value of your distribution for tax purposes is $20,000 ($10,000 of cash plus 250 shares of MacBlue stock × $40 per share). After the distribution, you will have no cash inside the IRA, but you will have 750 shares of MacBlue stock. The tax basis of the MacBlue stock in your hands will be $40 per share, not its original cost of $10 per share. Therefore, if you sell the stock at some time in the future, the taxable amount will be the sale price less your basis of $40 per share.

When you receive a distribution from your employer's retirement plan, the plan itself usually dictates which assets must be distributed; participants typically have little control over this issue.

You May Not Claim Losses

You may not claim on your tax return losses you incur inside your IRA or retirement plan. Instead, you simply pay tax on each distribution based on the cash value or the fair market value of the property on the date it is distributed from the plan. For example, if you purchased 100 shares of LM Corp. at $12,000 and the fair market value of the stock is $5,000 when you withdraw all 100 shares from your IRA, you are not permitted to take a loss of $7,000. But before you cry foul, remember that you didn't pay tax on the money you used to purchase the stock, either. It was purchased inside your retirement plan with tax-deferred money. The value of the stock at distribution is $5,000, and that is the entire taxable amount. In fact, you will have obtained a tax benefit from the loss through the reduction of the taxable distribution.

One extremely rare exception to this rule might occur if you have made contributions with after-tax dollars and never managed to withdraw all of your basis. For example, if your basis in your IRA exceeds the fair market value of the entire IRA (or all of your IRAs combined, if you have more than one) when you take a final distribution, you may claim the loss as a miscellaneous itemized deduction on your tax return. But the loss will be deductible only to the extent that it, along with other miscellaneous itemized deductions, exceeds 2% of your AGI.

> **EXAMPLE:** Ten years ago, you made a nondeductible $2,000 contribution to an IRA. You invested all of the money in junk bonds. Because the investment started to go bad immediately, you never made any additional contributions. Now the account is worth $1,500. If you take a distribution of the entire $1,500 and close the account, you may claim a loss of $500 on Schedule A of your tax return. When you combine this amount with your other miscellaneous itemized deductions (in the amount of $450), the total of your miscellaneous deductions is $950 ($500 + $450). You are permitted to deduct your miscellaneous deductions only to the extent that they exceed 2% of your AGI. If your AGI is $42,000, 2% of that is $840 ($42,000 × 2%). Therefore, you may deduct only $110 ($950 − $840).

> **TIP**
>
> **Roth IRAs and Roth 401(k) plans are different.** If you have a Roth IRA or a Roth 401(k) plan, all of your contributions (but not your investment returns) are after-tax, so your basis in your Roth IRA or Roth 401(k) is likely to be higher than in your regular IRA or 401(k) plan.

Divorce or Inheritance Doesn't Change the Basic Tax Rules

If you inherit a retirement plan or an IRA, or if you receive one from your spouse in a divorce settlement, the four rules just discussed apply to you as though you were the original owner. For example, when you take money or property out of an IRA you inherited from your mother, you pay tax on the fair market value of the assets on the date of distribution. And if your mother had some basis left in the account, that remaining basis is passed on to you.

> **CAUTION**
>
> **Step-up rules don't apply to retirement plans.** Many assets receive what is called a step-up in basis when the owner of those assets dies. In other words, the basis of an asset is deemed to be its value when the owner dies rather than what the owner originally paid for it. Because investment assets usually increase in value over time, this benefit is referred to as a step-up.
>
> Assets in IRAs and other retirement plans are not permitted a step-up in basis. The assets in the IRA will be subject to tax at their fair market value whenever they are distributed. Death only determines who will pay the tax. The original owner pays during his or her lifetime; after that, the beneficiary of the plan pays the tax.

Income Tax on Qualified Plans and Qualified Annuities

A variety of circumstances could lead to a distribution from your retirement plan during your working years. Or you might not take money out until you actually retire. If you wait until retirement, you have many options for paying the tax on the money you receive. If you take a distribution before retirement, you will encounter a minefield of restrictions, and you might even have to pay tax penalties.

Options for Paying Taxes at Retirement

In general, when you receive a distribution from a qualified plan or qualified annuity, you should consider four tax options:

- You can report the distribution on your return as ordinary income.
- You can roll over the distribution into a traditional IRA or another retirement plan, which means you can continue to delay paying taxes.
- If you qualify, you can use ten-year averaging, which is a method of computing the tax as though the distribution were spread over a ten-year period.
- If you qualify, you can roll over or transfer the distribution into a Roth IRA. This is called a conversion and you must pay tax on all of the pretax amounts that you transfer from the plan to the Roth IRA.

> (!) CAUTION
>
> **After-tax contributions aren't taxable.** If part of your distribution includes after-tax contributions you made to your plan, those amounts will not be taxable and should not be included when computing your income tax using any of the above methods.

Pay Ordinary Income Tax

Some people are tempted to choose the path of least resistance. This is true in life generally, but especially true in the part of life that requires dealing with the IRS. When taking distributions from a retirement plan, the easiest option is simply to take the money, deposit it in your regular bank account, and report the amount of the distribution as ordinary income on your tax return at tax time.

But if your retirement plan distribution is large, you ordinarily would not choose to pay tax on the entire amount unless you need the money immediately and don't qualify for any special tax options.

Another reason you might have to use the ordinary income tax option is if you made a procedural error when attempting to use one of the other tax options, which left you no choice but to use the ordinary income tax option.

Who Is Eligible?

Anyone who receives a distribution from a retirement plan can choose to have the distribution taxed in this way.

Which Distributions Are Eligible?

All distributions you receive from a retirement plan that are attributable to pretax contributions or to investment returns may be taxed at ordinary income tax rates. This is true whether the distribution represents only part of your account or the entire balance.

CAUTION

Roth 401(k)s are different. Note that in the case of a distribution from a Roth 401(k) plan, investment returns, as well as your original after-tax contributions, will not be subject to tax, provided you have met the age and holding period requirements. (See Chapter 10 for a complete discussion of Roth 401(k) plans.)

Advantages and Disadvantages

The advantage of this tax option is that once the money comes out of the retirement plan and you pay the taxes owed, you have unrestricted use of the funds. The money that you withdraw is no longer subject to the terms of the plan.

But that peace of mind is expensive. Paying tax at ordinary rates on the money in the same year you receive it is usually the least advantageous option, at least from a financial perspective. If your distribution is large, it could easily push you into a higher tax bracket. It's hardly cheery to think of starting your retirement by handing the government 40% or more of your nest egg.

Roll Over Your Distribution

Rather than paying ordinary income tax on your entire retirement plan distribution, you might consider a more versatile and attractive strategy: Rolling some or all of the distribution into a traditional IRA or another employer's plan.

A rollover is usually accomplished by having your employer transfer your funds directly to another employer's plan or an IRA through a transaction called a direct rollover. If the funds are distributed directly to you, however, you have 60 days to deposit them into another plan or an IRA. The portion that is rolled over will continue to be tax deferred and will be subject to all the rules of the new plan or IRA. Any portion that is not rolled over within 60 days will be subject to ordinary income tax.

CAUTION

Rollovers into Roth IRAs are not tax deferred. The one exception to continued tax deferral for rollovers occurs when you elect to roll your retirement plan into a Roth IRA. If you choose that option, all of your pretax money will be subject to income tax in the year the rollover takes place. See "Convert to a Roth IRA," below.

TIP

Rollovers into another qualified plan after retirement are unusual. This is because once a person retires, he or she probably doesn't have another plan. Distributions at retirement are usually rolled into an IRA, unless you are taking your benefits as an annuity, in which case, no rollover of any kind is permitted.

Who Is Eligible?

Any participant who receives a distribution from a qualified plan or qualified annuity is permitted to roll it over. It doesn't matter how old you are or how long you have been a participant in the plan.

Which Distributions Are Eligible?

Generally, all distributions and partial distributions from qualified plans and qualified annuities are eligible to be rolled over. The most significant exceptions are:

- distributions you are required to take because you have passed age 70½ (see Chapters 5–8 for information about required distributions)
- distributions in the form of a life annuity or periodic payments that last for ten years or more, and
- distributions that are made to a participant because of hardship (see "Hardship Distributions From Qualified Plans," below, for more information).

Advantages and Disadvantages

If you don't need to use your retirement money right away, rolling it over gives you a big advantage. It allows you to defer paying income tax until you are ready to spend the money (or until you are required to take it out by the new plan). If you take money out only when you need it, you may be able to withdraw it in small enough chunks to keep yourself in a low tax bracket. Meanwhile, whatever you don't need can be left to grow inside the new plan or IRA.

The disadvantage of rolling over the distribution is that you don't have unrestricted use of the money. As long as it's in an IRA or a qualified plan, it is subject to all the rules and restrictions of the plan.

Pitfalls

If you are about to receive a distribution from a qualified plan or qualified annuity and you want to roll it over into another plan or an IRA, arrange for a direct rollover. In other words, have the funds transferred directly from your old employer's plan into the new plan or IRA. If you don't and instead receive the funds yourself before delivering them to the new plan, the distribution will be subject to income tax withholding, which could cause you some serious problems. (See "Withholding Money to Pay Taxes," below, for more information about withholding.) Your employer is required to offer you the option of a direct rollover (except to a defined benefit plan) if the amount of the distribution is at least $200. In addition to the withholding problem, you could encounter other traps.

Trap One: 60-Day Rule. You have 60 days from the time you receive a distribution to roll it over into another plan or IRA. The clock starts ticking after you have the distribution in hand. Day 1 is the day after you receive the distribution. The distribution must be deposited in another plan or IRA on or before the 60th day.

> ⓘ **CAUTION**
>
> **Not all types of retirement plans can be mixed.** If you want to roll over your Roth 401(k) plan to a new employer's plan, the new employer must have a Roth 401(k) plan. Or if you want to roll over your Roth 401(k) plan to an IRA, it must be a Roth IRA.

Trap Two: Changing Your Mind. Once you actually complete the rollover of your retirement plan into another plan or IRA, there is no going back.

For example, suppose you instruct the plan administrator of your employer's plan to transfer your retirement money directly into an IRA. A week after the money is deposited to your IRA, you decide that you really should have taken the distribution and elected ten-year averaging. (Read on to learn more about this issue.) Unfortunately, you cannot undo a rollover. Once the rollover is complete, you may not pull the money out of the account and elect averaging, even if the 60 days has not yet expired.

If you do pull the money out, it will be treated as another retirement plan distribution, and you will have to pay income tax; you might even have to pay an early distribution tax. (See Chapter 3 for information about the early distribution tax.)

Trap Three: Rolling Over Ineligible Funds. Some of the money you receive from a retirement plan might not be eligible to be rolled over. You cannot roll over annuity payments, hardship distributions, or money that must be distributed to you when you are age 70½ or older.

If you accidentally roll over ineligible funds, you have a certain amount of time to correct the problem, usually until the due date of your tax return. (That's April 15 of the following year, unless you request an extension of time for filing your return. In that case, you will have until the extended deadline.) If you do not remove the funds in time, you will have to pay a penalty for each calendar year or part of a year those funds remain in the plan or IRA.

Trap Four: Plan Rules Govern. Sometimes you might find that the law permits you to take certain steps with your retirement plan, but the terms of your plan are more restrictive. In that case, the plan's rules will govern. For example, the law generally allows you to roll over qualified plans and qualified annuities into almost any other type of retirement plan. Some plans, however, do not permit mixing and matching. Qualified annuity plan administrators often will not accept rollovers from other qualified annuities. However, you can always roll over a qualified plan or qualified annuity distribution into a traditional IRA.

Convert to a Roth IRA

Not only are you permitted to roll over a qualified plan distribution to another plan or to a traditional IRA, but you may also roll over the distribution to a Roth IRA. If you choose this option, however, you are technically converting the assets to a Roth IRA and all of the usual rules for Roth IRA conversions will apply. Most important, you must pay income tax on all the pretax money that is transferred out of your employer's plan into your Roth IRA. And you must pay it in the year of the conversion. (See Chapter 9 for more information about converting to a Roth IRA.)

Who is Eligible?

Everyone qualifies to convert to a Roth IRA. There are no income or age restrictions.

Which Distributions Are Eligible?

As is the case with rollovers to other plans or to traditional IRAs, all distributions and partial distributions from qualified plans and qualified annuities are eligible to be rolled over to a Roth IRA, with the exception of required distributions, hardship distributions, and annuities or periodic payments that last for ten years or more.

Advantages and Disadvantages

Once you make the decision to roll over your employer's plan into an IRA, the next question you must ask yourself is: traditional IRA or Roth IRA? The decision involves a variety of factors. The disadvantage of converting to a Roth IRA is that you must pay tax on the entire amount of the distribution right away. The tax is not deferred. The advantage, however, is that all future distributions, including investment earnings, are potentially tax free no matter how large the account grows. Another advantage is that you are not required to take distributions from a Roth IRA during your lifetime, so the account can be left to grow tax free for as long as you live.

If you will not need to draw on the Roth IRA for living expenses during your retirement years, it is often right to convert to a Roth IRA. It can then be left alone to grow tax free for years until your beneficiaries must draw on the funds.

If you do need the Roth IRA to live on, then it makes sense to do some calculations, taking into account tax rates at the time of conversion compared with expected retirement tax rates, living expenses, and other factors to determine the optimum amount (if any) you should convert to a Roth IRA. You might want to consult with a tax professional to help with those calculations.

Pitfalls

As with any rollover, you will want to arrange a direct rollover from the plan to the Roth IRA to avoid mandatory income tax withholding (see "Withholding Money to Pay Taxes," below).

If you choose to receive the distribution and roll it over yourself, not only will you have mandatory withholding to deal with, but you have a 60-day window during which the transaction must be completed. If you fail to complete the rollover (actually, conversion), you won't owe any additional tax, but once the 60 days have passed, your opportunity to put that distribution into the Roth IRA will have expired.

See Chapter 9 for detailed information about conversions to Roth IRAs.

💡 TIP

You may roll over the pretax portion of your 401(k) or 403(b) plan to a traditional IRA and the after-tax portion to a Roth IRA. Because of the significant tax benefits of a Roth IRA, it often pays big dividends to transfer as much as possible into a Roth IRA. But, as described above, transferring pretax dollars from your 401(k) or tax-deferred annuity into a Roth IRA could result in a big tax bill. Eventually, some inventive taxpayers came up with a new strategy: They would roll over the after-tax portion of a plan distribution to a Roth IRA, and roll the pretax portion into a traditional IRA. Then there would be no taxes due at the time of the rollover.

Until recently, however, it was unclear whether or not the IRS would allow you to cherry-pick which dollars could be allocated to a Roth and which to a traditional IRA. In 2014, the IRS blessed the strategy with an official notice.

Now, if you are planning a direct rollover from a 401(k) plan or a 403(b) plan (a tax-deferred annuity) that is composed of both pretax and after-tax amounts, you may allocate the pretax and after-tax portions to different IRAs, provided you do both of the following:

- Schedule the rollovers to be completed at the same time. (However, the IRS has said it will allow for reasonable delays between the rollovers to facilitate administration).
- Inform the plan administrator about your allocation plans before the direct rollovers are scheduled to take place.

Use Ten-Year Averaging to Compute Tax

It may be that you cannot afford to roll over your retirement distribution because you need the money. And if you do need the money, you don't want to give up a large chunk of the distribution to income taxes. Although there is no way to avoid paying taxes if you elect not to roll over the distribution, you may be able to compute the tax using a method called ten-year averaging, which can reduce your total bill.

Who Is Eligible?

You are eligible to use ten-year averaging if you satisfy all of the following conditions:

- You were born before 1936.
- You have not used ten-year averaging on any distribution since 1986.
- You participated in the plan for at least five years, which means you or your employer made a contribution to your plan account in at least five separate years before the year of the distribution.

TIP

Figuring the length of participation. If your account is transferred from one plan to another, you don't have to start the participation clock ticking all over again. The years you participated in the old plan count toward the five-year requirement.

Which Distributions Are Eligible?

Even if you are eligible, you may use ten-year averaging only if your distribution also qualifies. Your distribution will qualify only if both of the following are true:

- The distribution to be averaged must be the entire amount of your qualified plan or qualified annuity. You cannot roll over part of the distribution and you cannot have rolled over part of it in the past.
- You must receive the distribution all within one tax year, even if you receive more than one payment.

CAUTION

You might have two plans that the IRS treats as one for ten-year averaging. For example, money purchase pension plans and defined benefit plans must be combined and considered one plan for purposes of the ten-year averaging rules. Let's say you receive a distribution of your defined benefit plan one year and roll it over. The next year you receive a distribution of your money purchase pension plan and want to use ten-year averaging. You cannot, however, because the distributions were received in different years.

How Is It Computed?

If you receive a distribution and elect to use ten-year averaging, the tax on the distribution itself is computed on IRS Form 4972 (see Appendix A) and recorded on a separate line of your tax return. You must pay that amount to the IRS even if you owe no other income taxes.

The tax is calculated as though you were a single individual (even if you are married) and as though you received the distribution in ten smaller installments over ten years. Despite this calculation, you pay the total tax due in the year of the distribution, not over ten years. These are the steps:

Step One: Determine the taxable amount of the distribution.

This is usually the entire amount of the distribution reduced by any after-tax contributions you made. Your employer or the administrator of the plan should provide this information.

Step Two: Determine the minimum distribution allowance.

If your distribution is less than $70,000, you may exclude some of it from your income when computing the tax. The excludable portion is called your minimum distribution allowance, or MDA. To determine the MDA:

1. Reduce the taxable amount of the distribution by $20,000, but not below zero.
2. Multiply the result by 0.2 or 20%.
3. Subtract the result from $10,000 or from one-half of the taxable amount (the number from Step One), whichever is less. The result is your MDA.

Step Three: Subtract your MDA from the taxable amount (Step One minus Step Two).

Step Four: Divide the result by 10.

Step Five: Compute the income tax on the amount from Step Four.

You must use the 1986 tax rates for a single person. (A schedule of 1986 tax rates is in Appendix A.)

Step Six: Multiply the result by 10.

> EXAMPLE: You receive a lump-sum distribution of $50,000 that qualifies for ten-year averaging. You want to use the money to build your retirement dream house, so you decide to keep the money and pay the tax. Here's how it is computed:
>
> Step One: Taxable amount = $50,000
>
> Step Two: Since the distribution is under $70,000, you will be entitled to an MDA as follows:
> $50,000 − $20,000 = $30,000
> $30,000 × 0.2 = $6,000
> $10,000 − $6,000 = $4,000 (your MDA)
>
> Step Three: $50,000 − $4,000 = $46,000
>
> Step Four: $46,000 ÷ 10 = $4,600
>
> Step Five: Tax on $4,600 at 1986 single rates = $597
>
> Step Six: $597 × 10 = $5,970

Thus, you will owe $5,970 of federal income tax on your $50,000 distribution in the year you receive it. By contrast, if you simply reported the $50,000 as additional income without using the special averaging, you could owe as much as $19,800 of federal income tax on that $50,000, if you are in the top tax bracket.

Advantages and Disadvantages

When should you use averaging? Although it is usually better to roll over a distribution and continue your tax deferral rather than pay a ten-year averaging tax, those guidelines go right out the window if you need the money. In such a situation, ten-year averaging could mean big tax savings.

You might also choose ten-year averaging if your distribution is small enough to be taxed at a rate (using 1986 rates) that is lower than you are likely to see in the future. But if your distribution is large, ten-year averaging is rarely a good choice. For one thing, you give up substantial compounded growth on the money that would otherwise remain in the retirement account. But also, the tax advantages of averaging decline as the distribution increases in amount. In addition, the top tax rates in 1986, which would apply to larger distributions, were quite a bit higher than top rates today.

> **EXAMPLE:** You receive a retirement plan distribution of $100,000. If you use ten-year averaging, the entire tax would be $14,470—all of it taxed at less than 15%. In contrast, if your distribution is $500,000 and you choose ten-year averaging, more than $150,000 would be taxed at rates higher than any current tax rate. In this case, you may be better off rolling over the $500,000 and spreading distributions out over your retirement years.

Bottom line: It's easy to be seduced by the lure of lower tax rates and ready money. But if your goal is to accumulate substantial sums for your retirement, you are usually better off rolling over your distribution and deferring the payment of tax.

Pitfalls

If you still think ten-year averaging is your best option, consider these traps.

Trap One: One-Time Election. Ten-year averaging is a once-in-a-lifetime election. If you choose to use it on a distribution, you may never again use ten-year averaging on a future distribution from any plan.

Trap Two: Multiple Distributions. If you receive distributions from more than one retirement plan in a single year and want to use ten-year averaging, you must use it on all the distributions you receive that year. If you want to use ten-year averaging on only one distribution, you must arrange to receive the distribution you want to average in a separate year, if possible. This rule is different from the aggregation rule covered above. Under the aggregation rule, if two plans are of the same type (for example, both are profit-sharing plans), they are considered one plan for ten-year averaging purposes. In that case, the distributions from both plans must be received in the same year or you may not use ten-year averaging on either distribution.

Use Capital Gain Rates to Compute Tax

If you were born before 1936 and you began participating in your employer's plan before 1974, you have another option available to you in addition to ten-year averaging: You may treat part of your distribution as capital gain subject to a flat 20% tax rate. The amount of your distribution that is eligible for this rate is computed by the plan administrator and is based on the number of years you participated in the plan before 1974. The administrator will report the eligible amount to you so that you can decide if you want to elect the 20% tax option. You may elect to use this special rate whether you choose to use ten-year averaging or ordinary income tax rates on the remaining portion of your distribution.

Special Rules for Employer Stock

Your retirement account distribution may include some shares of your employer's stock. If the total current value of the shares of stock purchased in your plan account is greater than the total basis, the difference is called the net unrealized appreciation.

Net unrealized appreciation is the difference between the fair market value of the stock and the stock's basis. Basis for this purpose means the cost of the stock when the plan purchased it. For example, suppose your employer contributed $1,000 to your retirement account on your behalf. The plan then used that $1,000 to purchase 100 shares of company stock at $10 per share. The stock's basis is $10 per share or $1,000 total. Many years later, when you retire, those 100 shares are worth $20,000. The net unrealized appreciation is $19,000, which is the fair market value less the plan's basis in those shares ($20,000 – $1,000).

You have several options for paying income taxes on the basis and the net unrealized appreciation of employer stock that is part of a retirement plan distribution:

- If you elect ten-year averaging, you can exclude the net unrealized appreciation when computing the tax. In that case, you would include only the plan's basis in the ten-year averaging calculation (assuming, of course, that the stock was purchased with pretax dollars). If you use this tax strategy, you will pay tax on the net unrealized appreciation using long-term capital gains rates when you later sell the company stock.

- You can include the net unrealized appreciation when calculating your tax using ten-year averaging. You might do this if your tax rate using averaging is lower than the long-term capital gains rate.
- You can pay ordinary income tax (as opposed to using ten-year averaging) on all but the net unrealized appreciation (paying tax on the plan's basis, for example, if the stock was purchased with pretax dollars). You would use this strategy if you did not qualify for ten-year averaging but did not want to roll over all of your employer stock into an IRA. Using this strategy, you would pay capital gains tax on the net unrealized appreciation only when you sell the stock.
- You can roll over your entire distribution, including employer stock, into a traditional IRA. If you do so, the net unrealized appreciation in the stock becomes irrelevant because all future distributions from the IRA will be taxed as ordinary income, not as capital gains.

TIP

Paying taxes to preserve capital gains rates. It might well be to your advantage not to roll over all of your employer stock into an IRA. This might be true if your net unrealized appreciation is large relative to the plan's basis in the stock, because the bulk of the distribution (the net unrealized appreciation) could be taxed at low capital gains rates when you eventually sell the stock. Remember, once the stock is rolled over into an IRA, all future distributions from the IRA will be taxed at ordinary rates, not capital gains rates. Note, too, that this strategy might work for you even if you are younger than age 59½. Although the portion of the distribution that you must pay tax on at the time of distribution (typically the basis) will be subject both to ordinary income tax and an early distribution penalty, the trade-off—taxing the bulk of the distribution at capital gains rates instead of ordinary rates—could easily offset any disadvantage. But just how large the net unrealized appreciation must be relative to the plan's basis for this strategy to work might require a calculation by you or your accountant.

CAUTION

No step-up for net unrealized appreciation. Your inclination may be to exclude the net unrealized appreciation from your income tax and keep the stock, passing it on to your heirs when you die. You might do this if you think your heirs will obtain a step-up in the basis of the stock when you die, which would allow them to avoid all tax on the net unrealized appreciation. But this strategy won't work. The tax code specifically denies any step-up in basis for net unrealized appreciation in employer stock.

Options for Paying Taxes Before Retirement

It is quite possible that you will receive a distribution from your retirement plan before you retire. Here are some common situations in which that might occur:

- You change jobs.
- Your company terminates its retirement plan.
- You are self-employed and terminate your own plan.

The retirement plan rules were written to discourage distributions before retirement. For this reason, you'll find your options for paying taxes somewhat limited if you receive a retirement plan distribution while the government thinks you are too young to be retired.

Pay Ordinary Income Tax

If you do not need the distribution you receive from your retirement plan for living expenses, you will almost certainly want to do something with it other than spend it or put it in a regular bank account. If you don't, you will have to report the distribution on your tax return and pay ordinary income tax on it. Furthermore, you might have to pay penalties for withdrawing the money early.

Roll Over Your Distribution

If you have not yet reached age 59½ and you receive a distribution from a qualified plan or qualified annuity, you can roll over the distribution into a traditional IRA or another retirement plan to continue deferring the tax and to avoid paying an early distribution penalty. Alternatively, you can roll over the distribution into a Roth IRA, which constitutes a conversion of the assets to a Roth IRA. If you choose this option, you must pay income tax on the converted amounts. See Chapter 9 for more information about converting to a Roth IRA.

CAUTION

Arrange a direct rollover. If you receive a distribution from a qualified plan, intending to roll it over into another plan or into an IRA, arrange to have the administrator of your old employer's plan transfer the funds directly into the new plan or IRA instead of sending the money to you. Otherwise, the administrator of the old plan may be required to withhold money to cover taxes you might owe. (See below for more information about withholding.)

Use Ten-Year Averaging to Compute Tax

As long as you satisfy the requirements for ten-year averaging described above, averaging is an option for you.

Options for Paying Taxes on Inherited Plans

If you are the beneficiary, rather than the owner, of a qualified plan and you receive a distribution as a result of the owner's death, the rules for paying income taxes are a little different from the general rules described in "Options for Paying Taxes at Retirement," above. You can do one of the following:

- Pay ordinary income tax.
- Roll over your distribution.
- Convert to a Roth IRA.
- Use ten-year averaging.

Pay Ordinary Income Tax

If the plan assets are distributed outright to you and you simply take the money and put it into your regular bank account, then you will have to report the distribution as income on your tax return and pay tax on it, as you might expect. You may be able to reduce the total amount of the tax or gain some breathing room in paying the tax, however, by taking the distribution in installments over a number of years.

There is a bit of good news, too. If you receive a distribution from a plan you inherited, you will not have to pay an early distribution tax, even if you are younger than 59½. The penalty is waived for inherited plans. (See Chapter 3 for information about the early distribution tax.)

Roll Over Your Distribution

If you inherit a qualified plan or qualified annuity and you were the spouse of the original owner, you can roll over the distribution into a traditional or Roth IRA in your name or into your employer's plan.

If you inherit a retirement plan, such as a 401(k) plan, and you were not the spouse of the original owner, then you may transfer the plan assets into a traditional IRA only if you follow these rules:

- You may not roll over the assets into a plan or an IRA that is in your own name. Instead, you must establish a new IRA that is titled in the name of the deceased with you as the designated beneficiary: "Father Doe, deceased, for benefit of Daughter Doe." When an IRA is titled this way, it is called an inherited IRA, even though it was just established.
- The transfer of assets from the qualified plan to the newly established inherited IRA must occur as a trustee-to-trustee transfer. In other words, the assets must go directly from the retirement plan into the new IRA without going through you first. You cannot take possession of the funds.
- You must not mix assets from any other qualified plan or IRA with the inherited funds.

See Chapters 7 and 8 for more information about inherited plans and IRAs, including how to title accounts.

Convert to a Roth IRA

When a spouse inherits a retirement plan or an IRA, the spouse is accorded virtually all of the distribution options offered to the deceased plan participant. For that reason, it has always been an easy matter for a spouse beneficiary to convert retirement assets to a Roth IRA if he or she wants to do so. In the past, nonspouse beneficiaries did not enjoy the same privileges. But in 2008, the IRS issued a notice indicating that not only is a nonspouse beneficiary now permitted to transfer qualified plan assets into a traditional IRA (in the decedent's name), but he or she also has the option to transfer (or convert) the assets to a Roth IRA. Again, there are some conditions:

- As is the case when transferring assets to a traditional IRA, the beneficiary must establish a new Roth IRA in the decedent's name. The new Roth IRA will be treated as an inherited Roth IRA.
- The transfer from a qualified plan to a new Roth IRA must occur as a trustee-to-trustee transfer.
- The new Roth IRA should not contain any other assets except those that were converted from the qualified plan.
- The beneficiary must pay income tax on the converted amounts for the year of conversion.

CAUTION

Different rules apply to inherited IRAs. The rule that allows a nonspouse beneficiary to transfer an inherited retirement plan (an employer plan) to a Roth IRA does not apply to inherited IRAs. If a nonspouse beneficiary inherits an IRA, the beneficiary may not convert that IRA to a Roth IRA.

See Chapter 9 for more information about converting assets to a Roth IRA and about how to take distributions from an inherited Roth IRA.

Use Ten-Year Averaging to Compute Tax

If you inherit a qualified plan or qualified annuity, you may use ten-year averaging provided the distribution is a qualified distribution and the original owner satisfied all the eligibility requirements for ten-year averaging (except the five-year participation requirement) at the time of death. These eligibility requirements are discussed in "Options for Paying Tax at Retirement," above.

> **CAUTION**
>
> **Meeting the eligibility requirements.** It is not you, the person who inherited the plan, who must meet the eligibility requirements for ten-year averaging: It is the original owner. It doesn't matter how old you are, nor would it matter if you had used averaging on one of your own distributions. As long as the original owner would have qualified for averaging, you qualify.

Options for Paying Taxes on Qualified Plans Received at Divorce

Congress has gone to great lengths to protect your qualified plan assets. The cornerstone of that protection is a provision known as the antialienation rule, which attempts to ensure that you cannot be forced to give away your qualified plan assets.

Divorce presents a unique problem, however. What if you want to use your retirement plan as part of a property settlement? Can you give away some or all of your plan assets in that situation? And if you can, who should be responsible for the taxes and penalties (if any) on the part you give away?

Congress addressed these concerns by giving divorcing couples a vehicle for protecting plan assets and minimizing tax penalties. It's called a Qualified Domestic Relations Order or QDRO (pronounced "quadro"). The QDRO rules spell out the circumstances under which your qualified plan benefits can go to someone else—an alternate payee—such as your soon-to-be former spouse.

A QDRO is a judgment, a decree, or an order (including a court-approved property settlement agreement) that satisfies all of the following requirements:

- It relates to child support, alimony, or the marital property rights of a spouse, a former spouse, a dependent child, or some other dependent of the qualified plan participant.
- It gives an alternate payee, such as a spouse, former spouse, dependent child, or another dependent, the right to receive all or a portion of the participant's plan benefits.
- It does not alter the form or the amount of the benefit originally intended for the participant even though the benefit might now go to an alternate payee. For example, the QDRO cannot require the plan to pay a larger annuity to the alternate payee than it would have paid to the participant.
- It contains certain language, specifically:
  - The alternate payee must be referred to as "the alternate payee" in the QDRO.
  - The QDRO must identify the plan, as well as the amount of each payment and the number of payments to be made.
  - The QDRO must contain the name and address of both the participant and the alternate payee.

If you are in the process of divorcing and you and your spouse agree that you will receive an interest in your spouse's qualified plan, you may be able to preserve some of the tax benefits of the plan for yourself. But this is possible only if there is a QDRO in place. If you and your spouse write up your agreement but it does not meet the above four requirements and is not court approved, then your agreement is not a QDRO. In such a situation, distributions to a spouse, former spouse, or child could be subject to penalties.

In most cases, QDRO payments are made to a spouse or former spouse as alimony or as part of a property settlement. Payments might also be used for child support. If you receive a qualified plan distribution under a QDRO, the rules for how it is taxed and what you can do with it will depend upon your relationship to the original owner or plan participant.

Options for a Nonspouse Alternate Payee

If the recipient of a QDRO payment is not the spouse or former spouse of the plan participant, then the plan participant must report all distributions from the qualified plan as income on the participant's own tax return and pay taxes on them. If the distribution qualifies for special tax treatment, however, the plan participant can opt for the special rules. For example, the plan participant may use ten-year averaging on a distribution to figure the tax liability, provided the participant is eligible (see "Options for Paying Taxes at Retirement," above). If you are the recipient, you would pay no taxes when you receive the distribution.

Although the tax burden falls heavily on the plan participant, a couple of special rules provide a little tax relief:

- The participant will not have to pay an early distribution tax on any QDRO distribution paid to a nonspouse recipient, no matter how old the participant is or how old the recipient is. (See Chapter 3 for more information about the early distribution tax.)
- If the participant separates the recipient's share of the plan, perhaps by rolling it over into a new IRA, the participant can use ten-year averaging on the remaining portion, provided the remaining portion would have qualified for averaging if it had been the participant's entire plan balance. The participant may not treat the recipient's portion alone as a distribution eligible for averaging, however, unless that portion constitutes the participant's entire plan balance.

Options for a Spouse or Former Spouse Alternate Payee

If you are a spouse or former spouse receiving a distribution under a QDRO, you are treated in almost every respect as though you are the plan participant. Specifically:

- You may roll over some or all of the distribution to your own IRA or employer plan.
- You must pay tax on the distribution if you do not roll it over.
- The distribution is subject to mandatory withholding rules as though you were the plan participant. (See "Withholding Money to Pay Taxes," below.)

As you might expect, there are exceptions to the general rule that you are to be treated as though you were the plan participant:

- Although you may elect ten-year averaging on the distribution you receive, your eligibility for averaging depends on the participant's eligibility. In other words, if the participant was born before 1936, has not made an averaging election since 1986, and has participated in the plan for at least five years, then you may elect ten-year averaging. If the plan participant does not qualify, neither do you.

- Although you may elect averaging, you are not permitted to use the special capital gain rules for pre-1974 accumulations, nor may you exclude from income the net unrealized appreciation in employer stock.

- Any distribution you keep in a regular account instead of rolling it over will not be subject to an early distribution tax, regardless of your age or the participant's age. (See Chapter 3 for information about early distributions.)

Once you do roll over the distribution into an IRA or another retirement plan in your name, the assets become yours in every respect, as though they never belonged to the original participant.

Withholding Money to Pay Taxes

Congress, in its increasingly creative efforts to improve the Treasury's cash flow, passed a mandatory withholding law in 1993 for qualified plans. The law requires your plan administrator to keep 20% of all qualified plan distributions to pay federal income tax before distributing the remainder to you.

> EXAMPLE: You leave your job and plan to travel around the world for six months. Your employer distributes your retirement plan to you. The total value of your account is $10,000. The plan administrator gives you $8,000 and sends the rest to the government to pay the taxes you will owe on the distribution.

Exceptions to Mandatory Withholding

There are some exceptions to the mandatory withholding law:

- Amounts that are transferred directly from the trustee of your retirement plan to the trustee of another plan or to the custodian of your IRA are not subject to the withholding. This is called a direct rollover and is the most appropriate action to take if your intention is to roll over your distribution.

> (!) CAUTION
>
> **Standard rollovers are not exempt from the mandatory withholding rule.** If you take a distribution of your retirement plan—for example, you receive a check payable to you—intending to roll it over into an IRA, your employer must withhold 20% for taxes. The direct rollover exception works only if the money is delivered directly from your retirement plan trustee to the trustee of another plan or to the custodian of your IRA. (Read on for more information about direct rollovers.)

- Any after-tax contributions you made to the plan are not subject to withholding when they are distributed to you.
- If you elect to receive your distribution in roughly equal periodic payments over ten or more years, those payments will not be subject to mandatory withholding.
- Small distributions of $200 or less are not subject to mandatory withholding.

Pitfalls of Mandatory Withholding

Unless you use a direct rollover, the withholding law can pose some serious problems for you and maybe even take a permanent bite out of your retirement nest egg by:

- reducing your retirement accumulation
- imposing penalties and taxes, and
- forcing you to sell assets to pay taxes.

Let's look at each of these in more detail.

Reducing Your Retirement Accumulation

If it is your intention to roll over your entire retirement plan distribution into an IRA or another retirement plan and continue the tax deferral, and you don't use a direct rollover, mandatory withholding could put a crimp in those plans. Because the withholding is usually paid out of the distribution, you will have a smaller amount to roll over.

> **EXAMPLE:** You have just retired. You accumulated $200,000 in your employer's retirement plan. You plan to roll over your distribution into an IRA. However, when you receive the check from your employer, it is only $160,000. Because of the mandatory withholding rules, your employer was required to send 20%, or $40,000, to the IRS to cover any income taxes you might owe on the distribution, even if it was always your intention to roll over the entire amount. So now you only have $160,000 in your retirement nest egg. (You may be able to replace the amount withheld, however. See "Avoiding or Correcting Mandatory Withholding," below.)

Imposing Penalties and Taxes

If your distribution was subject to withholding, you may claim a refund of the tax withheld for the portion that was rolled over (assuming you roll over part or all of the distribution). However, the portion of the distribution that was sent to the government for taxes was part of your distribution, too, and it wasn't rolled over, so it will be subject to income tax. Worse, if you are not yet 59½, you might have to pay an early distribution tax on the portion withheld for taxes, even though the withholding was mandatory. (See Chapter 3 for more information about the early distribution tax.)

> **EXAMPLE:** You decide to retire in November of the year you turn 61. You have accumulated $300,000 in your employer's retirement plan. When you receive your distribution, the amount is only $240,000 because your employer was required to send 20%, or $60,000, to the IRS for taxes. When you file your next tax return, you will report the $60,000 of withholding as tax you have already paid along with any other amounts withheld from your regular paychecks during the year.

In addition, you must report $60,000 of the retirement plan distribution as income. The $240,000 that was rolled over is not subject to tax, but the $60,000 that was sent to the IRS to pay taxes is. Even though the withholding was mandatory, it is still treated as a taxable distribution. In essence, you took money out of your retirement account to pay your taxes.

On the plus side, you should be entitled to a big tax refund when you file your tax return, since you paid $60,000 (through withholding) for taxes due on your distribution, but the taxable portion itself was only $60,000. The remaining $240,000 was rolled over.

Similarly, if you borrow money from your plan and don't pay it all back by the time you are to receive your distribution, the unpaid loan amount counts as part of your distribution and is subject to both income tax and mandatory withholding. You might need to liquidate assets (except employer securities) in order to cover the withholding.

EXAMPLE: When you retire, you will have $10,000 of cash in your retirement plan and 5,000 mutual fund shares valued at $20 per share. The total value of your account is $110,000. However, you also borrowed money from the plan last year and still owe $20,000 on that loan. The plan will report a distribution of $130,000 to the IRS ($10,000 in cash plus $100,000 in mutual fund shares plus the outstanding loan balance of $20,000). The mandatory 20% withholding is based on the full $130,000 and, therefore, is $26,000. Because you have only $10,000 in cash, the plan must sell 800 of your mutual fund shares to come up with enough cash to cover the withholding. Thus, although a distribution of $130,000 is reported to the IRS, the amount you actually receive will be only $84,000, which is $130,000 reduced by the loan amount and reduced further by the 20% withholding ($130,000 − $20,000 − $26,000 = $84,000).

Forcing You to Sell Assets to Pay Taxes

What happens if there's not enough cash in your account to cover the required withholding? The news is not good. The plan administrator must withhold taxes even if it means selling property in the account to generate enough cash. If you hold stock you don't want to sell, you might be out of luck, unless one of these exceptions applies:

- The plan permits you to come up with the money for withholding from sources outside the plan. This requires that you have a stash of cash.
- If your retirement assets consist solely of cash and employer securities (as opposed to other securities or property) and you don't have enough cash to cover the 20% mandatory withholding, the administrator will withhold only the cash. In other words, you are not required to liquidate employer securities in order to pay the withholding.

EXAMPLE: On the day you retire from Flush Corp., your retirement plan assets consist of $5,000 in cash and 3,000 shares of Flush Corp. stock valued at $50 per share, or $150,000. The total value of your retirement plan is $155,000, which means that the mandatory withholding is $31,000 (20% × $155,000). Because you do not have $31,000 in cash and you are not required to liquidate employer stock, your mandatory withholding is limited to the amount of cash in your retirement account, which is $5,000.

Avoiding or Correcting Mandatory Withholding

Happily, you can avoid the withholding pitfalls altogether through direct rollover, assuming you don't need the money. Simply request that the plan administrator transfer your entire distribution directly into another qualified plan or an IRA. If you never have access to the funds during the transfer, the administrator is not required to withhold any money. The rule applies even if your distribution check is sent to you personally, as long as it is payable to the trustee or custodian of the new plan and not to you.

It is possible to elect a direct rollover for part of your distribution, saving you at least some of the mandatory withholding. Only the portion paid directly to you will be subject to mandatory withholding.

If something goes awry and you receive a distribution check reduced by the 20% withholding amount, you may still be able to make yourself whole. If you can come up with the cash to cover the amount withheld, you can deposit it into the new plan or IRA as though you received it as part of your distribution. Then at tax time, you can claim a refund of the entire withholding amount. You avoid income taxes and penalties and manage to roll over every dollar of the distribution.

Although this approach works, you must have adequate cash on hand to take advantage of it. And of course, the government has free use of your money until you file your next tax return.

You can use a similar strategy if you have an outstanding loan from your plan. In other words, you can use cash you have outside the plan to roll over the amount of the loan into the new plan (more on this below).

Notification of Mandatory Withholding

Are you worried that if you miss the direct rollover option you'll feel foolish? Take heart: It's not as easy to miss as you might think. Not only must the plan administrator give you the option to elect a direct rollover, but the administrator must notify you of the option at least 30 days (and no more than 90 days, lest you forget) before the distribution is to take place. (Failure to give notice will cost the administrator $100 per incidence, up to $50,000 per year.) However, once the administrator provides notice, the obligation has been satisfied. The administrator is not required to make sure you read the notice.

Loans From Qualified Plans

The law generally permits employees to borrow money from their qualified plans, although some plans do not allow it. Most do, however, because employees consider the ability to borrow from their retirement plans an important benefit. But the borrowing rules are stringent.

A loan from a qualified plan is considered a taxable distribution unless it satisfies certain requirements:

- The loan must be repaid at a reasonable rate of interest with well-defined repayment terms.
- The loan amount cannot exceed $50,000.

- The loan amount also cannot exceed the greater of $10,000 or 50% of your vested account balance. (The vested amount is the portion you may take with you when you leave the company.) In other words, the loan is limited to 50% of your vested balance unless your account is under $20,000. Then you may borrow up to $10,000 as long as you have that much in your account and the plan allows it.

EXAMPLE: You have a vested account balance of $70,000 in your employer's retirement plan. You would like to borrow as much as you can from the plan. The loan may not exceed $50,000. But it also may not exceed 50% of your vested account balance, which is $35,000 (50% × $70,000). Thus the maximum you may borrow from the plan is $35,000.

- If you have more than one outstanding loan, the total of all loans from the plan cannot exceed $50,000 reduced by the difference between the highest loan balance for the previous 12 months and the current balance.

EXAMPLE: On January 15, your vested benefit in your employer's retirement plan is $150,000. You borrow $25,000 from the plan. In December of the same year, you realize that you need to borrow some additional money to get through the holiday season. Although you had begun to pay back the first loan, you still owe $20,000. To compute the amount you may borrow now, you begin with the $50,000 limit and reduce it by the amount of money you still owe to the plan. That reduces your limit to $30,000 ($50,000 − $20,000). The $30,000 must be reduced further by the difference between the highest outstanding balance in the last 12 months (which was $25,000) and the current outstanding balance (which is $20,000). That difference is $5,000. Thus, the $30,000 is further reduced to $25,000, which is the maximum you may now borrow from the plan.

- The loan must be repaid within five years, using a level amortization schedule (like a home mortgage) with payments to be made at least quarterly. There is an exception to the five-year repayment rule if the loan is used to purchase (but not improve) a principal residence. In that case, you may simply repay the loan in a reasonable amount of time. (The tax code does not define "reasonable"—however, the IRS has been known to approve loans outstanding for as long as 30 years when they are used to make mortgage payments.)

As long as the above five requirements are met, the amount of the loan will not be considered a taxable distribution to you, either at the time it is made or during the repayment period.

Outstanding Loans When You Leave Your Job

If you leave your job before you have finished paying off your loan, or if your employer terminates the retirement plan altogether, the company will typically reduce your retirement plan benefits by the amount of the loan that is still outstanding. (Some companies will allow you to pay it back in a lump sum.)

When that happens, the amount of the outstanding loan, which is called the "offset" amount, is considered a distribution. That means you must pay income tax, and possibly early-distribution penalties, on that amount (even though you didn't receive any actual funds), unless you roll it over.

In order to "roll over" the offset amount, you will need to come up with funds from another source. Because it might be difficult to quickly come up with funds, the IRS gives you until the due date of your tax return (including extensions) to roll over the offset amount. The rest of the distribution, if any, is still subject to the 60-day rollover rule.

> **EXAMPLE:** Milo, age 35, borrowed $5,000 from his 401(k) plan in 2016. In 2019, Milo decides to leave the company and go to work for its competitor. He still owes $2,000 on his loan and his employer intends to reduce (offset) his retirement plan distribution by the $2,000. Milo's 401(k) balance is $55,000, but because of the outstanding loan, the company will distribute only $53,000 to him.

To avoid taxes and penalties, Milo must roll over $55,000 into an IRA or another qualified plan. He must roll over $53,000 of the retirement plan distribution within 60 days of the time he receives it. He will have until the due date for filing his 2019 income taxes (including extensions) to come up an additional $2,000 (the offset amount withheld by his employer) to bring his rollover total to $55,000. That additional $2,000 may be rolled over to another retirement plan or an IRA.

> ! **CAUTION**
>
> **Rollover options for loan offset amounts do not apply to defaulted loans.** If you had not kept up with your loan payments to your plan and your loan is in default, or if you are not in compliance with any other of the plan's rules regarding loans, then the rollover option for the offset amount is not available to you. Consequently, you will owe taxes and penalties (if applicable) on the entire offset amount.

Hardship Distributions From Qualified Plans

A special relief provision in the tax code allows participants in 401(k) plans and other profit-sharing plans—but no other type of qualified plan—to withdraw money in the event of hardship. It is not sufficient that the law permits such withdrawals; the plan itself must specifically allow them as well.

The tax code defines a hardship withdrawal to be a distribution because of "immediate and heavy financial need." The plan must establish objective and nondiscriminatory ways of determining whether such a need exists and measuring the amount of money necessary to satisfy that need.

The IRS provides a list of expenses that qualify as hardship withdrawals. That means that if your expenses fall into one of the listed categories and your plan allows hardship withdrawals, your distribution will generally qualify as a hardship withdrawal. The IRS expenditures are as follows:

- medical expenses for you, your spouse, or your dependents
- expenses to purchase a principal residence (but not money to make mortgage payments)

- expenses to pay postsecondary education for a 12-month period, including tuition, room, and board, and
- expenses to stave off eviction from your principal residence or to forestall a foreclosure.

TIP

Congress sometimes passes relief legislation for specific natural disasters. In the wake of a disaster, Congress will occasionally pass legislation easing loan qualification requirements or hardship distribution requirements for qualified plans. This legislation typically applies only to specific catastrophes, such as a particular hurricane or wildfire, and comes with an expiration date.

Expenses can qualify for hardship withdrawals even if they don't fall into one of the above categories. Employers have broad discretion to define hardship for their employees. However, the plan document must provide some method of determining whether an expense constitutes immediate and heavy financial need. You must also provide a statement to the IRS declaring that you have exhausted other available resources. For example, if you have a vacation home, you would be required to sell it and use the proceeds before you would qualify to take money out of your plan.

Now the coup de grace. Suppose you jump through all the hoops and are eligible for a hardship withdrawal. What you gain is access to your funds without disqualifying the plan. But a hardship withdrawal is still subject to income tax (although it is not subject to the 20% mandatory withholding at the time of distribution). And you will also owe a 10% early distribution penalty if you are younger than 59½, unless the withdrawal qualifies for one of the exceptions described in Chapter 3.

CAUTION

Hardship distributions are not eligible to be rolled over into an IRA or another qualified plan. So if you take a distribution from your 401(k) plan under its hardship provisions, and then you decide you don't need the money after all, you are stuck. You cannot roll it into an IRA, nor can you put it back into the plan.

Special Income Tax Rules for Tax-Deferred Annuities

Although tax-deferred annuities, or TDAs, closely track the taxation rules for qualified plans, there are some important differences. (See Chapter 1 for more information about TDAs.)

Ordinary income tax applies. In general, distributions from TDAs will be taxed along with the rest of your income at normal tax rates unless you roll over the distribution. But you may not exclude from your income the net unrealized appreciation in employer stock, as you can with a qualified plan.

Rollover. As with qualified plan distributions, you may roll over any portion of a TDA distribution into an IRA or another retirement plan. However, if you roll over the TDA distribution into a qualified plan, you forfeit the right to use ten-year averaging on any future distribution from that qualified plan.

Averaging and capital gain treatment not allowed. Ten-year averaging is not permitted for distributions from TDAs, and neither is capital gain treatment for pre-1974 accumulations. Distributions from TDAs must be rolled over or they will be subject to ordinary income tax at the tax rates in effect in the year of distribution.

QDRO rules apply. The QDRO rules apply to TDAs just as they do to qualified plans, except that the alternate payee is not permitted to use ten-year averaging or the special capital gain treatment.

Hardship distributions permitted. Hardship distributions from TDAs are permitted and are subject to the same rules as hardship distributions from 401(k) plans.

Special Income Tax Rules for IRAs

Unlike TDAs, which mimic qualified plans in most respects, IRAs are quite different and in many ways more restrictive.

> **CAUTION**
>
> **Roth IRAs are not standard IRAs.** If you have a Roth IRA, the following rules might not apply. See Chapter 9 for a detailed description of Roth IRAs and the taxes, penalties, and distribution rules that apply to them.

Ordinary Income Tax Applies

All distributions from traditional IRAs are subject to ordinary income tax unless you have made nondeductible contributions to the IRA over the years. In that case, a portion of each distribution will be tax free. The fair market value of the taxable portion is simply included with your income and taxed at your normal rates. You may not use capital gain rates, nor may you claim losses.

Rollover Allowed

You can roll IRA distributions into another IRA or even into your employer's plan—with certain restrictions.

Roll to Another IRA

You may roll over an IRA or part of an IRA into a different IRA or even back into the same IRA, but you must follow two important rules.

Rule Number One: 60-Day Time Limit. If you take a distribution with the intention of rolling it into a different IRA, you have 60 days from the time you receive the distribution to deposit it into the new IRA. If you miss the deadline, you will owe income tax and perhaps penalties, such as an early distribution tax. (See Chapter 3.)

> **TIP**
>
> **If you need a short-term loan.** It is quite acceptable to take money from your IRA as long as you deposit it into another IRA, or back into the same IRA, within 60 days. The transaction is treated as a rollover rather than a loan. Just be careful to redeposit the precise amount of cash you distributed in the first place. Don't buy stock with the distributed funds and then try to deposit the stock into the IRA in lieu of the cash. If cash came out, cash must go back in.

Rule Number Two: Only One Per Year. You are permitted only one rollover per year from an IRA. If you own multiple IRAs, whether traditional, Roth, SEP, or SIMPLE, and roll over an amount from one, you may not roll over any additional amounts from any of your IRAs for 12 months. For example, let's say you have two IRAs. IRA #1 has a balance of $50,000 and IRA #2 has a balance of $80,000. You decide to roll over $20,000 from IRA #1 to IRA #2. After doing so, you may not roll over any amount from either IRA #1 or IRA #2 for 12 months. (Note that the restriction is for a full 12 months, not just until the end of the calendar year.)

This one-rollover-per-year rule for IRAs applies to spouse beneficiaries too. If you name your spouse as beneficiary of your IRA and if she decides to roll over your IRA into her own IRA when you die, that rollover will count as her one rollover for the year. (See Chapters 7 and 8 for more information about spousal rollovers.)

CAUTION

Conversions are excluded from the one-rollover-per-year rule. If you convert some or all of your traditional IRA to a Roth IRA, that transaction is not counted as a rollover for purposes of the one-rollover-per-year rule. You are not limited in the number of times you may convert assets from a traditional IRA to a Roth IRA.

TIP

The one-rollover-per-year rule applies only to rollovers, not direct transfers. This rule does not apply to transfers that go directly from one IRA custodian to another. For example, if you want to roll funds from IRA #1 to IRA #2, you could simply ask the custodian of IRA #1 to send you a check. When you receive it, you deliver it to the custodian of IRA #2. That is considered a rollover. But if you instruct the custodian of IRA #1 to transfer funds directly to the custodian of IRA #2, so that you never personally receive the funds, that is considered a transfer. The IRS is more lenient with transfers, because you don't have access to the funds and presumably can't do anything improper. The IRS allows you to make as many transfers as you like during the year.

Roll to an Employer Plan

You may also roll over some or all of your IRA distribution into your employer's plan, provided the plan permits such rollovers. Be careful, though; you are not permitted to roll over any after-tax amounts from the IRA to the employer plan. Thus, if you have made nondeductible contributions to the IRA, you cannot roll these into an employer plan.

60-Day Rule

For years, the IRS has been devilishly unforgiving of taxpayers who failed to complete a rollover in the allotted 60 days, regardless of the merits of their excuses. However, in 2016, the IRS issued a revenue procedure (Rev. Proc. 2016-47) listing 11 circumstances in which a taxpayer may claim eligibility for a waiver of the 60-day time limit. Here are the circumstances:

- An error was committed either by the financial institution receiving the contribution or by the financial institution making the distribution to which the contribution relates.
- The distribution, having been made in the form of a check, was misplaced and never cashed.
- The distribution was deposited into and remained in an account that the taxpayer mistakenly thought was an eligible retirement plan.
- The taxpayer's principal residence was severely damaged.
- A member of the taxpayer's family died.
- The taxpayer or a member of the taxpayer's family was seriously ill.
- The taxpayer was incarcerated.
- Restrictions were imposed by a foreign country.
- A postal error occurred.
- The distribution was made on account of a levy, and the proceeds of the levy have been returned to the taxpayer.
- The party making the distribution to which the rollover relates delayed providing information that the receiving plan or IRA required in order to complete the rollover despite the taxpayer's reasonable efforts to obtain the information.

If you claim a waiver for one of the above reasons, the IRS will take your word for it, provided you satisfy all of the following eligibility requirements:

- The IRS has not previously denied a waiver request for some or all of the same funds.
- You correct the problem by contributing the funds to the intended plan or IRA as soon as possible after one or more of the above circumstances no longer prevent you from making the contribution. According to the revenue procedure, the condition "as soon as possible" will be deemed satisfied if the contribution is completed no later than 30 days after you are no longer prevented from making the contribution.
- You make a written certification (which the IRS calls a self-certification) to your plan administrator or IRA custodian stating that you are eligible for a waiver. You do not need to send a copy of the certification to the IRS, but you should keep a copy in your files in case you are audited. The IRS has provided a template for the self-certification and suggests that you use it rather than creating your own. However, if you do create your own, it should be substantially similar. You will find a copy of the IRS's self-certification template in Appendix A.

The above circumstances make you eligible for an automatic waiver, but the IRS has the authority to grant you a waiver for other reasons as well.

Qualified Charitable Distribution

You may make a charitable donation directly from your IRA (or an IRA you inherited) and not pay tax on the amount you withdraw. Here's the fine print:

- You must be at least age 70½ on the day the money is distributed from the IRA.
- Only traditional IRAs and Roth IRAs qualify—not active SEPs or SIMPLE IRAs.
- The money must be sent directly from the custodian of the IRA to the charity. In other words, you cannot take the money out and deposit it in one of your bank accounts and then give it to charity.
- The amount you may give to charity without paying tax on the IRA distribution is limited to $100,000. This is a per-person limit.

If you and your spouse both have IRAs and you both otherwise qualify, you may each give up to $100,000 to charity from your respective IRAs.

- You may give the charity pretax money only. So, for example, your after-tax contributions in your Roth IRA are not eligible for donation under this provision.

If you follow the above rules, then you may exclude your IRA distribution from your income at tax time. Furthermore, you may use the distribution to satisfy part or all of your required minimum distribution from your IRA for the year. (See Chapter 6 for information about required minimum distributions.)

Averaging and Capital Gain Treatment Not Allowed

Neither ten-year averaging nor capital gain treatment is permitted on distributions from an IRA.

Special Rules at Divorce or Separation

The QDRO rules for qualified plans do not apply to IRAs. It is still possible to give a spouse or former spouse an IRA or a portion of an IRA, however, as part of a marital property settlement without subjecting the distribution to current income tax or penalties. To do so, you must have a valid divorce decree, a written instrument incident to divorce, a written agreement incident to a legal separation, or a maintenance or an alimony decree.

With one of those documents in place, the IRA may be transferred in whole or in part to a spouse or former spouse through one of the following methods:

- The custodian of the participant's IRA may transfer the IRA directly to the trustee of the spouse or former spouse's IRA.
- The participant may direct the custodian to change the title of the IRA to an IRA in the spouse's or former spouse's name.
- The original participant or owner may roll over the IRA into an IRA in the name of the spouse or former spouse.

Under no circumstances, however, should the spouse or former spouse initiate the transfer of the participant's IRA or take possession of the funds before they are deposited into an IRA in the spouse's name. Only the participant may direct the transfer or rollover. Once the funds are in an IRA in the name of the spouse or former spouse, the IRA is treated in every respect as though the spouse or former spouse were the original owner. When assets are later distributed, they will be subject to ordinary income tax and perhaps penalties, for which the spouse or former spouse will be liable.

> **CAUTION**
>
> **You'll still owe the early distribution tax.** Although there is an exception to the early distribution tax for distributions to an alternate payee under a QDRO, that exception does not apply to IRAs. (See Chapter 3 for more information about the early distribution tax.)

Mandatory Withholding Doesn't Apply

Distributions from IRAs are not subject to the mandatory withholding rules discussed earlier in this chapter that apply to distributions from qualified plans.

Loans Not Allowed

You are not permitted to borrow from an IRA (except for the 60-day short-term rollover discussed above). If you do, the consequences are disastrous. If you borrow any amount at all, the entire IRA is disqualified and all assets deemed distributed. The distribution will be subject to income taxes and perhaps other penalties as well, such as the early distribution tax.

Hardship Distributions Not Allowed

There is no such thing as a hardship distribution from any type of IRA. That's because hardship distributions are not necessary. Unlike a qualified plan, which restricts your access to funds, you can take money out of your IRA any time you want. Of course, you will have to pay income tax and, if you are younger than 59½, you'll also have to pay an early distribution tax. But you always have access to the money.

How Penalties Can Guide Planning

In this chapter and the previous one, we have defined the most common types of retirement plans, highlighted their differences, and discussed the income tax consequences of distributions. In the remaining chapters, we discuss distribution rules that apply across the board, to qualified plans, qualified annuities, TDAs, and IRAs. Those rules come with punishing penalties for violations. The penalties are in the form of an additional tax, but are usually avoidable if you understand the rules.

The following two penalty taxes will drive many of the decisions you make about your retirement plan or IRA.

Early distribution penalty. You will be hit with an early distribution tax if you take a retirement plan distribution too early—usually before age 59½. This penalty is discussed in depth in Chapters 3 and 4.

Required distribution penalty. Once you reach a certain age, usually 70½, you will be required to take a minimum amount from your retirement plan each year. If you don't, you will be subject to a huge penalty: 50% of the shortfall. Similar rules apply after you inherit a retirement plan. These required distributions are discussed in Chapters 5 through 8.

Permissible Rollovers	
Original Plan	**New Plan**
Qualified plan—401(a)	Traditional IRA Roth IRA SEP SIMPLE IRA Qualified plan—401(a) Qualified annuity plan—403(a) Tax-deferred annuity—403(b) In-plan conversion to designated Roth account
Qualified annuity plan—403(a)*	Traditional IRA SEP SIMPLE IRA Qualified plan—401(a) Qualified annuity plan—403(a) Tax-deferred annuity—403(b)

Permissible Rollovers (continued)	
Original Plan	**New Plan**
Tax-deferred annuity—403(b)	Traditional IRA Roth IRA SEP SIMPLE IRA Qualified plan—401(a) Qualified annuity plan—403(a) Tax-deferred annuity—403(b) In-plan conversion to designated Roth account
SEP	Traditional IRA Roth IRA SEP SIMPLE IRA Qualified plan—401(a)** Qualified annuity plan—403(a)** Tax-deferred annuity plan—403(b)**
SIMPLE IRA	SIMPLE IRA Traditional IRA (after two years) Roth IRA (after two years) SEP (after two years) Qualified plan—401(a) (after two years) Qualified annuity plan—403(a) (after two years) Tax-deferred annuity—403(b) (after two years)
Traditional IRA	Traditional IRA Roth IRA SEP SIMPLE IRA Qualified plan—401(a)** Qualified annuity plan—403(a)** Tax-deferred annuity plan—403(b)**
Roth IRA	Roth IRA
Roth 401(k) plan	Roth 401(k) plan Roth IRA

* 403(a) plans often don't permit rollovers to or from any other plan even though the law itself permits it.

** Can receive pretax portion only.

Key Tax Code Sections and Pronouncements

§ 401(a)(31)

Direct Rollover.

§ 402

Rollovers; Ten-Year Averaging.

§ 402A

Optional Treatment of Elective Deferrals as Roth Contributions.

§ 414(p)

Qualified Domestic Relations Orders (QDROs).

§ 3405

Qualified Plan Withholding Rules.

§ 4975

Prohibited Transactions.

Announcement 2014–15

Application of One-per-Year Limit on IRA Rollovers.

Notice 2014-54

Guidance on Allocating After-Tax Amounts to Rollovers.

Revenue Procedure 2016-47

Waiver of 60-day Rollover Requirement.

Early Distributions: Taking Your Money Out Before the Law Allows

---

Who Should Read Chapter 3

Read this chapter if you are younger than 59½ and want to withdraw money from your retirement plan or IRA. If you are older than 59½, this chapter does not apply to you.

I f you take money out of a qualified plan, qualified annuity, tax-deferred annuity, or an IRA before you reach age 59½, your withdrawal is called an early distribution, and you will have to pay a 10% early distribution tax on the money unless you can meet one of the exceptions.

This chapter describes those exceptions. It also explains how to calculate and report the tax just in case your distribution doesn't fit within one of those exceptions. In addition, it describes special rules for IRAs.

CAUTION

Don't forget regular income taxes. The exceptions we describe in this chapter help you escape the early distribution tax, not income taxes.

Exceptions to the Early Distribution Tax

The 10% early distribution tax feels more like a penalty than a tax, and no wonder: It is the cornerstone of the government's efforts to discourage us from plundering our savings before our golden years. Fortunately, there are many exceptions to the rule. You may not have to pay the early distribution tax if any of the following apply:

- You are age 59½.
- You die.
- You become disabled.
- You choose to take substantially equal periodic payments.
- You are at least 55 years old when you leave your job

Helpful Terms

Adjusted gross income (AGI). Total taxable income reduced by certain expenses, such as qualified plan or IRA contributions or alimony payments. Note: Adjusted gross income does not take into account any itemized deductions (see definition below).

After-tax contribution. A contribution to a retirement plan or an IRA for which no deduction was taken on an income tax return.

Ancestor. A person from whom an individual is descended. For example, an individual's parents, grandparents, and great grandparents are among his or her ancestors.

Distribution. A payout of property (such as shares of stock) or cash from a retirement plan or an IRA to the participant or a beneficiary.

Itemized deductions. Expenses, such as medical payments, mortgage interest, and charitable contributions, that may be used to reduce AGI to arrive at the total amount of income subject to tax.

Principal residence. The home in which an individual lives most of the time. ("Most" is not defined in the tax code. It is established by your actions.)

Separation from service. Termination of employment.

Standard deduction. A fixed dollar amount that may be used instead of itemized deductions to reduce AGI before computing tax liability.

- You are a qualified reservist called to active duty.
- The distributions are dividends from an ESOP.
- You withdraw the money to pay medical expenses.
- You withdraw the money to pay child support or alimony or as part of a QDRO (Qualified Domestic Relations Order).
- You use the money to pay a federal tax levy.
- The money is actually a refund.

You can read more about each of these exceptions in the sections below.

> ( ) **TIP**
>
> **Congress might pass legislation providing for additional exceptions.** In the wake of a natural disaster, Congress will occasionally pass legislation exempting certain distributions from the 10% early distribution penalty. This legislation typically applies only to specific events, such as a particular hurricane or wildfire, and the relief is available only for a limited period of time.

Age 59½

Although it's a little nonsensical to call being 59½ an exception to the tax on early distributions (after all, if you are 59½, your distribution isn't early in the first place), the tax code views it as an exception, so that is the way we discuss it here.

Before taking money out, make sure you will be at least 59½ on the day of the withdrawal. Otherwise, you'll pay the tax. In other words, it's not good enough that you turn 59½ during the year of the withdrawal. You must be at least 59½ on the day that you get the funds.

> ( ) **CAUTION**
>
> **Escaping the early distribution tax doesn't mean you get free access to your money.** Just because you have passed age 59½ doesn't guarantee that you can take money out of your retirement plan. Many qualified plans do not permit distributions before you terminate your employment. Attaining age 59½ simply ensures that if you are able to take money out, it will not be subject to the early distribution tax.

Death

Another straightforward exception to the tax, albeit a less attractive one, is death. None of the funds distributed from your retirement plan after your death will be subject to the early distribution tax, as long as the account is still in your name when the distribution occurs.

If you are the beneficiary of your spouse's retirement plan or IRA, then upon your spouse's death you may roll over a distribution from your spouse's retirement plan or IRA to a retirement plan or an IRA of your own. (See Chapters 7 and 8 for more information about post-death distributions.) This benefit is available only to you as a spouse beneficiary. But once the funds have been rolled over into an IRA in your name, the post-death exception to the early distribution tax no longer applies, because the account is no longer in the deceased owner's name.

If you want to roll over a post-death distribution from your deceased spouse's retirement plan into an IRA or a plan of your own, but need to hold back some of the money for living expenses, this could pose a problem. If you take a distribution from a retirement plan while the plan is still in your deceased spouse's name, the distribution will indeed avoid the 10% tax. But the IRS has ruled that when a surviving spouse invokes this exception, the spouse forfeits the option to roll over the remainder into an IRA in his or her own name. Although this conclusion arises from a private letter ruling (which means that other taxpayers may not rely on the result when planning their own tax strategies), it serves as a warning.

The logical solution to this problem is for the spouse to roll over only the amount that is not needed for living expenses, leaving the remainder in the deceased spouse's name (in other words, do the rollover first). The remaining portion could then be tapped to pay expenses without incurring the 10% tax. The IRS has not yet ruled on such a strategy, however.

About Private Letter Rulings

Many taxpayers who are unclear about how to proceed in a murky area of the tax law and who feel they have too much at stake to take a wait-and-see posture with the IRS will request private letter rulings. These rulings are just what their title implies—private—meaning the ruling applies only to the taxpayer who requested it and only to the situation in question. The result of the ruling will not serve as precedent and cannot be relied upon by anyone else with similar or even identical circumstances. But the rulings can provide valuable insights into which way the IRS leans on a particular issue.

Disability

If you become disabled, you can take money out of your retirement plan without worrying about the early distribution tax.

But what does it mean to be disabled? And who decides? The law defines disabled as the inability to "engage in any substantial gainful activity by reason of any medically determinable physical or mental impairment which can be expected to result in death or to be of long-continued and indefinite duration." Is this helpful?

The key to the disability exception seems to lie in the permanence of the condition, not the severity. Disability exceptions have been denied for chemical dependence and chronic depression, even when the taxpayers were hospitalized for those conditions. It also appears that the disability must be deemed permanent at the time of the distribution, whether or not it is later found to be permanent. For example, the IRS denied the disability exception for a taxpayer, even knowing that the taxpayer later qualified for Social Security disability benefits.

Successful disability claims have included a dentist who suffered nerve damage to his thumb and who produced documents from four insurance companies declaring his disability permanent. Another successful claim involved a taxpayer who had been granted a disability retirement by his company. The IRS relied on the company's determination of the individual's disability. These cases reveal that the IRS is most concerned about the timing and the nature of the disability. Using the cases as a guide, if your disability prevents you from working and is deemed permanent at the time you take your retirement plan distribution, then you should qualify for the disability exception. But there are no guarantees in this arena.

The IRS regulations do clarify one point, however. Gainful activity refers specifically to the type of work you were doing before becoming disabled. Thus it would seem that you need not be unfit for all work, just the work you customarily do.

Substantially Equal Periodic Payments

The substantially equal periodic payment exception is available to anyone with an IRA or a retirement plan, regardless of age, which makes it an attractive escape hatch. Theoretically, if you begin taking distributions from your retirement plan in equal annual installments, and those payments are designed to be spread out over your entire life or the joint life of you and your beneficiary, then the payments will not be subject to an early distribution tax.

The fly in the ointment is that you are not permitted to compute payments any way you please. The payment method must conform to IRS guidelines, which sanction three computation methods. Nonetheless, the guidelines are somewhat flexible, making the exception at once versatile and complex. For these reasons, Chapter 4 is devoted exclusively to interpreting the IRS's computational guidelines and related rulings.

If you think you might need to tap your retirement plan early, this is the option that is most likely to work for you. One caveat: If you want to begin taking substantially equal periodic payments from your employer's plan, you must have terminated your employment before payments begin. If the payments are from an IRA, however, the status of your employment is irrelevant.

Leaving Your Job After Age 55

If you are at least 55 years old when you leave your job, you will not have to pay the early distribution tax on money that you take out of your retirement plan. This exception applies per employer, meaning that you can go to work for another employer and still meet this exception to your previous employer's plan.

This exception is relevant only if you are between ages 55 and 59½. After age 59½, the early distribution tax does not apply to any retirement plan distribution.

As with other exceptions, you must pay attention to certain details. For example, you need not be age 55 on the day you leave your job, as long as you turn 55 by December 31 of the same year. The strategy falls apart if you retire in a year that precedes the year you turn 55, even if you postpone receiving the retirement benefits until you reach age 55.

> **EXAMPLE:** You retire at age 53 and convince your employer to keep your retirement plan benefits in the plan until you reach age 55. The day after your 55th birthday, you receive $100,000 from your former employer's plan. You buy a Jaguar and spend the rest of the money on a trip around the world. At tax time, you will owe regular income tax on the $100,000 plus a 10% early distribution tax.
>
> If, instead, you had retired in the same year you turned 55, the $100,000 would be subject to regular income tax, but you would not have to pay an early distribution tax.

TIP

Age 55 exception reduced to age 50 for certain public safety employees participating in government plans. Certain public safety employees who participate in government-sponsored retirement plans are able to take penalty-free distributions from their retirement plans if they separate from service after age 50. Public safety employees include:

- federal firefighters
- federal law enforcement officers
- federal customs and border protections officers
- air traffic controllers
- nuclear material couriers
- U.S. capitol police
- Supreme Court police, and
- State Department diplomatic security agents.

CAUTION

The age 50 and 55 exceptions described above are not available for IRAs. See "Special Rules for IRAs," below, for other rules that apply only to IRAs.

Qualified Reservist Distribution

If a member of the reserves is called to active duty for a period of more than 179 days or for an indefinite period, then distributions received on or after the date of the call to active duty, and before the end of the period of active duty, will not be subject to the early distribution tax. This exception applies only to individual retirement accounts and to salary deferral contributions to other types of plans.

> **TIP**
>
> **Qualified reservist distribution may be returned to the retirement plan.** The law provides an additional benefit to those who take qualified reservist distributions. After completing active duty, members of the reserves are permitted to return some or all of the distribution they received while on active duty, as long as it is returned within two years of the end of their active duty period.

Dividends From ESOPs

You do not have to pay the early distribution tax on distributions of dividends from employer stock held inside an ESOP, no matter when you receive the dividends. (See Chapter 1 for more information about ESOPs.)

Medical Expenses

If you withdraw money from a retirement plan to pay medical expenses, a portion of that distribution might escape the early distribution tax. But once again, the exception is not as simple or as generous as it sounds. The tax exemption applies only to the portion of your medical expenses that would be deductible if you itemized deductions on your tax return. Medical expenses are deductible if they are yours, your spouse's, or your dependent's. But they are deductible only to the extent they exceed 10% (up from 7.5% in 2018) of your adjusted gross income. Consequently, your retirement plan distribution will avoid the early distribution tax only to the extent it also exceeds the 10% threshold.

EXAMPLE: You are single and your adjusted gross income is $50,000. You had medical bills of $6,000 during the year, which you paid with funds you withdrew from your retirement plan. For income tax purposes, you are permitted to deduct medical expenses that exceed 10% of your adjusted gross income. Thus, your calculation is as follows:

Adjusted gross income (AGI)	=	$50,000
Nondeductible medical expenses 10% of AGI (0.10 × $50,000)	=	$ 5,000
Deductible medical expenses excess ($6,000 − $5,000)	=	$ 1,000

Although you took $6,000 from your retirement plan to pay medical expenses, only $1,000 will escape the early distribution tax. The remaining $5,000 will be subject to the 10% additional tax (unless you qualify for another exception). And don't forget that the entire $6,000 is subject to regular income tax, as well.

On the plus side, the medical expense exception to the early distribution tax is available even if you don't itemize deductions. It applies to those amounts that would be deductible if you did itemize.

EXAMPLE: As in the preceding example, your adjusted gross income is $50,000. You have $6,000 of medical expenses, which you paid with funds from your retirement plan. Only $1,000 of those expenses are deductible (as calculated above). Your deductible items for the year are as follows:

Deductible medical:	$1,000
Deductible taxes:	$1,500
Charitable contributions:	$ 700
Total	$3,200

The standard deduction for a single individual is greater than $3,200. When computing your tax liability, you are permitted to reduce your adjusted gross income by the larger of your itemized deductions or the standard deduction. In this case, because the standard deduction is larger, you will not itemize deductions on your tax return. You may still exclude $1,000 of your retirement plan distribution from the early distribution tax computation, however.

QDRO Payments

If you are paying child support or alimony from your retirement plan, or if you intend to distribute some or all of the plan to your former spouse as part of a property settlement, you will not have to pay an early distribution tax on any of those payments as long as there is a QDRO in place that orders the payments. (See Chapter 2 for more information about QDROs.) A QDRO usually arises from a separation or divorce agreement and involves court-ordered payments to an alternate payee, such as a former spouse or minor child. Although the QDRO exception applies to all distributions from a qualified plan to any named alternate payee, it is critical that the payments arise from a valid QDRO, not just a private agreement between you and your former spouse.

> CAUTION
>
> **The exception to the early distribution tax for QDRO payments does not apply to IRAs.** See "Special Rules for IRAs," below, for more information.

Federal Tax Levy

If you owe back taxes, you can be reasonably certain the government will try to collect them. If you have assets in a retirement plan, the government can take those assets (in other words, the IRS can put a levy on the assets of the plan) to pay your debt. If it does, then those amounts taken for taxes will not be subject to the early distribution penalty. This shouldn't be too much of a worry for you because IRS policy frowns on the government grabbing retirement plans to satisfy back tax debts unless the debtor is uncooperative and has no other assets.

Refunds

If you receive a refund of a contribution to your retirement plan because you contributed more than the law permits, you will not have to pay the early distribution tax on those corrective distributions.

Calculating the Tax

If you take money out a retirement plan before you reach age 59½ and cannot meet one of the exceptions described above, you will have to pay a 10% early distribution tax on the money. This tax applies to the taxable portion of your distribution only. So if you receive a distribution that includes after-tax contributions that you made to your retirement plan, the 10% tax will not apply to that portion. Similarly, if you receive a distribution of employer stock and elect to exclude the net unrealized appreciation from your taxable income, the excluded portion will not fall under the 10% tax. (See Chapter 2 for more information about employer stock and net unrealized appreciation.)

> EXAMPLE: You retire at age 51 and take $80,000 out of your retirement plan. The distribution includes $15,000 of after-tax contributions that you made to the plan over the years. The remaining $65,000 consists of employer contributions and investment returns. You plan to use the money to buy a vacation home, so you don't meet any of the exceptions to the early distribution tax. At tax time, you will owe regular income tax and the 10% early distribution tax on the $65,000 portion; you will owe no taxes on the $15,000 portion.

Reporting the Tax

If you take a distribution from a retirement plan during the year, the trustee or custodian of your retirement plan will send you a copy of IRS Form 1099-R, which reports the amount distributed to you. (See below for a sample Form 1099-R.) The trustee or custodian will also send a copy to the IRS. You don't need to attach a copy of Form 1099-R to your tax return unless income tax was withheld from your distribution. In that case, you must attach the 1099-R just as you would attach your W-2 to show how much tax was withheld.

Sample Form 1099-R From Plan Trustee or Custodian to Report Distribution

9898	☐ VOID	☐ CORRECTED			
PAYER'S name, street address, city or town, state or province, country, ZIP or foreign postal code, and phone no. Tech Inc. 401(k) Plan 786 Chipstone Way Sunburn, California 99999		**1** Gross distribution $ 1,500 **2a** Taxable amount $ 1,500	OMB No. 1545-0119 20**18** Form **1099-R**	**Distributions From Pensions, Annuities, Retirement or Profit-Sharing Plans, IRAs, Insurance Contracts, etc.**	
		2b Taxable amount not determined ☐	Total distribution ☐	**Copy A** **For**	
PAYER'S TIN 99-9999	RECIPIENT'S TIN 555-55-5555	**3** Capital gain (included in box 2a) $	**4** Federal income tax withheld $ 300	**Internal Revenue Service Center** File with Form 1096.	
RECIPIENT'S name Geoff Sute		**5** Employee contributions/ Designated Roth contributions or insurance premiums $	**6** Net unrealized appreciation in employer's securities $	For Privacy Act and Paperwork Reduction Act Notice, see the	
Street address (including apt. no.) 42 Rising Ave.		**7** Distribution code(s) 1	IRA/ SEP/ SIMPLE ☐	**8** Other $ %	**2018 General Instructions for Certain**
City or town, state or province, country, and ZIP or foreign postal code Sand City, CA 93955		**9a** Your percentage of total distribution %		**9b** Total employee contributions $	**Information Returns.**
10 Amount allocable to IRR within 5 years $	**11** 1st year of desig. Roth contrib.	FATCA filing requirement ☐	**12** State tax withheld $ $	**13** State/Payer's state no.	**14** State distribution $ $
Account number (see instructions)		Date of payment	**15** Local tax withheld $ $	**16** Name of locality	**17** Local distribution $ $

Form **1099-R**   Cat. No. 14436Q   www.irs.gov/Form1099R   Department of the Treasury - Internal Revenue Service

Do Not Cut or Separate Forms on This Page — Do Not Cut or Separate Forms on This Page

If you are younger than 59½ at the time of the distribution, a Code 1 should appear in Box 7 of the form, indicating that the early distribution tax applies. If you are younger than 59½ but you qualify for another exception (including having left your job after age 55), Box 7 should reflect that information as well. Code 3 indicates a disability exception, Code 4 is a post-death distribution, and Code 2 is for most other exceptions.

> **EXAMPLE:** At age 30, Geoff Sute quit his job with Tech Inc. for a higher paying job with another company. Tech Inc. distributed $1,500 to Geoff, which represented the entire balance of his 401(k) plan account. Geoff decided to spend the $1,500 on a new suit. At tax time, Tech Inc. sent Geoff a Form 1099-R reporting the distribution. (See sample form above.) Note that Box 7 correctly shows a Code 1.

Sample Form 1040 to Report Early Distribution

Form 1040 Department of the Treasury—Internal Revenue Service (99)
U.S. Individual Income Tax Return **2018** OMB No. 1545-0074 IRS Use Only—Do not write or staple in this space.

Filing status:	☐ Single	☐ Married filing jointly	☐ Married filing separately	☐ Head of household	☐ Qualifying widow(er)

Your first name and initial	Last name	Your social security number
Geoff	Sute	555 55 5555

Your standard deduction: ☐ Someone can claim you as a dependent ☐ You were born before January 2, 1954 ☐ You are blind

If joint return, spouse's first name and initial	Last name	Spouse's social security number

Spouse standard deduction: ☐ Someone can claim your spouse as a dependent ☐ Spouse was born before January 2, 1954 ☐ Full-year health care coverage
☐ Spouse is blind ☐ Spouse itemizes on a separate return or you were dual-status alien or exempt (see inst.)

Home address (number and street). If you have a P.O. box, see instructions.	Apt. no.	Presidential Election Campaign (see inst.)
42 Rising Ave.		☐ You ☐ Spouse

City, town or post office, state, and ZIP code. If you have a foreign address, attach Schedule 6.	If more than four dependents, see inst. and ✓ here ► ☐
Sand City, CA 93955	

Dependents (see instructions):

(1) First name Last name	(2) Social security number	(3) Relationship to you	(4) ✓ if qualifies for (see inst.):
			Child tax credit / Credit for other dependents
			☐ ☐
			☐ ☐
			☐ ☐
			☐ ☐

Sign Here
Joint return? See instructions.
Keep a copy for your records.

Under penalties of perjury, I declare that I have examined this return and accompanying schedules and statements, and to the best of my knowledge and belief, they are true, correct, and complete. Declaration of preparer (other than taxpayer) is based on all information of which preparer has any knowledge.

Your signature	Date	Your occupation	If the IRS sent you an Identity Protection PIN, enter it here (see inst.)
Spouse's signature. If a joint return, **both** must sign.	Date	Spouse's occupation	If the IRS sent you an Identity Protection PIN, enter it here (see inst.)

Paid Preparer Use Only

Preparer's name	Preparer's signature	PTIN	Firm's EIN	Check if:
				☐ 3rd Party Designee
Firm's name ►		Phone no.		☐ Self-employed
Firm's address ►				

For Disclosure, Privacy Act, and Paperwork Reduction Act Notice, see separate instructions. Cat. No. 11320B Form **1040** (2018)

Form 1040 (2018) Page **2**

	1	Wages, salaries, tips, etc. Attach Form(s) W-2	1
Attach Form(s) W-2. Also attach Form(s) W-2G and 1099-R if tax was withheld.	2a	Tax-exempt interest . . . 2a	b Taxable interest . . 2b
	3a	Qualified dividends . . . 3a	b Ordinary dividends . . 3b
	4a	IRAs, pensions, and annuities . 4a 1,500	b Taxable amount . . 4b 1,500
	5a	Social security benefits . . 5a	b Taxable amount . . 5b
	6	Total income. Add lines 1 through 5. Add any amount from Schedule 1, line 22	6
	7	Adjusted gross income. If you have no adjustments to income, enter the amount from line 6; otherwise, subtract Schedule 1, line 36, from line 6	7
Standard Deduction for— • Single or married filing separately, $12,000 • Married filing jointly or Qualifying widow(er), $24,000 • Head of household, $18,000 • If you checked any box under Standard deduction, see instructions.	8	Standard deduction or itemized deductions (from Schedule A)	8
	9	Qualified business income deduction (see instructions) .	9
	10	Taxable income. Subtract lines 8 and 9 from line 7. If zero or less, enter -0-	10
	11	a Tax (see inst.) _____ (check if any from: 1 ☐ Form(s) 8814 2 ☐ Form 4972 3 ☐ _____)	
		b Add any amount from Schedule 2 and check here ► ☐	11
	12	a Child tax credit/credit for other dependents b Add any amount from Schedule 3 and check here ► ☐	12
	13	Subtract line 12 from line 11. If zero or less, enter -0-	13
	14	Other taxes. Attach Schedule 4 .	14
	15	Total tax. Add lines 13 and 14	15
	16	Federal income tax withheld from Forms W-2 and 1099	16
	17	Refundable credits: a EIC (see inst.) _____ b Sch. 8812 _____ c Form 8863 _____	
		Add any amount from Schedule 5	17
	18	Add lines 16 and 17. These are your total payments	18
Refund Direct deposit? See instructions.	19	If line 18 is more than line 15, subtract line 15 from line 18. This is the amount you **overpaid**	19
	20a	Amount of line 19 you want **refunded to you**. If Form 8888 is attached, check here . . ► ☐	20a
	► b	Routing number _____ ► c Type: ☐ Checking ☐ Savings	
	► d	Account number _____	
	21	Amount of line 19 you want **applied to your 2019 estimated tax** . . ► 21	
Amount You Owe	22	**Amount you owe.** Subtract line 18 from line 15. For details on how to pay, see instructions . . ►	22
	23	Estimated tax penalty (see instructions) . . . . ► 23	

Go to www.irs.gov/Form1040 for instructions and the latest information. Form **1040** (2018)

Sample Form 1040, Schedule 4, to Report Early Distribution

SCHEDULE 4 (Form 1040) Department of the Treasury Internal Revenue Service	**Other Taxes** ▶ Attach to Form 1040. ▶ Go to *www.irs.gov/Form1040* for instructions and the latest information.	OMB No. 1545-0074 20**18** Attachment Sequence No. **04**	
Name(s) shown on Form 1040		Your social security number	

Other Taxes	57	Self-employment tax. Attach Schedule SE	57		
	58	Unreported social security and Medicare tax from: Form **a** ☐ 4137 **b** ☐ 8919	58		
	59	Additional tax on IRAs, other qualified retirement plans, and other tax-favored accounts. Attach Form 5329 if required	59	150	
	60a	Household employment taxes. Attach Schedule H	60a		
	b	Repayment of first-time homebuyer credit from Form 5405. Attach Form 5405 if required	60b		
	61	Health care: individual responsibility (see instructions)	61		
	62	Taxes from: **a** ☐ Form 8959 **b** ☐ Form 8960			
		c ☐ Instructions; enter code(s) _____	62		
	63	Section 965 net tax liability installment from Form 965-A	63		
	64	Add the amounts in the far right column. These are your **total other taxes.** Enter here and on Form 1040, line 14	64		

For Paperwork Reduction Act Notice, see your tax return instructions.	Cat. No. 71481R	Schedule 4 (Form 1040) 2018

If the Form 1099-R is accurate, your only responsibility is to compute and pay the extra 10%. This early distribution tax is reported as an additional tax under "other taxes" on Schedule 4 of Form 1040, your regular income tax form. Even if you do not owe the IRS any regular income tax, you must still report the early distribution tax on your tax return and pay it at tax time.

> **EXAMPLE:** Using the same facts as in the previous example, Geoff should report his $1,500 distribution on Form 1040, as shown above. Then he should report the early distribution tax of $150 on Schedule 4.

If the Form 1099-R is not properly coded, you must still compute and pay the additional tax, but you must also complete IRS Form 5329 to show your computation of the tax. Include it with your other forms when you file your tax return. (A Form 5329 along with instructions can be found in Appendix A.)

Sample 1: Form 5329 to Report Early Distribution, No Code on 1099-R

Form **5329**	**Additional Taxes on Qualified Plans (Including IRAs) and Other Tax-Favored Accounts**	OMB No. 1545-0074
Department of the Treasury Internal Revenue Service (99)	► Attach to Form 1040 or Form 1040NR. ► Go to *www.irs.gov/Form5329* for instructions and the latest information.	20**18** Attachment Sequence No. **29**

Name of individual subject to additional tax. If married filing jointly, see instructions.
Geoff Sute

Your social security number
555-55-5555

Fill in Your Address Only if You Are Filing This Form by Itself and Not With Your Tax Return ►

Home address (number and street), or P.O. box if mail is not delivered to your home — Apt. no.

City, town or post office, state, and ZIP code. If you have a foreign address, also complete the spaces below. See instructions.

If this is an amended return, check here ► ☐

Foreign country name — Foreign province/state/county — Foreign postal code

If you **only** owe the additional 10% tax on early distributions, you may be able to report this tax directly on Schedule 4 (Form 1040), line 59, or Form 1040NR, line 57, without filing Form 5329. See the instructions for Schedule 4 (Form 1040), line 59, or for Form 1040NR, line 57.

Part I **Additional Tax on Early Distributions.** Complete this part if you took a taxable distribution (other than a qualified 2017 disaster distribution) before you reached age 59½ from a qualified retirement plan (including an IRA) or modified endowment contract (unless you are reporting this tax directly on Form 1040 or Form 1040NR—see above). You may also have to complete this part to indicate that you qualify for an exception to the additional tax on early distributions or for certain Roth IRA distributions. See instructions.

1	Early distributions included in income. For Roth IRA distributions, see instructions	**1**	1,500
2	Early distributions included on line 1 that are not subject to the additional tax (see instructions). Enter the appropriate exception number from the instructions: _____	**2**	0
3	Amount subject to additional tax. Subtract line 2 from line 1	**3**	1,500
4	**Additional tax.** Enter 10% (0.10) of line 3. Include this amount on Schedule 4 (Form 1040), line 59, or Form 1040NR, line 57	**4**	150
	Caution: If any part of the amount on line 3 was a distribution from a SIMPLE IRA, you may have to include 25% of that amount on line 4 instead of 10%. See instructions.		

Part II **Additional Tax on Certain Distributions From Education Accounts and ABLE Accounts.** Complete this part if you included an amount in income, on Schedule 1 (Form 1040), line 21, or Form 1040NR, line 21, from a Coverdell education savings account (ESA), a qualified tuition program (QTP), or an ABLE account.

5	Distributions included in income from a Coverdell ESA, a QTP, or an ABLE account	**5**	
6	Distributions included on line 5 that are not subject to the additional tax (see instructions) . . .	**6**	
7	Amount subject to additional tax. Subtract line 6 from line 5	**7**	
8	**Additional tax.** Enter 10% (0.10) of line 7. Include this amount on Schedule 4 (Form 1040), line 59, or Form 1040NR, line 57	**8**	

Part III **Additional Tax on Excess Contributions to Traditional IRAs.** Complete this part if you contributed more to your traditional IRAs for 2018 than is allowable or you had an amount on line 17 of your 2017 Form 5329.

9	Enter your excess contributions from line 16 of your 2017 Form 5329. See instructions. If zero, go to line 15	**9**	
10	If your traditional IRA contributions for 2018 are less than your maximum allowable contribution, see instructions. Otherwise, enter -0-	**10**	
11	2018 traditional IRA distributions included in income (see instructions) .	**11**	
12	2018 distributions of prior year excess contributions (see instructions) .	**12**	
13	Add lines 10, 11, and 12	**13**	
14	Prior year excess contributions. Subtract line 13 from line 9. If zero or less, enter -0-	**14**	
15	Excess contributions for 2018 (see instructions)	**15**	
16	Total excess contributions. Add lines 14 and 15	**16**	
17	**Additional tax.** Enter 6% (0.06) of the **smaller** of line 16 **or** the value of your traditional IRAs on December 31, 2018 (including 2018 contributions made in 2019). Include this amount on Schedule 4 (Form 1040), line 59, or Form 1040NR, line 57 . . .	**17**	

Part IV **Additional Tax on Excess Contributions to Roth IRAs.** Complete this part if you contributed more to your Roth IRAs for 2018 than is allowable or you had an amount on line 25 of your 2017 Form 5329.

18	Enter your excess contributions from line 24 of your 2017 Form 5329. See instructions. If zero, go to line 23	**18**	
19	If your Roth IRA contributions for 2018 are less than your maximum allowable contribution, see instructions. Otherwise, enter -0-	**19**	
20	2018 distributions from your Roth IRAs (see instructions)	**20**	
21	Add lines 19 and 20	**21**	
22	Prior year excess contributions. Subtract line 21 from line 18. If zero or less, enter -0-.	**22**	
23	Excess contributions for 2018 (see instructions)	**23**	
24	Total excess contributions. Add lines 22 and 23	**24**	
25	**Additional tax.** Enter 6% (0.06) of the **smaller** of line 24 **or** the value of your Roth IRAs on December 31, 2018 (including 2018 contributions made in 2019). Include this amount on Schedule 4 (Form 1040), line 59, or Form 1040NR, line 57 . .	**25**	

For Privacy Act and Paperwork Reduction Act Notice, see your tax return instructions.   Cat. No. 13329Q   Form **5329** (2018)

Sample 2: Form 5329 to Report Exception to Early Distribution Tax

Form **5329**	**Additional Taxes on Qualified Plans (Including IRAs) and Other Tax-Favored Accounts**	OMB No. 1545-0074
Department of the Treasury Internal Revenue Service (99)	▶ Attach to Form 1040 or Form 1040NR. ▶ Go to *www.irs.gov/Form5329* for instructions and the latest information.	20**18** Attachment Sequence No. **29**

Name of individual subject to additional tax. If married filing jointly, see instructions.

Irwin Hirsh

Your social security number

444-44-4444

Fill in Your Address Only if You Are Filing This Form by Itself and Not With Your Tax Return ▶	Home address (number and street), or P.O. box if mail is not delivered to your home		Apt. no.
	City, town or post office, state, and ZIP code. If you have a foreign address, also complete the spaces below. See instructions.		If this is an amended return, check here ▶ ☐
	Foreign country name	Foreign province/state/county	Foreign postal code

If you **only** owe the additional 10% tax on early distributions, you may be able to report this tax directly on Schedule 4 (Form 1040), line 59, or Form 1040NR, line 57, without filing Form 5329. See the instructions for Schedule 4 (Form 1040), line 59, or for Form 1040NR, line 57.

Part I   **Additional Tax on Early Distributions.** Complete this part if you took a taxable distribution (other than a qualified 2017 disaster distribution) before you reached age 59½ from a qualified retirement plan (including an IRA) or modified endowment contract (unless you are reporting this tax directly on Form 1040 or Form 1040NR—see above). You may also have to complete this part to indicate that you qualify for an exception to the additional tax on early distributions or for certain Roth IRA distributions. See instructions.

1	Early distributions included in income. For Roth IRA distributions, see instructions	**1**	25,000
2	Early distributions included on line 1 that are not subject to the additional tax (see instructions). Enter the appropriate exception number from the instructions: 01	**2**	25,000
3	Amount subject to additional tax. Subtract line 2 from line 1	**3**	0
4	**Additional tax.** Enter 10% (0.10) of line 3. Include this amount on Schedule 4 (Form 1040), line 59, or Form 1040NR, line 57	**4**	0
	Caution: If any part of the amount on line 3 was a distribution from a SIMPLE IRA, you may have to include 25% of that amount on line 4 instead of 10%. See instructions.		

Part II   **Additional Tax on Certain Distributions From Education Accounts and ABLE Accounts.** Complete this part if you included an amount in income, on Schedule 1 (Form 1040), line 21, or Form 1040NR, line 21, from a Coverdell education savings program (ESA), a qualified tuition program (QTP), or an ABLE account.

5	Distributions included in income from a Coverdell ESA, a QTP, or an ABLE account	**5**	
6	Distributions included on line 5 that are not subject to the additional tax (see instructions) . . .	**6**	
7	Amount subject to additional tax. Subtract line 6 from line 5	**7**	
8	**Additional tax.** Enter 10% (0.10) of line 7. Include this amount on Schedule 4 (Form 1040), line 59, or Form 1040NR, line 57	**8**	

Part III   **Additional Tax on Excess Contributions to Traditional IRAs.** Complete this part if you contributed more to your traditional IRAs for 2018 than is allowable or you had an amount on line 17 of your 2017 Form 5329.

9	Enter your excess contributions from line 16 of your 2017 Form 5329. See instructions. If zero, go to line 15		**9**	
10	If your traditional IRA contributions for 2018 are less than your maximum allowable contribution, see instructions. Otherwise, enter -0-	**10**		
11	2018 traditional IRA distributions included in income (see instructions) .	**11**		
12	2018 distributions of prior year excess contributions (see instructions) .	**12**		
13	Add lines 10, 11, and 12		**13**	
14	Prior year excess contributions. Subtract line 13 from line 9. If zero or less, enter -0-		**14**	
15	Excess contributions for 2018 (see instructions)		**15**	
16	Total excess contributions. Add lines 14 and 15		**16**	
17	**Additional tax.** Enter 6% (0.06) of the **smaller** of line 16 **or** the value of your traditional IRAs on December 31, 2018 (including 2018 contributions made in 2019). Include this amount on Schedule 4 (Form 1040), line 59, or Form 1040NR, line 57 . . .		**17**	

Part IV   **Additional Tax on Excess Contributions to Roth IRAs.** Complete this part if you contributed more to your Roth IRAs for 2018 than is allowable or you had an amount on line 25 of your 2017 Form 5329.

18	Enter your excess contributions from line 24 of your 2017 Form 5329. See instructions. If zero, go to line 23		**18**	
19	If your Roth IRA contributions for 2018 are less than your maximum allowable contribution, see instructions. Otherwise, enter -0-	**19**		
20	2018 distributions from your Roth IRAs (see instructions)	**20**		
21	Add lines 19 and 20		**21**	
22	Prior year excess contributions. Subtract line 21 from line 18. If zero or less, enter -0-		**22**	
23	Excess contributions for 2018 (see instructions)		**23**	
24	Total excess contributions. Add lines 22 and 23		**24**	
25	**Additional tax.** Enter 6% (0.06) of the **smaller** of line 24 **or** the value of your Roth IRAs on December 31, 2018 (including 2018 contributions made in 2019). Include this amount on Schedule 4 (Form 1040), line 59, or Form 1040NR, line 57 . . .		**25**	

For Privacy Act and Paperwork Reduction Act Notice, see your tax return instructions.   Cat. No. 13329Q   Form **5329** (2018)

EXAMPLE 1: The facts are the same as in the previous example except that Tech Inc. failed to enter Code 1 in Box 7 of Form 1099-R. As a result, Geoff must complete Part I of Form 5329 and include the form when he files the rest of his tax return. Part I should be completed as shown in Sample 1, above.

EXAMPLE 2: Irwin retired from Tech Inc. at age 56. The company distributed $25,000 to Irwin, which represented the entire balance in his 401(k) plan. When Irwin received his Form 1099-R from Tech Inc. at tax time, the form showed a Code 1 in Box 7, indicating that Irwin had received an early distribution. Because Irwin left the company after age 55, his distribution is not subject to an early distribution tax. He must complete and attach Form 5329 to his tax return to tell the IRS which exception applies. The instructions for Form 5329 indicate that the age 55 exception is the number 01. Irwin must enter 01 on Line 2 of Part I. Irwin completes the rest of the form as shown in Sample 2, above.

Special Rules for IRAs

The early distribution tax applies to IRAs in much the same way it applies to qualified plans, with just a few exceptions and variations described in this section. Bear in mind, however, that the Roth IRA is not a typical IRA, so the following rules do not necessarily apply to it. For a complete discussion of the Roth IRA rules, see Chapter 9.

Rules Applicable to All IRAs Except Roth IRAs

Six special rules apply to rollover IRAs, contributory IRAs, SEP IRAs, and SIMPLE IRAs.

Rule One: No Age 55 Exception

As we explained earlier in this chapter, employees who are at least age 55 when they terminate their employment will not have to pay an early distribution tax on distributions from their former employer's qualified plan. This rule does not apply to IRAs, however. If you have an IRA, you must be at least 59½ to use the age exception to the early distribution tax. Of course, you may still qualify for an exception that is unrelated to your age.

Rule Two: No QDRO Exception

The special QDRO rules in the tax code do not apply to IRAs. This means the QDRO exception to the early distribution tax is available for qualified plan distributions, but not for IRA distributions. Even if your divorce agreement or court order mandates child support or alimony payments from an IRA, the payments will be subject to an early distribution tax unless one of the other exceptions applies. Sometimes the divorce agreement simply requires the distribution to a spouse of his or her interest in the IRA (for example, a community property interest), but in that case, too, the distribution could be subject to an early distribution tax.

There is one way around this, but it is available only to the former spouse of the IRA participant, and only if the spouse is to receive some or all of the IRA as directed by a divorce or maintenance decree or a written separation agreement. The IRA participant may direct the custodian of the IRA to transfer some or all of the IRA assets directly into an IRA in the former spouse's name. Alternatively, the participant could roll over the spouse's share into a new IRA in the participant's name and then direct the custodian to change title on the new IRA to the spouse's name. The participant might even roll over the spouse's interest into an IRA in the spouse's name (instead of using a direct transfer). The key in each case is for the spouse not to take possession of the funds before they are deposited into an IRA in the spouse's own name.

Once the funds are in an IRA in the spouse's name, however, they belong to the spouse in every way. Thereafter, all IRA rules apply to the assets as though the spouse had been the original IRA participant. If the spouse takes a distribution, the spouse will have to pay an early distribution tax unless an exception applies.

> **CAUTION**
>
> **Get it in writing!** The transfer of IRA assets to an account in the name of a spouse or former spouse must be as a result of a written divorce or separation agreement. You may not transfer funds from your IRA into your current spouse's IRA simply because you want to increase the value of his or her account for some reason.

> **CAUTION**
>
> **Child support cannot go into an IRA.** The above transfer strategy is available only for payments that are made to a separated or former spouse. Child support payments may not be transferred to an IRA in either the child's name or the former spouse's name.

Health Insurance Premiums

An early distribution tax exception unique to IRAs concerns health insurance premiums. If you are unemployed or were recently unemployed and use money from your IRA to pay health insurance premiums, the IRA funds used specifically for that purpose will not be subject to an early distribution tax, as long as you satisfy the following conditions:

- You received unemployment compensation for at least 12 consecutive weeks.
- You received the funds from the IRA during a year in which you received unemployment compensation or during the following year.
- The IRA distribution is received no more than 60 days after you return to work.

EXAMPLE: You are 45. You lost your job in 2018 and began receiving unemployment compensation on September 22, 2018. You want to maintain your health insurance even during your unemployment. You pay $400 per month on the first day of each month beginning October 1. Because you are short of cash, you withdraw the $400 from your IRA each month to cover the cost of the premiums. You land a job and begin working on March 15, 2019. Unfortunately, your new employer does not provide any health benefits, so you continue to pay premiums of $400 per month, withdrawing the money from your IRA each time. Only the premiums you pay after December 15, 2018 (12 weeks after your unemployment compensation payments began), and before May 15, 2019 (60 days after you began work), are eligible for the exception to the early distribution tax. Thus your distributions of $400 on January 1, February 1, March 1, April 1, and May 1 totaling $2,000 all escape the early distribution tax. Distributions after May 15 are subject to the early distribution tax unless another exception applies.

You may also make a penalty-free withdrawal from your IRA to pay for health insurance if you were self-employed before you stopped working, as long as you would have qualified for unemployment compensation except for the fact that you were self-employed.

Higher Education Expenses

Distributions that you use to pay higher education expenses will not be subject to the early distribution tax, as long as those distributions meet the following requirements:

- The distributions are used to pay for tuition, fees, books, supplies, and equipment, including computers and related equipment, software, and Internet access expenses that are used primarily by the student while in enrolled in school. Also, it is no longer necessary that the school require the student to purchase a computer as a condition of enrollment.
- The distributions are used for room and board, but only if the student is carrying at least half of a normal study load or is considered at least a half-time student.
- The expenses are paid on behalf of the IRA owner, spouse, child, or grandchild.
- The distributions do not exceed the amount of the higher education expenses. Furthermore, the total expenses (tuition, fees, and so on) must be reduced by any tax-free scholarships or other tax-free assistance the student receives, not including loans, gifts, or inheritances.

First Home Purchase

Many years ago, Congress enacted an exception to the early distribution tax to make it easier for people to buy their first homes. When the dust settled, the benefit was not as dramatic as people had hoped, not because it was difficult to qualify for, but because the lifetime distribution limit was only $10,000. Here are the details:

- The IRA distribution must be used for the acquisition, construction, or reconstruction of a home.

- The funds must be used within 120 days of receipt. If it happens that the home purchase is canceled or delayed, the funds may be rolled over into another IRA (or back into the same one) as long as the rollover is complete within 120 days of the initial distribution.

- The funds must be used to purchase a principal residence for a first-time homebuyer. A first-time homebuyer is someone who has had no interest in a principal residence during the two years ending on the date of purchase of the new home. If the individual happens to be married, then neither the individual nor the spouse may have owned any part of a principal residence during the preceding two-year period.

- The first-time homebuyer must be the IRA owner, the owner's spouse, or an ancestor (such as a parent, grandparent, or great grandparent), child, or grandchild of either the IRA owner or the owner's spouse.

- The lifetime limit of $10,000 applies regardless of whose home is purchased or improved. If the IRA owner withdraws $10,000 and gives it to his or her child, the lifetime limit for the IRA owner is used up. The IRA owner may not invoke the first home exception for any future distribution even if it is to buy a house for a different relative or for the IRA owner. The $10,000 does not have to be distributed all at once or even in a single year. For example, the IRA owner could withdraw $5,000 one year, giving it to a qualified person for a home purchase, and then withdraw another $5,000 in a later year.

Refunds

There is a limit to how much you may contribute to an IRA each year. If you contribute too much, then you have made an excess contribution. If you withdraw the excess by the time you file your tax return (including extensions, if you filed a request and were granted an extension), you will not have to pay an early distribution tax on the excess. You must also withdraw the income earned on the excess while it was in the IRA, however, and that portion will be subject to the early distribution tax, unless it qualifies for another exception.

> **EXAMPLE:** You are self-employed. In January, you open an IRA and contribute $5,500 for the current tax year. On December 31, when you compute your net income for the year, you discover that you only made $5,000 in self-employment income. Because your IRA contribution is limited to the lesser of $5,500 or your net income, you have made an excess contribution of $500. Also, you earned 10% on the IRA investment during the year. To correct the excess contribution, you must withdraw not only the $500, but the $50 of earnings on that excess (10% of $500) as well. If you withdraw these amounts by April 15 of the year after the excess contribution (or the due date of your tax return, if you received an extension of time for filing the return), there will be no penalty on the $500 distribution. The $50 of earnings will be subject to ordinary income tax and a 10% early distribution tax of $5.

If you fail to correct an excess contribution to an IRA by the time you file your tax return, but make a corrective distribution later, the entire amount of the distribution is subject to the early distribution tax unless it qualifies for another exception.

One Rule Applicable Only to SIMPLE IRAs

SIMPLE IRAs are described in Chapter 1. All the special IRA rules discussed above apply to SIMPLE IRAs, but there is one additional rule. If you are a participant in a SIMPLE IRA and you receive a distribution within two years of the date you began contributing to it, the early distribution tax increases from 10% to 25%. At the end of two years, it falls back to 10%. Of course, if the distribution qualifies for an exception, the early distribution tax will not apply at all.

Key Tax Code Sections and IRS Pronouncements

§ 72(t)
Early Distribution Tax.

§ 402(g)(2)(C)
Distribution of Excess Deferrals.

§ 4972
Nondeductible Contributions to Qualified Plans.

§ 4973
Excess Contributions to IRAs.

§ 4979
Excess Contributions to Qualified Plans
(in Violation of Nondiscrimination Rules).

Revenue Procedure 92-93
Treatment of Corrective Distributions.

Substantially Equal Periodic Payments

| **Who Should Read Chapter 4** |

Read this chapter if you are younger than 59½ and want to learn about using substantially equal periodic payments to escape the early distribution tax.

Chapter 3 introduced you to all of the exceptions to the early distribution tax. Here, we take an in-depth look at the most complicated of those exceptions: substantially equal periodic payments.

As you may recall, the exception essentially means that you do not have to pay the early distribution tax on money that you take out of your plan in regular payments over either your life expectancy or the joint life expectancy of you and your beneficiary, even if you are younger than 59½.

Here are some basic rules about the exception:

- There are no age restrictions. So, for example, you could be 25 and start taking substantially equal periodic payments.
- The payments must be substantially equal, which means you cannot alter the payment each year to suit your needs, perhaps by taking a few dollars one year and a few thousand the next.
- You must compute the payments as though you intend to distribute the retirement plan over your entire life, or over the joint life of you and your beneficiary.
- Payments from your employer's plan must begin after you leave your job. (This restriction does not apply to IRAs.)
- You may not discontinue payments or alter the computation method for at least five years. And if you have not reached age 59½ at the end of the five-year period, you must wait until you do reach that age before making a change. If you modify payments too soon, the early distribution tax (plus interest) will be applied retroactively to all of the payments you have received. There is one exception to the rule that you may not modify the payments: You are permitted a one-time switch to the required minimum distribution method if you started out using another method. ("Computing Periodic

Payments," below, discusses the various methods you can use to compute your payments. "Modifying the Payments," below, describes how to discontinue or alter the size of payments.)

RESOURCE

Learn more. If you'd like to read more about these guidelines, refer to IRS Revenue Ruling 2002-62, which you can find in Appendix A to this book.

Payments that are part of a series of substantially equal periodic payments (SEPP) are not eligible to be rolled over. Perhaps in your zeal to withdraw from your retirement plan precisely the amount you need and no more, you devise a plan to begin periodic withdrawals and then roll over into an IRA the portion of each payment you don't use. That strategy is creative, logical, reasonable—and prohibited. The tax code specifically denies rollover treatment to periodic payments. You should be able to achieve a similar result by splitting the account first before beginning periodic payments. At least that strategy is not specifically forbidden. (You can learn more about this strategy in "If You Don't Want to Withdraw All of Your Money," below.)

Helpful Terms
Amortize. To liquidate or reduce (as in the case of a debt) through periodic payments of principal and interest.
Annuity. A contract, sold by an insurance company, that promises to make monthly, quarterly, semiannual, or annual payments for life or for a specified period of time.
Distribution. A payout of property (such as shares of stock) or cash from a retirement plan or an IRA to the participant or a beneficiary.
Joint life expectancy. The number of years expected to pass before the second of two individuals dies.
Recalculated life expectancy. Life expectancy that is revised each year according to statistically accurate measures of mortality.

Periodic payments are also exempt from the mandatory income tax withholding rules for qualified plan distributions. (See Chapter 2 for more information about withholding.) Mandatory withholding applies only to those plan distributions that are eligible to be rolled over. Because periodic payments are not eligible to be rolled over, they are not subject to mandatory withholding.

If You Don't Want to Withdraw All of Your Money

Because the methods described below require that the whole plan be distributed eventually, some people find that they end up with larger payments from their plans than they need. That's not a good thing, because taking more money out of your plan than is necessary means paying income tax on money when you don't really have to.

If you have two or more retirement plans, you might be able to solve your problem by taking periodic payments from one plan and leaving the other(s) alone.

But if you have only one plan, you're in a bit of a pickle. Some taxpayers split an existing plan or IRA into two accounts so that one of the accounts is the right size to produce the payment they want. They then leave the other account alone. If you choose this method, however, be warned that no one knows for certain whether the IRS will routinely condone it.

Computing Periodic Payments

The basic requirement for periodic payments is that they be spread over your lifetime in roughly equal payments. This is trickier than it first appears. For one thing, you probably don't know how long you are going to live, and you also probably don't know how your investments are going to do over the years. If you did (and more important, if the IRS did), the calculation would be simple.

But because most of us have pretty murky crystal balls, the IRS requires us to use some generally accepted life expectancy assumptions and interest rates. Although the IRS does not hand us the numbers we are to use, the agency has put its stamp of approval on three methods for computing required distributions. These are the required minimum distribution, fixed amortization, and fixed annuitization methods. Each has its own set of guidelines for determining life expectancy and selecting an interest rate or an expected investment return. The section that follows discusses each method in detail.

You are permitted to use any of the methods you want, but before you choose, you should be aware of the principles that are common to all three computation methods:

- Using a joint life expectancy instead of your single life expectancy will reduce the size of your payments.
- Reducing the interest rate assumption will reduce the size of your payments.
- The IRS is more likely to object to large periodic payments than small ones.

If You Stray From the Guidelines

The computation methods outlined in Revenue Ruling 2002-62 and described in this chapter serve as safe harbors. As long as you use one of those methods, you can be certain that the IRS will not challenge you. You are free to stray from these guidelines, but if you do—by using an alternative method, for example, or by altering the variables (such as the interest rate) in one of the IRS methods—you will lose the safe harbor protection, and the IRS can challenge your method. You would then have to successfully defend your method or pay penalties. As a result, the IRS recommends that you request a private letter ruling if you will not be following one of the three methods precisely.

Method One: Required Minimum Distribution

In this relatively simple method, you determine your retirement account balance and divide it by a life expectancy factor each year. The result is your periodic payment for that year. The life expectancy factor can be plucked right out of tables provided by the IRS. (See Tables I, II, and III in Appendix B.) You don't have to worry about estimating an interest rate because your year-end account balance reflects the actual investment returns you earned during the year.

As simple as this method is, you must still decide whether to use your single life expectancy, the Uniform Lifetime Table, or the joint life expectancy of you and your beneficiary. A joint life expectancy and the Uniform Lifetime Table (which assumes a joint life expectancy) will produce a smaller payment than a single life expectancy will. The size of the payment you need should be the only factor in your decision, given that your choice will affect no other aspect of your retirement plan.

After you make your decision about life expectancies, follow the steps below to arrive at a payment.

Step One: Determine your life expectancy factor.

If you use your single life expectancy, you will look up your age each year in Table I in Appendix B and use the number from the table.

If you use the Uniform Lifetime Table, you will look up your age each year in Table III in Appendix B and use the number you find there.

If you have one or more beneficiaries, you may (but are not required to) use the joint life expectancy table (Table II in Appendix B, called the "Joint Life and Last Survivor Expectancy" table) to find the appropriate factor. To use a joint life expectancy, the person whose life you use along with your own must be your actual beneficiary. If you have named more than one beneficiary, then you must use the oldest beneficiary's age for determining your joint life expectancy.

If you choose to use either the single life table or the Uniform Lifetime Table, you must use the same table in all subsequent years.

If you choose the joint life table, you must continue to use that table while the beneficiary whose life you are using remains the oldest beneficiary of the account. If that beneficiary dies, is removed as a beneficiary, or is no longer the oldest beneficiary (for example, if you add an older beneficiary), do not change the calculation for the year of the change. For the next year, however, you must use the current oldest beneficiary's life when determining your joint life factor. If you have no beneficiary in that next year, you must use the single life table.

Step Two: Determine your account balance.

IRS guidelines state that the account balance you use to calculate your payment "must be determined in a reasonable manner." That statement in and of itself is not terribly useful. But fortunately, the statement is followed by an example in which the IRS makes it clear that using the account balance as of December 31 of the year before periodic payments are to begin is reasonable. And, according to the IRS, it is also reasonable to use the account balance for any date "within a reasonable period before the distribution." For example, if you take your first distribution on July 15, the IRS says it would be reasonable to choose an account balance as of any date between December 31 of the previous year and your distribution date.

Step Three: Calculate the payment.

Divide the account balance by the factor you determined in Step One, above. The result is the amount that must be distributed during the first year. For the second year, you follow a similar procedure, using the account balance either as of December 31 of the first payment year or as of a date within a reasonable period of your next distribution.

> **EXAMPLE:** You quit your job last year and rolled over your retirement plan into an IRA. The balance of your IRA at the end of the year you retired was $100,000. This year, you will turn 50. You need to draw on the IRA to help make ends meet, so you plan to begin periodic payments.
>
> **Year One**
>
> Step One: From Table I you see that your single life expectancy (for age 50) is 34.2 years.
>
> Step Two: Your December 31 balance for the year before payments are to begin was $100,000.
>
> Step Three: Your first annual periodic payment is $2,924, or $100,000 divided by 34.2.

Year Two

Assume that the balance of your IRA at the end of the first year of periodic payments was $110,000. (You earned more in interest than you withdrew the first year.) Follow these steps to compute the second year payment.

Step One: Refer again to Table I. You will turn 51 this year. Thus, your life expectancy is 33.3.

Step Two: Your account balance as of December 31 of the first year of periodic payments was $110,000.

Step Three: Your second periodic payment is $3,303, or $110,000 divided by 33.3.

CAUTION

Be exact. Although this method is referred to as the required minimum distribution method, the payment does not represent the minimum you must take, but the exact amount. Once you compute your periodic payment for the year, you must distribute precisely that amount, no more and no less.

Advantages of the Required Minimum Distribution Method

The IRS has declared that payments computed under the required minimum distribution rules will be considered substantially equal periodic payments. Nonetheless, the payments could vary significantly from one year to the next, depending on how well or poorly your portfolio performs. Thus, the advantage of this method is that it reflects your actual investment returns. And if your intention is to spread payments over your lifetime, this method can accomplish your goal. Not to be overlooked is the fact that this calculation method is simple and straightforward. And if you choose it, the IRS is unlikely to challenge your payment size or your methodology.

Disadvantages of the Required Minimum Distribution Method

Although this method might accurately reflect your investment returns, it is the least flexible. Except by choosing to use a joint life expectancy or the Uniform Lifetime Table, there is no way to tweak payments to produce the distribution you want. And because of market fluctuations, you might find your payments too large one year and not quite large enough the next. Even without market fluctuations, this method will tend to skew payments so that they are small in the early years and larger in later years. That's fine if you expect to need more income later, but if you need more now, there's no way to skew payments in the other direction.

Method Two: Fixed Amortization

This method is favored by many taxpayers because it is flexible enough to produce a range of payments, and the computation is straightforward. Once you compute your annual payment, the payment remains fixed for all subsequent years. To compute your payment under this method, you must first decide which table you will use: the single, joint life, or Uniform Lifetime Table. (Remember, a joint life expectancy produces lower payments.) Then you follow these steps.

Step One: Choose an interest rate.

This is where most of the flexibility comes in, although your choice isn't completely open-ended. IRS safe harbor guidelines (in Revenue Ruling 2002-62) state that you may use any interest rate that does not exceed 120% of the federal midterm rate for either of the two months before the month distributions begin.

You can find federal midterm rates at apps.irs.gov/app/picklist/list/federalRates.html. Because the payments must be made at least annually, you may use the "annual" interest rate found at this site.

Remember, the IRS guidelines provide a safe harbor, but nothing in the law prohibits you from using a higher rate. (Higher rates produce higher payments.) However, as mentioned above, the IRS recommends—but does not require—that you obtain a private letter ruling if you stray from the guidelines.

Step Two: Determine your life expectancy.

You may choose to use the Single Life Expectancy (Table I) or the Uniform Lifetime Table (Table III). If you have one or more designated beneficiaries of your account, you may use a Joint Life Expectancy (Table II) with the oldest beneficiary of the retirement plan.

Step Three: Determine your account balance.

As is the case with the required minimum distribution method, your account balance may be determined on one of two dates: as of December 31 of the year before your first distribution or as of a date "within a reasonable period" before the first distribution. Thus, presumably, if the account balance has dropped (or increased) dramatically between the end of the prior year and the date you take your first distribution, your choice of valuation date could make a significant difference in the size of your periodic payment.

Step Four: Calculate the payment.

Amortize your account balance using the life expectancy and interest rate you have chosen. Use the same method you would use to amortize a home mortgage or another loan. You can make the computation with a financial calculator, on a computer spreadsheet, or with an amortization program that might be included with other financial software you have.

Enter your account balance when asked for the loan amount and your life expectancy when asked for the number of years or months you will take to repay the loan. Then enter the interest rate you have chosen. The calculator then computes the payment amount.

Unfortunately, many mortgage calculators or amortization functions on financial calculators will allow you to use only whole numbers for your life expectancy. However, your actual life expectancy for most years is not a nice round number.

But at least one financial institution, Bankrate, offers on their website a free calculator designed specifically to calculate substantially equal periodic payments. That site is: www.bankrate.com/calculators/retirement/72-t-distribution-calculator.aspx.

If you use the Bankrate calculator, simply enter your account balance, the interest rate you plan to use, your age (Bankrate will determine your life expectancy automatically, based on the method you choose), your beneficiary's age (which will be taken into account only if you choose the joint life expectancy table), and finally, which life expectancy table you would like to use.

EXAMPLE: You have decided to start taking substantially equal periodic payments annually from your IRA beginning in the year you turn 52. Your IRA account balance as of December 31 of the preceding year was $82,000.

Step One: You decide to use 120% of the federal midterm rate for December of the year before you begin distributions. That rate is 2.28%.

Step Two: You will take distributions over your own single life expectancy, which is 32.3 (from Table I) for age 52.

Step Three: Your account balance on December 31 of the year before payments are to begin was $82,000.

Step Four: Using a financial calculator, you compute your annual payment to be $3,615 ($82,000 amortized over 32.3 years at 2.28%). Your payment for the second and future years will also be $3,615.

Advantages of the Fixed Amortization Method

One significant attraction of this method is its simplicity. Once you determine your payment, you never have to compute it again. No looking up numbers in tables every year or trying to remember computation formulas. You do it once and it's done.

Along with the simplicity comes some flexibility. You can choose from a range of interest rates, and you may use one of three life expectancy tables. That flexibility should get you close to the payment you want unless you need an exceptionally large amount. And if you really want to use a higher interest rate than the guidelines suggest, you can always request a private letter ruling.

Disadvantages of the Fixed Amortization Method

The amortization example in the IRS guidelines, as well as in most of the favorable private letter rulings, computes a fixed payment, which doesn't vary at all from year to year. Fixed payments, by definition, do not take into account recalculation of life expectancies, actual investment returns on your account, or inflation. The payments are constant. Consequently, if inflation surges, you might find yourself stuck with a payment that is too low for your needs and that doesn't reflect either the real returns on your investments or the changing economic climate.

However, recent private letter rulings give hope to taxpayers who want to modify their payments to keep up with inflation. In one case, for example, the taxpayer amortized his account balance anew each year, using 120% of the current federal midterm rate and his updated life expectancy. The IRS took the position that although the payment changed, the method of computing the payment was exactly the same each year. If you choose to do something like this, keep in mind that it doesn't follow the guidelines precisely and therefore does not enjoy safe harbor protection.

Method Three: Fixed Annuitization

Although the underlying arithmetic in the annuitization method is essentially the same as in the amortization method, the computation is performed simply by dividing your account balance by an annuity factor. The annuity factor is derived from a formula used mostly by actuaries.

As with the amortization method, once you determine your annual payment, it should remain the same every year, if you want to stay within the safe harbor.

The factor is based on certain interest rate and mortality assumptions. Those of us who are inexperienced with these calculations rely on actuaries and other number crunchers to produce tables we can use to look up the appropriate factor.

IRS regulations state that you may use any reasonable mortality table to come up with your annuity factor. The IRS has provided a safe harbor mortality table in Revenue Ruling 2002-62. As you might expect, this mortality table produces a smaller payment than many of the mortality tables used by insurance companies or even in other sections of the tax code.

Step One: Choose an interest rate.
Your criterion for choosing an interest rate should be no different for this method than for the amortization method. Higher rates will produce

higher payments; but the safe harbor is an interest rate that does not exceed 120% of the federal midterm rate.

Step Two: Find your annuity factor.

Although the IRS provided a safe harbor mortality table, it didn't go so far as to actually compute the factors for us. Does that mean you need to hire your own actuary? No. Fortunately, at least one webpage, https://72t.net/72t/calculator/distributions, has popped up to fill this gap. The calculator that comes up will not only calculate your payment under the annuitization method, but it will also allow you to choose another safe harbor method and compare the payment sizes (you need to fill out the first seven fields only and click the "calculate" heading).

Step Three: Determine your account balance.

You use the same guidelines for determining your account balance under the annuitization method as you would under the amortization method. You may use the balance as of December 31 of the year before the first distribution, or you may use the balance as of a date within a reasonable period before the date of your first distribution.

Step Four: Compute the payment.

Divide the account balance by the annuity factor to arrive at your payment.

> **EXAMPLE:** You will turn 52 this year. You decide to begin substantially equal periodic payments from your IRA, and you plan to use your own single life expectancy. Your IRA account balance as of December 31 of the preceding year was $82,000.
>
> Step One: You choose an interest rate of 3.69%, which is 120% of the federal midterm rate.
>
> Step Two: You use the online annuity factor calculator to come up with an annuity factor of 18.807.
>
> Step Three: Your account balance on December 31 of last year was $82,000.
>
> Step Four: Your periodic payment for this year, your first payment year, is $4,360 (Step Three divided by Step Two, or $82,000 divided by 18.807).

> ! CAUTION
>
> **Only fixed payments are officially approved by the IRS.** Bear in mind that although some private letter rulings sanction variable payments under the annuity factor method, only fixed payments have been approved officially by the IRS.

Advantages of the Fixed Annuitization Method

The only substantive difference between this method and the amortization method is that this method allows you to use mortality figures other than those provided by the IRS. Thus, theoretically, you have the flexibility to choose a table that accurately reflects your situation or produces a payment that better suits your needs.

If you choose a mortality table other than the IRS's, however, you fall outside the safe harbor.

Disadvantages of the Fixed Annuitization Method

The disadvantages of this are the same as those under the amortization method: Because your payment is fixed (if you use the safe harbor), it will not reflect a changing economy or the actual performance of your investments.

Implementing and Reporting Your Decision

Once you have selected your computation method, prepare a worksheet illustrating the computation. (See sample, below.) Keep it with your other important tax papers in case the IRS should ever ask you to explain the methodology you chose. Next, arrange with your plan administrator or IRA custodian to begin periodic payments. After that, your only remaining task is to report the payments on your tax return.

After the end of the year, you will receive a Form 1099-R from either the trustee of your plan or the custodian of your IRA. This form will report the total amount of distributions you received during the year. If the form shows a Code 2 in Box 7, you do not need to file any special forms with your tax return. (Code 2 means that the distribution qualifies for an exception to the early distribution tax.) You will simply report your periodic payments as ordinary income on your tax return. (See Chapter 3 for more information about Form 1099-R codes and the reporting requirements for IRA and qualified plan distributions.)

> ⚠ CAUTION
>
> **A portion of each payment might be nontaxable.** If you have multiple IRAs and have made nondeductible contributions to any of them, remember that every distribution from any IRA will be partially taxable and partially tax free. That's because all of your IRAs are aggregated for purposes of determining how much basis is allocated to a distribution. The basis is recovered pro rata with every distribution you take from any of your IRAs. See "Your Basis Is Not Taxable" in Chapter 2 to see how to determine the taxable portion of each substantially equal periodic payment.

If Box 7 of Form 1099-R does not show Code 2, you must complete Part I of Form 5329 and file it with the rest of your tax return. Part I of Form 5329 asks you to report the total amount of your early distributions (on Line 1) and the distributions that are eligible for an exception to the early distribution tax (Line 2). Line 2 also provides a space for you to write in the exception number. The exception number for substantially equal periodic payments is 02. You can find exception codes in the instructions for Form 5329, which is in Appendix A.

> EXAMPLE: At age 52, you began receiving substantially equal periodic payments of $2,000 per month from your IRA. After the end of the year, you receive your 1099-R from your IRA custodian, reporting distributions of $24,000 from your IRA. Box 7 incorrectly shows Code 1. Consequently, you must complete Part I of Form 5329 and file it with the rest of your tax return. Lines 1–4 of Form 5329 should look like the sample form below.

Sample Worksheet for Your Tax Files

Computation of Substantially Equal Periodic Payments Using Amortization Method

Annual distributions to be made each February 1, beginning in the year 2019

December 31, 2018, value of IRA Account # 01234: $82,000

My single life expectancy at age 52 in the year 2019 (from IRS Publication 590, Appendix C, Table 1): 32.3 years

120% of the federal midterm rate for January 2019: 3.69%

Annual payment ($82,000 amortized over 32.3 years at 3.69%): $4,387

Modifying the Payments

In general, the substantially equal periodic payment exception will save you from the early distribution tax only if you do not discontinue your payments or alter your computation method (other than in the approved ways, such as recalculation based on annual changes in life expectancy or account balance under the required minimum distribution method) once payments have begun. If you change your computation method, the early distribution tax can be applied retroactively to all distributions.

Fortunately, Congress didn't intend that your payments remain fixed until your death, just for a well-defined period of time. And, of course, there are exceptions to the no-modification rule that allow you to change the payments under certain circumstances, even if you don't satisfy the time period requirement.

Sample: Form 5329 to Report Incorrectly Coded 1099-R

Form **5329**	**Additional Taxes on Qualified Plans (Including IRAs) and Other Tax-Favored Accounts**	OMB No. 1545-0074 **2018**
Department of the Treasury Internal Revenue Service (99)	▶ Attach to Form 1040 or Form 1040NR. ▶ Go to *www.irs.gov/Form5329* for instructions and the latest information.	Attachment Sequence No. **29**

Name of individual subject to additional tax. If married filing jointly, see instructions.	Your social security number

Fill in Your Address Only if You Are Filing This Form by Itself and Not With Your Tax Return

Home address (number and street), or P.O. box if mail is not delivered to your home	Apt. no.
City, town or post office, state, and ZIP code. If you have a foreign address, also complete the spaces below. See instructions.	If this is an amended return, check here ▶ ☐

Foreign country name	Foreign province/state/county	Foreign postal code

If you **only** owe the additional 10% tax on early distributions, you may be able to report this tax directly on Schedule 4 (Form 1040), line 59, or Form 1040NR, line 57, without filing Form 5329. See the instructions for Schedule 4 (Form 1040), line 59, or for Form 1040NR, line 57.

Part I   Additional Tax on Early Distributions. Complete this part if you took a taxable distribution (other than a qualified 2017 disaster distribution) before you reached age 59½ from a qualified retirement plan (including an IRA) or modified endowment contract (unless you are reporting this tax directly on Form 1040 or Form 1040NR—see above). You may also have to complete this part to indicate that you qualify for an exception to the additional tax on early distributions or for certain Roth IRA distributions. See instructions.

1	Early distributions included in income. For Roth IRA distributions, see instructions	**1**	24,000
2	Early distributions included on line 1 that are not subject to the additional tax (see instructions). Enter the appropriate exception number from the instructions: __02__	**2**	24,000
3	Amount subject to additional tax. Subtract line 2 from line 1	**3**	0
4	**Additional tax.** Enter 10% (0.10) of line 3. Include this amount on Schedule 4 (Form 1040), line 59, or Form 1040NR, line 57	**4**	0
	Caution: If any part of the amount on line 3 was a distribution from a SIMPLE IRA, you may have to include 25% of that amount on line 4 instead of 10%. See instructions.		

Part II   Additional Tax on Certain Distributions From Education Accounts and ABLE Accounts. Complete this part if you included an amount in income, on Schedule 1 (Form 1040), line 21, or Form 1040NR, line 21, from a Coverdell education savings account (ESA), a qualified tuition program (QTP), or an ABLE account.

5	Distributions included in income from a Coverdell ESA, a QTP, or an ABLE account	**5**	
6	Distributions included on line 5 that are not subject to the additional tax (see instructions) . . .	**6**	
7	Amount subject to additional tax. Subtract line 6 from line 5	**7**	
8	**Additional tax.** Enter 10% (0.10) of line 7. Include this amount on Schedule 4 (Form 1040), line 59, or Form 1040NR, line 57	**8**	

Part III   Additional Tax on Excess Contributions to Traditional IRAs. Complete this part if you contributed more to your traditional IRAs for 2018 than is allowable or you had an amount on line 17 of your 2017 Form 5329.

9	Enter your excess contributions from line 16 of your 2017 Form 5329. See instructions. If zero, go to line 15		**9**	
10	If your traditional IRA contributions for 2018 are less than your maximum allowable contribution, see instructions. Otherwise, enter -0-	**10**		
11	2018 traditional IRA distributions included in income (see instructions) .	**11**		
12	2018 distributions of prior year excess contributions (see instructions) .	**12**		
13	Add lines 10, 11, and 12		**13**	
14	Prior year excess contributions. Subtract line 13 from line 9. If zero or less, enter -0-		**14**	
15	Excess contributions for 2018 (see instructions)		**15**	
16	Total excess contributions. Add lines 14 and 15		**16**	
17	**Additional tax.** Enter 6% (0.06) of the **smaller** of line 16 **or** the value of your traditional IRAs on December 31, 2018 (including 2018 contributions made in 2019). Include this amount on Schedule 4 (Form 1040), line 59, or Form 1040NR, line 57 . . .		**17**	

Part IV   Additional Tax on Excess Contributions to Roth IRAs. Complete this part if you contributed more to your Roth IRAs for 2018 than is allowable or you had an amount on line 25 of your 2017 Form 5329.

18	Enter your excess contributions from line 24 of your 2017 Form 5329. See instructions. If zero, go to line 23		**18**	
19	If your Roth IRA contributions for 2018 are less than your maximum allowable contribution, see instructions. Otherwise, enter -0-	**19**		
20	2018 distributions from your Roth IRAs (see instructions)	**20**		
21	Add lines 19 and 20		**21**	
22	Prior year excess contributions. Subtract line 21 from line 18. If zero or less, enter -0-		**22**	
23	Excess contributions for 2018 (see instructions)		**23**	
24	Total excess contributions. Add lines 22 and 23		**24**	
25	**Additional tax.** Enter 6% (0.06) of the **smaller** of line 24 **or** the value of your Roth IRAs on December 31, 2018 (including 2018 contributions made in 2019). Include this amount on Schedule 4 (Form 1040), line 59, or Form 1040NR, line 57 . . .		**25**	

For Privacy Act and Paperwork Reduction Act Notice, see your tax return instructions.	Cat. No. 13329Q	Form **5329** (2018)

The No-Modification Rule

Once you establish a schedule and begin receiving substantially equal periodic payments, you may not modify them or discontinue them for five years or until you attain age 59½, whichever period is longer. For example, if you are age 49 when you begin receiving payments, you will be only 54 after five years. Therefore, you must continue the payments until you reach 59½. On the other hand, if you begin payments when you are 58, you must continue them for five full years, even though you will have passed the age 59½ milestone in the meantime.

The time period requirement is quite literal. If you begin monthly payments at 49 and wish to stop at age 59½, you must take your last payment on or after the day you reach age 59½. You may not simply stop payments on January 1 of the year you turn 59½. Similarly, if you begin monthly payments on your 58th birthday, you must continue them at least until your 63rd birthday, when five full years will have passed.

As mentioned above, the no-modification rule means you may not prematurely discontinue or alter the size of the payments. Furthermore, if you transfer any additional amounts into the account or transfer any amounts to another retirement account, the IRS will consider those actions to be modifications of your payment. And of course, you may not withdraw additional amounts in excess of the periodic payment because the IRS sees that as a simple (and disallowed) increase in the amount of the annual payment.

Exceptions to the No-Modification Rule

There are four exceptions to the rule that payments cannot be modified.

Death

If you die before the required period has passed, your beneficiary may discontinue the payments.

Disability

If you become disabled, you are no longer tied to your periodic payment schedule, and subsequent distributions will not be subject to the early distribution tax. For this exception to apply, you must satisfy the IRS's definition of disabled. (See Chapter 3 for more information on the disability exception.)

Complete Depletion of Assets

If your account balance goes to zero while you are taking substantially equal periodic payments, the IRS will not penalize you for failing to continue the payments. Even the IRS recognizes that your investment losses should be penalty enough.

One-Time Change to Required Minimum Distribution Method

In the early years of the new millennium, taxpayers watched their retirement funds shrink in lockstep with the tumbling stock market. The IRS sought to offer some relief to those who had started periodic payments at the market peak and now faced a rapidly depleting retirement nest egg because of high periodic payments.

Had taxpayers chosen to use the required minimum distribution method at the outset, their payments would have fluctuated with their retirement plan account balance. If you now think you would be better off with that method, the IRS will allow anyone currently using either the amortization or the annuitization method to make a one-time permanent switch to the required minimum distribution method.

If you choose to switch, you may not switch back to either of the other methods. Furthermore, if you are currently using the required minimum distribution method, you may not switch to the amortization or the annuitization methods. Once you choose the required minimum distribution method, you are stuck with it.

Bear in mind that if you switch to the required minimum distribution method, you will almost certainly be reducing your payments, so make some calculations first to be sure you can get by on the smaller amounts.

Penalties for Breaking the No-Modification Rule

If you modify your payments in any but the approved ways before the required period has expired, then all distributions you have received since you initiated periodic payments will be subject to the early distribution tax. Because a modification invalidates the substantially equal periodic payment exception, all of the payments are treated (retroactively) as though they were normal discretionary distributions. Therefore, funds that were distributed before you turned 59½ are subject to an early distribution tax, but amounts received after age 59½ are not.

The cumulative payments for all years must be reported on your tax return for the year in which you first modify the payments. You must pay the early distribution taxes with that return. You must also pay interest on any early distribution taxes that would have been due from and after the year of the first periodic payment.

EXAMPLE 1: You began taking substantially equal periodic payments of $6,000 per year on July 1 of the year you turned 49. You took the last one on July 1 of the year you turned 54. Then you stopped the payments altogether. Because you were required to continue payments until you reached age 59½, the substantially equal periodic payment exception became invalid in the year you turned 55 when you failed to take a payment. When you file the tax return for that year, you must report all distributions received and pay the early distribution tax with your tax return. The tax is 10% of all distributions that would have been subject to the early distribution tax if you had not been using the substantially equal periodic payment exception. The total of all distributions is $36,000 (six payments multiplied by $6,000). The early distribution tax is $3,600 ($36,000 × 0.10).

In addition, you will owe interest retroactively on the early distribution tax itself, as if the tax had been imposed on the due date of the tax return for the year in which you received the early distribution. In this example, your early distribution tax for each year was $600. You didn't pay any of it until the year you turned 55. For the distribution you took during the year you were 49, you owe six years of interest on the $600. For the distribution you took during the year you were 50, you owe five years of interest on $600. You get the idea. The rate used to compute the interest you owe is the IRS's standard rate on underpayment of tax. The rate is based on the applicable federal short-term rate and therefore changes from time to time. As of the fourth quarter of 2016, the rate for underpayment of tax was 4%.

EXAMPLE 2: Your birthday is August 1. You began taking substantially equal periodic payments of $6,000 per year on December 31 of the year you turned 58. You took an identical payment every December 31 through the year you turned 61 and then stopped. Because you were required to continue payments for five full years, you will be subject to an early distribution tax of 10% on the distributions that would have been subject to the tax if you had never invoked the substantially equal periodic payment exception. You took four payments of $6,000, the last one in December of the year you turned 61. However, if you had not been using the substantially equal period payment exception, only the distributions you took in the years you turned 58 and 59 would have been subject to an early distribution tax. All other distributions occurred after age 59½ and thus would not have been subject to penalty. (Note that because your birthday is August 1, you didn't turn 59½ until the same year you turned 60. So the distribution you took in December of the year you turned 59 was an early distribution, because you weren't yet 59½.)

Your early distribution tax will be $1,200 ($6,000 × 2 years × 0.10), plus interest.

Key Tax Code Sections, Regulations, and Notices

§ 72(t)(2)(A)(iv)
Substantially Equal Period Payment Exception.

§ 72(t)(3)(B)
Separation From Service Requirement for Age 55 Exception.

§ 1.72-9
IRS Life Expectancy Tables.

§ 402(c)(4)
Prohibition Against Rollover of Periodic Payment.

§ 1.401(a)(9)
Regulations for Minimum Distribution Calculation.

Revenue Ruling 2002-62
IRS Guidelines for Computing Substantially Equal Payments.

Required Distributions:
Taking Money Out When You Have To

> ## Who Should Read Chapter 5
>
> This chapter gives an overview of situations in which you are required to take money out of your retirement plan or IRA. Chapter 6 provides the details you will need to compute required distributions during your lifetime. Chapters 7 and 8 provide the information your heirs will need to compute distributions after your death.

Someone once said that the government's strategy for encouraging people to use their retirement money is a lot like herding cattle through a gate. If a cow heads off to the left of the gate, a cattle prod nudges her back on track. Similarly, if you wander off the retirement trail and withdraw your funds too early, you're brought up short with an early distribution tax. If our proverbial cow meanders too far to the right, she receives another painful poke, just as you are hit with another penalty if you wait too long to withdraw your retirement money. That penalty—for waiting too long—is the focus of this chapter.

To avoid being penalized for delaying distributions, you must comply with what are called the required distribution rules. Those rules mandate that you take a minimum amount from your retirement plan each year, beginning in the year you turn 70½ or, under certain circumstances, in the year you retire if you work past age 70½. The minimum amount is calculated according to a formula in the income tax regulations. You may take more than the minimum, but you may not take less. If you do take less, you will be fined 50% of the amount that should have come out of your plan but didn't (the shortfall, in penalty parlance).

The required distribution rules evolved from Congress's desire that you use up your retirement funds during your own retirement, instead of passing the assets on to your heirs. The law presents you with a date by which you must start withdrawing money from your retirement plan. It also answers questions such as: What happens if you die before the date you are supposed to begin distributions? Does the law provide income

Helpful Terms

Beneficiary. The person or entity entitled to receive the benefits from insurance or from trust property, such as a retirement plan or an IRA, usually after the insured or the owner of the property dies.

Deferral period. The number of years over which distributions from a retirement plan or an IRA can be spread.

Distribution. A payout of property (such as shares of stock) or cash from a retirement plan or an IRA to the participant or a beneficiary.

Grandfather provision. A part of a new law that exempts an individual or entity from the new law and allows the individual or entity to use the old law or special transitional laws.

TDA or tax-deferred annuity. Many university professors, public school employees, and employees of nonprofit organizations are covered by TDAs, which are retirement annuity plans for public charities or public schools. These retirement plans are usually funded with individual annuity contracts purchased from insurance companies. Retirement benefits are frequently paid as a monthly annuity for life.

Waiver. Intentional dismissal, as of a penalty.

tax relief to your heirs? Is your beneficiary allowed to defer distributions from your plan even though the funds were never intended for his or her retirement? Does your spouse have special privileges?

As if those issues didn't complicate matters enough, there is a flip side to the premature death issue: What happens if you die after you have started receiving required distributions but before you have used up all your retirement money? Does this change anything? Are your heirs given relief in this situation? And, again, does your spouse have special privileges?

The required distribution rules attempt to address all of these questions and more. In this chapter, we offer a summary of these rules.

Required Distributions During Your Lifetime

You don't have to worry about taking required distributions from your own retirement plan until the year in which you turn 70½. At that time, however, you must start taking distributions under one of the following two scenarios:

- You may withdraw everything by your required beginning date, or RBD, which for most people is April 1 of the year after turning 70½, but for some people will be April 1 of the year after they retire. (See Chapter 6 for more information about determining your RBD.)

- Alternatively, you may distribute your retirement plan money over a period of years. Most people will use the Uniform Lifetime Table (see Table III in Appendix B) to determine the number of years over which they may spread distributions. If your spouse is your beneficiary and is more than ten years younger than you are, however, you will use a different and more favorable table called the Joint Life and Last Survivor Table. (See Table II in Appendix B.)

When faced with those two distribution options, few people would choose the first—to distribute the entire amount of their retirement plan at once—because of the income tax implications. A whopping distribution all in one year could put you in the top tax bracket for that year, allowing the government to take a huge tax bite out of your nest egg.

In contrast, the second option allows people to spread distributions over a period of years, thereby keeping their tax burden lower. As an added bonus, the second option is flexible: If people want to take only the minimum required amount, they can, but they also have the option of taking more money out when they need it.

Chapter 6 describes the steps involved in determining your required distributions during your lifetime.

Death Before Required Beginning Date

If you die before your RBD, your beneficiary generally may spread distributions from your retirement plan over his or her life expectancy.

If your retirement plan requires or permits it, your beneficiary might also take distributions according to the five-year rule. This is almost always a less favorable method, so if your beneficiary has a choice, he or she should probably choose another method.

Under the five-year rule, your retirement plan assets must be completely distributed by December 31 of the year containing the fifth anniversary of your death. The law does not prescribe a distribution method. In order to mitigate the tax impact, your beneficiary might choose to take money out of the plan in annual installments over that five-year period. This strategy is perfectly acceptable as long as the plan administrator will allow it. But the plan has the authority to determine the distribution method during the five-year period. Some plans will permit installment payments; others will require a lump-sum payment.

If you have no beneficiary, the five-year rule is mandatory.

If your beneficiary is someone other than your spouse, upon your death your beneficiary will have the option to transfer your retirement plan assets into a new inherited IRA and spread distributions over his or her own life expectancy. However, the new IRA must be in your name, as the original owner, and distributions to the beneficiary must begin in the year after your death.

Your nonspouse beneficiary will also have the option to transfer your retirement plan assets to a new inherited Roth IRA in your name. This is called a conversion. If your beneficiary chooses this option, he or she must first pay taxes on the converted amounts, and must take distributions over his or her life expectancy beginning in the year after your death. Note that this strategy works only for conversions from an inherited retirement plan to an inherited Roth IRA. Beneficiaries may not convert inherited traditional IRAs to Roth IRAs.

If your beneficiary is your spouse, he or she has some additional privileges. After your death, your spouse may defer distributions from your retirement plan until you would have been 70½. At that point, the distributions will be spread over your spouse's own life expectancy. Alternatively, your spouse can roll over your retirement plan (whether a qualified plan or an IRA) into an IRA or plan of his or her own. Your spouse would then name new beneficiaries and begin distributions in the year he or she turns 70½. If your spouse rolls the plan into a Roth IRA, taxes will be due in the year of the rollover but no distributions will be required during your spouse's lifetime.

> **CAUTION**
>
> **If there are multiple beneficiaries.** If your spouse is not the sole beneficiary but is instead one of several, then he or she might lose some of these special privileges.

Chapter 7 describes the effect of premature death on your retirement distributions, and it includes a detailed explanation of the life expectancy rule, the five-year rule, and the special privileges accorded a surviving spouse.

Death After Required Beginning Date

If you survive to your RBD, you must begin taking required distributions as described above. If money is left in your retirement plan when you die, your beneficiary must continue to take distributions every year, generally based on his or her life expectancy. Your beneficiary can elect to receive more than the prescribed amount, but not less.

As is the case when you die before your RBD, your nonspouse beneficiary may transfer the assets from your retirement plan into an inherited IRA in your name, and then take distributions over his or her life expectancy. Alternatively, your beneficiary may convert your retirement plan to an inherited Roth IRA in your name. Again, distributions from the Roth IRA must begin in the year after your death.

If you did not name a beneficiary, the assets will generally be distributed to your estate over your own remaining life expectancy as of the year of your death.

Some special rules apply if your spouse is your sole beneficiary. For example, your spouse may take distributions as though he or she were a nonspouse beneficiary. Alternatively, your spouse can roll over your retirement plan into an IRA or a plan of his or her own. After the rollover, the retirement assets belong to the spouse, and the required distribution rules apply as though the spouse had been the original owner.

Chapter 8 explains your beneficiary's options if you die after you begin receiving required distributions.

Special Rules for Tax-Deferred Annuities

If you were a participant in a tax-deferred annuity (also known as a TDA or 403(b) plan) established before 1987, some special required distribution rules apply. Specifically, all contributions and earnings added to your account after 1986 are subject to the same required distribution rules described above.

However, the amount in your account on December 31, 1986 was grandfathered under an older set of rules and is not subject to the current required distribution rules.

Because of this grandfathering, when it comes time for you to start required distributions from your TDA, you may subtract your pre-1987 balance and compute your required distribution on the difference. You may continue to subtract the pre-1987 balance when computing required distributions every year until you reach age 75, at which time your entire account, including the pre-1987 balance, will be subject to current required distribution rules.

CAUTION

Grandfathering rules are strict. Although you may exclude the pre-1987 balance when computing required distributions, you may not exclude any subsequent earnings attributable to the grandfathered amount. The grandfathered portion is a fixed dollar amount: the precise balance of your account on December 31, 1986.

EXAMPLE: On December 31, 1986 the balance in your TDA was $130,000. You are now retired and will turn 70½ this year. The total value of your account is $220,000. Because you are not yet 75, you may exclude $130,000 (your pre-1987 balance) when you compute your first required distribution, which means the required distribution will be based on an account balance of $90,000 ($220,000 − $130,000). You may use this approach until the year you turn 75. From that year forward, you must use the total value of your account when computing your required distribution.

All required distributions you take before age 75 are deemed to come from your post-1986 accumulation. Any amount you withdraw in excess of the required amount, however, is deemed to come from the pre-1987 portion.

EXAMPLE: As in the previous example, your pre-1987 account balance is $130,000, and your post-1986 accumulation is $90,000. You compute your first required distribution to be $5,625, but decide to take an extra $5,000 to pay some unexpected medical expenses. Your total distribution for the year is $10,625. The minimum required amount of $5,625 is deemed to come from your post-1986 account (the $90,000 portion). The remaining $5,000 is deemed to come from your pre-1987 accumulation. Therefore, next year when you subtract your pre-1987 balance before computing your required distribution, you will subtract $125,000 (which is $130,000 − $5,000), instead of $130,000.

CAUTION

Be careful not to forfeit your option to defer. If at any time before you reach age 75, you roll over your entire TDA into an IRA, then you forfeit the option to defer until age 75 distributions on your pre-1987 accumulation. Similarly, if you roll over your TDA assets to another TDA (that is, you, yourself, take the money from one TDA and move it to another), you lose the deferral option. To avoid this, request a direct transfer of the funds (trustee to trustee) from the first TDA to the second. Transfers to an IRA don't work, though.

In addition, if the trustee or custodian of your TDA at any time ceases to keep accurate records of the year-end balances of your grandfathered and nongrandfathered portions, the entire balance of your TDA will be subject to current required distribution rules, and you will no longer have the option of deferring distributions on your pre-1987 accumulation.

Special Rules for Roth IRAs

Roth IRAs conform to some of the required distribution rules described above, but not to others. Specifically, you are not required to take lifetime distributions. But if you die leaving a balance in your Roth IRA, the post-death rules introduced above, and described fully in Chapter 7, will apply whether you die before or after your RBD. Chapter 9 contains a detailed discussion of the Roth IRA rules.

CAUTION

Roth 401(k) plans are hybrids. A Roth 401(k) plan is treated like a traditional 401(k) plan for purposes of lifetime required distributions. In other words, Roth 401(k) plans are not exempt from lifetime required distributions. However, if you roll over your Roth 401(k) plan into a Roth IRA, either at retirement or when you leave your job, then once the assets are in the Roth IRA (and no longer in the Roth 401(k) plan), the Roth IRA rules would apply and no distributions would be required during your lifetime. See Chapter 10 for more information about Roth 401(k) plans.

Penalty

The penalty for failing to take a required distribution is one of the worst in all the tax code: 50% of the shortfall. Some call it onerous, others call it Draconian, but everyone calls it punitive. If you were required to take a $10,000 distribution but took only $4,000, you would owe the IRS $3,000 for your mistake, 50% of the $6,000 you didn't take.

And don't think your failure to take a distribution will go unnoticed. The IRS requires trustees and custodians of IRAs to identify on IRS Form 5498 those IRAs for which a minimum distribution is required.

When meting out punishment for failure to comply with a rule or regulation, enforcers of the law sometimes attempt to discern your intent so that the punishment better fits the crime. For example, in the case of a required distribution violation, did you make an inadvertent error? A once-in-a-blue-moon blunder? Or are your failures chronic? Perhaps you attempted to cash in on a perceived loophole? The more egregious the violation, the more severe the penalty is likely to be. Some scenarios are discussed in the following sections.

Innocent Blunders

If you simply forget to take your required distribution one year, the 50% penalty is probably the worst you'll face. And as painful as it is, at least it hits only once. So even if you don't correct the shortfall the next year, the excise tax will not be assessed again with respect to the first transgression.

> **EXAMPLE:** You forgot to take your required distribution of $6,000 for the year 2017. In 2018 you computed your required distribution for 2018 and withdrew it, but you still hadn't discovered your error for the year 2017. Your mind cleared sometime in the year 2019 and you withdrew the $6,000 for 2017 along with your distribution for the year 2019. You must pay a penalty of $3,000 (50% of $6,000) plus interest for the year 2017 mistake. However, you only have to pay it once, even though the mistake remained uncorrected for all of 2018. (See below for information on how to report the distribution and penalty.)

Once you stumble and are faced with an unavoidable penalty, you might think there is nothing to be gained by distributing the required amount. But here are two good reasons to withdraw it:

- Only if you correct your mistake can you hope to obtain an official waiver of the penalty. (See below for more information about waivers.)

- If you don't correct the shortfall, you risk disqualifying the plan, which would force a total distribution of the account and loss of all future tax-deferred growth. The tax code states that a plan will not be a qualified plan unless it complies with the required distribution rules. Arguably, you will not be in compliance for as long as a shortfall remains uncorrected.

Chronic Errors

Make no mistake, the IRS will look askance at the taxpayer who habitually fails to take proper required distributions, whether those distributions are late, incorrect, or nonexistent. Once a problem becomes chronic, not only will the IRS's sympathy wane, but plan disqualification becomes a serious risk.

Ineligible Rollovers

There is one more way for you or the trustee of your retirement plan to mess up your required distribution. You might roll it over. Required distributions from plans and IRAs are not eligible for rollover. (See Chapter 2 for more information about rollovers.) If they were, you would be able to withdraw your required distribution each year and roll what you don't need into another plan or IRA. That strategy might fit in with your financial and estate planning goals, but it flies in the face of Congressional intent, which is to encourage you to deplete your retirement account during your retirement, instead of preserving the assets for your heirs.

When Congress enacted the no-rollover rule, lawmakers recognized the rule would be difficult to enforce without help. Consequently, income tax regulations were fashioned to push the rule a step further, tacking on penalties for ineligible rollovers and requiring trustees of qualified plans to lend a hand in enforcement. The regulations for IRAs and TDAs are slightly different from those for qualified plans and qualified annuities.

Qualified Plans and Qualified Annuities

If you decide to roll over an amount from one qualified plan to another qualified plan or to an IRA during a year you are required to take a distribution, then only the amount that exceeds the required distribution is eligible for rollover. The amount of the required distribution itself must be distributed to you, and if it is not, it must be included in your taxable income for the year anyway.

> **EXAMPLE:** When you retired, you left your 401(k) assets with your employer. When you turned 70½ several years ago, your employer began distributing your minimum required distributions to you. On January 1 of this year, you decide to roll over your remaining 401(k) account balance into an IRA so that you can manage your own investments. The balance of your 401(k) is $500,000. Your minimum distribution for the current year is $40,000. When you receive your 401(k) distribution, you are permitted to roll over only $460,000, because your required distribution for the current year is not eligible for rollover. If you roll over the entire $500,000 anyway, you must still report $40,000 of income on your tax return as though you had not rolled over the required distribution. And there could be other penalties, as well.

If you roll over an ineligible amount into an IRA, the consequences extend beyond including the ineligible portion in your income for the year. The ineligible amount is considered an excess contribution to the IRA. If it is not promptly withdrawn, it will be subject to excess contribution penalties in the year of the contribution (rollover) and again each year the excess remains uncorrected. (See below for more about excess contributions.)

To help ensure that the required distribution is not rolled over, the regulations require trustees of retirement plans to compute required distributions for all participants. There is good reason for placing this burden on a trustee: The portion of any distribution that exceeds the participant's required distribution is eligible for rollover. When a trustee distributes any amount that is eligible for rollover, the trustee must comply with a host of procedural rules and regulations related to withholding, disclosure, and participant notification of tax options. In order to comply with these administrative rules, the trustee must determine whether or not some or all of a distribution is eligible for rollover. That, in turn, requires computation of the required distribution.

> ⚠ CAUTION
>
> **Required distributions are not only ineligible for rollover, they are also ineligible for transfer.** This means that a trustee must compute the minimum required distribution not only during a rollover, but also when benefits are being transferred by the trustee directly to a new plan. Consequently, the trustee must distribute the required amount to the participant either at the time of transfer or segregate the amount and distribute it before the required distribution deadline for the year.

IRAs and TDAs

Required distributions from IRAs and TDAs also are ineligible for rollover, but compliance can be a little tricky. If you have more than one IRA (whether traditional, SEP, or SIMPLE IRA), you must compute the required distribution for each one. You are then permitted to withdraw the total required amount from one or more of the IRAs. This aggregation rule applies to TDAs as well. So if you have more than one TDA, you may calculate the required distribution for each and withdraw the total from only one. Note, however, that you may not mix and match. You may not calculate a required distribution from your IRA and withdraw it from your TDA, or vice versa.

> **EXAMPLE:** You have two IRAs and a TDA. Your required distribution from IRA #1 is $3,000 and from IRA #2 is $2,500. Your required distribution from your TDA is $4,000. You may total the required distributions from your two IRAs and withdraw the entire $5,500 from either IRA #1 or IRA #2 (or part from both). But the $4,000 required distribution from the TDA must be distributed from the TDA, not from one of the IRAs.

> ⚠ CAUTION
>
> **Aggregation does not apply to qualified plans or qualified annuities.** For example, if you have more than one 401(k) plan, you must compute the distribution for each and withdraw the required amount from the respective plan.

CAUTION

Inherited IRAs and inherited TDAs. You are not permitted to aggregate inherited IRAs and inherited TDAs with your own IRAs and TDAs for required distribution purposes. For example, assume you have an IRA to which you have made contributions over the years. You also have an IRA that you inherited from your father. When the time comes to take required distributions, you must compute the distribution for each IRA separately and withdraw the required amount from the respective IRA. However, if you have inherited multiple IRAs from the same decedent and the divisor used for computing required distributions is the same for each account, you may aggregate those inherited IRAs, provided they are all either traditional, SEP, or SIMPLE IRAs. Inherited Roth IRAs may be aggregated only with other inherited Roth IRAs from the same decedent and with the same divisor. TDAs also may be aggregated with other TDAs from the same decedent and with the same divisor.

Because of this aggregation option for IRAs, the IRS cannot really require IRA custodians to distribute to you the required amount before moving the funds. After all, what if you already computed and withdrew the requisite amount from another IRA, or you intend to do so? Because of this potential problem, the IRS relaxed the IRA transfer rules a little. But just a little. If you transfer your funds from one IRA to another in a direct custodian-to-custodian transfer, then the IRS will not require the custodian to withhold (and distribute to you) a required distribution from that IRA. The entire IRA can be transferred.

But if you roll over the funds instead (that is, you, yourself, take the funds out of one IRA and deposit them in another IRA), it is a different story. The law says required amounts cannot be rolled over. Therefore, the custodian would have to withhold a computed required distribution from the IRA funds you want to roll over, even though you intend to take—or already did take—the required amount from another IRA.

Excess Contributions

One of the most intimidating characteristics of the tax law is that penalties sometimes seem to come out of nowhere. One small mistake can turn a manageable tax liability into a financial disaster.

A rollover into a plan or an IRA of an amount that is not permitted to be rolled over can lead to catastrophe. Unless the mistake is corrected promptly, usually by the filing deadline for the tax return, the IRS will consider the rollover an excess contribution to the plan or IRA. Excess contributions are subject to a penalty of 6% for excess contributions to an IRA or 10% for excess contributions to a qualified plan. This penalty is assessed in addition to any other penalties or taxes that might apply, and it will be imposed every year until the excess is removed.

> **EXAMPLE:** In 2017, you received a required distribution of $6,000 from your 401(k) plan and rolled it over into an IRA. Because required distributions are ineligible for rollover, the $6,000 is an excess contribution. You were unaware of the problem until the IRS audited your 2017 tax return in late 2019. You removed the $6,000 in December 2019. The $6,000 must be reported as income on your tax return for the year 2019. In addition, you will owe an excess contribution penalty of $360 (6% of $6,000) for each of the years 2017 and 2018. Because you distributed the excess before filing your 2019 tax return, you will owe no penalty for the year 2019.

Reporting the Penalty

If you owe a penalty for failing to take your required distribution, you must complete IRS Form 5329 (you can find a copy of this form in Appendix A) and include it when you file your tax return. If you have already filed your tax return for the year, then you must file an amended tax return for the year of the error and pay the penalty plus interest.

EXAMPLE: You began taking required distributions from your IRA in 2013 and took them regularly until 2015. In 2017, you inherited some money, so you didn't need to draw on the IRA for living expenses as you had in the past. Consequently, you simply forgot to take your required distribution of $6,000. In fact, you forgot to take your 2018 distribution, too, which would have been $6,500. Finally, in February of 2019, you realized your error.

For 2017, you must file an amended tax return and include a completed Form 5329. You must also pay a penalty of $3,000 (50% of $6,000), plus interest, for which the IRS will bill you.

For 2018, because you have not yet passed the filing deadline for your tax return, you may simply file as usual by April 15, 2019 and include a completed Form 5329. Along with any regular income tax you owe, you will owe a penalty of $3,250 (50% of $6,500). You will not have to pay interest, though, as long as the tax return and payment are filed on time.

Finally, you should correct the distribution errors by withdrawing the required amounts for both 2017 and 2018. If you correct the problem in 2019, you must report the distributions of $6,000 (for 2017) and $6,500 (for 2018) on your 2019 tax return. In addition, you will have to take a required distribution for 2019 and include it as income on your tax return.

In general, you have until December 31 to take your required distribution for any given year. If you miss the deadline, you must pay the penalty when you file your tax return (or pay the penalty with an amended return). The one exception to the December 31 deadline is the first year of required distributions. A grace period gives you until April 1 of the following year to withdraw your first required distribution. (See Chapter 6 for more information about when distributions must begin.) Thus, if you don't take a distribution by December 31 of the first year of required distributions, you won't owe a penalty unless you miss the April 1 deadline as well. If you happen to miss that one, too, you must pay the penalty, but you would pay it when you file your tax return for the year containing the April 1 distribution deadline.

EXAMPLE: You turned 70½ in 2017, so your required beginning date (with the grace period) was April 1, 2018, although your first distribution year was officially 2017. This means that you were supposed to take your first required distribution by April 1, 2018 and your second distribution by December 31, 2018. Unfortunately, you forgot to take any distribution at all until January 2019. You will owe penalties for 2017 and 2018, because you missed the deadline for both required distributions. But because both distribution deadlines were in 2018, you can simply complete a Form 5329 and attach it to your tax return for the 2018 tax year (which is due by April 15, 2019). At that time, you must pay the 50% penalty on the required distribution shortfalls for both 2017 and 2018. You do not have to file an amended return for 2017, because the distribution for 2017 did not have to be made until April 1, 2018.

Waiver

Mistakes happen. Even Congress knows it. That's why a waiver has been written into the penalty provisions of the required distribution law.

Terms of the Waiver

There are four short paragraphs in the tax code section that assesses a penalty for delaying distributions from your retirement plan. But the entire fourth paragraph is devoted to a waiver of the penalty. It says that if you demonstrate that your failure to withdraw the proper amount was due to reasonable error and you are taking steps to correct the shortfall, the penalty may be waived. "May" is the operative word, though. The IRS is not required to waive the penalty; it simply has the authority to do so.

TIP

Sometimes, the penalty will be waived automatically. Remember: The required distribution rules apply to inherited plans and IRAs, too. If a beneficiary inherits a retirement plan, he or she must generally take distributions over his or her life expectancy beginning in the year after the original participant's death (the life expectancy rule). But if the beneficiary fails to take the first distribution on time, he or she can fall back on the five-year rule to avoid a penalty. The five-year rule requires that all assets be distributed by December 31 of the year containing the fifth anniversary of the participant's death. To fall back on the five-year rule, the plan must permit the five-year rule as an option. If it does and if the beneficiary chooses to use it, the penalty for failing to take a distribution under the life expectancy rule will be waived automatically. (See Chapter 7 for more information about the life expectancy rule and the five-year rule.)

Requesting a Waiver

To request a waiver, you must first explain how the mistake came about. Perhaps you didn't understand the computation formula. Or maybe you wrote a letter to the custodian of your plan requesting a distribution, but you broke your leg on the way to the post office to mail the letter and forgot to drop the letter in a mail box after you were released from the hospital.

Your excuse must accompany a description of the steps you have taken to correct the mistake. For example, you might report that as soon as you discovered that you didn't take the appropriate amount from your IRA, you asked the custodian to distribute the funds, which the custodian did the following week.

These explanations must be attached to a completed Form 5329 and filed along with the rest of your return at tax time. If you are submitting an amended return, send it in right away.

The IRS has been generous with these waivers, so don't assume your excuse is too lame to pass muster. For example, taxpayers have argued that they didn't understand the formula for computing the required distribution or that they made an arithmetic error. One taxpayer claimed that he signed the request for a distribution but forgot to mail it to his custodian. In all of those cases, the taxpayers had corrected their mistakes by the time they reported the error to the IRS, and they were all granted waivers.

If you have a plausible explanation for your error and you have taken steps to correct it, you stand a good chance of obtaining a waiver. Even the IRS is aware that 50% is a stiff penalty and is more interested in curbing abuse than punishing the computationally challenged. But if you consistently fail to take appropriate distributions, or if the IRS discovers your mistake during an audit, the IRS is likely to be less forgiving.

Key Tax Code and Regulation Sections

§ 401(a)(9)
Required Distributions From Qualified Plans.

§ 402(e)(4)
Eligible Rollover From Qualified Plan.

§ 408(d)(3)(E)
Ineligible Rollover From IRA.

§ 4974
50% Excise Tax on Required Distributions.

§ 1.403(b)-2
Treatment of Pre-1987 Accumulation in TDA.

Required Distributions During Your Lifetime

Who Should Read Chapter 6
Everyone will need to read this chapter. It tells you precisely when you are required to begin taking money out of your own retirement plan or IRA, how you compute the amount to withdraw, and what other decisions you must make at that time.

Comedians and accountants have long pondered the origin of the numbers that appear in the tax code, particularly the ones that don't seem to make any sense. Why must we start taking money out of our retirement plans at age 70½? Why not 70? Or even 71? Some of us like to think Congress has a sense of humor, although cynics believe there's a conspiracy to keep the tax code complex. More likely, it's the result of a compromise.

Whatever its history, 70½ has become an important milestone; it's the age when most people must crack open their retirement nest eggs, even if they don't want to. Before age 59½, you have to worry about penalties for tapping your retirement money too early. (See Chapter 3 for information on the early distribution penalty.) Age 59½ to 70½ is the penalty-free zone. You can take distributions any time you want—or not—without penalty. But once you reach 70½, you are required to begin taking distributions.

Some or all of your retirement plan nest egg might be paid to you as an annuity after you retire. This means you will receive your money in installments, usually in the form of monthly payments. The payments might continue for a fixed number of years (a term certain) but more often will be spread over your lifetime. Annuities are a common form of payment if you were covered by your employer's defined benefit plan while you were working.

Annuity payments must also satisfy the required distribution rules described in this chapter. Annuity plan administrators are aware of the distribution rules, and the plans are generally structured to ensure that your payments satisfy the requirements; however, ultimately the responsibility is yours.

Helpful Terms

Annuity. A contract, sold by an insurance company, that promises to make monthly, quarterly, semiannual, or annual payments for life or for a specified period of time.

Applicable distribution period (ADP). The divisor used for determining a required distribution. An account balance is divided by an ADP to arrive at the required distribution for a given year.

Contingent beneficiary. A person or an entity that is entitled to receive the benefits of a retirement plan or an IRA only if and when a specific event occurs, such as the death of a primary beneficiary.

Distribution. A payout of property (such as shares of stock) or cash from a retirement plan or an IRA to the participant or a beneficiary.

Irrevocable trust. A trust that cannot be changed or terminated by the person who created it. Once assets are transferred to an irrevocable trust, the assets are subject to the terms of trust for as long as the trust exists.

Primary beneficiary. A person or an entity entitled to receive benefits from a retirement plan or an IRA upon the death of the original participant.

Revocable trust. A trust whose terms allow the creator of the trust to alter its provisions, cancel it, or remove some or all of the property from the trust and return the property to the creator.

Term certain or period certain. A fixed, identifiable period, such as a specific number of years. For example, a retirement plan that is distributable over a term certain of 20 years must be completely liquidated (distributed) after 20 years.

If, instead of an annuity, some or all of your nest egg is in an IRA or another type of retirement plan account, then when it is time for you to begin required distributions, it is your responsibility to compute and withdraw the appropriate amount each year.

In this chapter, we discuss in detail the rules governing required distributions that you must take during your lifetime.

> **CAUTION**
>
> **Roth IRAs are different.** You are not required to take a distribution from your own Roth IRA during your lifetime. But after your death, your nonspouse beneficiaries will be required to start taking distributions. See Chapter 9 for detailed information about Roth IRAs.

Required Beginning Date

The absolute deadline for taking your first required distribution (withdrawal) from your retirement plan is called your "required beginning date," or RBD. If you are the original owner of your retirement plan (as opposed to the beneficiary of someone else's plan), then your RBD is April 1 of the year after you turn 70½.

> **EXAMPLE:** You were born January 15, 1949. You will turn 70½ on July 15, 2019. Your RBD is April 1, 2020.

Your RBD marks the deadline for taking the required distribution for your first distribution year only. For all subsequent years, the deadline is December 31.

You can defer your RBD for an employer plan if you work past age 70½. In that case, your RBD for that particular plan is April 1 of the year after you retire, no matter what age you are.

> **CAUTION**
>
> **Self-employed people beware.** This special deferral option is not available if you own 5% or more of the business that sponsors the retirement plan, which of course includes virtually all self-employed individuals.

You generally cannot defer your RBD for any IRAs you have. There are exceptions for people who are covered by a federal or state government plan or by a church plan. (A church plan is one maintained by a church for church employees. This would include any type of religious organization or house of worship, as long as the organization qualifies as a tax-exempt organization.) If neither of those situations applies, the RBD for an IRA is April 1 of the year after you turn 70½, even if you continue to work.

As you can see, it's possible to have more than one RBD if you work beyond age 70½, one for an employer plan and one for an IRA.

> **RESOURCE**
>
> **If you inherit a retirement plan.** You must use a different set of rules to determine your RBD for plans that you inherit. We discuss those rules in Chapters 7 and 8.

Because April 1 of the year after age 70½ is the RBD for most people, that is the date we will use for discussion purposes in this chapter.

First Year

You must withdraw at least the required minimum amount from your retirement plan account by your RBD or you will face a stiff penalty. To satisfy this requirement, you may count all distributions that take place between January 1 of the year you turn 70½ and April 1 of the following year (which is your RBD). In other words, you have 15 months to complete your first distribution.

Although you are permitted to take the required distribution in one big chunk, you don't have to. You can take it out as you need it, for example in monthly installments, as long as you have removed the minimum required amount for the first year by your RBD.

It is important to remember that amounts distributed before January 1 of the year you turn 70½ do not count toward your first required distribution, nor do amounts distributed after your RBD.

> **EXAMPLE 1:** You turn 70½ in 2019, and 2019 is your first distribution year. Although you were not required to take money out of your IRA in 2018, you took $20,000 on October 1, 2018 to buy a car. In 2019, your required minimum distribution is $10,000. You may not count the $20,000 you took in 2018 toward your 2019 required distribution.

EXAMPLE 2: You turn 70½ in 2019, and your RBD is April 1, 2020. Your required distribution for 2019 is $10,000. You decide to wait until 2020 to take the distribution for your first year. You take $9,000 on March 1, 2020 and another $1,000 on May 1, 2020. Because the $1,000 that you took on May 1 is after your RBD, you cannot use it as part of your required distributions. Because you are $1,000 short of the amount required to be distributed, you will owe the IRS penalties on the $1,000 shortfall.

Second Year and Beyond

For the second and all future distribution years, you must take at least the required amount out of your retirement account between January 1 and December 31. There are no more three-month grace periods.

> CAUTION
>
> **Waiting can be costly.** If you decide to wait until your RBD (which is April 1 of your second distribution year) to take your first required distribution, you must still take the full required distribution for the second year by December 31. That means you would have to take two required distributions in the same year, which could push you into a higher income tax bracket. For example, let's say you turn 70½ in 2019, which is your first distribution year, and your RBD is April 1, 2020. Your required distribution for your first distribution year is $30,000 and for the second year is $32,000. You are single and have no other taxable income. You also use the standard deduction. If you take your first distribution in 2019 and the second in 2020, the tax rate for both distributions is 12%. If you take both distributions in the same year, however, your gross income will be $62,000. At that level, some of your distributions will be taxed at a 22% rate.

Again, you may take the distribution in bits and pieces during the 12-month period, or you may take the entire amount on December 31. If you happen to take more than the required amount in one year, which is permissible, you may not count the excess toward your required distributions for the next year (or beyond).

> **EXAMPLE:** Your required distribution for your second distribution year is $10,000 and for your third distribution year is $12,000. If you take $16,000 in your second distribution year, you may not apply the extra $6,000 to your third distribution year and withdraw only $6,000. Instead you must withdraw the full $12,000 during the third year.

Computing the Required Amount

To compute your required distribution for a given year, simply divide your account balance by what the IRS calls the "applicable distribution period," or ADP. The resulting number is the minimum amount you must withdraw from the account for that year. The sections that follow give detailed instructions on computing the required distribution.

Determining the Account Balance

According to tax regulations, the account balance for computing your required distribution each year is determined as of "the last valuation date in the calendar year before the distribution calendar year." For the vast majority of people who are computing their own required distributions, this would be December 31 of the year before the distribution year.

If your retirement assets are in a qualified plan when you begin required distributions instead of in an IRA, however, it is possible that the plan itself specifies a date other than December 31 for valuing the plan assets and computing required distributions. Nevertheless, we will use December 31 for discussion purposes in this book.

> **EXAMPLE:** You turn 70½ in 2019. To compute the required distribution for your first distribution year (2019), you use your account balance as of December 31, 2018. To compute the required distribution for the year 2020, you look at your account balance as of December 31, 2019 and so on.

Recall that you are permitted to take your first required distribution in the year after you turn 70½, as long as you take it on or before your RBD (which is April 1 of the year after you turn 70½). Deferring your first distribution, however, does not alter the date for determining the appropriate account balance. For example, if you turn 70½ in 2019 and decide to take your first distribution in March of 2020, you must still use your account balance as of December 31, 2018 to compute the amount of your first distribution.

What If You Fail to Take Your Required Distribution?

Almost without exception, you will use the prior year's December 31 balance of your retirement account to compute the required distribution for the current year. But one important exception crops up when you fail to take some or all of your required distribution one year. To avoid penalties, you will want to correct this error as soon as possible for each year you failed to take the appropriate amount out of the account.

When determining the appropriate account balance for each year's calculation, the IRS has indicated that you may reduce the actual account balance by the amount of any required distribution that should have been distributed by that date but was not.

EXAMPLE: You forgot to take your required distributions for the years 2017 and 2018. Now, in 2019, you want to correct the errors and take all required distributions for prior years. To calculate the 2017 required distribution, you will use the actual December 31, 2016 account balance. To calculate the 2018 distribution, you will use the December 31, 2017 balance, reduced by the required distribution for 2017 (which you failed to take). For your 2019 distribution, you will use the December 31, 2018 account balance, reduced by the required distributions for 2017 and 2018 (which you failed to take).

Determining the Applicable Distribution Period

Once you have determined the appropriate account balance to use for a particular distribution year, you must divide it by the applicable distribution period, or ADP, to arrive at your required distribution.

First Year

To find your ADP for your first distribution year, you must use one of two tables provided by the IRS. Most people will use what the IRS calls the Uniform Lifetime Table (Table III in Appendix B), but some people will be able to use the Joint Life and Last Survivor Table (Table II in Appendix B). The table you use depends on whom you designate as your beneficiary.

General Rule

The vast majority of people will use the Uniform Lifetime Table to find their ADP. The only time you would not do so is when your spouse is the sole beneficiary of your retirement account and is more than ten years younger than you are. In all other cases, you will use the Uniform Lifetime Table. Thus, if your beneficiary is a child, grandchild, friend, charity, your estate, or a spouse who is not more than ten years younger than you are, you will use the Uniform Lifetime Table.

If you haven't yet named a beneficiary, you will still use the Uniform Lifetime Table.

To find the ADP for your first distribution year, you determine your age as of your birthday in the year you turn 70½. If that age is 70, then find the ADP next to age 70 in the Uniform Lifetime Table (Table III in Appendix B). That number is 27.4.

If your age is 71 on your birthday in the year you turn 70½, the ADP from the table is 26.5.

CAUTION

It depends on when your birthday is. You are not always age 70 in your first distribution year. If your birthday falls after June 30, you will turn 70½ in the same year in which you turn 71. In that case, you must use age 71 when looking up the ADP for your first distribution year.

Spouse More Than Ten Years Younger

If your beneficiary is your spouse and he or she is more than ten years younger than you are, the rules are slightly more favorable. You do not use the Uniform Lifetime Table. Instead, you use the Joint Life and Last Survivor Table (Table II in Appendix B) to find your ADP: the actual joint life expectancy of you and your spouse.

To determine your ADP, look up the number that corresponds to your age and your spouse's age on your respective birthdays in your first distribution year. For example, if you are age 70 on your birthday in your first distribution year (the year you turn 70½) and your spouse is age 55 in that year, your ADP from Table II is 31.1.

Be careful, though. In order to use Table II for your ADP, you must satisfy both of the following requirements:

- Your spouse must be more than ten years younger than you are.
- Your spouse must have been the sole designated beneficiary of your retirement account for the entire year.

For purposes of this last requirement, your marital status is determined as of January 1 of the distribution year. For example, if you would have been eligible to use Table II except for the fact that your spouse died during the year—or that you and your spouse divorced during the year—you would still be able to use Table II in the year of the death or divorce. However, in the following year, you would use the Uniform Lifetime Table (assuming you were still single on January 1 of that following year).

Second Year and Beyond

Determining the ADP for the second and future distribution years is done in precisely the same way you determined the ADP for the first year.

General Rule

In your second distribution year, you will again use the Uniform Lifetime Table, or Table III, to find your ADP—unless your spouse beneficiary is more than ten years younger than you are. (In that case, see just below.) For the second year calculation, use your age as of your birthday in the second year. If your age in that year is 71, find the ADP next to age 71 in Table III. That number is 26.5. For the third year, assuming you are age 72 on your birthday, your ADP is 25.6, and so on.

Spouse More Than Ten Years Younger

If your spouse is more than ten years younger than you are, and if he or she was the sole designated beneficiary of your retirement plan or IRA for the entire year, then you use Table II to find the ADP for your second distribution year. Look up the number that corresponds to your age and your spouse's age on your respective birthdays in your second distribution year. For example, if you are age 71 on your birthday in your second distribution year and your spouse is age 56 in that year, Table II indicates that your joint life expectancy—your ADP—for the second year is 30.1.

> **EXAMPLE:** You turned 70½ in February 2019. At that time, your brother was the beneficiary of your IRA. In November of 2019, you married someone 20 years younger than you and changed the beneficiary designation of your IRA to your new spouse. For 2019, you must use the Uniform Lifetime Table—Table III—to compute your first required distribution. For 2020, you may use Table II to find your ADP, as long as your new spouse remains the beneficiary for all of 2020.

Computing the Required Distribution

Once you have determined the appropriate account balance and ADP, you simply divide the account balance by the ADP to arrive at your required minimum distribution. You can withdraw more than the required amount each year, but you may not withdraw less without incurring a penalty. (See Chapter 5 to learn more about the penalty.)

EXAMPLE: You turn 70 on March 1, 2019 and your IRA account balance on December 31, 2018 is $50,000. Your niece is the beneficiary of your IRA. Your ADP for your first distribution year is 27.4 (from Table III). Therefore, your first required distribution is $1,824 ($50,000 ÷ 27.4).

TIP

Special opportunity for after-tax contributions. If you retire and receive a lump-sum distribution from your employer's plan, your distribution might include after-tax contributions that you made to the plan. Because these amounts are not taxable, you have an interesting planning opportunity if your retirement date is in the year you turn 70½ or later. Specifically, you may count the distribution of after-tax amounts as part of your required distribution from the plan for that particular year. By doing so you can reduce your income tax while leaving additional pretax amounts in the account to grow for another year.

EXAMPLE: You retire in 2019, which is also the year you turn 70½. Over the years, you created quite a nest egg of pretax dollars inside your employer's qualified retirement plan. You have also made $10,000 in after-tax contributions. Your required distribution for your first distribution year is $19,000. When you retire in 2019, your employer distributes your retirement benefits to you as a lump sum. You decide to take your first required distribution by December 31, 2019. Your intention is to roll over into an IRA all but your required distribution for 2019. You keep out your after-tax contributions of $10,000 and an additional $9,000. You then roll over the remainder of the lump sum into an IRA. Thus, you have distributed from your retirement plan the entire amount of your first required distribution ($19,000), but only $9,000 of it is taxable.

Special Aggregation Rule for IRAs and TDAs

If you have more than one IRA, you must compute the required distribution for each IRA separately, but then you may add up all the computed amounts and take the total from only one or several IRAs, as long as the aggregate or total amount is distributed before the deadline.

This strategy also works if you have more than one TDA plan. You may compute the required distribution for each plan, and then distribute the total from just one plan or more. You may not mix and match IRAs and TDAs, however. If you have one IRA and one TDA, you must calculate and distribute the required amount from each separately.

! CAUTION

You are not permitted to aggregate either inherited IRAs or inherited TDAs with your own IRAs or TDAs for required distribution purposes. For example, let's assume you have an IRA to which you have made contributions over the years. You also have an IRA that you inherited from your father. Your required distribution must be computed separately for each IRA and withdrawn from the respective account. However, if you have inherited multiple IRAs from the same decedent and the divisor used for computing required distributions is the same for each account, you may aggregate those inherited IRAs, provided they are all either traditional, SEP, or SIMPLE IRAs. Inherited Roth IRAs may be aggregated only with other inherited Roth IRAs from the same decedent and with the same divisor. TDAs also may be aggregated with other TDAs from the same decedent and with the same divisor.

! CAUTION

No aggregation for other types of plans. You are allowed to use the aggregation rule only for IRAs and TDAs. If you have another type of plan (such as an employer plan or a Keogh), you must compute the required amount separately for each plan and take the computed amount from the respective plan account.

Reporting Distributions From IRAs

It's up to you to compute the correct required distribution and report it on your tax return. However, in the case of an IRA, help is available. The law requires IRA custodians to tell IRA owners who have reached age 70½ either the amount of the required distribution or the fact that a distribution is required. If the custodian simply gives notice of the required distribution, the custodian must offer to calculate the amount for the IRA owner.

Custodians also must identify for the IRS those IRAs for which a minimum distribution must be made. They must do this each year. They do not, however, have to report to the IRS the amount of the required distribution.

Designating a Beneficiary

In the old days, if you did not name a person as beneficiary of your IRA or retirement plan, you would feel the impact of that decision as soon as you reached age 70½. That was because, without a designated beneficiary, you would have been required to distribute your retirement plan a lot faster than you would have if you had named a designated beneficiary.

Eventually, the IRS relaxed that requirement, and now it doesn't matter who your beneficiary is when you start taking required distributions. You are permitted to use the Uniform Lifetime Table even if you fail to name any beneficiary at all.

But even though the IRS won't punish you for not naming a beneficiary by your RBD, naming a designated beneficiary is still important. First, if your spouse is more than ten years younger than you are and you want to use Table II to compute required distributions, you can do so only if your spouse is your designated beneficiary.

Second, if you die without a designated beneficiary of your retirement plan or IRA, the distribution of the plan or IRA assets could be accelerated after your death, possibly leaving your heirs with significant tax problems. (See Chapters 7 and 8 for more information about what happens if you die without a designated beneficiary.)

Bear in mind that you may name any person or entity as the beneficiary of your retirement plan. But not all beneficiaries are "designated" beneficiaries. If you choose a beneficiary who does not fall within the definition of a designated beneficiary, you are deemed to have no beneficiary at all for required distribution purposes. (To find out who is, and who is not, a designated beneficiary, see immediately below.)

Definition of Designated Beneficiary

A designated beneficiary must be a natural person, as opposed to an entity such as a charity or a corporation. There is one exception to this natural person rule: A trust that has certain qualifications (known as a qualified trust, covered below) can be a designated beneficiary.

If you fail to name a natural person or a qualified trust as your beneficiary and instead name your estate, a charity, a corporation, or a nonqualified trust, then you are deemed to have no designated beneficiary for required distribution purposes.

> CAUTION
>
> **Just because you do not complete a beneficiary designation form and record the name of a beneficiary does not necessarily mean that you have no designated beneficiary.** Some plans provide for a default beneficiary, usually a spouse, when the owner does not name a beneficiary. Be sure to find out if your plan has such a default provision. If it does not, then you are deemed to have no designated beneficiary even if the laws of your state dictate who should receive your assets. Similarly, some plans or IRAs automatically revoke the designation of a spouse as beneficiary if you divorce. Again, be sure to check the plan provisions to ensure that your retirement plan assets will go to the beneficiaries you intend.

Designated beneficiaries fall into the following three categories:
- spouse
- nonspouse natural person, and
- qualified trust.

We look at each category in the following sections.

Spouse

If your spouse is your designated beneficiary, your spouse will have certain privileges after your death—such as a rollover option—that other beneficiaries will not have. (See Chapters 7 and 8.)

Nonspouse Natural Person

Any human being—what the tax code calls a "natural person"—qualifies as a designated beneficiary. For example, your designated beneficiary could be a friend, relative, or nonmarital partner.

Qualified Trust

A trust can be a designated beneficiary if it meets all of the following requirements:

- The trust must be valid under state law, meaning its terms must be enforceable.
- The trust must be either irrevocable while you are alive (meaning you cannot change its terms or cancel it) or irrevocable upon your death.
- The beneficiaries of the trust must be natural persons (humans) and must be identifiable. They don't have to be identified by name, however. For example, you may use the terms "spouse" or "children."
- You must provide a copy of the trust to the trustee or custodian of your retirement plan or IRA. If the trust is revocable (meaning you can change or amend it), you must give the trustee or custodian a copy of any subsequent amendments. As an alternative to submitting the entire trust agreement, you may also provide a list of beneficiaries with a description of the amount each is to receive and the conditions, if any, under which they will receive benefits.

If the trust meets all of the above qualifications, then the beneficiary of the trust is treated as the designated beneficiary for purposes of computing your required distributions. If your spouse is sole beneficiary of the trust and is more than ten years younger than you are, you can use Table II to find your ADP each year when computing required distributions. If there is more than one beneficiary of the trust, however, the multiple beneficiary rules discussed below will apply.

The trust must satisfy all of the above for any period during which the trust is named beneficiary and during which the beneficiary of the trust is being used to determine required distributions.

So, for example, if you want to use the joint life expectancy of you and your spouse to compute required distributions when you turn 70½, then in order to satisfy the fourth requirement (the fourth bullet point, above), you must provide the custodian with a copy of the trust document by your RBD.

Multiple Beneficiaries

If you want to name more than one person as the beneficiary of your retirement plan, you should be aware of the consequences.

Primary Beneficiaries

You can name several primary beneficiaries of your retirement plan who may or may not share equally in the plan assets after your death. If any one of the primary beneficiaries fails to qualify as a designated beneficiary, then you are deemed to have no designated beneficiary at all. This is true even if all other beneficiaries would qualify as designated beneficiaries. For example, if you name your sister to receive 50% of your IRA and a charity to receive the rest, you are deemed to have no designated beneficiary (because the charity is not a natural person).

You can avoid this problem by setting up a separate IRA for each beneficiary. For example, you can direct the custodian of the IRA, in writing, to set up a second IRA and transfer half of your existing IRA assets into the new IRA. You would name the charity as sole beneficiary of the new IRA and your sister as sole beneficiary of the old IRA.

> **TIP**
>
> **Sometimes, your heirs can cure the problem.** If you die having named multiple beneficiaries of your retirement plan and if one of those beneficiaries is not a designated beneficiary, all is not lost. Your heirs might be able to cure the problem by splitting the account or by distributing assets to one or more beneficiaries by December 31 of the year after your death. For more information about these strategies, see the "Multiple Beneficiaries, One Account" sections of Chapters 7 and 8.

Contingent Beneficiaries

A contingent beneficiary is a beneficiary you name to receive your retirement plan assets in the event your primary beneficiary does not qualify to receive the benefits. Usually a primary beneficiary fails to qualify because he or she has already died. If you name a primary beneficiary and then name a contingent beneficiary who will receive the retirement benefits only if the primary beneficiary predeceases you, then the contingent beneficiary has no effect on required distributions.

If the contingent beneficiary could become the primary beneficiary for any reason other than the death of the original primary beneficiary, then the contingent beneficiary is treated as one of multiple beneficiaries (along with the primary beneficiary) when determining required distributions.

> **EXAMPLE:** You have instructed the custodian of your IRA in writing that you name your spouse, who is 15 years younger than you, as primary beneficiary of your IRA, but only if you are married at the time of your death. In the event you and your spouse divorce, your father will become the primary beneficiary of your IRA. Because your father's interest is not contingent solely on the death of your spouse, both your spouse and your father are considered beneficiaries of your retirement plan. Consequently, because your spouse is not the sole designated beneficiary, you may not use Table II to compute required distributions. Instead you must use the Uniform Lifetime Table (Table III).

Special Rules for Annuities

If you are taking some or all of your retirement plan benefits in the form of an annuity, those annuity payments must also satisfy the required distribution rules described in this chapter.

Although the required distribution rules for annuities are essentially the same as those for IRAs and other retirement plans, there are some differences worth noting.

Types of Annuities

In order to understand how the required distribution rules apply to your annuity, you must first know what type of annuity you have.

Life annuity. A life annuity makes payments to you or to you and your beneficiary for your entire life. You might have a single life annuity or a joint and survivor annuity. Payments from a single life annuity continue throughout your lifetime and stop when you die, regardless of how much has been paid. No further payments are made to any heirs or to your estate. In the case of a joint and survivor annuity, payments continue until your death or the death of your beneficiary—whichever occurs later—and then the payments stop. No additional payments are made to any other heirs or to your estate.

Term certain annuity. A term certain annuity makes payments for a fixed number of years regardless of when you die or when your beneficiary dies. If you die before the term is over, payments will be made to your beneficiary, your estate, or your heirs for the remainder of the term.

Life annuity with term certain. A life annuity with a term certain will make payments for your lifetime or for a term certain if you die before the term is up. For example, assume you are taking a single life annuity with a term certain of ten years. If you live more than ten years, the annuity payments will continue throughout your life and stop when you die. If you die after five years, the annuity will continue payments for five more years. Similarly, if you have a joint and survivor annuity with a term certain, and both you and your beneficiary die before the term is up, the annuity will continue to be paid to your heirs for the remainder of the term.

Form of Payment

To satisfy the required distribution rules, annuity payments must come at regular intervals of at least once a year. For example, you can receive payments monthly, quarterly, semiannually, or annually, but not every 18 months.

The payments may be in the form of either a life annuity or a term certain. If you choose a life annuity, the payments must last for your lifetime or the joint lifetime of you and your beneficiary.

If you choose a term certain, the term must satisfy one of the following:

- It must be no longer than the ADP for your age (from Table III).
- It must be no longer than the joint life expectancy of you and your spouse beneficiary (from Table II), if your spouse beneficiary is more than ten years younger than you are.

Once payments begin, the term certain may not be lengthened and payments generally must be level, although they might be increased to reflect changes in cost of living or benefit increases under the plan.

Required Beginning Date

When you receive your retirement benefits as an annuity, the first payment must be made on or before your RBD to satisfy the required distribution rules. The amount of the first required payment is simply your regular annuity payment for that period. For example, if the terms of your annuity require that you be paid $2,000 per month for life, then you must receive your first $2,000 payment on or before your RBD. You are not required to receive any payments before that date.

Starting Early

If you elect to start receiving your annuity before your RBD, and if you comply with the form of payment rules described above, then the start date of your annuity becomes your RBD for all purposes. For example, the designated beneficiary is determined as of your annuity start date. And distributions must continue according to the established schedule even if you die before turning 70½.

Young Beneficiaries

If the beneficiary of your annuity is more than ten years younger than you are (and is not your spouse), then you must use special tables to determine whether or not your annuity satisfies the required distribution rules. You will need to know what type of annuity you have in order to determine which table to use.

If You Have a Term Certain Annuity

If you have elected to take your annuity over a term certain and have named a nonspouse beneficiary who is more than ten years younger than you are, you may still use Table II to find your joint life expectancy, but only until your RBD. Once you reach your RBD, you must satisfy the required distribution rules, which means the term certain may not exceed the period found in Table III (see Appendix B) beginning in the year you turn 70½ and for all subsequent years.

> **EXAMPLE:** You retire and begin taking your annuity when you are age 65. You name your grandson as beneficiary. He is 35 years old and your joint life expectancy, according to Table II, is 48.9 years. You elect to begin taking distributions over a term certain of 48.9 years. Five years later, when you turn 70½, the remaining term certain will be 43.9 years (48.9 – 5). According to Table III, however, which you must use when you reach age 70½, the remaining term certain may not exceed 27.4 years. In order to satisfy required distribution rules, your annuity plan must automatically adjust your payments beginning in the year you turn 70½ so that the annuity is paid out over 27.4 years (instead of 43.9 years).

Joint and Survivor Annuity

If you elect to receive a life annuity (without a term certain) over the joint life of you and a nonspouse beneficiary who is more than ten years younger than you are, then at all times from and after your first distribution year (the year you turn 70½), the projected payment to your beneficiary cannot exceed a certain percentage of the payment you are currently receiving. The percentage is based on the difference in your ages and is determined from Table IV (see Appendix B).

As in the case of a term certain annuity, if you begin receiving payments before your RBD and they do not satisfy the required distribution rules, the payments must be adjusted beginning in the year you turn 70½.

> EXAMPLE: You are taking your retirement benefits as a joint and survivor annuity over the joint life of you and your daughter. The year you turn 70½, your monthly payment is $3,000. The age difference between you and your daughter is 21 years. From Table IV, you see that your daughter's projected benefit when you die cannot exceed 72% of your current benefit; that is, it cannot exceed $2,160 per month ($3,000 × 0.72). So when you die, the payment to your daughter must drop from $3,000 per month to no more than $2,160 per month.

If you name more than one beneficiary of your annuity, then you must use the youngest beneficiary to determine the percentage from Table IV. And similarly, if you change your beneficiary to a younger beneficiary (for any reason other than the death of a primary beneficiary), your payments may need to be adjusted so that projected payments to the beneficiary satisfy the percentage requirements from Table IV.

Joint and Survivor Annuity With Term Certain

If you have a life annuity with a term certain, you must satisfy both the term certain requirements and the survivor benefit limitations described above. In other words, the term of your annuity may not exceed the number corresponding to your age in Table III, and the projected payments to your beneficiary after your death may not exceed the percentage in Table IV.

TIP

It's not always this difficult. Although the annuity rules seem (and can be) complex, most people's annuities take the form of a single life annuity or a joint life annuity with a spouse. If you have selected either of these forms of payment, then you should not have to make new computations every year. It is only when you name a much younger nonspouse beneficiary or when you change beneficiaries that your situation could become more complicated.

Divorce or Separation

If you are divorced or separated, part of your qualified plan, qualified annuity, or TDA might be payable to an "alternate payee" (such as a spouse, former spouse, or child) under the terms of a QDRO: a court-approved divorce or maintenance agreement. (See Chapter 2 for more information about QDROs.)

When you reach your RBD, the required distribution rules will apply to the alternate payee's portion, as well as to your own. And because you are the plan participant, it is your RBD that determines when distributions must begin. Furthermore, if the required amount is not withdrawn in timely fashion, you, not the alternate payee, must pay the penalty. As for other required distribution rules, the way in which they are applied will depend on whether or not the alternate payee's portion is in a separate account.

> **CAUTION**
>
> **Alternate payee must wait.** The terms of your QDRO might provide that the alternate payee is to receive immediate and total distribution of his or her share of the plan. Unless the plan itself permits such a distribution, however, the alternate payee must wait to receive his or her share until the time when you distribute assets from the plan, either at your retirement, when you begin required distributions, or at some other time specified by the plan.

Separate Account

A QDRO might require that an alternate payee's portion be divided and separately accounted for. If so, the following variations in the required distribution rules apply:

- The alternate payee's separate share is not to be combined, or aggregated, with the rest of your plan benefits when you compute required distributions. In other words, you would separately compute the required distribution amount for your portion and the alternate payee's portion. You would then distribute the alternate payee's portion from his or her share.

- In computing the required distribution from the alternate payee's portion, you may use one of the following to determine the ADP:
  - the Uniform Lifetime Table (Table III) based on your age
  - the joint life of you and the alternate payee, if the alternate payee is your ex-spouse and is more than ten years younger than you are, or
  - the alternate payee's single life expectancy.

The decision about which ADP to use belongs to you—not to the alternate payee—even though the distribution will come from the alternate payee's portion and will be distributed to the alternate payee.

> **CAUTION**
>
> **If the alternate payee dies.** Although you have several options for selecting a distribution period to compute required distributions from the alternate payee's portion, one option that you do not have is to use the joint life expectancy of the alternate payee and his or her beneficiary. If the alternate payee dies before your RBD, however, the alternate payee's beneficiary will be treated as the beneficiary for required distribution purposes.

> EXAMPLE: Your ex-husband is entitled to half of your pension plan under the terms of your QDRO. The pension plan administrator separated your ex-husband's share into a separate account, and your ex-husband named his sister as beneficiary of his separate share of the pension. The plan provides that no distributions can be made until you retire or reach your RBD. If your ex-husband dies before your RBD, then your ex-husband's sister becomes the designated beneficiary when computing distributions from your ex-husband's portion of the pension.

Even if a QDRO mandates dividing the retirement benefit between you and the alternate payee, the terms of the plan might not permit physically separating the shares. The plan administrator can get around this using a reasonable method to separately account for the alternate payee's portion. For example, a reasonable method would be to allocate on a pro rata basis all investment gains and losses, as well as contributions and forfeitures (if applicable).

No Separate Account

In some instances, you will not physically separate your share from the alternate payee's share. Some QDROs do not require an actual separation of the alternate payee's share, and some plans don't permit actual separation.

In either case, the retirement plan remains undivided, and a portion of each distribution goes to the alternate payee. Under this scenario, the alternate payee's portion does not have to separately satisfy the minimum distribution requirement. Instead, it is combined, or aggregated, with your other plan assets for purposes of determining the account balance and calculating your required distribution for the year.

Thus, aggregation means that the required distribution rules work as though there was no alternate payee. When calculating required distributions, you may use either the Uniform Lifetime Table or Table II (if your spouse beneficiary is more than ten years younger than you are). But you may not use the alternate payee's single life expectancy.

Income Taxes and Penalties

Generally speaking, the rules governing the payment of taxes and penalties on QDRO distributions are essentially the same whether the alternate payee is a spouse, former spouse, or child.

There are, however, two exceptions to that general rule.

Spouse or former spouse alternate payee. If the alternate payee named in the QDRO is your spouse or former spouse, the alternate payee must pay all income taxes on distributions he or she receives. But you are responsible for penalties on any shortfall in required distributions, even though the alternate payee is receiving a portion.

Nonspouse alternate payee. If the alternate payee is someone other than your spouse or former spouse (for example, your child), you must pay all income taxes, as well as any penalties that might apply. This is true even though the distribution actually goes to the alternate payee.

Rollovers

The option to roll over a distribution from a qualified plan into an IRA or another qualified plan is a big tax benefit. Traditionally, the benefit has been reserved for plan participants and, occasionally, the participant's spouse. Under the QDRO rules, the privilege is extended to a former spouse.

Spouse or former spouse alternate payee. A spouse or former spouse may roll over any distributed portion of his or her interest in your plan if there is a QDRO in place. This is the case whether or not the spouse or former spouse's portion was held in a separate account. Once the spouse or former spouse completes the rollover to an account in his or her name, the account belongs to the spouse or former spouse in every way, and the required distribution rules apply to that account as though the alternate payee were the original owner.

> ⓘ **CAUTION**
>
> **The plan has the final word.** Although the QDRO rules permit your spouse or former spouse to roll over an interest in your retirement plan, some plans will not permit it. Furthermore, some plans will not make any distribution at all until you have reached a certain retirement age, which is specified in the plan. Because the plan rules ultimately govern distributions, spouses and former spouses often have little control over how they receive QDRO payments.

Nonspouse alternate payee. Nonspouse alternate payees may not roll over their interest in your retirement plan under any circumstances. The law does not allow it.

> ⓘ **CAUTION**
>
> **When the rules don't apply.** Remember: The special rules described in this section apply only to qualified plans, qualified annuities, and TDAs, and they apply only if there is a QDRO in place. If there is no QDRO, your retirement plan is treated as though it is entirely yours for required distribution purposes. If your divorce agreement states that your former spouse is to share in your plan, you must generally give your former spouse his or her share as it is distributed from the plan. In other words, a portion of each distribution would go to your former

spouse and you would keep your share. As for IRAs, there are no corresponding QDRO rules. As long as the IRA remains in your name, the required distribution rules apply as though your former spouse had no interest in the IRA. But if some or all of your IRA is transferred into your former spouse's name as a result of a written divorce or separation agreement, then from the time the transfer is complete, the transferred portion belongs to your former spouse in every respect. That means the required distribution rules apply as though your former spouse were the original owner. (See Chapter 2 for more information about IRAs and divorce.)

Key Tax Code and Regulation Sections

§ 401(a)(9)
Required Distributions From Qualified Plans.

§ 1.401(a)(9)
Required Distribution Regulations.

§ 1.408-8
Required Distribution Rules for IRAs.

Distributions to Your Beneficiary
If You Die Before Age 70½

Who Should Read Chapter 7
Read this chapter to find out what happens to your own retirement plan after you die or if you inherit a retirement plan or an IRA from someone who died before age 70½. This chapter describes how the account must be distributed and explains other procedures to help avoid unnecessary penalties and taxes.

The law says you must start taking money out of your retirement plan by a certain date, called your "required beginning date" (RBD). But what if you never make it to that date? What would your premature death mean for your beneficiaries (other than the obvious sadness), and how can you prepare for it?

In this chapter, we look at the answers to those questions, paying particular attention to the ways you can help your beneficiaries avoid onerous taxes and penalties.

Determining the Designated Beneficiary

For most people, the RBD is April 1 of the year after they turn 70½ (see Chapter 6 for information about determining your RBD). If you die before your RBD, your designated beneficiary (if you have one) generally must begin taking distributions from your retirement plan in the year after your death, with some exceptions. Just how rapidly the assets must be distributed and according to what schedule depends primarily on who the designated beneficiary is. So before we look at distribution methods, let's see how the IRS will determine who your designated beneficiary is.

Recall that you can name any person or organization you want as the beneficiary of your retirement plan or IRA. However, when determining how your retirement plan assets should be distributed after your death, only designated beneficiaries are taken into account. (See Chapter 6 for more information about designated beneficiaries.) If one or more of your named beneficiaries is not a designated beneficiary, you are deemed to have no designated beneficiary and distributions must be accelerated.

Helpful Terms

Annuity. A contract, sold by an insurance company, that promises to make monthly, quarterly, semiannual, or annual payments for life or for a specified period of time.

Contingent beneficiary. A person or an entity that is entitled to receive the benefits of a retirement plan or an IRA only if and when a specific event occurs, such as the death of a primary beneficiary.

Deferral period. The number of years over which distributions from a retirement plan or an IRA can be spread.

Disclaimer. A renunciation of or a refusal to accept property to which a person is entitled by gift, by law, or under the terms of a will or a trust.

Distribution. A payout of property (such as shares of stock) or cash from a retirement plan or an IRA to the participant or a beneficiary.

Estate. All property that a person owns.

Irrevocable trust. A trust that cannot be changed or terminated by the person who created it. Once assets are transferred to an irrevocable trust, the assets are subject to the terms of the trust for as long as the trust exists.

Primary beneficiary. A person or an entity entitled to receive benefits from a retirement plan or an IRA upon the death of the original participant.

Revocable trust. A trust whose terms allow the creator of the trust to alter its provisions, cancel it, or remove some or all of the property from the trust and return the property to the creator.

Term certain. A fixed, identifiable period, such as a specific number of years. For example, a retirement plan that is distributable over a term certain of 20 years must be completely liquidated after 20 years.

Deadline for Determining Designated Beneficiary

The designated beneficiary of your retirement plan is determined as of September 30 of the year after your death. Although the determination date occurs after you die, this doesn't mean that someone can come along and name beneficiaries of your retirement plan after your death.

If you fail to name any beneficiary of your retirement plan, you generally will be deemed to have no designated beneficiary.

But if nobody can add a beneficiary after your death, why, you might ask, is the deadline for determining the beneficiary so long after your death? That's the issue that we address in the following section.

Changing Beneficiaries Before the Deadline

Even though no one can add beneficiaries to your retirement plan after you die, your beneficiary could change after your death. For example, suppose you name your spouse as primary beneficiary and your children as contingent beneficiaries. After your death, your spouse decides she has enough money to live on for the rest of her life without using any of your retirement plan assets. She might disclaim (renounce) her interest in your retirement plan. In that case, the plan assets would go to your children, the contingent beneficiaries.

The IRS inserted this extended deadline into the regulations as a relief provision. It gives beneficiaries an opportunity to do some postmortem planning, whether to make administration of distributions easier or to clean up a disadvantageous situation you left behind.

For example, suppose you named your wife and your favorite charity as equal beneficiaries of your retirement account. When you die, if the charity and your spouse are still equal beneficiaries on September 30 of the year after your death, you are deemed to have no designated beneficiary (because the charity isn't a designated beneficiary), and distributions to all beneficiaries must be accelerated. This could have disastrous tax consequences for your spouse.

As a cleanup measure, however, the charity can receive its entire distribution before September 30 of the year after death, leaving only your spouse as beneficiary. Then the post-death rules apply as though your spouse were sole beneficiary of the account. This would produce a much more favorable result.

Distribution Methods

If you die before your RBD, your retirement plan benefits will be distributed using one of three methods: the life expectancy rule, the five-year rule, or a spousal rollover. Read on to learn more about each of these methods.

Life Expectancy Rule

The life expectancy rule allows your beneficiary to spread distributions over his or her life expectancy after your death, if both of the following conditions are met:

- The beneficiary of your plan or IRA as of September 30 of the year after your death is a designated beneficiary.
- The plan itself either permits the life expectancy rule or is silent (meaning it doesn't indicate one way or another which rule should be used).

Your beneficiary can look up the appropriate life expectancy factor in Table I (see Appendix B).

> **TIP**
>
> **What if the plan specifies the five-year rule?** Even if the plan specifies that the retirement plan assets must be distributed to the beneficiary according to the five-year rule, plans are required to offer a rollover option.

Distributions under the life expectancy rule generally must begin in the year after your death and continue until the entire account has been depleted. (Some unusual twists apply if your spouse is your beneficiary. See "Spouse Beneficiary," below.)

Five-Year Rule

The five-year rule is mandatory in cases where both of the following are true:

- You die before your RBD.
- Your retirement plan or IRA is deemed to have no designated beneficiary as of September 30 of the year after your death. (See Chapter 6 for more information about which beneficiaries qualify as designated beneficiaries.)

If the five-year rule applies, all of your retirement plan assets must be distributed within five years after your death.

However, spouse beneficiaries may roll over distributions from the retirement plan into an account in their own name, deferring taxes (see below).

TIP

Actually, it's five years plus. Practically speaking, your beneficiary has a little more than five years to withdraw the assets when the five-year rule applies. This is because the official distribution deadline is December 31 of the year containing the fifth anniversary of your death. For example, if you die on March 3 in the year 2019, your retirement plan need not be completely distributed until December 31, 2024—five years and almost ten months later.

Required Beginning Date

The five-year rule applies only if you die before your RBD. If you live past that milestone, a different set of rules will apply when you die without a designated beneficiary. If you have passed your RBD, you can forget about the five-year rule (and you should be reading Chapter 8). But be careful: It is your RBD that counts, not the year you turn 70½. For example, if your RBD is April 1, 2019, but you die on March 15, 2019, the five-year rule will apply even though you have already passed age 70½ and even if you have already taken a distribution for your first distribution year. Technically, you have not begun required distributions until you pass your RBD.

EXAMPLE: You turned 70½ in June 2018, which makes your RBD April 1, 2019. On December 30, 2018 you withdrew $6,000 from your IRA, which was the amount of your first required distribution. But then you died on March 15, 2019, before reaching your RBD. Because you died before your RBD, the five-year rule will apply even though you had already withdrawn an amount that would have satisfied your first required distribution.

Distributing the Account

The five-year rule mandates that all assets be distributed from your retirement plan by December 31 of the year containing the fifth anniversary of your death, but it places no restriction on the form of payment. This means, for example, that your beneficiary could receive the entire amount as a lump sum in the month after your death, monthly installments spread over the five-year period, or perhaps nothing at all until the December 31 deadline in the fifth year.

Although the IRS would accept any of those approaches, the retirement plan itself might have more stringent distribution requirements. The plan controls how payments will be made. (See below for more about plan rules.) Some plans allow beneficiaries to receive installment payments or to leave the funds in the plan until the five-year period is up. If the plan requires immediate distribution of the entire account, however, then that's what your beneficiary will be stuck with, unless the beneficiary opts for a rollover.

Rollover

If your spouse is the beneficiary of your retirement plan, your spouse will generally have an alternative to the life expectancy rule or the five-year rule. That alternative is to roll over your retirement plan, or the spouse's share of your retirement plan, into an IRA in the spouse's own name. (See below for more information about spousal rollovers.)

If your beneficiary is not your spouse, your beneficiary still may roll over your retirement plan (but not your IRA) into a traditional IRA or a Roth IRA. However, in this case, the IRA or Roth IRA into which the retirement plan is rolled cannot be in the beneficiary's own name. Instead the new IRA or Roth IRA must be an inherited IRA (i.e., it must remain in the name of the decedent). See below for more information about spousal and nonspousal rollovers.

Effect of the Retirement Plan's Rules

Although the law provides a framework for required distributions within which retirement plans may operate, the plan's own rules can be—and usually are—more restrictive. In that case, the plan's rules govern. For example, even though the law allows a designated beneficiary to use the life expectancy rule and take distributions over his or her life expectancy, the plan itself might require that even designated beneficiaries use the five-year rule. Or sometimes the plan will allow the designated beneficiary to choose a method of distribution.

Optional Provisions

Sometimes, plans give beneficiaries a choice of which rule to use. For example, in the best of all worlds (from the taxpayer's perspective), plans would allow beneficiaries to choose between the five-year rule and the life expectancy rule. And if a beneficiary didn't have a choice and was saddled with the five-year rule, the beneficiary would certainly like to be able to choose how the assets were distributed over that five-year period.

> **TIP**
>
> **If you do get to choose.** Generally, a beneficiary who has the option to use the life expectancy rule would choose it and not the five-year rule. However, if a beneficiary failed to take a timely distribution under the life expectancy rule, he or she might want to fall back on the five-year rule to avoid the hefty penalty for failing to take a required distribution.

But this isn't the best of worlds, and plan administrators don't always put taxpayers' needs first. In fact, some plans offer no options at all to beneficiaries, instead mandating distribution of the entire plan in the year of death. At the other extreme, some plans might distribute nothing at all until the end of the fifth year.

Furthermore, many plans have different policies for different beneficiaries. For example, the terms of a plan might require that nonspouse beneficiaries receive a distribution of the entire plan immediately following the participant's death (without the five-year grace period), but allow a spouse beneficiary to use the life expectancy rule.

Default Provisions

If the plan is resolutely silent on how distributions will occur after the death of the plan participant, certain default provisions kick in by law. Specifically, if the plan has a designated beneficiary, the life expectancy rule applies by default. And, remember, beneficiaries always have a rollover option (except nonspouse beneficiaries can't roll over IRAs).

Spouse Beneficiary

If your spouse is the beneficiary of your retirement plan, he or she has two options for taking distributions from your retirement plan after your death. Your spouse can:

- leave the account in your name and use the life expectancy rule to take distributions over his or her own life expectancy beginning in the year you would have been 70½—or the year after your death if that is later, or
- roll over the plan or IRA into a plan or an IRA in his or her own name.

Read the section immediately below to learn more about these options.

CAUTION

For purposes of this section, we assume that the spouse was the sole beneficiary of the retirement plan. The rules change if a spouse is one of several beneficiaries. (See "Multiple Beneficiaries, One Account," below.)

Life Expectancy Rule

If your spouse is the beneficiary of your retirement account, he or she can wait until the year you would have turned 70½ to begin receiving required distributions. This additional deferral—until the deceased participant would have turned 70½—is available only to a spouse. Your spouse can choose this option even if he or she has already turned 70½ as long as he or she leaves the account in your name.

If your spouse chooses the life expectancy rule, he or she would use the following steps to compute the first required distribution from your account.

Step One: Determine the account balance.

Your spouse must use your retirement account balance as of December 31 of the year before you would have turned 70½ to compute the first required distribution.

Step Two: Determine the ADP.

Using his or her age in the year you would have turned 70½, your spouse must look up the appropriate life expectancy factor in Table I (see Appendix B). That factor is the applicable distribution period—or ADP—for the first year.

Step Three: Calculate the required distribution.

To determine the first required distribution, your spouse divides the account balance by the ADP—which is Step One divided by Step Two. The resulting amount must be distributed by December 31 of the year you would have turned 70½ (not April of the following year).

> EXAMPLE: Ed was born March 15, 1949 and died on June 1, 2016, at age 67, before reaching his RBD. His wife, Bertha, is the beneficiary of his retirement plan. Bertha intends to use the life expectancy rule to determine required distributions from the plan. She chooses to defer distributions until 2019 (the year Ed would have turned 70½). To calculate the first required distribution, she must do the following:

Step One: To compute the required distribution, Bertha must use the account balance as of December 31, 2018, the year before Ed would have turned 70½. That amount is $100,000.

Step Two: Bertha will be age 68 on her birthday in 2019, the year Ed would have turned 70½. Her single life expectancy at age 68 (from Table I in Appendix B) is 18.6 years.

Step Three: Bertha's first required distribution is $100,000 ÷ 18.6 (Step One ÷ Step Two), or $5,376. Bertha must withdraw at least that amount by December 31, 2019.

For the second and future years, your spouse would find the ADP from Table I each year, using his or her age for the current year. Your spouse would then divide the account balance as of December 31 of the previous year by the new ADP.

EXAMPLE: Continuing the example, above, for the year 2020, Bertha will use the December 31, 2019 balance of Ed's retirement account and divide it by her ADP. The ADP for age 69 (from Table I) is 17.8.

TIP

If you turned 70½ in the year of your death. Remember, if you turned 70½ (or would have turned 70½) in the same year that you died, your spouse does not have to begin distributions that same year. Instead, he or she can delay the start of distributions until the year after your death. In that case, your spouse would use the account balance as of December 31 of the year of your death and his or her age in the year after your death to compute the first required distribution.

Rollover

If your spouse is the beneficiary of your retirement plan or an IRA, he or she has another quite valuable deferral option. A spouse can roll over the plan assets into a plan or an IRA of his or her own. (Note: This option is available only to a spouse.)

If your plan is not an IRA, the only way your spouse can make the plan his or her own is by rolling the plan assets over into an IRA or a plan in his or her own name.

But if your retirement plan is an IRA, your spouse has several ways to make your IRA his or her own. Your spouse can do so by:

- rolling over the assets into a new or preexisting IRA or plan in his or her own name
- failing to take one of your post-death required distributions at the proper time, or
- contributing additional amounts of his or her own to your IRA.

Convert to Spouse's Plan or IRA by Rollover

A spouse can roll over a deceased participant's IRA into a plan or an IRA in the spouse's own name. This method is the cleanest because there is a clear record of what happened and when.

Once the account becomes the spouse's own, it belongs to the spouse in every way, as though he or she were the original owner. Required distributions will begin when the spouse reaches his or her own RBD and will be based on the ADP for the spouse's age at that time.

> **EXAMPLE:** Grace died in 2013 at the age of 69. Her husband, George, was the beneficiary of her IRA, and he turned 64 on February 14, 2013. At the end of 2013, George rolled over Grace's IRA into an IRA in his own name. George will not need to begin required distributions until his own RBD, which is April 1 of the year after he turns 70½, or April 1, 2020.

If a surviving spouse rolls over a deceased participant's IRA into a new IRA in his or her name, the spouse may name a new beneficiary of his or her own choosing.

> **EXAMPLE:** Your husband is the primary beneficiary of your IRA, and your brother will inherit the plan if your husband dies before you do. But let's say you predecease your husband and he decides to roll over your IRA into

an IRA in his own name. He completes the rollover and names his sister as primary beneficiary. His action is completely legal under the rollover rules. Once he rolls over your IRA, the assets are his. His sister will receive the IRA assets; your brother will not.

Your spouse may roll over your retirement plan and name a new beneficiary after you die, even if your spouse has passed his or her RBD at the time of the rollover. In that case, your spouse's RBD for purposes of the new IRA is December 31 of the year of the rollover, and required distributions must begin at that time.

> **EXAMPLE:** You died in 2018 at the age of 69. Your wife turned 72 in 2018. In March 2019, she rolled over your retirement plan into an IRA in her name and designated your children as beneficiaries. Your wife must take her first required distribution by December 31, 2019.

Convert to Spouse's IRA by Failing to Take Required Distribution

If you die before your RBD, and your spouse fails to take a required distribution under the life expectancy rule—either by December 31 of the year after your death or by December 31 of the year you would have been 70½—your spouse is deemed to have made an election to treat your IRA as his or her own (regardless of the spouse's age). The IRA becomes your spouse's own on December 31 of the year of the failure, and your spouse will not be required to take a distribution until his or her own RBD.

> **EXAMPLE:** Your wife died in the year 2012 at age 63. You were the beneficiary of her IRA. You did not take any distributions in 2013, nor had you taken any distributions by December 31, 2019—the year your wife would have been 70½. Therefore, by missing all of the deadlines for taking a distribution from your wife's retirement account, the account is deemed to be your own as of December 31, 2019.

Convert to Spouse's IRA by Contributing Additional Amounts

If your spouse makes a contribution to your IRA from his or her own funds after your death, or rolls over one of his or her own existing retirement plans into your IRA, your spouse is deemed to have made your IRA his or her own.

Timing a Rollover

The IRS imposes no deadline for a spouse to roll over a deceased participant's retirement plan into the spouse's own plan or IRA. That means a spouse can begin taking distributions as a beneficiary under the life expectancy rule and then some years later roll over the assets into a plan or an IRA of his or her own.

As a practical matter, if a spouse is past age 59½ and intends to roll over a participant's retirement plan, there is nothing to be gained from waiting. If the spouse needs money, the spouse can take it freely from the IRA even after rolling it over, because there is no penalty for taking distributions after age 59½.

If the spouse is younger than 59½, however, free use of the IRA funds could be dicey. Recall that one of the exceptions to the early distribution tax is a distribution to a beneficiary after the death of the original participant. (See Chapter 3 for more information on the early distribution tax.) But that particular exception is not available to a spouse after the spouse rolls over the deceased person's plan into a plan or an IRA in the spouse's name. Once it is rolled over, it is the spouse's, and because the spouse is still alive, the after-death exception does not apply. Thus, the spouse must generally postpone distributions until age 59½ to avoid the early distribution tax.

Consequently, if the spouse is younger than 59½ and needs to use the retirement plan money to live on, the spouse might be better off leaving the plan or IRA in the name of the deceased so that the after-death exception can be used. Once the spouse reaches age 59½, or no longer needs access to the funds, the spouse may roll over the remainder of the decendent's plan or IRA into her own retirement plan or IRA.

Convert to Roth IRA

A surviving spouse may also convert the retirement plan (but not an IRA) directly to a Roth IRA in the spouse's own name. If this option is chosen, the spouse will generally pay income tax on the pretax converted amounts in the year of conversion, but because the Roth IRA will be in the spouse's name, no further distributions will be required during the spouse's lifetime.

When the spouse dies, the assets will be distributed to the beneficiaries that the spouse designated when the Roth IRA was established. See Chapter 9 for more information about converting to a Roth IRA and taking distributions from Roth IRAs.

If the spouse is the beneficiary of a traditional IRA (rather than an employer's plan, for example), in order to convert the traditional IRA to a Roth IRA, the spouse must first roll over the plan assets to a traditional IRA in his or her own name. Once the assets are in the spouse's IRA, he or she may convert them to a Roth IRA, also in the spouse's name.

Death of Spouse Beneficiary

If a spouse beneficiary inherits a retirement plan or an IRA and begins taking required distributions on December 31 of the year after the participant's death (or December 31 of the year the deceased participant would have turned 70½) but dies before all assets of the retirement account are distributed, the spouse's beneficiary must take distributions in the following way:

- In the year of the spouse's death, the spouse's beneficiary will divide the account balance (as of December 31 of the year before the spouse's death) by the ADP for the spouse in the year of the spouse's death (using the spouse's age on his or her birthday in the year of death and looking up the respective ADP in Table I in Appendix B).

- In the second year and beyond, the spouse's beneficiary will reduce the ADP determined in the previous paragraph by one and divide it into the account balance as of the previous December 31. The computation continues in this way each year until the entire account is depleted.

EXAMPLE: You died in 2016 at age 69. Your wife was the beneficiary of your IRA and began taking required distributions from your IRA in 2017. She died in 2018. She would have been 64 on her birthday. Her sister is the sole beneficiary of her estate. On December 31, 2018 the balance in the IRA was $60,000. Your wife's ADP in 2019 (for age 64) is 21.8 (from Table I). The required distribution for 2019 is $2,752 ($60,000 ÷ 21.8).

In the second year—2020—the ADP will be reduced by one. On December 31, 2019, the balance in the IRA was $63,000. The ADP for 2020 is 20.8 (which is 21.8 − 1). Therefore, the sister's required distribution for 2020 is $3,029 ($63,000 ÷ 20.8).

If a spouse beneficiary dies after the participant, but before beginning required distributions under the life expectancy rule (and before rolling over the account into an IRA in the spouse's own name), then the following rules apply:

- In general, the life expectancy rule or the five-year rule will apply to the spouse's beneficiary as though the spouse had been the original participant. Specifically, the age of the spouse's beneficiary will determine how required distributions are computed under the life expectancy rule. (If the spouse remarries and names his or her new spouse as beneficiary, however, the new spouse will be treated as a nonspouse beneficiary. See the next bullet point.)

EXAMPLE: You die in 2015 at age 65. Your wife is the beneficiary of your retirement plan account and, therefore, is not required to begin distributions until you would have been age 70½ (in the year 2020). Her sister is the sole beneficiary of your wife's estate. Your wife died in 2018 before beginning required distributions from your retirement account. The life expectancy rule will apply to distributions to her sister, the beneficiary. Under the life expectancy rule, your wife's sister must begin distributions by December 31, 2019, and take them over her life expectancy. For her first distribution, she would use her age in 2019 and find the ADP in Table I. For subsequent years, she would reduce the ADP by one.

- If your surviving spouse remarried and named his or her new spouse as beneficiary, the special additional deferral option, described above, is not available to the new spouse beneficiary. Specifically, the spouse's new wife or husband is not permitted to wait until the spouse would have been 70½ to begin required distributions. The spouse's beneficiary is simply treated as a nonspouse and is subject to the rules in the previous bullet point.

EXAMPLE: You die in 2015 at age 65. Your wife is the beneficiary of your retirement plan account and therefore is not required to begin distributions until you would have been age 70½ (in 2020). Your wife remarried in 2017 and named her new husband as beneficiary of her entire estate. She died in 2018 before beginning required distributions from your retirement account. The life expectancy rule applies and your wife's new husband must begin distributions by December 31, 2019 and take them over his life expectancy. He is not entitled to use the special deferral option of a spouse, however. He may not wait until his spouse (your wife) would have been 70½ to begin distributions.

Nonspouse Beneficiary

As a participant in a retirement plan, or as the spouse of a participant, it is easy to take for granted the special privileges, exceptions, and additional distribution options the tax code offers. But options for a nonspouse beneficiary are more limited. In the case of a retirement plan that is not an IRA, the nonspouse beneficiary typically has two options: the life expectancy rule or a rollover to an IRA. If the inherited plan is an IRA, the nonspouse beneficiary does not have a rollover option and is limited to the life expectancy rule.

CAUTION

If there is more than one beneficiary. The rules in this section apply if there is only one beneficiary named on the account. If there is more than one beneficiary, a different set of rules applies. The multiple beneficiary rules are discussed later in this chapter.

Life Expectancy Rule

The law allows a nonspouse beneficiary to use the life expectancy rule to calculate required distributions after the plan participant's death. Those distributions must begin no later than December 31 of the year after the participant's death. No additional deferral is permitted.

Don't forget, however, to check the plan to see what it says. Remember: When the plan rules are more restrictive than the law, the plan controls. For example, the plan can require that benefits be paid out according to the five-year rule, in which case the beneficiary is stuck with it. (But see "Nonspouse Beneficiaries Might Not Be Stuck With the Five-Year Rule," below, for a possible escape hatch.) On the other hand, if the plan is silent on post-death distributions, the life expectancy rule applies by default.

> **EXAMPLE:** You died on March 15, 2018, before reaching your RBD. Your son is the beneficiary of your retirement plan, and he turns 48 in 2019. Your account was valued at $100,000 on December 31, 2018. Your son will use the life expectancy rule to compute required distributions.
>
> Step One: To compute the first payment, your son must use the account balance as of December 31, 2018, the year of your death. That amount is $100,000.
>
> Step Two: Your son will be age 48 on his birthday in the year after your death (2019). His single life expectancy—or ADP—at age 48 (from Table I in Appendix B) is 36.0 years.
>
> Step Three: Your son's first required distribution is $100,000 ÷ 36.0 (Step One ÷ Step Two), or $2,778. Your son must withdraw at least that amount by December 31, 2019.

For distributions in years after the first year, a nonspouse beneficiary must reduce the previous ADP by one. A nonspouse beneficiary is not permitted to use Table I for any year but the first year of required distributions.

> **EXAMPLE:** Continuing the above example, for the year 2020, your son will use the December 31, 2019 balance of your retirement account and divide it by the new ADP, which is 35.0 (36.0 − 1).

Nonspouse Beneficiaries Might Not Be Stuck With the Five-Year Rule

Generally, nonspouse beneficiaries may use the life expectancy rule when taking distributions from an inherited retirement plan. However, if the plan itself requires that distributions to nonspouse beneficiaries be paid out according to the five-year rule, the beneficiary will be bound by the rules of the plan, unless the plan documents contain a provision that allows the beneficiary to transfer the plan's assets into an inherited IRA. If so, the beneficiary might be able to get out from under the five-year rule, depending on when the transfer actually occurs. Specifically:

- If the beneficiary transfers the assets in the year of death into an inherited IRA in the decedent's name, the beneficiary may transfer all of the assets and then begin taking distributions over the beneficiary's life expectancy beginning in the year after death.

- If the transfer to the inherited IRA occurs in the year after death, the beneficiary may transfer all but the required distribution amount for the year after death. In subsequent years, the beneficiary will take distributions based on his or her life expectancy in the year after death reduced by one each subsequent year (as described under the life expectancy rule, above).

- In the second, third, and fourth years after the year of death, the transfer might be permitted, but the five-year rule will still apply. In other words, the transfer must be completed by December 31 of the year after death in order for the beneficiary to be able to use the life expectancy rule. If the transfer is completed in the second through fourth years, the beneficiary may transfer the entire amount (without taking any required distributions), but then the inherited IRA to which the assets were transferred must be distributed in its entirety by December 31 of the fifth year after death.

- And finally, no transfer will be permitted during the fifth year after the year of death. Instead, the retirement plan must be distributed to the beneficiary by December 31 of that year and the beneficiary must pay income tax on the entire distribution.

Remember, too, that a beneficiary can always take more than the minimum amount each year, but not less.

Rollover

The law also allows a nonspouse beneficiary to transfer the assets of an inherited retirement plan (an employer plan, not an IRA) into a new inherited IRA. The new inherited IRA must be established in the name of the deceased and the assets must be transferred directly from the plan trustee to the custodian of the new IRA. The beneficiary may not take possession of the funds at any time or those funds will be deemed distributed and taxable.

A nonspouse beneficiary is never permitted to roll over a deceased person's retirement plan or IRA into the beneficiary's own IRA. If the beneficiary attempts to do so, the entire rollover could be considered a taxable distribution and an excess contribution to an IRA, and it would be subject to penalties. Even if the excess contribution is corrected, the retirement plan assets cannot be redeposited into the deceased participant's account. Consequently, the beneficiary will owe income tax on the entire amount, whether or not penalties are assessed.

A nonspouse beneficiary must leave the retirement account in the name of the deceased participant (or transfer the account into an IRA in the name of the deceased) until the account is completely distributed under the life expectancy rule (or more rapidly).

Convert to a Roth IRA

The same rule (described above) that would allow a nonspouse beneficiary to transfer an inherited retirement plan (an employer plan, not an IRA) into an IRA in the decedent's name would also allow the beneficiary to transfer the plan assets into a new inherited Roth IRA in the decedent's name. If the beneficiary chooses this action, the transfer constitutes a conversion from a retirement plan to a Roth IRA, and the following rules would apply:

- The beneficiary must accomplish the conversion by means of a trustee-to-trustee transfer, which means the funds must go directly from the trustee of the decedent's retirement plan to the custodian of the new inherited IRA.

- The new inherited IRA must be in the name of the decedent, for the benefit of the beneficiary (see "Name on Account," below).
- The beneficiary must pay income tax on the pretax portion of the amount that is transferred from the retirement plan to the new inherited Roth IRA. The income tax will be due with the tax return for the year of the conversion.
- The beneficiary must take required distributions from the inherited Roth IRA according to the same schedule that would apply to an inherited retirement plan or to an inherited traditional IRA.

Note that if a nonspouse beneficiary inherits an IRA instead of a retirement plan (an employer plan), the beneficiary does not have the option to convert the traditional inherited IRA into a Roth IRA.

For more information about converting retirement plan assets to a Roth IRA and taking distributions from Roth IRAs, see Chapter 9.

Death of Nonspouse Beneficiary

If a nonspouse beneficiary dies after the participant has died, but before the retirement plan has been completely distributed, the distribution method remains the same. For example, if distributions were made under the life expectancy rule, distributions will continue to be made over the life expectancy of the deceased beneficiary, using the beneficiary's age on his or her birthday in the year after the participant's death, reduced by one in each subsequent year.

> **EXAMPLE:** Sara named her brother, Archie, as beneficiary of her retirement plan. She died in 2017 at the age of 68. Archie intended to begin taking distributions over his life expectancy beginning in 2018. He would have turned 55 on March 1, 2018, but he died on February 15, 2018. Nonetheless, distributions will be made to his beneficiary as though he were still alive. Archie's ADP at age 55 would have been 29.6 years (from Table I). The ADP will be reduced by one each year until the entire account is distributed.

If the plan had required the beneficiary to use the five-year rule, the entire account must still be distributed by December 31 of the year containing the fifth anniversary of the original participant's death, even though the beneficiary has since died.

> 💡 **TIP**
>
> **Who is the beneficiary's beneficiary?** When a primary beneficiary dies after the original participant has died but before all the retirement plan assets have been distributed, where does the remainder go? The answer depends on the laws of your state. If the primary beneficiary had designated a beneficiary, the path is clear. If not, typically, the retirement plan will be distributed according to the terms of the primary beneficiary's will. In the absence of a will, the assets would be distributed to the heirs of the primary beneficiary according to state law.

No Designated Beneficiary

If you have no designated beneficiary for your retirement account, then payout options at your death are restricted. Recall that a designated beneficiary must usually be a natural person, although it may also be a special type of trust. (See Chapter 6 for more information about designated beneficiaries.) And although you are permitted to name any beneficiary you choose, whether a person or an entity, some privileges are reserved for beneficiaries that qualify as designated beneficiaries.

Five-Year Rule

If the beneficiary of your retirement plan is not a designated beneficiary and you die before your RBD, the five-year rule applies and the entire account must be distributed by December 31 of the year containing the fifth anniversary of your death.

No Life Expectancy Rule

If your beneficiary is not a designated beneficiary, the life expectancy rule is never an option under any circumstances. The five-year rule is mandatory, and all of the assets in the plan must be distributed by December 31 of the year containing the fifth anniversary of your death.

TIP
The law allows installments. Even if the life expectancy rule is not an option, it is still permissible for the beneficiary to take distributions in installments over the five-year period, if the plan will allow it.

Multiple Beneficiaries, Separate Accounts

If you have several IRAs or retirement plans, each with a different beneficiary, then each plan is treated separately for purposes of the required distribution rules. You are not considered to have multiple beneficiaries.

Even if you do name multiple beneficiaries of a single retirement plan, your beneficiaries might still be deemed to have separate accounts. If the plan administrator or custodian agrees to do so, he or she can segregate each beneficiary's share and treat each as a separate account payable to one beneficiary. And even if the administrator does not segregate the shares, the shares may be treated as separate accounts if the administrator or custodian sets up separate accounting procedures (under which, for example, investment gains and losses are allocated to beneficiaries on a pro rata basis). Under either of these scenarios, each beneficiary could take distributions over his or her own life expectancy after your death without being subject to the multiple beneficiary rules. (See below for more information about multiple beneficiaries with one account.)

CAUTION
Don't count on administrators allowing separate accounting. As a practical matter, many qualified plan administrators are reluctant to shoulder the burden of separate accounting or even to physically split the account. Consequently, the beneficiaries may be stuck with the multiple beneficiary/one account rules described in the next section. IRA custodians, too, are often unwilling to provide a separate accounting for each beneficiary when multiple beneficiaries are named on one account. In the case of an IRA, however, there is nothing to prevent you from splitting the account during your lifetime into separate IRAs, one for each beneficiary. And in most cases, the account can be split after your death, as well.

Multiple Beneficiaries, One Account

The rules change significantly if there is more than one beneficiary of a single retirement account. Bear in mind, the date for determining the beneficiaries is September 30 of the year following your death. If on that date all beneficiaries are designated beneficiaries, then they have until December 31 to split the account so that each beneficiary gets his or her separate share. (See below for more about splitting accounts.) If the accounts are split in timely fashion, the required distribution rules apply separately to each share or account. Then, for example, each beneficiary could use his or her own life expectancy to compute required distributions.

CAUTION

This won't work if one or more beneficiaries is not a designated beneficiary. Splitting accounts in this manner will work only if all beneficiaries are designated beneficiaries as of September 30 of the year after your death. If on that date there are multiple beneficiaries named on the account and even one of them fails to qualify as a designated beneficiary, then you are deemed to have no designated beneficiary and the five-year rule will apply.

But let's assume that multiple designated beneficiaries remain on the account through December 31 of the year after your death. What are the consequences?

First of all, the beneficiaries are not free to use their own life expectancies to take distribution of their respective shares. Also, a spouse might lose some special privileges if both your spouse and child are beneficiaries of a single account.

When you have multiple beneficiaries, for purposes of the life expectancy rule and the five-year rule, all beneficiaries are treated as nonspouse beneficiaries, even if one of them is your spouse. As a result, the most restrictive rules—those that generally produce the worst result—will apply to all beneficiaries. For example, if you name your spouse and your children as beneficiaries, they must choose from the options available to your children because children have fewer options than spouses.

Life Expectancy Rule

The life expectancy rule still applies when there are multiple beneficiaries on a single account (as long as the plan does not require accelerated payments). But the least favorable distribution period is the one your beneficiaries must use: The account must be distributed over the single life expectancy of the oldest beneficiary. This will yield the largest distribution and deplete the account most rapidly, which is exactly what Congress wants. The oldest beneficiary's life expectancy is determined (from Table I) as of his or her age in the first distribution year (the year after your death). Once the distribution amount is calculated and withdrawn, it is divided among the beneficiaries in proportion to their interests in the account.

> **EXAMPLE:** You name your mother and your three children as equal beneficiaries of your retirement plan. You die in 2019. Under the terms of the plan, your beneficiaries are permitted to use the life expectancy rule when distributing your retirement account. Because your mother is the oldest beneficiary, the account must be distributed over her life expectancy. She will turn 85 in 2020, the first distribution year. Her life expectancy—or ADP—at that time will be 7.6 years (from Table I). To compute the first distribution, your beneficiaries must divide the December 31, 2019 account balance by 7.6. That amount will then be distributed and divided equally among your mother and your three children. Each will get a fourth. The ADP will drop by one each subsequent year, and the account will be completely distributed in just eight years.

Five-Year Rule

Again, it's important to remember that the plan can require that distributions be made according to the five-year rule. If the plan provides that the five-year rule applies to nonspouse beneficiaries, but the life expectancy rule is available for a spouse, the spouse is nonetheless prohibited from using the life expectancy rule if the spouse is one of multiple beneficiaries.

Splitting Accounts After Death

If you die before your required beginning date having named multiple beneficiaries of your single retirement account, and as of September 30 of the year after your death all beneficiaries are designated beneficiaries, your beneficiaries have until December 31 of the year after your death to separate their respective shares. If they complete the separation in time, the distribution rules will apply separately to each beneficiary and his or her respective share.

As we explained above, the biggest benefit will be that each beneficiary will be able to use his or her own life expectancy to calculate distributions from his or her share. Furthermore, the separation will give each beneficiary autonomy over investment decisions and will also simplify accounting and other record keeping. As long as the plan itself permits the separation, the law won't prevent it.

One cautionary note: Beneficiaries may use their own life expectancies beginning in the year after the accounts are separated. So if the accounts are separated in the year after death, the required distribution for that year must be based on the life expectancy of the oldest beneficiary (presumably because there were, in fact, multiple beneficiaries named on the account for part of the year). Confused? Here's an example.

> **EXAMPLE:** You named your mother, Josephine, and your three children, Holly, Herman, and Hank, as equal beneficiaries of your retirement plan. You died in 2018. In March 2019, your mother and the three children instructed the custodian to split your IRA into four separate but equal IRAs. All of the new IRAs remain in your name, but one names your mother as beneficiary, one names Holly, one names Herman, and one names Hank. For the year 2019 (the year of the split), the beneficiaries must use your mother's life expectancy to compute required distributions. But then beginning in 2019 (the year after the split), each beneficiary can take required distributions from his or her share of the IRA over his or her own life expectancy.

TIP

Splitting the account in the year of death. If, in the above example, the account were split in 2018 (the year of death), each beneficiary could use his or her own life expectancy to compute the 2019 required distribution (as well as future distributions) from his or her share.

CAUTION

If you name a trust as beneficiary. Splitting the account will not work when a trust is named beneficiary of your retirement account and the trust itself has multiple beneficiaries. (See "Trust Beneficiary," below, for more information.)

Transfer

When separating each beneficiary's share into a separate account after your death, assets must be transferred directly from the trustee or custodian of the original single plan account to the trustee or custodian of each separate account. The beneficiary must not have control of the funds at any time. If the beneficiary is deemed to have control, the IRS will consider the assets fully distributed and fully taxable in the current year.

Furthermore, in the case of nonspouse beneficiaries, the account must remain in the name of the deceased, so it cannot be transferred to one or more of the beneficiaries' existing retirement plans or even into a new retirement account in a beneficiary's name. If a spouse is one of the beneficiaries, however, the spouse could presumably separate his or her share and roll it over to either an existing or a new IRA in the spouse's name.

Name on Account

When transferring a portion of the plan assets to a new account, the IRS requires that the new account also be in the original participant's name. But financial institutions generally do not like to maintain accounts, let alone set up new ones, in the name of a deceased person. To accommodate both the IRS requirements and their own internal accounting procedures, many custodians construct account titles that identify both the original participant (now deceased) and the beneficiary who is to receive distributions.

EXAMPLE: Joe Corpus died leaving a substantial IRA equally to his three children, Dan, Irwin, and Bruce. The children want to split the IRA into three separate IRAs so that each can manage his own investments. The IRA custodian set up three new IRA accounts in Joe's name and transferred a third of Joe's original IRA into each one. The title on Dan's account reads: "Joe Corpus, Deceased, for the benefit of (or FBO) Dan Corpus." The other two accounts are titled "Joe Corpus, Deceased, FBO Irwin Corpus" and "Joe Corpus, Deceased, FBO Bruce Corpus."

Reporting Requirements

The IRS has issued what is called a "revenue procedure" outlining a set of reporting requirements that IRA custodians must adhere to after an IRA participant dies. The custodian must file IRS Form 5498 (you can find a sample in Appendix A) for each beneficiary. The form reports the name of the original owner, the name of the beneficiary, the beneficiary's tax ID or Social Security number, and the value of the beneficiary's share of the IRA as of the end of the year.

With this information, the IRS can trace the source of the IRA for income tax purposes and determine who is liable for the deferred tax. The form must be filed every year until the account is depleted.

CAUTION

Nonspouse beneficiaries, beware! Some nonspouse beneficiaries and, unfortunately, even some custodians are under the mistaken impression that a beneficiary may roll over a deceased participant's retirement plan into an IRA in the beneficiary's own name. This option, however, is available only to a spouse beneficiary. Nonspouse beneficiaries are never permitted to roll over retirement plan assets into new or existing IRAs in their own names.

Choosing a Distribution Option

As we explained above, the effect of naming multiple beneficiaries of one retirement plan account (assuming the account is not split by December 31 of the year after death) is to limit the deferral period to the life expectancy of the oldest beneficiary. As long as the plan permits, however, there is nothing to prevent one beneficiary from accelerating distributions of his or her share while the remaining beneficiaries use the life expectancy rule. The remaining beneficiaries' deferral period would be limited to the life expectancy of the oldest, even if the oldest had already withdrawn some or all of his or her share.

> **EXAMPLE:** Mary, Paul, and Peter inherited an IRA from their father, Jake. The children had not split the account by December 31 of the year after Jake's death. Now, Mary, the oldest child, wants to take her share and use it to buy a house. The boys don't need the money right now and want to take their portions out slowly, spreading distributions over as many years as possible. Mary may take her share outright, and the boys may continue to spread distribution of their shares over Mary's life expectancy.

When a Spouse Is One of the Beneficiaries

If your spouse is one of multiple beneficiaries of your retirement account, your spouse loses the option to defer distributions until you would have been 70½. Also, even if your spouse is the oldest beneficiary, your spouse would not be permitted to use his or her ADP in the Single Life Table (Table I) each year. Instead, your spouse would look up his or her ADP only in the year after death (using Table I), but in subsequent years, would reduce the ADP by one each year.

If the account is an IRA, your spouse also would lose the option to make the IRA his or her own by failing to take a required distribution or by making a contribution of his or her own. However, he or she can still roll over any distribution he or she receives into an IRA in his or her own name, whether or not he or she is the sole beneficiary of your retirement account.

A spouse is the sole beneficiary of your retirement account if he or she is the sole beneficiary on September 30 of the year after your death. If your spouse is one of several designated beneficiaries (see immediately below) as of September 30, all is not lost. If your spouse's share is then separated on or before December 31 of the year after death, making your spouse the sole beneficiary of his or her share, then your spouse is deemed to be the sole beneficiary of his or her share, and all the special privileges accorded a spouse beneficiary would apply to that separate share.

Designated and Nondesignated Beneficiaries

If, as of September 30 of the year after your death, any one of the beneficiaries of your retirement account is not a designated beneficiary, the account is deemed to have no designated beneficiary, even if one or more of the other beneficiaries on the account would otherwise be a designated beneficiary. If the account is deemed to have no designated beneficiary, the life expectancy rule is not available. Instead, the assets must be distributed under the five-year rule. Many a charitably inclined taxpayer, wanting to leave a portion of his or her retirement plan to charity and a portion to a spouse or child, has been blindsided by this unfavorable application of the rules.

> **EXAMPLE:** Paul named his son and the American Cancer Society as equal beneficiaries of his IRA. Paul died in 2018. The beneficiaries did not get around to splitting the account or paying out the charity's portion by September 30, 2019. Because the American Cancer Society is not a natural person or a qualified trust, it is not considered a designated beneficiary. Therefore, the IRA is deemed to have no designated beneficiary, even though Paul's son would have qualified had he been the sole beneficiary. As a result, the entire account must be distributed by December 31, 2023, with half going to Paul's son and half to the American Cancer Society.

Remember, though, this problem can be cured by separating the account or by distributing the charity's share before September 30 of the year after death.

> ⊘ CAUTION
>
> **All beneficiaries must be designated beneficiaries.** The December 31 deadline for splitting accounts applies only if all beneficiaries are designated beneficiaries as of September 30 of the year after death.

Trust Beneficiary

Generally, a beneficiary must be a natural person to qualify as a designated beneficiary and be eligible for the life expectancy rule. The exception to this general rule applies when the beneficiary is a trust that meets certain stringent requirements. As explained in Chapter 6, if the trust satisfies all of those requirements, then the beneficiaries of the trust will be treated as designated beneficiaries for purposes of the life expectancy rule. In other words, the trustee or custodian of the retirement plan may look through the trust to find the designated beneficiary whose life expectancy can be used to compute required distributions.

One of those requirements is to provide a copy of the trust to the trustee or custodian of your retirement plan. For purposes of post-death distributions, the trust document must be in the hands of the trustee or custodian by October 31 of the year after death.

Nonspouse Beneficiary of Trust

If you name a trust as beneficiary and it meets the requirements of a designated beneficiary (see Chapter 6), distributions under the life expectancy rule or the five-year rule will be computed as though there were no trust in place (in other words, as though the beneficiary of the trust had been named beneficiary of the retirement plan). Therefore, if the beneficiary of the trust is not your spouse, the life expectancy rule would apply and the beneficiary may spread required distributions over the beneficiary's life expectancy beginning in the year after your death. In any case, all distributions would go into the trust and become subject to the terms of the trust, which may or may not call for an immediate distribution to the beneficiary.

Spouse Beneficiary of Trust

If your spouse is sole beneficiary of the trust, your spouse will be treated as the designated beneficiary for purposes of the life expectancy rule. That means your spouse could take distributions over his or her life expectancy either beginning on December 31 of the year you would have been 70½ or beginning the year after your death if that is later. In either case, your spouse would use his or her age each year to find the corresponding ADP in Table I.

> TIP
>
> **Your spouse cannot make your IRA his or her own.** If you name a trust as beneficiary of your IRA, IRS regulations state that even if your spouse is the sole beneficiary of your trust, he or she cannot make the IRA his or her own, either by failing to take a required distribution or by making additional contributions. However, he or she might be able to receive a distribution of IRA assets from the trust and then roll them over into his or her own IRA. See "Trust Beneficiary and Spousal Rollovers," below.

Multiple Beneficiaries of Trust

If a trust has multiple beneficiaries and meets the criteria for looking through the trust for a designated beneficiary, then for purposes of applying the life expectancy rule, the multiple beneficiary rules described above will apply as though the individuals themselves were named beneficiaries of the retirement plan.

> CAUTION
>
> **Splitting the account won't work if a trust is the beneficiary.** If you have named a trust as beneficiary of your retirement plan and there are multiple beneficiaries of the trust, splitting the retirement plan into separate accounts for each beneficiary of the trust—whether it is done before or after your death— won't allow beneficiaries to use their own life expectancies to compute required distributions. The multiple beneficiary rules would still apply, and distributions would have to be taken over the life expectancy of the oldest beneficiary of the trust.

Trusts and Estate Planning

You must jump through a raft of hoops to name a trust as beneficiary of a retirement plan and feel confident that you have accomplished what you intended. Sometimes you never do achieve a high level of confidence. With all the risk and uncertainty, why would anyone bother?

Before 2018, people often named trusts as beneficiaries of retirement plans in order to minimize estate taxes and other costs. However, in 2017, Congress dramatically increased the size of an estate that is subject to estate taxes for decedents dying in 2018 or later. For example, in 2019, an individual can exclude $11,400,000 from his or her estate, and for a married couple, that amount is $22,800,000. Because of this change, the vast majority of people do not need to direct retirement assets to a trust to save estate taxes.

However, a trust can be useful for other reasons. For example, you might want to control the manner in which the retirement plan assets are distributed to beneficiaries. Perhaps one of your beneficiaries is a spendthrift, and you worry that the beneficiary might squander his or her inheritance if given easy access to it. Or perhaps you have a blended family and want to make sure that all members of that blended family receive their intended shares, while also providing financial security to your surviving spouse.

Another reason you might want to name a trust as beneficiary is to extend the deferral period of an IRA. For example, if you have a minor grandchild and would like to direct a portion of your IRA to that grandchild, you can establish a trust to which the IRA is payable. Required distributions would be based on that grandchild's life expectancy. Because a grandchild has a relatively long life expectancy, required distributions would be smaller than they would be if your spouse or even your children are the beneficiaries. Thus, more of the assets in the IRA can be left to grow tax deferred for a longer period of time. This might ensure that there will be funds available for the grandchild's college education, and, in any event, will almost certainly increase the amount the grandchild will inherit.

Trusts and Estate Planning (continued)

How does this work? The law won't allow a trust to "own" a retirement plan, which means it is not possible to simply transfer the assets in the plan into the trust. To fund the trust, a person would have to create the trust and name the trust as beneficiary, so that after-death distributions from the plan would be directed into the trust, and the terms of the trust would dictate how the funds are distributed. Making this strategy work as you intend can be complex, so it is important that you confer with a professional who has experience with this approach.

Trust Beneficiary and Spousal Rollovers

When a trust is named beneficiary of a retirement plan, it is often the spouse who is the beneficiary of the trust. Distributions from the plan go into the trust when the participant dies, and then the trust makes distributions to the spouse.

But sometimes the surviving spouse discovers after the participant dies that there is no longer any need for the retirement plan assets to be held in trust. In that case, the surviving spouse might prefer to simply roll over the retirement plan assets into his or her own IRA, name his or her own beneficiary, and begin a new schedule of required distributions.

Unfortunately, the law says that only a spouse beneficiary (and not a trust) may roll over retirement plan assets, and then only if the spouse acquires the assets directly from and by reason of the participant's death.

But taxpayers have argued that if the spouse is the sole beneficiary of the trust and can distribute all of the assets without interference from any third party, then the assets essentially pass directly from the deceased to the spouse, making the rollover within the spirit of the law.

Between 1987 and 2001, the IRS established a pattern of approving such actions in private letter rulings, despite the lack of explicit legal approval.

In final regulations issued in April 2002, however, the IRS stated specifically that a spouse cannot make a deceased participant's IRA his or her own if a trust is named primary beneficiary of the IRA, even if the spouse is the sole beneficiary of the trust.

Nonetheless, some practitioners believe that if the spouse has the power to distribute all assets of the trust, he or she could distribute the IRA assets to the trust and then distribute the assets from the trust to the spouse. Having done so, the spouse could then roll over the assets into an IRA of his or her own. Although this strategy is not specifically sanctioned by the IRS, some practitioners believe it will pass muster, even under the current regulations.

We think you should proceed with caution. If you name a trust as beneficiary of your retirement plan with the expectation that your spouse can fall back on a rollover, you are taking a risk.

As an alternative to taking this risk, consider naming your spouse as primary beneficiary (thus preserving the rollover opportunity) and your trust as contingent beneficiary. After your death, your spouse would have the option of disclaiming some or all of his or her interest in your retirement plan, allowing it to flow to the trust. Ultimately, however, no strategy involving a trust is completely simple or safe.

Estate as Beneficiary

In cases in which an estate was named beneficiary of a retirement plan, private letter rulings issued before 2001 closely paralleled those in which a trust was named beneficiary (see above). If the participant's spouse was the sole beneficiary of the estate, and no one had the authority to restrict the spouse's access to the estate, several IRS private letter rulings permitted the spouse to take a distribution of the plan assets and roll them over into an IRA in the spouse's name.

It is still unclear, however, how much weight these old private letter rulings will carry under the newer regulations. We believe it is safest to avoid using this strategy.

CAUTION

Think twice before naming your estate as beneficiary. Although many people name their estate as beneficiaries of their retirement plans or IRAs, there are few advantages to doing so and some significant disadvantages. For example, because your estate is not a designated beneficiary, you are deemed to have no designated beneficiary for required distribution purposes. As a result, distributions could be accelerated after your death unless your spouse is the sole beneficiary of your estate and is permitted to roll over the plan assets. Relying on such an option for your spouse is risky business, however, given that the strategy has thin support from only a few IRS private letter rulings. Whatever it is you want to accomplish by naming your estate as beneficiary of your retirement plan can almost certainly be achieved through another strategy.

Annuities

If your retirement plan benefits are to be paid in the form of an annuity, whether to you or to your beneficiary, the required distribution rules must still be satisfied.

Start Date

If you die before your RBD, the date by which payments to your beneficiary must begin (the start date) depends on whether or not your beneficiary is your spouse.

If you have named a nonspouse beneficiary, the start date is December 31 of the year after your death.

If your beneficiary is your spouse, however, the start date is the later of December 31 of the year after your death or December 31 of the year you would have turned 70½.

If you had already started receiving your annuity payments and died before your RBD, payments still must satisfy the required distribution rules described below as of the start date.

Form of Payment

In order to satisfy required distribution rules, payments must be in a particular form, although the form varies with the type and terms of the annuity. (See Chapter 6 for more information about types of annuities.) After your death, your beneficiary must take his or her first payment by one of the start dates described above. That payment, however, can be a normal payment. For example, if your beneficiary intends to take monthly payments over his or her life expectancy, the first monthly payment can be paid in December of the year after your death and monthly thereafter. Your beneficiary need not take the full annual amount in December of that first year.

Irrevocable Annuity

If you had already begun receiving payments under an irrevocable annuity at the time of your death, your beneficiary must continue to receive payments with no break in the distribution schedule.

Divorce or Separation

If you were divorced or separated at some time during your life, part of your qualified plan, qualified annuity, or TDA may be payable to an alternate payee (such as a spouse, former spouse, or child) under the terms of a QDRO (a court-approved divorce or maintenance agreement; see Chapter 2 for more information about QDROs).

If the alternate payee's entire share has not yet been paid at the time of your death, then the alternate payee's distribution options are determined by whether or not the alternate payee's interest was held in a separate account or aggregated with the rest of your benefit.

Separate Account

If an alternate payee's share is segregated or separately accounted for (see Chapter 6 for more information about separate accounts), then the life expectancy rule applies to that share, and the alternate payee may take distributions over his or her own life expectancy, beginning no later than December 31 of the year after your death. Remember, though, the plan itself could require application of the five-year rule, in which case the alternate payee's share must be distributed by December 31 of the year containing the fifth anniversary of your death.

Spouse or Former Spouse Alternate Payee

A spouse or former spouse alternate payee has all the rights and privileges of a surviving spouse beneficiary as long as the alternate payee's share is in a separate account. The life expectancy rule would apply unless it is prohibited under the plan. Distributions may be made over the ex-spouse's life expectancy, and must begin by the later of December 31 of the year following the death of the participant or December 31 of the year the participant would have turned 70½.

And if the plan permits, the spouse or former spouse alternate payee may roll over his or her share distribution into a retirement plan or an IRA in his or her own name.

Death of Alternate Payee

If the alternate payee dies before his or her interest has been completely distributed, the alternate payee's beneficiary will be treated as the designated beneficiary of the alternate payee's portion for purposes of the life expectancy rule and the five-year rule.

> **EXAMPLE:** Your former wife is entitled to one-half of your retirement plan benefits under the terms of a QDRO. Your former wife has named her brother as beneficiary of her share of the retirement plan. Your ex-wife died when you were age 60, before she had received any portion of your retirement plan. You die a year later at the age of 62. Your beneficiary may take distribution of his or her share of the account over his or her own life expectancy. At the same time, your ex-wife's brother can receive your ex-wife's portion over his own life expectancy.

No Separate Account

If the plan administrator has not maintained a separate account for the alternate payee of your retirement plan, the beneficiary designation will determine how distributions will be made after your death. Specifically, the multiple beneficiary rules, described above, will apply. The distribution would then be divided among the alternate payee and the beneficiaries in proportion to their interests.

> EXAMPLE: Your former husband is entitled to one-half of your retirement plan benefits under the terms of a QDRO. You have named your father as beneficiary of the other half. Your former husband's share has not been segregated or separately accounted for. You die an untimely death at the age of 56. Under the terms of the plan, your beneficiary will use the life expectancy rule. Because the interests of your father and your former husband are aggregated in one account, your father, as beneficiary, is the one whose life expectancy must be used to determine required distributions. Each distribution will be split equally between your former husband and your father.

Reporting Distributions From IRAs

If you are the beneficiary of an IRA, it is up to you to compute the required distribution each year and report it on your tax return. If you were the original owner of the IRA, the custodian would be required to help you compute the proper amount. However, the law does not currently extend this benefit to beneficiaries. As a beneficiary, you will still receive a Form 5498, reporting the value of the IRA each year, but when it comes to calculating the required distribution, you're on your own.

Key Tax Code and Regulation Sections, IRS Pronouncements

§ 401(a)(9)
Required Distributions From Qualified Plans.

§ 1.401(a)(9)
Required Distribution Regulations.

§ 402(c)
Rollovers From Qualified Plans.

§ 408
Individual Retirement Accounts.

§ 1.408-8, A-5
Election by Spouse to Treat Decedent's IRA as Own.

Rev. Proc. 89-52
After-Death IRA Reporting Requirements.

Distributions to Your Beneficiary
If You Die After Age 70½

Who Should Read Chapter 8
Read this chapter if you want to know what happens to your own retirement plan after you die or if you inherit a retirement plan or an IRA from someone who died after reaching age 70½ and who had already begun mandatory distributions from the plan or IRA. This chapter describes how the remainder of the account must be distributed.

E ven though you are required to start taking money out of your retirement account on your required beginning date (which, for most people, is April 1 of the year after they turn 70½), the account might not be empty when you die. It might even be quite large, especially if you had been withdrawing only the minimum required amount each year or you die soon after your RBD. So what happens to the leftovers? The answer to that question is the subject of this chapter.

Administrative Details

Although the rules for computing required distributions after your death might vary depending on who your beneficiary is, the following administrative procedures apply almost across the board.

Name on the Account

Unless your beneficiary is your spouse, your retirement account must remain in your name until the account is entirely depleted. If a beneficiary other than your spouse attempts to change the name on the retirement plan account to his or her own name, the action could be deemed a distribution of the entire account. Worse, if the beneficiary attempts to roll over your account into the beneficiary's own IRA, not only will it be deemed a distribution, but penalties for contributing more to an IRA than is allowed may be assessed as well.

Helpful Terms

Annuity. A contract, sold by an insurance company, that promises to make monthly, quarterly, semiannual, or annual payments for life or for a specified period of time.

Beneficiary. The person or entity entitled to receive the benefits from insurance or from trust property, such as a retirement plan or an IRA.

Deferral period. The number of years over which distributions from a retirement plan or an IRA can be spread.

Distribution. A payout of property (such as shares of stock) or cash from a retirement plan or an IRA to the participant or a beneficiary.

Estate. All property that a person owns.

Primary beneficiary. A person or an entity entitled to receive benefits from a retirement plan or an IRA upon the death of the original participant.

Term certain. A fixed, identifiable period, such as a specific number of years. For example, a retirement plan that is distributable over a term certain of 20 years must be completely liquidated after 20 years.

Despite the above rule, the trustee or custodian might want to retitle the account to show that you have died. This is permissible as long as the custodian complies with certain procedures for titling the account and reporting distributions. (See Chapter 7 for more information about titling accounts.)

The account can also be transferred to a new IRA as long as the new IRA is titled in the name of the deceased and the funds are transferred directly from the trustee or custodian of the original plan to the trustee or custodian of the new IRA. (See "Nonspouse Beneficiary," below, for more information.)

A special rule allows your spouse to treat your retirement plan account as his or her own. See "Spouse Beneficiary," below, to learn how this can be done.

Timing of Distributions

Once you pass your RBD, distributions from your account must continue, even after your death. There can be no hiatus in distributions. If you failed to take some or all of your required distribution in the year of your death, your beneficiary must take the remainder before the end of the year. Then your beneficiary must continue to take distributions in all subsequent years until the account is depleted.

The only exception to this rule occurs if your spouse elects to treat the account as his or her own. In that case, required distributions from the account (after the spouse makes it his or her own) will be determined as if the spouse had been the original owner of the account. (See "Spouse Beneficiary," below, for more about this strategy.)

Designated Beneficiary

Recall that you can name any person or organization you choose as the beneficiary of your retirement plan or IRA. When determining how your retirement assets should be distributed after your death, however, only designated beneficiaries are taken into account. (See Chapter 6 for more information about designated beneficiaries.) If one or more of your beneficiaries is not a designated beneficiary, you are deemed to have no designated beneficiary.

Deadline for Determining Designated Beneficiary

For purposes of computing post-death required distributions, your designated beneficiary is determined as of September 30 of the year after your death. That doesn't mean someone else can name a new beneficiary of your retirement plan after you die. In fact, no new beneficiaries can be added. Therefore, it is important that you carefully consider and then formally select a beneficiary before you die (using the plan's designation of beneficiary form). Not only will that beneficiary receive the assets of your plan, but his or her life expectancy will determine how quickly assets must be distributed after your death.

Changing Beneficiaries Before the Deadline

The IRS allows this extended deadline for determining beneficiaries specifically to give those beneficiaries an opportunity to do some postmortem planning: to make administration of the retirement plan easier or to clean up a disadvantageous situation you left behind. For example, suppose you name your spouse as primary beneficiary and your daughter as contingent beneficiary. After your death, your spouse might decide she has no need for the assets in your retirement plan. She might disclaim (renounce) her interest in those assets. If she does, the plan assets would go to your daughter, and your daughter's life expectancy would determine the period over which your retirement plan assets are ultimately distributed.

Reporting Distributions

If you are the beneficiary of an IRA or another retirement plan, it is up to you to compute the required distribution each year and report it on your tax return. In the case of an IRA, the custodian will send you a Form 5498, reporting the value of the IRA each year, but you are responsible for the calculation. If you had been the original owner of the IRA, the law would require the custodian to help you compute the proper amount. (See Chapter 6.) However, the law does not extend this benefit to beneficiaries.

Spouse Beneficiary

If your spouse is the beneficiary of your retirement account, he or she may take distributions under the rules described in this section.

> **CAUTION**
>
> **For sole beneficiaries only.** For purposes of this section, we assume that the spouse was the sole beneficiary of the retirement plan. The rules change if a spouse is one of several beneficiaries. (See "Multiple Beneficiaries, One Account," below, for the multiple beneficiary rules.)

Year of Death

The required minimum distribution for the year of your death will be computed in exactly the same way you would have computed it if you had lived to the end of the year. If you did not take a distribution of the required amount before your death, your spouse beneficiary must do so on your behalf by December 31 of the year of your death. In other words, your spouse would use the Uniform Lifetime Table and find the ADP for your age on your birthday in the year of your death. Then your spouse would divide the account balance as of December 31 of the previous year by the ADP.

If your spouse is more than ten years younger than you are, and if you had been using Table II (Joint and Last Survivor Table) to compute lifetime distributions, your spouse would use Table II to find the ADP in the year of your death, as well.

> CAUTION
>
> **Spouse must take required distribution for year of death.** A spouse beneficiary has the option to treat a deceased participant's retirement plan as the spouse's own. Nonetheless, if you die after your RBD, your spouse must take your required distribution for the year of your death (if you had not already done so) before your spouse can make the account his or her own. Once the account is in the spouse's name, all the required distribution rules apply as though the spouse were the original owner. (See "Rollover," below, to learn what happens when the account is rolled over or placed in the name of a surviving spouse.)

Second Year and Beyond

If your spouse is younger than you are, beginning in the second year (and assuming your spouse does not roll over the account into a retirement account in his or her own name), your spouse will use his or her own age and Table I (Single Life Table) to look up the ADP each year.

EXAMPLE: Richard died on October 14, 2018, at the age of 75. Richard's wife, Pat, was the sole beneficiary of his IRA. She was 74 in 2018. Richard had been computing required distributions using the Uniform Lifetime Table (Table III). Richard withdrew his required distribution for 2018 before he died.

To compute the required distribution for 2019, Pat uses Table I to find her ADP for her age in 2019. Pat turned 75 in 2019, so her ADP from Table I is 13.4. Pat will divide the December 31, 2018 balance of Richard's IRA by 13.4 to determine the required distribution for 2019.

In 2020, Pat turns 76. Her ADP (from Table I) is 12.7. Pat will divide the December 31, 2019 balance of Richard's IRA by 12.7 to determine the required distribution for 2020.

If your spouse is older than you, your spouse will compute required distributions using the greater of:

- your remaining life expectancy at the time of your death, reduced by one each subsequent year, or
- your spouse's life expectancy, redetermined each year using his or her age and looking up the ADP in the Single Life Table.

Because you are permitted to use the most favorable (larger) ADP, it is quite possible that your surviving spouse will start out using your life expectancy and then switch to his or her own once the ADP surpasses your remaining life expectancy. (To find your remaining life expectancy, see the life expectancy tables in Appendix B.)

EXAMPLE: You died in 2018 at age 73, after having taken your required distribution from your IRA for the year. Your spouse, who was the sole beneficiary of your IRA, turned 74 in 2018.

For 2019, the ADP is the greater of:

- your life expectancy (from the Single Life Table) in 2018, reduced by one, which is 13.8 (14.8 − 1), or
- your spouse's life expectancy in 2019 at age 75 (from the Single Life Table), which is 13.4.

Because your remaining life expectancy of 13.8 exceeds your surviving spouse's life expectancy of 13.4 in 2019, your spouse would use 13.8 to compute the required distribution for 2019.

For 2020, the ADP is the greater of:

- your life expectancy as of the year of your death reduced by one for each subsequent year, which is 12.8 (14.8 − 2), or
- your spouse's life expectancy in 2020 at age 76 (from the Single Life Table), which is 12.7.

Because your remaining life expectancy of 12.8 exceeds your surviving spouse's life expectancy in 2020, your spouse would use 12.8 to compute the required distribution for 2020.

For 2021, the ADP is the greater of:

- your life expectancy as of the year of your death reduced by one for each subsequent year, which is 11.8 (14.8 − 3), or
- your spouse's life expectancy in 2021 at age 77 (from the Single Life Table), which is 12.1.

Because your surviving spouse's life expectancy of 12.1 in 2021 now exceeds your remaining life expectancy of 11.8, your spouse would switch to using his or her own life expectancy to compute the required distribution for 2021 and beyond.

Rollover

When you die, your spouse may choose to leave your retirement plan or IRA in your name, applying all the distribution rules described above until the account has been completely liquidated.

Fortunately for your spouse, however, there is another, usually more favorable, option. Your spouse can roll over the plan assets into a plan or an IRA of his or her own. (Note that this option is available only to a spouse beneficiary.)

If your plan is not an IRA, a rollover to a plan in the spouse's name is the only way to make the plan the spouse's own.

But if the retirement plan is an IRA, your spouse has several ways to make the IRA his or her own. Your spouse can do so by:

- rolling over the assets into a new or preexisting IRA or plan in the spouse's own name
- failing to take your post-death required distribution at the proper time, or

• contributing additional amounts of the spouse's own to your IRA. The following sections look at each of these in more detail.

Convert to Spouse's Plan or IRA by Rollover

Most spouses choose the rollover method because it is convenient and because it leaves a clear trail. Once the rollover is complete, the account belongs to your spouse in every way. Not only can your spouse name a new beneficiary, but your spouse's RBD will determine when future required distributions must begin.

If your surviving spouse is not 70½ or older when he or she rolls over your retirement plan or IRA, required distributions may be discontinued until your spouse reaches his or her RBD. Then on your spouse's RBD, your spouse must begin required distributions anew, using the Uniform Lifetime Table to determine the ADP (or using Table II, if your spouse has since married someone else and if the new spouse is more than ten years younger).

> **CAUTION**
>
> **Spouse must take a distribution in the year of death.** As mentioned above, if you had not withdrawn your required distribution before your death and your spouse wants to roll over the account into his or her own name, your spouse must withdraw the required amount for the year of your death before he or she can complete the rollover.

After you die, your spouse may roll over your retirement plan or IRA even if your spouse has passed his or her own RBD. In this case, however, there can be no hiatus in required distributions. If your spouse rolls over your IRA in the year of your death, he or she must take a distribution on your behalf (if you had not done so). The following year, your spouse must take a distribution on his or her own behalf (because it is now your spouse's IRA and his or her RBD has passed).

EXAMPLE: Richard died on October 14, 2018 at the age of 75. Richard's wife, Pat, was the sole beneficiary of his IRA. She was 74 in 2018. Richard had already withdrawn the required distribution for 2018.

On January 19, 2019, Pat opened an IRA in her own name and rolled over Richard's IRA into her new account. She named her daughter Tash as beneficiary of the new account. To determine her required distribution for 2019, Pat will use the December 31, 2018 IRA balance. She will divide that balance by the ADP for her age in 2019, which is 75. Her ADP (from the Uniform Lifetime Table—Table III) is 22.9.

Convert to Spouse's IRA by Failing to Take a Required Distribution

If you die after your RBD, and your spouse fails to take a required distribution on your behalf in any year after the year of your death, your spouse is deemed to have made an election to treat your IRA as his or her own. (Remember that because you are past your required beginning date, your spouse must take your required distribution for the year of your death if you had not already done so.) The IRA becomes the spouse's own on December 31 of the year of the failure, and the spouse will not be required to take a distribution until his or her own RBD.

If your spouse has passed his or her own RBD, then your spouse must take a distribution in the year your spouse makes the IRA his or her own. The distribution will be based on your spouse's age in that year, and the ADP will be determined from the Uniform Lifetime Table. If your spouse has remarried someone who is more than ten years younger, the ADP will be determined from Table II, using the surviving spouse's and his or her new spouse's ages.

Convert to Spouse's IRA by Contributing Additional Amounts

If your spouse makes a contribution to your IRA from his or her own funds after your death, or rolls over one of his or her own existing retirement plans into your IRA, your spouse is deemed to have made your IRA his or her own.

Timing of Rollover

The income tax regulations give your spouse no deadline for converting or rolling over your retirement account to his or her own IRA after your death. Your spouse should be able to make the election at any time—even years after your death—as long as he or she continues to take timely required distributions on your behalf for as long as the account remains in your name.

As a practical matter, if a spouse is past age 59½ and intends to roll over a participant's retirement plan into the spouse's own IRA, there is nothing to be gained from waiting. If the spouse needs money, the spouse can take it freely from his or her own IRA even after rolling it over, because there is no penalty for taking distributions after age 59½.

If the spouse is younger than age 59½, however, free use of the IRA funds could be dicey. Recall that one of the exceptions to the early distribution tax is a distribution to a beneficiary after the death of the original participant. (See Chapter 3 for more information on the early distribution tax.) But that particular exception is not available to a spouse after the spouse rolls over the deceased person's plan into the spouse's own plan or IRA. Once it is rolled over, it is the spouse's IRA. Because the spouse is still alive, the after-death exception does not apply. Thus, the spouse must generally postpone distributions until age 59½ to avoid the early distribution tax, if the spouse rolls over the plan.

Consequently, if the spouse is younger than age 59½ and needs to use the retirement plan money to live on, the spouse might be better off leaving the plan in the name of the deceased so that the after-death exception can be used. Once the spouse reaches age 59½ or no longer needs access to the funds, the spouse may roll over the remainder of the deceased spouse's plan or IRA into her own retirement plan or IRA.

Convert to a Roth IRA

If a spouse qualifies, he or she may also convert the retirement plan (but not an IRA) directly to a Roth IRA in the spouse's own name. Under this option, the spouse will generally pay income tax on the pretax converted amounts in the year of conversion, but because the Roth IRA will be in the spouse's name, no further distributions will be required during the spouse's lifetime. When the spouse dies, the assets will be distributed to the beneficiaries that the spouse designated when the Roth IRA was established. See Chapter 9 for more information about converting to a Roth IRA and taking distributions from Roth IRAs.

If the spouse is the beneficiary of a traditional IRA (rather than an employer's plan, for example), in order to convert the traditional IRA to a Roth IRA, the spouse must first roll over the plan assets to a traditional IRA in his or her own name. Once the assets are in the spouse's IRA, he or she may convert them to a Roth IRA, also in the spouse's name.

Death of Spouse Beneficiary

When your spouse dies, assuming your spouse did not make your retirement plan his or her own (by rolling over the assets, failing to take a required distribution, or adding to your account), the spouse's beneficiary must continue to take distributions according to the rules discussed in this section.

Year of Spouse's Death

If the spouse had not taken a required distribution in the year of his or her death, the spouse's beneficiary must take the distribution before the end of the year. The beneficiary will use Table I to find the ADP that corresponds to the spouse's age on his or her birthday in the year of death, and then the beneficiary will divide the account balance as of December 31 of the year before the spouse's death by the ADP for the year of death.

Second Year and Beyond

For subsequent years, the ADP is reduced by one each year. The account balance for the previous December 31 is divided by the ADP for the current year to determine the required distribution. This calculation method continues until the account is completely distributed, regardless of whether or not the spouse's beneficiary survives until the account is empty.

226 IRAS, 401(K)S & OTHER RETIREMENT PLANS

EXAMPLE: Pierre was born on January 10, 1946 and turned 70½ in 2016. Pierre's wife, Zoe, was his designated beneficiary. She turned 68 in 2016. To compute his required distribution for 2016, Pierre used an ADP of 27.4, which he found in the Uniform Lifetime Table next to his age of 70.

2016 Distribution:
Pierre's December 31, 2015 IRA account balance was $100,000. Thus, Pierre's first required distribution (for 2016) was $3,650 ($100,000 ÷ 27.4).

2017 Distribution:
Pierre died in 2017 before taking his required distribution. Zoe found Pierre's ADP of 26.5 (for age 71) from the Uniform Lifetime Table (Table III in Appendix B). The IRA account balance on December 31, 2016 was $106,000. The required distribution for 2017, the year of Pierre's death, was $4,000 ($106,000 ÷ 26.5).

2018 Distribution:
Zoe decided not to roll over Pierre's IRA into an IRA in her own name. The required distribution for 2018 was based on Zoe's single life expectancy. Therefore, she used Table I. Zoe turned 70 in 2018. The ADP for age 70 is 17. The December 31, 2017 IRA balance was $111,000. Therefore, the 2018 required distribution was $6,529 ($111,000 ÷ 17).

2019 Distribution:
Zoe died in 2019 before taking her required distribution. Her beneficiaries will again use Table I to find Zoe's ADP for 2019, the year of her death. The ADP for Zoe's age that year, which was 71, is 16.3. The December 31, 2018 balance of the IRA was $115,000. The required distribution is $7,055 ($115,000 ÷ 16.3).

2020 Distribution:
For the year after Zoe's death and each subsequent year, Zoe's beneficiaries must reduce the ADP for the previous year by one. Therefore, the ADP for 2020 is 15.3 (16.3 − 1). The December 31, 2019 balance of the IRA was $120,000. The required distribution is $7,843 ($120,000 ÷ 15.3).

Nonspouse Beneficiary

If the beneficiary of your retirement plan or IRA is not your spouse, distributions after your death are computed according to the rules described in this section.

> ⚠ CAUTION
>
> **If there is more than one beneficiary.** The rules in this section apply if there is only one beneficiary named on the account. If there is more than one beneficiary, a different set of rules applies. Those rules are discussed in the multiple beneficiaries sections later in this chapter.

Year of Death

In the year of your death, if you had not yet taken your required distribution for the year, your beneficiary must do so before the end of the year. Your beneficiary will use the Uniform Lifetime Table (Table III in Appendix B) one last time, looking up the ADP for your age on your birthday in the year of your death. If you had already taken your required distribution, your beneficiary need not take another distribution in the year of your death.

Second Year and Beyond

Beginning in the year after your death, required distributions are calculated differently depending on whether you were younger or older than your beneficiary.

First, let's assume that your beneficiary was younger than you. In that case, your beneficiary would compute required distributions for the second year and beyond using the beneficiary's single life expectancy in the year after your death (from Table I). In subsequent years, the beneficiary will reduce the ADP by one each year.

> **EXAMPLE:** You turned 70½ in 2013 and began taking required distributions from your IRA at that time. Your designated beneficiary was your daughter, Prudence, who turned 45 in 2013. You had been using the Uniform Lifetime Table (Table III, Appendix B).
>
> You died in the year 2017 after having taken your required distribution for the year. In 2018, the year after your death, Prudence must take a distribution based on her own single life expectancy, determined as of her birthday in 2018. Prudence turned 50 in 2018, and her single life expectancy, or ADP (from Table I), was 34.2. To determine the required distribution for 2018, Prudence divides the December 31, 2017 IRA balance by 34.2.
>
> In 2019, Prudence will reduce the ADP by 1 and divide the December 31, 2018 balance by 33.2 (34.2 − 1). In future years, the ADP will be reduced by one until the entire IRA is depleted.

Second, let's assume you were younger than your beneficiary. In that case, your beneficiary would calculate the required distribution for the year after your death using your single life expectancy (from Table I) in the year of your death, reduced by one (that is, the ADP for the year after your death). In subsequent years, your beneficiary will reduce the ADP by one each year.

> **EXAMPLE:** You turned 70½ in 2007 and began taking required distributions from your IRA at that time. Your designated beneficiary was your brother Ernest, who turned 73 in 2007. You had been using the Uniform Lifetime Table (Table III, Appendix B).
>
> You died in 2017 after taking your required distribution for the year. In 2018, the year after your death, Ernest must take a distribution based on your single life expectancy. He must determine your life expectancy in 2017 (the year of death) and reduce it by one. In 2017, you would have been 80 on your birthday. Your single life expectancy in that year (from Table I) was 10.2. Therefore, Ernest must use an ADP of 9.2 (10.2 − 1) to compute the required distribution for the year 2018. He will divide the December 31, 2017 balance by 9.2.
>
> In 2019, Ernest will reduce the ADP by one. Therefore, he must divide the December 31, 2018 balance by 8.2 (9.2 − 1). In future years, he will reduce the ADP by one until the entire account is depleted.

Death of Nonspouse Beneficiary

If your nonspouse beneficiary dies after you do but before the account is completely empty, the computation method for required distributions will not change at the beneficiary's death. Distributions will be made to the beneficiary's beneficiary according to the schedule established at your death, using the original beneficiary's life expectancy (or yours if you were younger) as the ADP in the year after your death and reducing the ADP by one each subsequent year. Bear in mind, however, that beneficiaries are always permitted to take more than the minimum required distribution.

Rollover

The law also allows a nonspouse beneficiary to transfer the assets of an inherited retirement plan (an employer plan, not an IRA) into a new inherited IRA. The new inherited IRA must be established in the name of the deceased and the assets must be transferred directly from the plan trustee to the custodian of the new IRA. The beneficiary may not take possession of the funds at any time or those funds will be deemed distributed and taxable.

On the other hand, a nonspouse beneficiary is never permitted to roll over a deceased participant's retirement plan or IRA into the beneficiary's own IRA. Furthermore, the consequences are the same whether or not the deceased had passed his or her RBD at the time of death. Any rollover attempt will be deemed a distribution, and if the assets are actually deposited into an IRA in the beneficiary's name, the deposit will be considered an excess contribution to an IRA and will be subject to penalties if not withdrawn in a timely fashion.

Convert to a Roth IRA

The same rule (described above) that allows a nonspouse beneficiary to transfer an inherited retirement plan (an employer plan) into an IRA in the decedent's name also allows the beneficiary to transfer the plan assets into a new inherited Roth IRA in the decedent's name. If the beneficiary chooses this action, the transfer constitutes a conversion from a retirement plan to a Roth IRA, and the following rules apply:

- The beneficiary must accomplish the conversion by means of a trustee-to-trustee transfer, which means the funds must go directly from the trustee of the decedent's retirement plan to the custodian of the new inherited IRA.
- The new inherited IRA must be in the name of the decedent, for the benefit of the beneficiary (see "Name on Account," below).
- The beneficiary must pay income tax on the pretax portion of the amount that is transferred from the retirement plan to the new inherited Roth IRA. The income tax will be due with the tax return for the year of the conversion.
- The beneficiary must take required distributions from the inherited Roth IRA according to the same schedule that would apply to an inherited retirement plan or to an inherited traditional IRA.

Note that if a nonspouse beneficiary inherits an IRA instead of a retirement plan (an employer plan), the beneficiary does not have the option to convert the traditional inherited IRA into a Roth IRA.

For more information about converting retirement plan assets to a Roth IRA and taking distributions from Roth IRAs see Chapter 9.

No Designated Beneficiary

If you did not name a beneficiary of your retirement plan or the beneficiary does not qualify as a designated beneficiary, then distributions are based on your own single life expectancy in the year of your death, reduced by one for each subsequent year until the account is depleted.

> **EXAMPLE:** You turned 70½ in 2014. You named your estate as beneficiary and never got around to changing the designation before your death.
>
> You died in the year 2018 before taking your required distribution for the year. Your beneficiary (that is, the beneficiary of your estate) must use the Uniform Lifetime Table (Table III in Appendix B) and your age in 2018 to compute the required distribution for 2018. The ADP for age 74 is 23.8.

For 2019, your beneficiary must find your single life expectancy (from Table I) for your age in 2018 (the year of your death) and reduce it by one. Your single life expectancy for age 74 is 14.1. Therefore, the ADP for the 2019 required distribution is 13.1 (14.1 − 1). In the future, the ADP will be reduced by one each year.

Multiple Beneficiaries, Separate Accounts

If you have several IRAs or retirement plans, each with a single beneficiary, then the required distribution rules are applied separately to each plan. You are not considered to have multiple beneficiaries.

Multiple Beneficiaries, One Account

If you name more than one designated beneficiary of a single retirement account, then you have multiple beneficiaries for that account, and required distributions after your death will be computed as though the beneficiary with the shortest life expectancy were your sole beneficiary.

For example, if you name your sister and your children as equal beneficiaries of your IRA, and your sister is the oldest beneficiary, then distributions are computed after your death as though your sister were your sole beneficiary. But once calculated and withdrawn, the distribution will be divided equally among the beneficiaries.

Note, however, that if the beneficiary with the shortest life expectancy is older than you are, your beneficiaries will use your remaining single life expectancy to compute required distributions after your death. This is the same exception that applies if you die on or after your RBD having named a person who is older than you as your only beneficiary.

Determining the Designated Beneficiary

As is the case if you die before your RBD, the date for determining the beneficiaries is September 30 of the year following your death. If you had more than one beneficiary as of your date of death, your beneficiaries would still have time to make some changes. For example, one or more beneficiaries could disclaim an interest. Or perhaps the interests of one or more beneficiaries could be distributed by September 30 of the year after your death. (See Chapter 7 for more information about changes that can be made after your death.)

There's one other cure for multiple beneficiaries. If on September 30 of the year after your death all beneficiaries are designated beneficiaries, then they have until December 31 of that year to split the account so that each beneficiary has his or her separate share. (See below for more about splitting accounts.) If the accounts are split in timely fashion, the required distribution rules would apply separately to each share or account. Then, for example, each beneficiary could use his or her own life expectancy to compute required distributions.

> **CAUTION**
>
> **If one or more beneficiaries are not designated beneficiaries.** If on September 30 of the year after death there are multiple beneficiaries named on the account and one of them is not a designated beneficiary, then you are deemed to have no designated beneficiary. Splitting the account after September 30 will not cure the problem.

Computing the Required Distribution

If there are multiple beneficiaries named on your retirement account and they do not cure the problem, as described above, distributions must be spread over the life expectancy of the oldest beneficiary. In other words, the ADP is determined as though the oldest beneficiary were the sole beneficiary. Once the distribution is calculated, each beneficiary will receive his or her proportionate share.

> **EXAMPLE:** You have only one IRA, and you name your three children, Tanya, Durf, and Trina, as equal beneficiaries. You die in 2018 at age 74 after having taken your required distribution for the year. As of December 31,

2019, your children were all still named equal beneficiaries of the account. In 2019, Tanya was 40, Durf was 30, and Trina was 22. Because Tanya is the oldest, distributions must be spread over her single life expectancy in the year after your death, reduced by one each subsequent year. In 2019, the ADP for Tanya's age 40 (from Table I) is 43.6. Each child receives one-third of the distribution. In the future, the ADP will be reduced by one each year.

Splitting Accounts

Accountants and taxpayers alike rejoiced when the IRS simplified matters by allowing accounts to be split among beneficiaries after the original owner died, whether the owner died before or after the required beginning date.

If you die having named multiple beneficiaries of your single retirement account, and if all beneficiaries are designated beneficiaries as of September 30 of the year after death, your beneficiaries have until December 31 of the year after your death to separate their respective shares. If they complete the separation in time, the distribution rules will apply separately to each beneficiary and his or her respective share.

The biggest benefit of timely separation is that each beneficiary can use his or her own life expectancy to calculate distributions from his or her share. A nonspouse beneficiary would use his or her own ADP from Table 1 for the year after the accounts were separated, then reduce it by one for each subsequent year. A spouse beneficiary would use his or her own ADP from Table 1, looking up a new ADP each year. Furthermore, the separation gives each beneficiary autonomy over investment decisions and simplifies accounting and other record keeping. As long as the plan itself permits the separation, the law won't prevent it.

A word of caution, however: Beneficiaries may use their own life expectancies to compute required distributions beginning in the year after the accounts were separated. So if the accounts are separated in the year *after* death, the required distribution for that year must be based on the life expectancy of the oldest beneficiary (presumably because there were, in fact, multiple beneficiaries named on the account for part of the year).

EXAMPLE: You name your brother, Joseph, and your three children, Holly, Herman, and Hank, as equal beneficiaries of your retirement plan. You die in 2018 at the age of 72 after taking your required distribution for the year. In March 2019, your brother and the three children instructed the custodian to split your IRA into four separate but equal IRAs. All of the new IRAs remain in your name, but one names only your brother as beneficiary, one names Holly, one names Herman, and one names Hank. Because your IRA was split into separate IRAs for each beneficiary before December 31, 2019 (the year after your death), each beneficiary can take required distributions from his or her share of the IRA over his or her own life expectancy—beginning in 2020.

However, for the year 2019 (the year the IRA was split), each beneficiary must use your brother's life expectancy to compute his or her required distribution, because your brother is the oldest beneficiary.

TIP

Splitting in the year of death. If, in the above example, the account were split in 2018 (the year of death), each beneficiary could use his or her own life expectancy to compute the 2019 required distribution (as well as future distributions) from his or her share.

CAUTION

When a trust is beneficiary. Splitting the account will not work when you name a trust as beneficiary of your retirement account and the trust itself has multiple beneficiaries. (See below for more information.)

Transfer

When separating each beneficiary's share into a separate account after your death, assets must be transferred directly from the trustee or custodian of the original single account to the trustee or custodian of each separate account. The beneficiary must not have control of the funds at any time. If the beneficiary is deemed to have control, the IRS will consider the assets fully distributed and fully taxable in the current year.

Furthermore, in the case of nonspouse beneficiaries, the account must remain in the name of the deceased, so it cannot be transferred to one or more of the beneficiaries' existing retirement plans or even into a new retirement account in a beneficiary's name. If a spouse is one of the beneficiaries, however, the spouse can separate his or her share and roll it over to an existing or a new IRA in the spouse's name.

Name on Account

When transferring a portion of the plan assets to a new account, the IRS requires that the new account also be in the original participant's name. But financial institutions generally do not like to maintain accounts, let alone set up new ones, in the name of deceased people. To accommodate both the IRS requirements and their own internal accounting procedures, many custodians construct account titles that identify both the original participants (now deceased) and the beneficiaries who are to receive distributions.

Choosing a Distribution Option

As we explained above, the effect of naming multiple beneficiaries of one retirement plan account (assuming the account is not split by December 31 of the year after death) is to limit the deferral period to the life expectancy of the oldest beneficiary. As long as the plan permits, however, there is nothing to prevent one beneficiary from accelerating the distribution of his or her share while the remaining beneficiaries use the life expectancy rule. The remaining beneficiaries' deferral period would be limited to the life expectancy of the oldest, even if the oldest had already withdrawn some or all of his or her share.

When a Spouse Is One of the Beneficiaries

If your spouse is one of several beneficiaries of your retirement account, he or she can still take a distribution of his or her share of the account and roll it over into an IRA in his or her own name. If a spouse does not roll over his or her share, the spouse must use the ADP of the oldest beneficiary for the year after death (using Table I) and reduce it by one in each subsequent year.

If your account was an IRA and your spouse was not the sole beneficiary, your spouse loses the option to make the IRA his or her own by failing to take a required distribution or by making a contribution of his or her own.

A spouse is the sole beneficiary of your retirement account if he or she is the sole beneficiary on September 30 of the year after your death. If your spouse is one of several designated beneficiaries as of September 30 but separates his or her share on or before December 31 of the year after death (making your spouse the sole beneficiary of his or her share), then your spouse is deemed to be the sole beneficiary of his or her share, and your spouse gets all the special privileges accorded a spouse beneficiary.

Specifically, the spouse would be able to use Table I to look up a new ADP each year, instead of simply reducing the original ADP by one each year.

Trust Beneficiary

If you name a trust as beneficiary of your retirement plan or IRA and that trust meets certain requirements (see Chapter 6 for a discussion of those requirements), then the trustee or custodian of the plan is permitted to look through the trust to find the beneficiary of the trust. The trust beneficiary can then be treated as a designated beneficiary for purposes of computing required distributions.

All of the retirement plan distributions would go into the trust and become subject to the terms of the trust.

Nonspouse Beneficiary of Trust

A nonspouse beneficiary of the trust will use the required distribution rules described above. This means the beneficiary may spread required distributions over his or her life expectancy. The beneficiary would find the ADP (from Table I) corresponding to his or her age in the year after your death. The ADP would then be reduced by one each subsequent year.

> **TIP**
>
> **Older nonspouse beneficiary.** If your nonspouse beneficiary is older than you, he or she may use your remaining life expectancy to compute required distributions after your death.

Spouse Beneficiary of Trust

If your spouse is sole beneficiary of the trust, your spouse will be treated as the designated beneficiary for purposes of computing post-death distributions. That means your spouse can take distributions over his or her single life expectancy beginning on December 31 of the year after your death by looking up the ADP for his or her age each year in Table I.

> **TIP**
>
> **Older spouse beneficiary.** As is the case when you name your spouse directly as beneficiary of your retirement plan, if your spouse is older than you, he or she would use your remaining life expectancy to compute required distributions after your death.

> **CAUTION**
>
> **Your spouse cannot make your IRA his or her own.** If you name a trust as beneficiary of your IRA, IRS regulations state that even if your spouse is the sole beneficiary of your trust, your spouse cannot make the IRA his or her own, either by failing to take a required distribution or by making additional contributions. However, your spouse might be able to receive a distribution of IRA assets from the trust and then roll them over into his or her own IRA, as explained below.

Multiple Beneficiaries of Trust

If a trust has multiple beneficiaries, then for purposes of post-death required distributions, the multiple beneficiary rules described above apply as though the individuals themselves were named beneficiaries of the retirement plan.

> ⊘ **CAUTION**
>
> **Splitting the account won't work if a trust is the beneficiary.** If
> you name a trust as beneficiary of your retirement plan and there are multiple
> beneficiaries of the trust, splitting the retirement plan into separate accounts for
> each beneficiary of the trust—whether it is done before or after your death—
> won't allow beneficiaries to use their own life expectancies to compute required
> distributions. The multiple beneficiary rules still apply, requiring your beneficiaries
> to take distributions over the life expectancy of the oldest beneficiary of the trust.

Trust Beneficiary and Spousal Rollovers

When a trust is named beneficiary of a retirement plan, it is often the spouse who is the beneficiary of the trust. Distributions from the plan go into the trust and then the trust makes distributions to the spouse.

But sometimes the surviving spouse discovers after the participant dies that there is no longer any need for the retirement plan assets to be held in trust. In that case, the surviving spouse might prefer to simply roll over the retirement plan assets into his or her own IRA, name his or her own beneficiary, and begin a new schedule of required distributions.

Unfortunately, the law says that only a spouse beneficiary (and not a trust) may roll over retirement plan assets, and then only if the spouse acquires the assets directly from and by reason of the participant's death.

But taxpayers have argued that if the spouse is the sole beneficiary of the trust and can distribute all of the assets without interference from any third party, then the assets essentially pass directly from the deceased to the spouse, making the rollover within the spirit of the law.

Between 1987 and 2001, the IRS established a pattern of approving such actions in private letter rulings, despite the lack of explicit legal approval.

In final regulations issued in April 2002, however, the IRS stated specifically that a spouse cannot make a deceased participant's IRA his or her own if a trust is named primary beneficiary of the IRA, even if the spouse is the sole beneficiary of the trust.

Nonetheless, some practitioners believe that if the spouse has the power to distribute all assets of the trust, he or she could distribute the

IRA assets to the trust and then distribute the assets from the trust to him- or herself. Having done so, the spouse could then roll over the assets into an IRA of his or her own. Although this strategy is not specifically sanctioned by the IRS, some practitioners believe it will pass muster, even under the newer regulations.

We think you should proceed with caution. If you name a trust as beneficiary of your retirement plan with the expectation that your spouse can fall back on a rollover, you are taking a risk.

As an alternative to taking this risk, consider naming your spouse as primary beneficiary (thus preserving the rollover opportunity) and your trust as contingent beneficiary. After your death, your spouse would have the option of disclaiming some or all of his or her interest in your retirement plan, allowing it to flow to the trust. Ultimately, however, no strategy involving a trust is completely simple or safe.

Estate as Beneficiary

Recall that an estate does not qualify as a designated beneficiary. If an estate is named beneficiary, then the plan assets must be distributed over the original participant's life expectancy. The ADP for the year after death is the participant's single life expectancy (from Table I) in the year of death, reduced by one. The ADP is reduced by one for each subsequent year, as well. This is true even if the participant's spouse or child is beneficiary of the estate. There is no look-through rule for an estate as there is for certain qualified trusts. Consequently, if a participant was elderly at death, the plan might have to be entirely distributed in a short time.

TIP

Rollover risky. The IRS has frequently allowed a spouse to roll over the assets of a retirement plan into an IRA in the spouse's own name when an estate is named beneficiary of the plan and the spouse is the sole beneficiary of the estate. But the strategy is not sanctioned by the tax code or by tax regulations, so it remains risky.

Annuities

If you die on or after your RBD and if you had been receiving your retirement benefits as an annuity, the form of the annuity determines how the remaining benefits will be paid to your beneficiary. (See Chapter 6 for more information about types of annuities.)

For example, the annuity might have been a joint and survivor annuity that must continue to pay your beneficiary the same benefits you were receiving. Or the annuity might have been a term certain annuity; if you survive only part of the term, your beneficiary receives payments for the remainder of the term.

Divorce or Separation

If you were divorced or separated during your lifetime, some or all of your retirement plan might be distributable to an alternate payee, such as a spouse, former spouse, or child, under the terms of a QDRO (a court-approved divorce or maintenance agreement; see Chapter 2 for more information about QDROs).

In such cases, some portion of each distribution during your lifetime was payable to the alternate payee (unless, of course, the alternate payee's share was distributed outright). That doesn't change when you die.

If you die after your RBD, payments from your account will continue to be computed using your beneficiary's ADP in the year after death, reduced by one each subsequent year. If an alternate payee has been receiving a portion of each distribution, the alternate payee is entitled to his or her share of post-death distributions, as well.

> **EXAMPLE:** On September 30 of the year after your death, the designated beneficiary of your retirement plan was your sister. Under the terms of a QDRO, your former spouse is entitled to half of your retirement plan, and you had been giving your former spouse 50% of each distribution. You died after taking your required distribution for the year. In the year after your death, your sister must take a distribution from your retirement plan using the ADP (from Table I) for her age in that year. Half of the distribution will go to your sister and half to your former spouse.

In subsequent years, your sister will reduce the previous year's ADP by one when computing required distributions. Half of all distributions must go to your former spouse.

If the alternate payee is a nonspouse (for example, a child), he or she may never roll over a distribution from your retirement plan. However, a spouse or former spouse with an interest in your retirement plan under the terms of a QDRO has all the rights of a surviving spouse beneficiary. When you die, your former spouse may roll over any distribution he or she receives from your plan into an IRA or a retirement plan in his or her own name, provided the former spouse first takes a required distribution on your behalf in the year of your death. If your former spouse has not yet reached his or her RBD, future required distributions may be deferred until that time.

Key Tax Code and Regulation Sections, IRS Pronouncements

§ 401(a)(9)
Required Distributions From Qualified Plans.

§ 1.401(a)(9)
Required Distribution Regulations.

§ 402(c)
Rollovers From Qualified Plans.

§ 408
Individual Retirement Accounts.

§ 1.408-8, A-5
Election by Spouse to Treat Decedent's IRA as Own.

Rev. Proc. 89-52
After-Death IRA Reporting Requirements.

Announcement 95-99
Employee Plans Examination Guidelines.

Roth IRAs

Who Should Read Chapter 9

Read this chapter if you have a Roth IRA, if you are considering opening one, or if you would like to convert another retirement plan to a Roth IRA.

I n its eternal quest for the most effective way to encourage people to save for retirement, Congress created in 1997 one of the biggest sugarcoated carrots we've ever seen: the Roth IRA.

Congress designed the Roth IRA to be much like a traditional IRA, but with a few attractive modifications. When the modifications began to fill pages rather than paragraphs, the new creature was given its own section in the tax code, Section 408A. The section begins with the statement that all the traditional IRA rules apply to Roth IRAs except as noted. This chapter focuses on the exceptions, with special attention to the unusual treatment of distributions.

The lure of the Roth IRA is powerful. Although contributions are not deductible (meaning they are made with after-tax dollars), all distributions, including the earnings on contributions, are potentially tax free, as explained below.

Unfortunately, Roth IRAs don't work for everyone. Here's a summary of the key differences between traditional IRAs and Roth IRAs:

- You may make a contribution to a traditional IRA no matter how high your income is, as long as you (or your spouse, if you are married and filing a joint return) have earned income (income from employment) and are younger than 70½. But in the case of a Roth IRA, you may not make any contribution if your income exceeds a certain level. If you are married filing a joint return, the amount that you are allowed to contribute to a Roth IRA is gradually reduced when your modified AGI exceeds $193,000 (for tax year 2019). You may not make any contribution at all once your income reaches $203,000. If you are single, the phaseout

Helpful Terms

Adjusted gross income (AGI). Total taxable income reduced by certain expenses, such as qualified plan contributions, IRA contributions, and alimony payments.

After-tax dollars. The amount of income left after all income taxes have been withheld or paid.

Beneficiary. The person or entity entitled to receive the benefits from insurance or from trust property, such as a retirement plan or an IRA.

Deferral period. The number of years over which distributions from a retirement plan or an IRA can be spread.

Distribution. A payout of property (such as shares of stock) or cash from a retirement plan or an IRA to the participant or a beneficiary.

Earned income. Income received for providing goods or services. Earned income might be wages, salary, or net profit from a business.

Nondeductible contribution. A contribution to a retirement plan or an IRA that may not be used as a business expense or an adjustment to offset taxable income on an income tax return.

Traditional IRA. Any contributory or rollover IRA that is not a Roth IRA or a SIMPLE IRA.

begins at $122,000 and is complete when your income reaches $137,000. If you are married filing separate returns, the phaseout begins with your first dollar of income and is complete when your income reaches $10,000. (Note: These numbers will increase for inflation from time to time.)

- No contribution to a traditional IRA is permitted after age 70½. However, you may continue to make contributions to a Roth IRA after age 70½, as long as you or your spouse have earned income and your modified AGI doesn't exceed the limits described above.

- A contribution to a traditional IRA is always deductible if neither you nor your spouse is covered by a qualified plan. If even one of you is covered by a plan, the deduction is phased out as your income increases. On the other hand, no contribution to a Roth IRA is ever deductible, whether or not you are covered by another plan.
- Earnings that accumulate inside a traditional IRA are always subject to income tax when withdrawn. But earnings in a Roth IRA can be completely tax free when distributed if certain requirements are satisfied.
- If you have a traditional IRA, you must begin required distributions on or before your required beginning date (RBD). If you have a Roth IRA, you are not required to withdraw any amount during your lifetime.

Calculating Your Modified Adjusted Gross Income

You are not permitted to make a Roth IRA contribution if your modified adjusted gross income (modified AGI) exceeds a certain amount. When calculating your modified AGI, you make the following adjustments to your regular AGI:

- Exclude from income any amounts converted from a retirement plan or an IRA to a Roth.
- Exclude any distributions from traditional IRAs or other retirement plans that you were required to withdraw because you are older than 70½.
- Add back income from U.S. savings bonds used for higher education expenses.
- Add back employer-paid adoption expenses.
- Add back excluded foreign earned income and payments received for foreign housing.
- Add back any deduction claimed for a traditional IRA contribution.
- Add back the deduction for educational loan interest.

> CAUTION
>
> **Roth 401(k) plans are different from Roth IRAs.** Roth 401(k) plans are not exempt from the lifetime required distribution rules. See Chapter 10 for more information about Roth 401(k) plans.

The contrast between traditional IRAs and Roth IRAs is most stark in the treatment of distributions. The differences turn up not only in the ordinary income tax rules, but also in the application of the early distribution tax and the required distribution rules.

Taxation of Distributions

The income tax rules for traditional IRAs are straightforward. Generally, distributions are taxed as ordinary income unless they are rolled over into another retirement plan or IRA. If you made nondeductible (after-tax) contributions to your traditional IRA over the years, those amounts are not subject to tax when distributed. That's the good news. The bad news is that those after-tax contributions are deemed to come out pro rata, not all at once. In other words, the nondeductible portion of a traditional IRA comes out as only a part of each distribution you ever take from the IRA. Consequently, only a percentage of each distribution is tax free. (See Chapter 2 for more information about calculating the nontaxable portion of a distribution from a traditional IRA.)

The basic rule for Roth IRAs is similar: The taxable portion of any distribution must be reported on your income tax return, and it will be taxed as ordinary income unless you roll it over. But that's where the similarity ends.

The key to squeezing the maximum benefit from a Roth IRA is to be aware of which distributions are taxable and which are not. Maintaining that vigilance is not difficult; you must simply view your Roth IRA as the sum of two distinct parts. One part consists of the contributions you have made. The second part consists of the earnings on those contributions, such as interest earned on bond investments or gains from stock sales.

Distribution of Nondeductible Contributions

The portion of your Roth IRA that consists of your contributions is never subject to income tax when it comes out. Never. Even if you take it out the day after you put it in. That's because all contributions you made were nondeductible, which means you have already paid tax on the money. You don't have to pay tax a second time when you take it out. Fair is fair.

Furthermore, any distribution you take from a Roth IRA is presumed to be a return of your contributions until you have withdrawn all contributions you made to it over the years (or to all Roth IRAs, if you have more than one). In other words, all contributions are recovered before earnings are recovered. This simple rule gives the Roth IRA an advantage over a traditional IRA. It means you may retrieve your contributions whenever you want without incurring any income tax. In this way, the contributions can serve as an emergency fund.

> **EXAMPLE:** Dain began making contributions to a Roth IRA three years ago. By the beginning of this year, the Roth IRA had grown to $8,000. Of that amount, $6,000 was from Dain's annual contributions and $2,000 was from investment returns. In February of this year, Dain had an auto accident and totaled his car. Dain needed to purchase a new car but didn't have any resources other than his Roth IRA. He decided to withdraw $6,000 from his Roth IRA. The $6,000 is not subject to tax because Dain's distribution is deemed to be a return of his contributions.

Distribution of Investment Returns

When you contribute to an IRA, you ordinarily use the contributed funds to purchase investments that will earn money for you. For example, you might invest in bonds or CDs to generate interest. Or you might buy stock, hoping the price will shoot up so you can make a bundle on a later sale. As long as those earnings—the interest and the stock proceeds—stay inside the IRA, they are not taxed. But what happens when they come out? In the case of a traditional IRA, all of the earnings are subject to ordinary income tax. The advantage of the Roth IRA is that when you distribute earnings, they are tax free—even though they have never been taxed before—as long as the distribution is considered a qualified distribution.

Qualified Distributions

It will pay you handsomely to nail down the tax-free advantage a Roth IRA offers. All you have to do is follow a few simple rules. First, don't take a distribution of your investment returns for five years. A distribution within five calendar years of when you first establish a Roth IRA can never be a qualified distribution.

(!) CAUTION

If you die before the five years are up. If you die before satisfying the five-year holding period, your beneficiary must wait until you would have satisfied it, or the distribution will not be qualified.

So, counting the year of your first contribution as Year One, you will satisfy the five-year requirement if you wait until the sixth year before withdrawing any earnings.

> EXAMPLE: Jessica opened a Roth IRA in June 2015. At the end of 2016, her account was worth $15,000, of which $8,000 was from contributions and $7,000 was from investment earnings. In June 2019, Jessica withdrew $10,000 to pay for a trip to China. Of that amount, $8,000 is deemed to be from contributions and will not be subject to income tax. The remaining $2,000 is deemed to come from earnings. Because the distribution did not satisfy the five-year holding requirement, the $2,000 will be subject to income tax. (It might also be subject to an early distribution penalty.)

Although you are permitted to make a contribution to a Roth IRA after the end of the year (until April 15), the five-year holding period for a qualified distribution begins on the first day of the calendar year to which your very first contribution relates, which might be an earlier year than the one during which the contribution was actually made.

> **EXAMPLE:** Soren wanted to set up a Roth IRA and make a contribution for 2018. He finally got around to doing so in February 2019, well before the April 15, 2019 deadline. Because the contribution is for 2018, Soren will count 2018 as Year One when computing the five-year holding period, even though he didn't actually make the contribution until 2019. Soren's five-year requirement will be satisfied January 1, 2023.

Simply satisfying the five-year requirement will not automatically make a distribution qualified. It must also be at least one of the following:

- a distribution you take after reaching age 59½
- a distribution you take after becoming disabled
- a distribution to your beneficiary or your estate after your death, or
- a distribution you take to purchase a first home (up to a lifetime withdrawal limit of $10,000).

The four items above are defined in the same way they are defined for purposes of the early distribution tax exceptions, described in Chapter 3. If your distribution satisfies the five-year requirement and falls into one of the above categories, it will be qualified and thus entirely tax free.

CAUTION

Remember, contributions are never subject to income tax when they come out of a Roth IRA. So even if they are part of a nonqualified distribution, they are tax free. Only the earnings will be taxed if they are part of a nonqualified distribution. (Earnings may also be subject to an early distribution penalty if they are part of a nonqualified distribution that doesn't qualify for an exception; see below.)

Municipal Bonds Offer Another Form of Tax-Free Investment

Typically, when you purchase municipal bonds, all of the interest you earn on the bonds is tax free. As an investment vehicle, a Roth IRA has two distinct advantages over a municipal bond. First, inside a Roth IRA, money can be invested in stocks and other diverse investments that are likely to yield a greater return over the long term than do municipal bonds. Second, although the interest on municipal bonds is tax free, you must be diligent about reinvesting the interest or you will soon have taxable income.

For example, if you invest $10,000 in a municipal bond that pays 4% interest, you receive $400 of tax-free interest during the year. But if you place that interest in a regular interest-bearing account or another investment that generates taxable income, the earnings on the $400 will be taxable. To ensure that all future earnings are tax free, you must reinvest in more municipal bonds, which might be difficult with only $400 of cash. Municipal bonds are rarely sold in increments of $400.

In contrast, all distributions from a Roth IRA are potentially tax free, whether you invest in stocks, corporate bonds, or CDs. Thus, not only can you invest in a variety of securities, but also you won't have the same reinvestment concerns you would have if municipal bonds were your only investment option. For example, if you invest in a CD that generates $500 of interest income, you could reinvest in stocks, bonds, or another CD.

EXAMPLE: Lara began making contributions to a Roth IRA in 2017. By June 2019, she had accumulated $7,500. Of that amount, $7,000 was from contributions she made in the years 2017, 2018, and 2019. The remaining $500 was from earnings on her investments. In December 2019, Lara withdrew $7,200 from the IRA. The distribution is a nonqualified distribution because it occurred within five years of her initial contribution. Only $200 is subject to tax, however, because her contributions, which total $7,000, are deemed to come out first; they are never subject to tax.

Nonqualified Distributions

Any distribution from a Roth IRA that does not satisfy the requirements of a qualified distribution is automatically nonqualified. Nonqualified distributions are treated very much like traditional IRA distributions. Any after-tax contributions you made will come out tax free, but the earnings are taxable. There is one critical difference, however: As mentioned above, the contributions you made to the Roth IRA (which were made with after-tax dollars) are presumed to come out first, before any earnings. This means if you must take a nonqualified distribution, some or all of it will escape income tax, as long as you have not previously withdrawn all of your contributions.

> **EXAMPLE:** JJ contributed to a Roth IRA in each of the years 2016, 2017, and 2018. By June 2018, he had accumulated $10,000, of which $9,000 was from contributions and $1,000 was from earnings. In December, JJ withdrew $9,000 from his IRA. Although the distribution was nonqualified, the $9,000 was nontaxable because it was all attributable to his contributions. In April 2019, JJ contributed another $4,000 to his Roth IRA. By December, he had a total of $5,200 in the IRA. Only $4,000 was attributable to contributions because he had already withdrawn all contributions for prior years. The remaining $1,200 represented earnings. JJ decided to withdraw $5,000. The entire distribution is nonqualified, but the $4,000 attributable to contributions would be tax free. Only $1,000 of the distribution is attributable to earnings, and that portion will be subject to income tax.

Conversions and Rollovers

When you have a Roth IRA, your opportunities for rolling over the assets are limited. In fact, you may roll them over only to another Roth IRA. In contrast, your opportunities for rolling over assets from other retirement plans and IRAs to a Roth IRA have expanded considerably in recent years.

You have long been able to roll over—or convert—traditional IRAs, SEPs, and SIMPLE IRAs to a Roth IRA.

> !
>
> **CAUTION**
>
> **SEPs and SIMPLEs.** This section applies to SEPs in exactly the same way it applies to traditional IRAs. In other words, a SEP can be converted to a Roth IRA. In the case of a SIMPLE IRA, you may convert to a Roth IRA only after two years from the date you first established the SIMPLE IRA. Before the two years have expired, the SIMPLE IRA is ineligible for conversion.

Then, beginning in 2008, you were also able to convert other types of retirement plans to a Roth IRA, including qualified plans (such as 401(k) plans), tax-deferred annuities (403(b) plans), or government plans (457 plans).

Although you might be permitted to roll over assets from a retirement plan or an IRA to a Roth IRA, you may not do the reverse. You are not permitted to roll over assets from a Roth IRA to any other type of plan or IRA. A Roth IRA may only be rolled over to another Roth IRA.

As explained in the paragraphs below, some special rules apply to amounts that have been converted or rolled over to a Roth IRA.

Rollover From Roth IRA

If you take a distribution from a Roth IRA with the intention of rolling it over, you may roll it over only to another Roth IRA. This is logical when you think about it. Distributions from Roth IRAs are all potentially tax free, whereas most, if not all, distributions from a traditional IRA or a qualified plan are taxable. If you were allowed to mix plans indiscriminately, the IRS would have a hard time tracking the source of the various distributions to determine which funds are taxable.

Except for the fact that you may only roll a Roth IRA to another Roth IRA, all the rules governing rollovers between IRAs apply to rollovers between Roth IRAs. (See Chapter 2 for more about IRA rollovers.) Among the most important of those rules are the following:

- Once you take a distribution from a Roth IRA, you have only 60 days to complete the rollover to another Roth IRA.
- You are permitted only one Roth-to-Roth rollover per year.
- Rollover distributions between IRAs are not subject to income tax withholding.

Rollover to Roth IRA

Rollovers to a Roth IRA may come from another Roth IRA, a traditional IRA, a qualified plan, a tax-deferred annuity, or a government plan.

A Roth IRA may be rolled into another Roth IRA without any restrictions other than those that apply to rollovers between traditional IRAs, as described in the previous section. A rollover from a traditional IRA or from another retirement plan is called a conversion and is more complex, as explained below.

Conversion to Roth IRA

If you want to convert assets from a traditional IRA or another retirement plan to a Roth IRA, you must be prepared to pay the piper. Specifically, the entire pretax amount of the conversion will be subject to income tax at ordinary rates. (If you made nondeductible contributions to your plan or IRA, those amounts will not be taxed a second time when you convert to a Roth IRA.) Congress wasn't about to wipe out all of those deferred taxes with one stroke of the pen. Once you've ponied up the money and converted the assets, however, all future distributions of the converted amounts will be free of income tax. Furthermore, distributions of future earnings on converted amounts will be tax free as long as those distributions satisfy the five-year holding period and are qualified.

> **EXAMPLE:** In 2013, you converted your $20,000 traditional IRA to a Roth IRA. On your tax return for 2013, you included the $20,000 and paid tax on it. By 2019, your Roth IRA has grown to $35,000, and you withdraw $30,000 to throw yourself a 65th birthday party. The entire $30,000 distribution is tax free because you are older than 59½ and you have satisfied the five-year holding period.

As a practical matter, it may be difficult for people with sizable retirement plans or IRAs to convert entire accounts to Roth IRAs unless they have large amounts of cash outside the IRA. Imagine paying regular income tax on a $100,000 IRA. One way around this problem would be to convert the retirement plan or IRA to a Roth IRA in bits and pieces over a number of years to keep the tax at a manageable level. Nothing in the law prevents you from converting part of your retirement plan or IRA instead of the whole thing. Furthermore, there is no time limit on conversion. As long as the law doesn't change, you can simply wait and convert some or all of your retirement funds when it makes the most sense for you.

For older IRA participants, converting to a Roth IRA is not necessarily the correct decision. If you must include a large retirement plan or IRA in income, some or all of it could easily be taxed at the maximum tax rate, and you might not recover from that financial outlay (through tax-free compounded growth) before your death. If your primary concern is passing wealth to your beneficiaries, however, a conversion could save estate taxes and also give your beneficiaries an opportunity for additional tax-free growth after your death.

The decision to convert or not to convert can involve some complex calculations. You must factor in age, health, income and estate tax rates, Social Security benefits, and investment returns. If you are young, healthy, and able to pay the taxes with separate money, the conversion is likely to pay off for you.

TIP

Can you find separate funds to pay the tax? The conversion of a retirement plan or an IRA to a Roth IRA can be a real boon to young investors who can pay the tax from funds outside of the retirement plan or IRA. These folks have years of tax-free compounding ahead of them. However, if the tax is paid out of retirement plan or IRA funds, the advantage of the conversion declines and may even disappear altogether.

CAUTION

If you are younger than 59½ and you elect to use some of the converted amounts to pay the tax, the portion that goes to taxes could be subject to the early distribution tax. (See below.)

> (!) CAUTION
>
> **You are not permitted to roll over or convert a required distribution.**
> Therefore, any required distribution must be placed in a regular account, not an
> IRA account of any kind.

If you decide to proceed with the conversion of a retirement plan or an IRA to a Roth IRA, you will find that Congress has provided even more tax relief for you:

- The conversion is ignored for purposes of the one-rollover-per-year rule. (See Chapter 2 for more information about this rule.)
- Even if you are younger than 59½, the converted amount will not be subject to the early distribution tax, as long as the entire taxable amount is rolled over. (Beware of using part of the rollover to pay income tax, though; as explained below, this money could be subject to the early distribution tax.)
- For income tax purposes, later distributions of converted amounts from your Roth IRA are treated like distributions of nondeductible contributions. The converted portion will not be subject to income tax when it is distributed in future years, but the earnings will be subject to tax unless they are part of a qualified distribution. (See above for the definition of a qualified distribution.)

Correcting Errors: Recharacterizing

Before 2018, there was little risk to converting retirement plan assets to a Roth IRA because you could simply undo it later—by the due date (or the extended due date) of your tax return. This was called a recharacterization.

However, effective January 1, 2018, the recharacterization rules were radically changed. Most significantly, recharacterizations of conversions to Roth IRAs are no longer allowed. If you convert assets from your retirement plan or IRA to a Roth IRA, you may not change your mind and return the assets to a traditional IRA. (You were never permitted to return assets to an employer retirement plan, even if that's where they came from.)

On the other hand, you may still elect to recharacterize a contribution you made to either a traditional IRA or a Roth IRA. In other words, you may elect to treat a contribution made to a traditional IRA as made to a Roth IRA. Or you may elect to treat a contribution to a Roth IRA as made to a traditional IRA.

Recharacterizations can sometimes also be used to correct administrative errors.

Mechanics of Recharacterizing a Contribution

As is often the case when moving retirement plan money around, it is important to pay attention to details. Here are the rules must follow if you want to recharacterize a contribution.

- A recharacterization must occur as a trustee-to-trustee transfer.
- Amounts to be recharacterized may be transferred to an existing IRA or to a new IRA.
- You must recharacterize assets that were actually contributed. You may not replace the funds with assets from another IRA, for example.
- You must include in the recharacterized amount the net income (or loss) allocable to the contribution that is now being recharacterized.
- You must make an election to recharacterize. You do this by notifying the custodian or trustee of both IRAs of your intention ("election") to recharacterize the earlier contribution. You should provide notice on or before the date the funds are recharacterized. Your notice should include:
  - a statement that you elect to treat the original contribution as having been made to the second IRA instead of the first
  - the amount of the original contribution
  - the amount of the contribution that is to be recharacterized in a trustee-to-trustee transfer
  - the amount of investment income allocable to the recharacterized amount that must also be transferred
  - the date of the original contribution, and
  - the tax year for which the original contribution was made
- You must then report the recharacterization as described in the next section. Use Form 8606. (See a copy of Form 8606 in Appendix A.)

Deadlines

If you decide to recharacterize, you must do so before the deadline. Specifically:

- You have until the extended due date of your tax return to recharacterize funds. Then you report the recharacterization on the tax return for the year for which the original contribution was made.
- If you already filed your return and reported the contribution, you still have until October 15 of that year to recharacterize the contribution. But in that case, you must amend the return for the year for which the contribution was made in order to report the recharacterization.

Partial Recharacterizations

Partial recharacterizations are permissible, but be careful to follow the rules for recharacterizing allocable earnings, as well as the original contribution amount. The general rule is that when the time comes to recharacterize, you must either choose a dollar amount (of the original contribution) to recharacterize, or you must choose to recharacterize an amount contributed on a specific date. Once you have settled on an amount to be recharacterized, you must allocate a pro rata portion of the earnings or losses since the time of the contribution. The IRS provides a worksheet in Publication 590 that will help you with the math.

Early Distribution Tax

Understanding how the early distribution tax applies to Roth IRAs is complicated by the fact that there are two types of distributions (qualified and nonqualified) and a special set of rules for converted amounts. (Early distribution tax rules for traditional IRAs and other retirement plans are discussed in Chapter 3.)

Qualified Distributions

Qualified distributions from Roth IRAs are not subject to the early distribution tax. It's as simple as that. This rule, too, has some logic to it. The early distribution tax applies only to distributions that are included in income—those that are required to be reported on your tax return. Because all qualified distributions from Roth IRAs are tax free, they are all exempt from the early distribution tax. (The requirements for qualified distributions are listed above.)

Nonqualified Distributions

Nonqualified distributions from Roth IRAs are treated in most respects like distributions from traditional IRAs. Any portion of the distribution that is required to be included on your income tax return is subject to the early distribution tax, unless the distribution qualifies for an exception. The exceptions for nonqualified distributions from Roth IRAs are the same as those for traditional IRA distributions. (See Chapter 3 for a detailed description of all the exceptions to the early distribution tax.) The key exceptions to the early distribution tax include distributions:

- after you reach age 59½
- because of your death or disability
- that are substantially equal periodic payments
- for certain medical expenses
- for certain health insurance
- for higher education expenses, or
- for a first home purchase (limited to $10,000).

Distributions of Nondeductible Contributions

Bear in mind that all of your nondeductible contributions to a Roth IRA will come out before any earnings. Because the contributions are nondeductible, they are not subject to tax when distributed, even if they are part of a nonqualified distribution. And because they are tax free and not includable on your income tax return, they automatically escape the early distribution tax.

Any earnings that are distributed as part of a nonqualified distribution are subject to the early distribution tax, unless an exception applies.

Again, for planning purposes, this means you can take your contributions out of a Roth IRA at any time, and they will be subject neither to income tax nor to the early distribution tax.

> **EXAMPLE:** In 2016, you established a Roth IRA. You contributed $3,000 in 2016, 2017, and 2018. By November of the year 2019, the account had grown to $9,600. Finding yourself a little strapped for cash, you withdraw $6,000 from the account in late November. Because the distribution is less than your total contributions of $9,000, the $6,000 will not be subject to either income tax or the early distribution tax.

Distribution of Converted Amounts

A special rule exempts converted amounts from the early distribution tax in the year of the conversion, as long as the entire amount of the conversion goes into the Roth IRA. There are two ways to get caught by an early distribution tax when you convert to a Roth IRA. You might use some of the converted amount to pay the income tax you owe on the conversion, or you might withdraw the converted amount too soon. But remember, the early distribution tax would never apply if you were older than 59½ at the time of the distribution (or if another exception, described in Chapter 3, applies).

Paying Income Tax With Converted Amounts

If you qualify to convert a retirement plan or an IRA to a Roth IRA, the amount actually deposited into the Roth IRA will not be subject to an early distribution tax. Even though it is included on your tax return and you pay income tax on the converted amount, you are spared the early distribution tax if you roll over everything. But if you use some of the money from the plan or IRA to pay the income tax liability instead of rolling it over, the portion used for taxes will be subject to the early distribution tax, unless you are older than 59½ or another exception applies. (See Chapter 3 for more information about the early distribution tax and exceptions to the tax.)

Withdrawing Converted Amounts Too Soon

Converted amounts in a Roth IRA are after-tax amounts (because you paid tax in the year of conversion). However, if you withdraw any converted dollars within five years, that portion of the distribution will be treated as though it is taxable, but only for purposes of determining the early distribution tax. (Recall that the early distribution tax generally does not apply to amounts that are excluded from your income for tax purposes. This is an exception to that rule.)

> **EXAMPLE:** You have a traditional IRA to which you have been making deductible contributions each year. By the time you are 50, the account has grown to $15,000. You convert the IRA to a Roth IRA, paying tax on the entire $15,000. The following year, you withdraw $10,000 from the Roth IRA to bail your son out of jail. Because you are younger than 59½ and you withdrew the $10,000 within five years of converting your traditional IRA to a Roth IRA, you must pay an early distribution tax of $1,000 ($10,000 × 10%). You will not owe regular income tax on the $10,000.

The portion of a distribution that is subject to the early distribution tax is limited to the amount that you included in your taxable income and reported on your tax return in the year of conversion.

> **EXAMPLE:** You have a traditional IRA to which you have made deductible contributions of $4,000 and nondeductible (after-tax) contributions of $6,000. By the time you are 51, the account has grown to $17,000. You convert the IRA to a Roth IRA, paying tax on $11,000. (You don't have to pay tax on the $6,000 of nondeductible contributions.) The next year, when you are 52, you withdraw $17,000 to help your daughter start a new business. You must pay an early distribution tax on the $11,000, because that is the amount that was included on your income tax return in the year of conversion. The early distribution tax is $1,100 ($11,000 × 10%).

TIP

How the earnings are treated. The earnings on converted amounts are treated exactly the same as earnings on contributory amounts. Only qualified distributions of earnings escape the early distribution tax, unless another early distribution tax exception applies.

Ordering of Distributions

You might think you should be able to pick and choose which amounts come out of your Roth IRA first. For example, if you take a distribution before the five-year holding period is up, you would want to take your contributions first, because they are not subject to tax or penalties. Or if you converted one of your traditional IRAs six years ago and another two years ago, you would want to take a distribution from the one that was converted six years ago, because those converted amounts satisfy the five-year holding period and would not be subject to an early distribution tax.

Sadly, you cannot pick and choose the origin of each distribution you take. But serendipitously, the ordering rules you are required to use are quite favorable. Distributions are deemed to come out in the following order:

- Regular Roth IRA contributions are distributed first.
- Next come converted amounts, starting with the amounts first converted. If you converted a traditional IRA containing both taxable and nontaxable amounts (for example, if you had made deductible and nondeductible contributions), the taxable portion is deemed to come out first.
- Earnings come out last.

The benefits can be dramatic. For example, if you take a distribution before the five-year holding period is up or you fail to satisfy the other requirements of a qualified distribution, the withdrawal still won't be subject to the early distribution tax as long as you have taken less than the total amount of all contributions you have made to all your Roth IRAs. Note that for purposes of these ordering rules, all Roth IRAs are considered a single Roth IRA.

EXAMPLE: You have two traditional IRAs: IRA #1 and IRA #2. In 2011, you converted IRA #1, then valued at $10,000, to a Roth IRA. In 2015, you converted IRA #2, valued at $20,000, to a Roth IRA. You also have a separate contributory Roth IRA, which you established in 2011 and to which you have been making annual contributions. By 2019, the contributory Roth IRA has grown to $15,000, of which $8,000 is contributions and $7,000 is earnings. In November 2019, on your 40th birthday, you withdraw $25,000 to pay for your trip to India. The source of the distribution is deemed to be:

- $8,000 from Roth IRA contributions
- $10,000 from the oldest converted amount (IRA #1), and
- $7,000 from the next oldest converted amount (IRA #2).

The $8,000 of contributions are not subject to either income tax or the early distribution tax because they are all from nondeductible after-tax contributions. The $10,000 deemed to be from IRA #1 is also not subject to either income tax (which you already paid in the year of conversion) or the early distribution tax (because the conversion occurred more than five years before). The remaining $7,000 will not be subject to income tax, because it was converted from a traditional IRA and you already paid tax on it in 2015. However, it will be subject to an early distribution tax of $700 (10% of $7,000), because it was distributed within five years of the conversion and you are younger than 59½.

Required Distributions

The required distribution rules—those that will eventually force you to start taking money out of your retirement plan or your traditional IRA—have a broad reach. (See Chapter 5 for a summary of the required distribution rules.) They apply to IRAs, qualified plans, plans that behave like qualified plans, and even some nonqualified plans. But as broad as that reach is, a significant exception has been carved out for Roth IRAs.

During Your Lifetime

During your lifetime, you are not required to take distributions from a Roth IRA. Ever. In fact, you could die without ever having removed a cent. This rule, which allows Roth IRA participants to accumulate a tax-favored nest egg and then simply pass it on to another generation, seems to conflict with the government's long-standing policy to ensure that tax-favored retirement plans primarily benefit the original participant.

But there is a logical, if cynical, explanation. Because the Roth IRA was structured to allow all qualified distributions to be tax free, the government has no real incentive to force distributions. There are no deferred taxes to collect. So much for public policy.

After Your Death, Before Your RBD

Once you die, the distribution rules for Roth IRAs again merge with those for traditional IRAs. All of the post-death required distribution rules apply to Roth IRAs in the same way they apply to traditional IRAs. Thus, if you die before your RBD, the life expectancy rule or the five-year rule will apply. Those rules, as well as other required distribution rules that kick in if you die before your RBD, are explained in Chapter 7.

TIP

Roth IRAs can be a boon to your beneficiaries. Although the post-death required distribution rules for traditional IRAs are essentially the same as those for Roth IRAs, the planning implications could be quite different because of different taxation rules. If a Roth IRA has been in place for five years before the owner died, making all distributions qualified distributions (see "Qualified Distributions," above), then all distributions will be tax free to beneficiaries (unless some of it must be used to pay estate taxes). In addition, the early distribution tax does not apply to inherited IRAs, regardless of the age of the beneficiary. For this reason, there will undoubtedly be a real temptation for beneficiaries to take distribution of their shares immediately upon the participant's death. Free money. But because assets inside the Roth IRA could continue to grow tax free, it is usually to the beneficiary's advantage to defer distributions for as long as possible.

After Your Death, After Your RBD

If you have a traditional IRA, you must begin required distributions when you reach your required beginning date, or RBD. If you die after your RBD, a special set of distribution rules applies. (See Chapter 8.) But because you are not required to take distributions from a Roth IRA during your lifetime, you have no RBD for that purpose. In other words, you are always deemed to have died before your RBD.

Key Tax Code and Regulation Sections

§ 72(t)
Early Distribution Tax and Exceptions.

§ 72(t)(2)(F)
First-Home-Purchase Exception to Early Distribution Tax.

§ 401(a)(9)
Required Distributions From Qualified Plans.

§ 1.401(a)(9)
Required Distribution Regulations.

§ 408A
Roth IRAs.

§ 1.408A
Roth IRA Regulations.

Roth 401(k) Plans

Who Should Read Chapter 10

Read this chapter if you are younger than 59½ and want to withdraw money from your retirement plan or IRA. If you are older than 59½, this chapter does not apply to you.

The plan commonly called a Roth 401(k) plan is a bit of a hybrid. Although it is technically a type of 401(k) plan, it has some of the features of a Roth IRA. Sorting out which 401(k) plan rules and which Roth IRA rules apply to the Roth 401(k) can be tricky. The safest approach is to assume that the 401(k) plan rules apply unless you can find a particular exception.

To start with, a Roth 401(k) plan is simply an option that can be added to a traditional 401(k) plan. A Roth 401(k) plan cannot exist on its own. So if your employer wants to establish a Roth 401(k) plan, it must establish a regular 401(k) plan and then add a provision to the plan documents that would establish a separate Roth 401(k) account, called a designated Roth account. Employees would then be able to contribute part of their salaries to either the regular 401(k) account or the Roth 401(k) account— or perhaps split the contribution between the two accounts.

Only after-tax salary deferral contributions may be deposited in the Roth 401(k) account. No employer contributions and no pretax employee contributions are permitted.

The one exception to this rule applies if you elect an "in-plan" conversion. When you transfer funds directly from your traditional 401(k) plan account to your designated Roth account within the plan (the Roth 401(k)), that is an in-plan conversion. As long as you satisfy certain requirements, you may transfer both employer and employee contributions to the Roth account. For more information about in-plan conversions, see "Rollover to a Roth 401(k)" below.

Helpful Terms

401(k) plan. A type of qualified profit-sharing plan that allows an employee to contribute a portion of his or her salary to the plan instead of receiving that portion in cash.

After-tax contribution. A contribution to a retirement plan on which income taxes have already been paid. Those contributions will be tax free when distributed from the plan.

Beneficiary. The person or entity entitled to receive the benefits from insurance or from trust property, such as a retirement plan or an IRA.

Distribution. A payout of property, such as shares of stock or cash, from a retirement plan or an IRA to the participant or a beneficiary.

Pretax earnings. The investment returns earned on retirement plan contributions. Those earnings will be taxable when they are distributed from the retirement plan.

Pro rata. Proportionately. For example, an amount distributed pro rata over four years is distributed evenly over those four years. Property that is distributed pro rata to its owners is distributed according to the percentage of each owner's interest.

Salary deferral contribution. A contribution to a retirement plan that is paid from salary that would otherwise be paid to the employee in cash.

In any case, the funds in the designated Roth account will consist entirely of after-tax contributions and conversions, plus the pretax earnings on those amounts.

Because the Roth 401(k) is actually just part of a regular 401(k) plan, most of the rules that apply to a regular 401(k) plan also apply to a Roth 401(k) plan. For example, the vesting rules and the contribution limits are the same. But there are significant differences in how the contributions will be taxed when they come out of the plan.

Taxation of Distributions

If you have been participating in a Roth 401(k) plan at work and you leave your job, you will generally have three options (assuming you do not simply take the money and spend it):

- You may transfer your Roth 401(k) plan into the Roth 401(k) plan of your new employer, if your new employer has such a plan. If you choose this option, the rules that you must follow are the same as the rules for transferring a traditional 401(k) plan to a new employer's 401(k) plan. (See Chapter 2.) Just remember: The only employer plan to which you may transfer your Roth 401(k) plan is another Roth 401(k) plan.

- You may roll over or transfer your Roth 401(k) plan to a Roth IRA. If you choose this option, once your Roth 401(k) plan assets have been deposited into the Roth IRA, the Roth IRA rules will apply to all of the assets as though they had always been part of the Roth IRA. The rules described in Chapter 2 for rolling over qualified plans into IRAs also apply to rollovers from Roth 401(k) plans to Roth IRAs.

- You may leave your Roth 401(k) plan assets with your employer. If you choose this option, the distribution rules described in the remainder of this chapter will apply when you eventually take money out of the plan.

Distribution of After-Tax Amounts

The portion of your Roth 401(k) plan that consists of your salary deferral contributions and in-plan conversion amounts is never subject to income tax when it comes out. That's because those contributions were subject to income tax in the year they were contributed to the plan. You don't have to pay tax a second time when you take the money out.

However, when you take money out of a Roth 401(k) plan, a portion of the distribution is deemed to be from your contributions and conversions, and a portion from earnings. In other words, your after-tax amounts come out pro rata.

EXAMPLE: Ricky has $10,000 in his Roth 401(k) plan. Of that amount, $9,000, or 90%, is attributable to after-tax salary deferral contributions and $1,000 (10%) is from earnings on his contributions. If Ricky takes $3,000 out of his account, $300 (which is 10% of $3,000) will be attributable to earnings and will be subject to income tax, while $2,700 will be attributable to after-tax contributions and will be free of income tax.

CAUTION

Roth IRA rules are different. Note that this distribution rule is different from the rule that applies to Roth IRAs. When you take money out of a Roth IRA, all of your contributions come out first. Earnings come out last.

Distribution of Pretax Earnings

As is the case with Roth IRAs, the contributions you make to a Roth 401(k) plan are invested and earn money for you. Those earnings—the interest and stock gains—will not be subject to income tax while they are inside the plan. When it comes time to take money out of the Roth 401(k) plan, the earnings portion, as well as the contributions, will be tax free, *if* the distribution is considered a qualified distribution.

Qualified Distributions

Remember that when you take a distribution from a Roth 401(k) plan, a portion of that distribution will be from your after-tax amounts and a portion will be from the earnings on those amounts. The after-tax portion of the distribution will never be subject to income tax, because you already paid the tax. However, the earnings will be subject to tax unless the distribution is a qualified distribution.

The first requirement for a qualified distribution is a five-year holding period. If you take a distribution within five calendar years of when you first contribute to your Roth 401(k) plan, the distribution will not be a qualified distribution.

As with a Roth IRA, if you count the year of your first contribution as Year One, you satisfy the five-year requirement if you wait until the sixth year before taking money out of the plan. The five-year holding period begins on the first day of the calendar year for which your contribution was made.

However, unlike its application to Roth IRAs, the five-year holding period applies to each Roth 401(k) plan separately. So if you have more than one Roth 401(k) plan, a distribution will not be a qualified distribution if it is taken from a plan that has not been in place for at least five years.

! CAUTION

Roth IRA rules are different. This five-year holding period rule for Roth 401(k) plans is different from the five-year holding period rule for Roth IRAs. If you hold multiple Roth IRAs, you satisfy the five-year holding period for all such IRAs once you have held any Roth IRA for five years.

! CAUTION

Five-year holding period applies to beneficiaries. As is the case with a Roth IRA, if you die before satisfying the five-year holding period, your beneficiary must wait until you would have satisfied it, or the distribution will not be qualified.

Simply satisfying the five-year requirement will not automatically make a distribution qualified. It must also be at least one of the following:

- a distribution you take after reaching age 59½
- a distribution you take after becoming disabled, or
- a distribution to your beneficiary or your estate after your death.

If your distribution satisfies the five-year requirement and falls into one of the above categories, it will be qualified and thus entirely tax free.

Nonqualified Distributions

Any distribution from a Roth 401(k) plan that does not satisfy the requirements of a qualified distribution described above is automatically nonqualified. Although the portion of your nonqualified distributions that is attributable to your contributions will not be taxable, the portion that is attributable to earnings will be subject to income tax and perhaps penalties, as well. (See below for information about penalties that might apply.)

Conversions and Rollovers

When you have a Roth 401(k) plan, your rollover and conversion opportunities are limited. The sections that follow take a closer look at your rollover options.

Rollover to a Roth 401(k)

In late 2010, Congress passed a new law allowing an employee to transfer assets from a traditional 401(k) plan account to a designated Roth account within the 401(k) plan. This new transaction is called an in-plan conversion because assets may be transferred only between two accounts in the same plan. There are some requirements and restrictions, but most people should be able to satisfy them. They are as follows:

- The 401(k) plan must have a provision that permits the addition of a designated Roth account. In other words, the plan documents must state that the plan administrator may establish Roth 401(k) accounts for employees.
- The 401(k) plan documents must also specifically state that in-plan conversions are permitted.
- The conversions must be in the form of a direct rollover, which means that the trustee of the plan must transfer the funds from the traditional 401(k) plan account to the Roth 401(k) account.

As is the case for a conversion from a traditional IRA to a Roth IRA, you are not permitted to undo, or recharacterize, an in-plan conversion of traditional 401(k) plan assets to a Roth 401(k). So, if you convert some or all of your traditional 401(k) plan assets to a Roth 401(k), there is no going back.

Rollover to Another Roth 401(k)

You are permitted to transfer your Roth 401(k) plan to another Roth 401(k) plan if you change jobs and your new employer has a Roth 401(k) plan. If you decide to move the assets of your old plan, you must transfer them directly from the trustee of your old plan to the trustee of your new plan. You are not permitted to take possession of the funds yourself. Technically, this is a trustee-to-trustee transfer, rather than a rollover. If you do not transfer the entire amount to the new plan, the earnings are presumed to be transferred first. (Note: This is an exception to the pro rata rule described above.)

Once you have transferred the assets from your old Roth 401(k) plan to the new one and the assets for both plans have been commingled, a new and favorable rule kicks in. Specifically, the five-year holding period requirement for qualified distributions will be based on the oldest plan. So, for example, if you had satisfied the five-year holding period for your old plan but not the new one, once the old plan's assets have been commingled with the new plan's assets, all are deemed to satisfy the five-year holding period.

Rollover to a Roth IRA

You are also permitted to roll over your Roth 401(k) plan assets into a Roth IRA. If you choose to do this, the assets can be transferred in a trustee-to-trustee transfer (also known as a direct rollover) to avoid mandatory income tax withholding on the earnings. Alternatively, you can take the funds yourself and roll them over within 60 days to a Roth IRA.

Once the assets of the Roth 401(k) plan have been deposited in your Roth IRA account, all the Roth IRA rules apply to the combined assets. None of the Roth 401(k) plan rules will apply once the funds have been commingled with the Roth IRA assets. This applies also to the five-year holding period requirement for qualified distributions. All of the assets in the Roth IRA will be subject to the original Roth IRA holding period even if the Roth 401(k) plan had been in place for more than five years and the Roth IRA had not.

No Rollover From a Roth IRA to a Roth 401(k) Plan

Although you are permitted to roll over the assets of a Roth 401(k) plan to a Roth IRA, you may not do the reverse—that is, you are not permitted to roll over the assets of a Roth IRA to a Roth 401(k) plan.

> ! CAUTION
>
> **Traditional IRAs are different.** This rule is different from the rollover rules for traditional IRAs. You are permitted to roll over a traditional IRA into a qualified plan, if the plan allows it.

Early Distribution Tax

When making decisions about retirement plans, it is important to take into consideration both income taxes and penalties. The early distribution tax is an income tax that functions like a penalty. The penalty is for taking money out of a retirement plan too soon. The beginning of this chapter discussed income taxes. Now it's time to look at those situations in which an early distribution penalty might apply.

Qualified Distributions

All distributions from Roth 401(k) plans are either qualified distributions or nonqualified distributions. If the distribution is a qualified distribution as described above, the early distribution tax does not apply. The early distribution tax applies only to those distributions that are subject to income tax. Because all qualified distributions from Roth 401(k) plans are tax free, they are all exempt from the early distribution tax as well.

Nonqualified Distributions

Any portion of a nonqualified distribution from your Roth 401(k) plan that is required to be included on your income tax return is subject to the early distribution tax, unless an exception applies. The exceptions to the early distribution tax are the same as those that apply to a regular 401(k) plan distribution. Those exceptions can be found in Chapter 3. Because nonqualified distributions typically comprise after-tax contributions and earnings, only the earnings portion will be subject to the early distribution tax, unless an exception applies.

Ordering of Distributions

The special ordering rules for Roth IRAs that allow you to take your after-tax contributions out first do not apply to Roth 401(k) plans. Consequently, when you take a distribution from your Roth 401(k) plan, the distribution will comprise after-tax contributions and pretax earnings on those contributions in proportion to the total amount of each in your account. (See the example at the beginning of this chapter.)

Required Distributions

The required distribution rules that force you to begin taking money out of your retirement plans and traditional IRAs during your lifetime also apply to Roth 401(k) plans. The required distribution rules also force your beneficiaries to take distributions from the account after your death, whether they need the money or not. The following sections discuss both sets of distribution rules.

Required Distributions During Your Lifetime

The lifetime required distribution rules described in Chapter 6 also apply to distributions from your Roth 401(k) plan. Note that the rules for a Roth 401(k) plan are different from those for a Roth IRA. If you have a Roth 401(k) plan, you must begin taking distributions from the account when you reach age 70½, or after you retire, if that is later.

> TIP
>
> **A rollover to a Roth IRA might be a good strategy.** Recall that if you roll over your Roth 401(k) plan into a Roth IRA, once the assets are commingled, the Roth IRA rules will apply to all the assets in the account. Because you are not required to take distributions from a Roth IRA during your lifetime, if you roll over your Roth 401(k) plan into a Roth IRA, you will be able to bypass the lifetime required distribution rules that would otherwise apply to your Roth 401(k) plan.

Required Distributions After Your Death

All of the post-death required distribution rules apply to Roth 401(k) plans in the same way they apply to other qualified plans and traditional IRAs. Thus, if you die before your RBD, the life expectancy rule or the five-year rule will apply. Chapter 7 explains those rules in detail. If you die after your RBD, the rules described in Chapter 8 will apply.

Key Tax Code Sections Regulations

§ 72(t)
Early Distribution Tax and Exceptions.

§ 401(a)(9)
Required Distributions From Qualified Plans.

§ 402A
Optional Treatment of Elective Deferrals as Roth Contributions.

§ 1.401(a)(9)
Required Distribution Regulations.

§ 1.401(k)-1(f)
401(k) Regulations Related to Roth 401(k) Contributions.

§ 1.402A
Designated Roth Accounts.

IRS Forms, Notices, and Schedules

Certification for Late Rollover Contribution

Name
Address
City, State, ZIP Code
Date

Plan Administrator/Financial Institution
Address
City, State, ZIP Code

Dear Sir or Madam:

Pursuant to Internal Revenue Service Revenue Procedure 2016-47, I certify that my contribution of $[*enter amount*] missed the 60-day rollover deadline for the reason(s) listed below under Reasons for Late Contribution. I am making this contribution as soon as practicable after the reason or reasons listed below no longer prevent me from making the contribution. I understand that this certification concerns only the 60-day requirement for a rollover and that, to complete the rollover, I must comply with all other tax law requirements for a valid rollover and with your rollover procedures.

Pursuant to Revenue Procedure 2016-47, unless you have actual knowledge to the contrary, you may rely on this certification to show that I have satisfied the conditions for a waiver of the 60-day rollover requirement for the amount identified above. You may not rely on this certification in determining whether the contribution satisfies other requirements for a valid rollover.

Reasons for Late Contribution

I intended to make the rollover within 60 days after receiving the distribution but was unable to do so for the following reason(s) (*check all that apply*):

- ☐ An error was committed by the financial institution making the distribution or receiving the contribution.
- ☐ The distribution was in the form of a check and the check was misplaced and never cashed.
- ☐ The distribution was deposited into and remained in an account that I mistakenly thought was a retirement plan or IRA.
- ☐ My principal residence was severely damaged.
- ☐ One of my family members died.
- ☐ I or one of my family members was seriously ill.
- ☐ I was incarcerated.
- ☐ Restrictions were imposed by a foreign country.
- ☐ A postal error occurred.
- ☐ The distribution was made on account of an IRS levy and the proceeds of the levy have been returned to me.
- ☐ The party making the distribution delayed providing information that the receiving plan or IRA required to complete the rollover despite my reasonable efforts to obtain the information.

Signature

I declare that the representations made in this document are true and that the IRS has not previously denied a request for a waiver of the 60-day rollover requirement with respect to a rollover of all or part of the distribution to which this contribution relates. I understand that in the event I am audited and the IRS does not grant a waiver for this contribution, I may be subject to income and excise taxes, interest, and penalties. If the contribution is made to an IRA, I understand you will be required to report the contribution to the IRS. I also understand that I should retain a copy of this signed certification with my tax records.

Signature: _____

Form **4972**	**Tax on Lump-Sum Distributions** (From Qualified Plans of Participants Born Before January 2, 1936) ▶ Go to *www.irs.gov/Form4972* for the latest information. ▶ Attach to Form 1040, Form 1040NR, or Form 1041.	OMB No. 1545-0193 20**18**

Department of the Treasury
Internal Revenue Service (99)

Attachment Sequence No. **28**

Name of recipient of distribution | Identifying number

Part I	**Complete this part to see if you can use Form 4972**		Yes	No
1	Was this a distribution of a plan participant's entire balance (excluding deductible voluntary employee contributions and certain forfeited amounts) from all of an employer's qualified plans of one kind (for example, pension, profit-sharing, or stock bonus)? If "No," **don't** use this form	1		
2	Did you roll over any part of the distribution? If "Yes," **don't** use this form	2		
3	Was this distribution paid to you as a beneficiary of a plan participant who was born before January 2, 1936?	3		
4	Were you **(a)** a plan participant who received this distribution, **(b)** born before January 2, 1936, **and (c)** a participant in the plan for at least 5 years before the year of the distribution?	4		
	If you answered "No" to both questions 3 **and** 4, **don't** use this form.			
5a	Did you use Form 4972 after 1986 for a previous distribution from your own plan? If "Yes," **don't** use this form for a 2018 distribution from your own plan	5a		
b	If you are receiving this distribution as a beneficiary of a plan participant who died, did you use Form 4972 for a previous distribution received as a beneficiary of that participant after 1986? If "Yes," **don't** use this form for this distribution	5b		

Part II	**Complete this part to choose the 20% capital gain election** (see instructions)		
6	Capital gain part from Form 1099-R, box 3	6	
7	Multiply line 6 by 20% (0.20) . . . . ▶	7	
	If you also choose to use Part III, go to line 8. Otherwise, include the amount from line 7 in the total on Form 1040, line 11; Form 1040NR, line 42; or Form 1041, Schedule G, line 1b. Be sure to check box **2** on Form 1040, line 11, or check box **b** on Form 1040NR, line 42.		

Part III	**Complete this part to choose the 10-year tax option** (see instructions)				
8	If you completed Part II, enter the amount from Form 1099-R, box 2a, minus box 3. If you didn't complete Part II, enter the amount from box 2a. Multiple recipients (and recipients who elect to include net unrealized appreciation (NUA) in taxable income), see instructions		8		
9	Death benefit exclusion for a beneficiary of a plan participant who died before August 21, 1996 .		9		
10	Total taxable amount. Subtract line 9 from line 8		10		
11	Current actuarial value of annuity from Form 1099-R, box 8. If none, enter -0-		11		
12	Adjusted total taxable amount. Add lines 10 and 11. If this amount is $70,000 or more, **skip** lines 13 through 16, enter this amount on line 17, and go to line 18		12		
13	Multiply line 12 by 50% (0.50), but **don't** enter more than $10,000 . .	13			
14	Subtract $20,000 from line 12. If line 12 is $20,000 or less, enter -0-	14			
15	Multiply line 14 by 20% (0.20)	15			
16	Minimum distribution allowance. Subtract line 15 from line 13		16		
17	Subtract line 16 from line 12		17		
18	Federal estate tax attributable to lump-sum distribution		18		
19	Subtract line 18 from line 17. If line 11 is zero, **skip** lines 20 through 22 and go to line 23 . . .		19		
20	Divide line 11 by line 12 and enter the result as a decimal (rounded to at least three places)	20	.		
21	Multiply line 16 by the decimal on line 20	21			
22	Subtract line 21 from line 11	22			
23	Multiply line 19 by 10% (0.10)		23		
24	Tax on amount on line 23. Use the Tax Rate Schedule in the instructions		24		
25	Multiply line 24 by 10.0. If line 11 is zero, **skip** lines 26 through 28, enter this amount on line 29, and go to line 30		25		
26	Multiply line 22 by 10% (0.10)	26			
27	Tax on amount on line 26. Use the Tax Rate Schedule in the instructions	27			
28	Multiply line 27 by 10.0		28		
29	Subtract line 28 from line 25. Multiple recipients, see instructions . . . . ▶		29		
30	**Tax on lump-sum distribution.** Add lines 7 and 29. Also include this amount in the total on Form 1040, line 11 (check box **2**); Form 1040NR, line 42 (check box **b**); or Form 1041, Schedule G, line 1b . . . . ▶		30		

For Paperwork Reduction Act Notice, see instructions.   Cat. No. 13187U   Form **4972** (2018)

Section references are to the Internal Revenue Code.

Future developments. For the latest information about developments related to Form 4972 and its instructions, such as legislation enacted after they were published, go to *www.irs.gov/Form4972.*

General Instructions

Purpose of Form

Use Form 4972 to figure the tax on a qualified lump-sum distribution (defined below) you received in 2018 using the 20% capital gain election, the 10-year tax option, or both. These are special formulas used to figure a separate tax on the distribution that may result in a smaller tax than if you reported the taxable amount of the distribution as ordinary income.

You pay the tax only once, for the year you receive the distribution, not over the next 10 years. The separate tax is added to the regular tax figured on your other income.

Related Publications

For more information related to this topic, see the following publications.
- Pub. 575, Pension and Annuity Income.
- Pub. 721, Tax Guide to U.S. Civil Service Retirement Benefits.
- Pub. 939, General Rule for Pensions and Annuities.

What Is a Qualified Lump-Sum Distribution?

It is the distribution or payment in one tax year of a plan participant's entire balance from all of an employer's qualified plans of one kind (for example, pension, profit-sharing, or stock bonus plans) in which the participant had funds. The participant's entire balance doesn't include deductible voluntary employee contributions or certain forfeited amounts. The participant must have been born before January 2, 1936.

Distributions upon death of the plan participant. If you received a qualified distribution as a beneficiary after the participant's death, the participant must have been born before January 2, 1936, for you to use this form for that distribution.

Distributions to alternate payees. If you are the spouse or former spouse of a plan participant who was born before January 2, 1936, and you received a qualified lump-sum distribution as an alternate payee under a qualified domestic relations order, you can use Form 4972 to figure the tax on the distribution using the 20% capital gain election, the 10-year tax option, or both. For details, see Pub. 575.

Distributions That Don't Qualify for the 20% Capital Gain Election or the 10-Year Tax Option

The following distributions aren't qualified lump-sum distributions and don't qualify for the 20% capital gain election or the 10-year tax option.
- The part of a distribution not rolled over if the distribution is partially rolled over to another qualified plan or an IRA.

- Any distribution if an earlier election to use either the 5- or 10-year tax option had been made after 1986 for the same plan participant.
- U.S. Retirement Plan Bonds distributed with the lump sum.
- A distribution made during the first 5 tax years that the participant was in the plan, unless it was made because the participant died.
- The current actuarial value of any annuity contract included in the lump sum (Form 1099-R, box 8, should show this amount, which you use only to figure tax on the ordinary income part of the distribution).
- A distribution to a 5% owner that is subject to penalties under section 72(m)(5)(A).
- A distribution from an IRA.
- A distribution from a tax-sheltered annuity (section 403(b) plan).
- A distribution of the redemption proceeds of bonds rolled over tax free to a qualified pension plan, etc., from a qualified bond purchase plan.
- A distribution from a qualified plan if the participant or his or her surviving spouse previously received an eligible rollover distribution from the same plan (or another plan of the employer that must be combined with that plan for the lump-sum distribution rules) and the previous distribution was rolled over tax free to another qualified plan or an IRA.
- A distribution from a qualified plan that received a rollover after 2001 from an IRA (other than a conduit IRA), a governmental section 457(b) plan, or a section 403(b) tax-sheltered annuity on behalf of the plan participant.
- A distribution from a qualified plan that received a rollover after 2001 from another qualified plan on behalf of that plan participant's surviving spouse.
- A corrective distribution of excess deferrals, excess contributions, excess aggregate contributions, or excess annual additions.
- A lump-sum credit or payment under the alternative annuity option from the Federal Civil Service Retirement System (or the Federal Employees' Retirement System).

How To Report the Distribution

If you can use Form 4972, attach it to Form 1040 (individuals), Form 1040NR (nonresident aliens), or Form 1041 (estates or trusts). The payer should have given you a Form 1099-R or other statement that shows the amounts needed to complete Form 4972. The following choices are available.

20% capital gain election. If there is an amount in Form 1099-R, box 3, you can use Form 4972, Part II, to apply a 20% tax rate to the capital gain portion. See *Capital Gain Election,* later.

10-year tax option. You can use Part III to figure your tax on the lump-sum distribution using the 10-year tax option whether or not you make the 20% capital gain election.

Taxable amount. If Form 1099-R, box 2a, is blank, you must figure the taxable amount to complete Form 4972. For details, see Pub. 575.

Where to report. Report amounts from your Form 1099-R either directly on your tax return (Form 1040, 1040NR, or 1041) or on Form 4972.

1. If you don't use Form 4972, and you file:

a. **Form 1040.** Report the entire amount from box 1 (Gross distribution) of Form 1099-R on line 4a, and the taxable amount on line 4b. If your pension or annuity is fully taxable, enter the amount from box 2a (Taxable amount) of Form 1099-R on line 4b; don't make an entry on line 4a.

b. **Form 1040NR.** Report the entire amount from box 1 (Gross distribution) of Form 1099-R on line 17a, and the taxable amount on line 17b. If your pension or annuity is fully taxable, enter the amount from box 2a (Taxable amount) of Form 1099-R on line 17b; don't make an entry on line 17a.

c. **Form 1041.** Report the amount on line 8.

2. If you don't use Part III of Form 4972, but use Part II, report only the ordinary income portion of the distribution on Form 1040, lines 4a and 4b; on Form 1040NR, lines 17a and 17b; or on Form 1041, line 8. The ordinary income portion is the amount from box 2a of Form 1099-R, minus the amount from box 3 of that form.

3. If you use Part III of Form 4972, don't include any part of the distribution on Form 1040, lines 4a and 4b; on Form 1040NR, lines 17a and 17b; or on Form 1041, line 8.

The entries in other boxes on Form 1099-R may also apply in completing Form 4972.

- Box 6 (Net unrealized appreciation in employer's securities). See *Net unrealized appreciation (NUA),* later.
- Box 8 (Other). Current actuarial value of an annuity.

How Often You Can Use Form 4972

After 1986, you can use Form 4972 only once for each plan participant. If you receive more than one lump-sum distribution for the same participant in 1 tax year, you must treat all those distributions the same way. Combine them on a single Form 4972.

If you make an election as a beneficiary of a deceased participant, it doesn't affect any election you can make for qualified lump-sum distributions from your own plan. You can also make an election as the beneficiary of more than one qualifying person.

Example. Your mother and father died and each was born before January 2, 1936. Each had a qualified plan of which you are the beneficiary. You also received a qualified lump-sum distribution from your own plan and you were born before January 2, 1936. You can make an election for each of the distributions: one for yourself, one as your mother's beneficiary, and one as your father's beneficiary. It doesn't matter if the distributions all occur in the same year or in different years. File a separate Form 4972 for each participant's distribution.

TIP *An earlier election on Form 4972 or Form 5544 for a distribution before 1987 doesn't prevent you from making an election for a distribution after 1986 for the same participant, provided the participant was under age 59½ at the time of the pre-1987 distribution.*

When To File Form 4972

You can file Form 4972 with either an original or amended return. For an amended return, you generally must file within 3 years after the date the original return was filed or within 2 years after the date the tax was paid, whichever is later, to use any part of Form 4972.

Capital Gain Election

If the distribution includes a capital gain amount, you can (a) make the 20% capital gain election in Part II of Form 4972, or (b) treat the capital gain as ordinary income.

Only the taxable amount of distributions resulting from pre-1974 participation qualifies for capital gain treatment. The capital gain amount should be shown in Form 1099-R, box 3. If there is a net unrealized appreciation (NUA) in Form 1099-R, box 6, part of it will also qualify for capital gain treatment. Use the NUA Worksheet on this page to figure the capital gain part of NUA if you make the election to include NUA in your taxable income.

You can report the ordinary income portion of the distribution on Form 1040, line 4b; Form 1040NR, line 17b; or Form 1041, line 8; or you can figure the tax using the 10-year tax option. The ordinary income portion is generally the amount from Form 1099-R, box 2a, minus the amount from box 3 of that form.

Net unrealized appreciation (NUA). Normally, NUA in employer securities received as part of a lump-sum distribution isn't taxable until the securities are sold. However, you can elect to include NUA in taxable income in the year received.

The total amount to report as NUA should be shown in Form 1099-R, box 6. Part of the amount in box 6 will qualify for capital gain treatment if there is an amount in Form 1099-R, box 3. To figure the total amount subject to capital gain treatment including the NUA, complete the NUA Worksheet on this page.

Specific Instructions

Name of recipient of distribution and identifying number. At the top of Form 4972, fill in the name and identifying number of the recipient of the distribution.

If you received more than one qualified distribution in 2018 for the same plan participant, add them and figure the tax on the total amount. If you received qualified distributions in 2018 for more than one participant, file a separate Form 4972 for the distributions of each participant.

If you and your spouse are filing a joint return and each has received a lump-sum distribution, complete and file a separate Form 4972 for each spouse, combine the tax, and include the combined tax in the total on Form 1040, line 11. Be sure to check box **2** on Form 1040, line 11.

Multiple recipients of a lump-sum distribution. If you are filing for a trust that shared the distribution only with other trusts, figure the tax on the total lump sum first. The trusts then share the tax in the same proportion that they shared the distribution.

If you shared in a lump-sum distribution from a qualified retirement plan when not all recipients were trusts (a percentage will be shown in Form 1099-R, boxes 8 and/or 9a), figure your tax on Form 4972 as follows.

Step 1. Complete Form 4972, Parts I and II. If you make the 20% capital gain election in Part II and also elect to include NUA in taxable income, complete the NUA Worksheet below to determine the amount of NUA that qualifies for capital gain treatment. Then, skip Step 2 and go to Step 3.

Step 2. Use this step only if you don't elect to include NUA in your taxable income or if you don't have NUA.

• If you aren't making the capital gain election, divide the amount from Form 1099-R, box 2a, by your percentage of distribution in box 9a. Enter this amount on Form 4972, line 8.

• If you are making the capital gain election, subtract the amount from Form 1099-R, box 3, from the amount in box 2a. Divide the result by your percentage of distribution from Form 1099-R, box 9a. Enter the result on Form 4972, line 8.

• Complete Form 4972, lines 9 and 10. Divide the amount from Form 1099-R, box 8, by the percentage in box 8. Enter the result on Form 4972, line 11. Then, skip Step 3 and go to Step 4.

Step 3. Use this step only if you elect to include NUA in your taxable income.

• If you aren't making the capital gain election, add the amount from Form 1099-R, box 2a, to the amount in box 6. Divide the result by your percentage of distribution from Form 1099-R, box 9a. Enter the result on Form 4972, line 8. On the dotted line next to line 8, write "NUA" and the amount of NUA included (Form 1099-R, box 6, divided by your percentage of distribution in box 9a).

• If you are making the capital gain election, subtract the amount from Form 1099-R, box 3, from the amount in box 2a. Add to the result the amount from line F of your NUA Worksheet. Then, divide the total by your percentage of distribution from Form 1099-R, box 9a. Enter the result on Form 4972, line 8. On the dotted line next to line 8, write "NUA" and the amount of NUA included (line F of your NUA Worksheet divided by your percentage of distribution from Form 1099-R, box 9a).

• Complete Form 4972, lines 9 and 10. Divide the amount from Form 1099-R, box 8, by the percentage in box 8. Enter the result on Form 4972, line 11.

Step 4. Complete Form 4972 through line 28.

Step 5. Complete the following worksheet to figure the entry for Form 4972, line 29.

A. Subtract line 28 from line 25 . _____

B. Enter your percentage of the distribution from box 9a _____

C. Multiply line A by line B. Enter here and on Form 4972, line 29. Also, write "MRD" on the dotted line next to line 29 . . . . _____

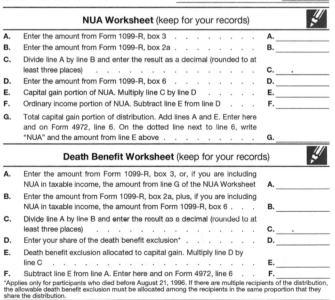

NUA Worksheet (keep for your records)

A. Enter the amount from Form 1099-R, box 3 . . . .   **A.** _____

B. Enter the amount from Form 1099-R, box 2a . . . .   **B.** _____

C. Divide line A by line B and enter the result as a decimal (rounded to at least three places)   . . . .   **C.** . _____

D. Enter the amount from Form 1099-R, box 6 . . . .   **D.** _____

E. Capital gain portion of NUA. Multiply line C by line D   . . . . .   **E.** _____

F. Ordinary income portion of NUA. Subtract line E from line D   . . .   **F.** _____

G. Total capital gain portion of distribution. Add lines A and E. Enter here and on Form 4972, line 6. On the dotted line next to line 6, write "NUA" and the amount from line E above . . . .   **G.** _____

Death Benefit Worksheet (keep for your records)

A. Enter the amount from Form 1099-R, box 3, or, if you are including NUA in taxable income, the amount from line G of the NUA Worksheet   **A.** _____

B. Enter the amount from Form 1099-R, box 2a, plus, if you are including NUA in taxable income, the amount from Form 1099-R, box 6 . . .   **B.** _____

C. Divide line A by line B and enter the result as a decimal (rounded to at least three places)   . . . .   **C.** . _____

D. Enter your share of the death benefit exclusion* . . . .   **D.** _____

E. Death benefit exclusion allocated to capital gain. Multiply line D by line C   . . . .   **E.** _____

F. Subtract line E from line A. Enter here and on Form 4972, line 6   .   **F.** _____

*Applies only for participants who died before August 21, 1996. If there are multiple recipients of the distribution, the allowable death benefit exclusion must be allocated among the recipients in the same proportion that they share the distribution.

Form 4972 (2018)   Page **4**

Part II

See *Capital Gain Election,* earlier, before completing Part II.

Line 6. Leave this line blank if your distribution doesn't include a capital gain amount or you aren't making the 20% capital gain election, and go to Part III.

Generally, enter on line 6 the amount from Form 1099-R, box 3. However, if you elect to include NUA in your taxable income, use the NUA Worksheet, earlier, to figure the amount to enter on line 6. If you are taking a death benefit exclusion (see *Line 9* below for the definition), use the Death Benefit Worksheet, earlier, to figure the amount to enter on line 6. The remaining allowable death benefit exclusion should be entered on line 9 if you choose the 10-year tax option.

If any federal estate tax was paid on the lump-sum distribution, you must decrease the capital gain amount by the amount of estate tax applicable to it. To figure this amount, you must complete the Death Benefit Worksheet, earlier, through line C, even if you don't take the death benefit exclusion. Multiply the total federal estate tax paid on the lump-sum distribution (get this amount from the administrator of the deceased's estate) by the decimal on line C of the Death Benefit Worksheet. The result is the portion of the federal estate tax applicable to the capital gain amount. Then, use that result to reduce the amount in Form 1099-R, box 3, if you don't take the death benefit exclusion, or reduce line F of the Death Benefit Worksheet if you do. Enter the remaining capital gain on line 6. If you elected to include NUA in taxable income and you didn't take the death benefit exclusion, subtract the portion of federal estate tax applicable to the capital gain amount from the amount on line G of the NUA Worksheet. Enter the result on line 6. Enter the remainder of the federal estate tax on line 18.

If you take the death benefit exclusion and federal estate tax was paid on the capital gain amount, the capital gain amount must be reduced by both the procedures discussed above to figure the correct entry for line 6.

Part III

Multiple recipients, see *Multiple recipients of a lump-sum distribution,* earlier.

Line 8. If Form 1099-R, box 2a, is blank, you must first figure the taxable amount. For details on how to do this, see Pub. 575.

If you made the 20% capital gain election, enter only the ordinary income portion of the distribution on this line. The ordinary income portion is the amount from Form 1099-R, box 2a, minus the amount from box 3 of that form. Add the amount from line F of the NUA Worksheet if you included NUA capital gain in the 20% capital gain election. On the dotted line next to line 8, write "NUA" and the amount from line F of the NUA Worksheet.

If you didn't make the 20% capital gain election and didn't elect to include NUA in taxable income, enter the amount from Form 1099-R, box 2a. If you didn't make the 20% capital gain election but did elect to include NUA in your taxable income, add the amount from Form 1099-R, box 2a, to the amount from Form 1099-R, box 6. Enter the total on line 8. On the dotted line next to line 8, write "NUA" and the amount from Form 1099-R, box 6.

 Community property laws don't apply in figuring tax on the amount you report on line 8.

Line 9. If you received the distribution because of the plan participant's death and the participant died before August 21, 1996, you may be able to exclude up to $5,000 of the lump sum from your gross income. This exclusion applies to the beneficiaries or estates of common-law employees, self-employed individuals, and shareholder-employees who owned more than 2% of the stock of an S corporation.

Enter the allowable death benefit exclusion on line 9. If you made the 20% capital gain election, enter the amount from line D of the Death Benefit Worksheet minus the amount from line E of that worksheet.

Multiple recipients. If there are multiple recipients of the distribution not all of whom are trusts, and you didn't complete Part II, enter the full allowable death benefit exclusion on line 9. Don't allocate the exclusion among the recipients; the computation under *Multiple recipients of a lump-sum distribution,* earlier, effectively allocates the exclusion.

If you completed Part II, multiply the full allowable death benefit exclusion (don't allocate among the recipients) by the percentage on line C of the Death Benefit Worksheet. Subtract the result from the full allowable death benefit exclusion. Enter the result on line 9.

Line 18. A beneficiary who receives a lump-sum distribution because of a plan participant's death must reduce the taxable part of the distribution by any federal estate tax paid on the lump-sum distribution (get this amount from the administrator of the deceased's estate). Do this by entering on line 18 the federal estate tax attributable to the lump-sum distribution. Also see *Line 6* above if you made a capital gain election.

Lines 24 and 27. Use the following Tax Rate Schedule to complete lines 24 and 27.

Line 29. Multiple recipients, see *Multiple recipients of a lump-sum distribution,* earlier.

Tax Rate Schedule

If the amount on line 23 or 26 is:		Enter on line 24 or 27:	
Over	But not over—		Of the amount over—
$ 0	$ 1,190	- - - - - 11%	$ 0
1,190	2,270	$130.90 + 12%	1,190
2,270	4,530	260.50 + 14%	2,270
4,530	6,690	576.90 + 15%	4,530
6,690	9,170	900.90 + 16%	6,690
9,170	11,440	1,297.70 + 18%	9,170
11,440	13,710	1,706.30 + 20%	11,440
13,710	17,160	2,160.30 + 23%	13,710
17,160	22,880	2,953.80 + 26%	17,160
22,880	28,600	4,441.00 + 30%	22,880
28,600	34,320	6,157.00 + 34%	28,600
34,320	42,300	8,101.80 + 38%	34,320
42,300	57,190	11,134.20 + 42%	42,300
57,190	85,790	17,388.00 + 48%	57,190
85,790	- - - - -	31,116.00 + 50%	85,790

Paperwork Reduction Act Notice. We ask for the information on this form to carry out the Internal Revenue laws of the United States. You are required to give us the information. We need it to ensure that you are complying with these laws and to allow us to figure and collect the right amount of tax.

You aren't required to provide the information requested on a form that is subject to the Paperwork Reduction Act unless the form displays a valid OMB control number. Books or records relating to a form or its instructions must be retained as long as their contents may become material in the administration of any Internal Revenue law. Generally, tax returns and return information are confidential, as required by section 6103.

The time needed to complete this form will vary depending on individual circumstances. The estimated burden for individual taxpayers filing this form is approved under OMB control number 1545-0074 and is included in the estimates shown in the instructions for their individual income tax return. The estimated burden for all other taxpayers who file this form is shown below.

Recordkeeping	. 19 min.
Learning about the law or the form	1 hr., 36 min.
Preparing the form . . .	2 hr., 7 min.
Copying, assembling, and sending the form to the IRS .	. 20 min.

If you have comments concerning the accuracy of these time estimates or suggestions for making this form simpler, we would be happy to hear from you. See the instructions for the tax return with which this form is filed.

Tax Rate Schedule for 1986				
If the amount on line 30 or 33 is:		**Enter on line 31 or 34:**		
Over—	But not over—	Amount	Plus percentage	Of the amount over—
$0	$1,190	- - - - -	11%	$0
1,190	2,270	$130.90	+ 12%	1,190
2,270	4,530	260.50	+ 14%	2,270
4,530	6,690	576.90	+ 15%	4,530
6,690	9,170	900.90	+ 16%	6,690
9,170	11,440	1,297.70	+ 18%	9,170
11,440	13,710	1,706.30	+ 20%	11,440
13,710	17,160	2,160.30	+ 23%	13,710
17,160	22,880	2,953.80	+ 26%	17,160
22,880	28,600	4,441.00	+ 30%	22,880
28,600	34,320	6,157.00	+ 34%	28,600
34,320	42,300	8,101.80	+ 38%	34,320
42,300	57,190	11,134.20	+ 42%	42,300
57,190	85,790	17,388.00	+ 48%	57,190
85,790	- - - - -	31,116.00	+ 50%	85,790

Form **5329**	**Additional Taxes on Qualified Plans (Including IRAs) and Other Tax-Favored Accounts**	OMB No. 1545-0074
Department of the Treasury Internal Revenue Service (99)	▶ Attach to Form 1040 or Form 1040NR. ▶ Go to *www.irs.gov/Form5329* for instructions and the latest information.	20**18** Attachment Sequence No. **29**

Name of individual subject to additional tax. If married filing jointly, see instructions.		Your social security number

Fill in Your Address Only if You Are Filing This Form by Itself and Not With Your Tax Return ▶

Home address (number and street), or P.O. box if mail is not delivered to your home		Apt. no.
City, town or post office, state, and ZIP code. If you have a foreign address, also complete the spaces below. See instructions.		If this is an amended return, check here ▶ ☐
Foreign country name	Foreign province/state/county	Foreign postal code

If you **only** owe the additional 10% tax on early distributions, you may be able to report this tax directly on Schedule 4 (Form 1040), line 59, or Form 1040NR, line 57, without filing Form 5329. See the instructions for Schedule 4 (Form 1040), line 59, or for Form 1040NR, line 57.

Part I   **Additional Tax on Early Distributions.** Complete this part if you took a taxable distribution (other than a qualified 2017 disaster distribution) before you reached age 59½ from a qualified retirement plan (including an IRA) or modified endowment contract (unless you are reporting this tax directly on Form 1040 or Form 1040NR—see above). You may also have to complete this part to indicate that you qualify for an exception to the additional tax on early distributions or for certain Roth IRA distributions. See instructions.

1	Early distributions included in income. For Roth IRA distributions, see instructions	**1**	
2	Early distributions included on line 1 that are not subject to the additional tax (see instructions). Enter the appropriate exception number from the instructions: _____	**2**	
3	Amount subject to additional tax. Subtract line 2 from line 1	**3**	
4	**Additional tax.** Enter 10% (0.10) of line 3. Include this amount on Schedule 4 (Form 1040), line 59, or 1040NR, line 57	**4**	
	Caution: If any part of the amount on line 3 was a distribution from a SIMPLE IRA, you may have to include 25% of that amount on line 4 instead of 10%. See instructions.	**8**	

Part II   **Additional Tax on Certain Distributions From Education Accounts and ABLE Accounts.** Complete this part if you included an amount in income, on Schedule 1 (Form 1040), line 21, or Form 1040NR, line 21, from a Coverdell education savings account (ESA), a qualified tuition program (QTP), or an ABLE account.

5	Distributions included in income from a Coverdell ESA, a QTP, or an ABLE account	**5**	
6	Distributions included on line 5 that are not subject to the additional tax (see instructions) . . .	**6**	
7	Amount subject to additional tax. Subtract line 6 from line 5	**7**	
8	**Additional tax.** Enter 10% (0.10) of line 7. Include this amount on Schedule 4 (Form 1040), line 59, or Form 1040NR, line 57	**8**	

Part III   **Additional Tax on Excess Contributions to Traditional IRAs.** Complete this part if you contributed more to your traditional IRAs for 2018 than is allowable or you had an amount on line 17 of your 2017 Form 5329.

9	Enter your excess contributions from line 16 of your 2017 Form 5329. See instructions. If zero, go to line 15		**9**	
10	If your traditional IRA contributions for 2018 are less than your maximum allowable contribution, see instructions. Otherwise, enter -0-	**10**		
11	2018 traditional IRA distributions included in income (see instructions) .	**11**		
12	2018 distributions of prior year excess contributions (see instructions) .	**12**		
13	Add lines 10, 11, and 12		**13**	
14	Prior year excess contributions. Subtract line 13 from line 9. If zero or less, enter -0-		**14**	
15	Excess contributions for 2018 (see instructions)		**15**	
16	Total excess contributions. Add lines 14 and 15		**16**	
17	**Additional tax.** Enter 6% (0.06) of the **smaller** of line 16 **or** the value of your traditional IRAs on December 31, 2018 (including 2018 contributions made in 2019). Include this amount on Schedule 4 (Form 1040), line 59, or Form 1040NR, line 57 . . .		**17**	

Part IV   **Additional Tax on Excess Contributions to Roth IRAs.** Complete this part if you contributed more to your Roth IRAs for 2018 than is allowable or you had an amount on line 25 of your 2017 Form 5329.

18	Enter your excess contributions from line 24 of your 2017 Form 5329. See instructions. If zero, go to line 23		**18**	
19	If your Roth IRA contributions for 2018 are less than your maximum allowable contribution, see instructions. Otherwise, enter -0-	**19**		
20	2018 distributions from your Roth IRAs (see instructions)	**20**		
21	Add lines 19 and 20		**21**	
22	Prior year excess contributions. Subtract line 21 from line 18. If zero or less, enter -0-		**22**	
23	Excess contributions for 2018 (see instructions)		**23**	
24	Total excess contributions. Add lines 22 and 23		**24**	
25	**Additional tax.** Enter 6% (0.06) of the **smaller** of line 24 **or** the value of your Roth IRAs on December 31, 2018 (including 2018 contributions made in 2019). Include this amount on Schedule 4 (Form 1040), line 59, or Form 1040NR, line 57 . .		**25**	

For Privacy Act and Paperwork Reduction Act Notice, see your tax return instructions.   Cat. No. 13329Q   Form **5329** (2018)

Form 5329 (2018)   Page **2**

Part V — Additional Tax on Excess Contributions to Coverdell ESAs. Complete this part if the contributions to your Coverdell ESAs for 2018 were more than is allowable or you had an amount on line 33 of your 2017 Form 5329.

26	Enter the excess contributions from line 32 of your 2017 Form 5329. See instructions. If zero, go to line 31	**26**	
27	If the contributions to your Coverdell ESAs for 2018 were less than the maximum allowable contribution, see instructions. Otherwise, enter -0-	**27**	
28	2018 distributions from your Coverdell ESAs (see instructions) . . .	**28**	
29	Add lines 27 and 28	**29**	
30	Prior year excess contributions. Subtract line 29 from line 26. If zero or less, enter -0- . . .	**30**	
31	Excess contributions for 2018 (see instructions)	**31**	
32	Total excess contributions. Add lines 30 and 31	**32**	
33	**Additional tax.** Enter 6% (0.06) of the **smaller** of line 32 **or** the value of your Coverdell ESAs on December 31, 2018 (including 2018 contributions made in 2019). Include this amount on Schedule 4 (Form 1040), line 59, or Form 1040NR, line 57	**33**	

Part VI — Additional Tax on Excess Contributions to Archer MSAs. Complete this part if you or your employer contributed more to your Archer MSAs for 2018 than is allowable or you had an amount on line 41 of your 2017 Form 5329.

34	Enter the excess contributions from line 40 of your 2017 Form 5329. See instructions. If zero, go to line 39	**34**	
35	If the contributions to your Archer MSAs for 2018 are less than the maximum allowable contribution, see instructions. Otherwise, enter -0-	**35**	
36	2018 distributions from your Archer MSAs from Form 8853, line 8 . .	**36**	
37	Add lines 35 and 36	**37**	
38	Prior year excess contributions. Subtract line 37 from line 34. If zero or less, enter -0-	**38**	
39	Excess contributions for 2018 (see instructions)	**39**	
40	Total excess contributions. Add lines 38 and 39	**40**	
41	**Additional tax.** Enter 6% (0.06) of the **smaller** of line 40 **or** the value of your Archer MSAs on December 31, 2018 (including 2018 contributions made in 2019). Include this amount on Schedule 4 (Form 1040), line 59, or Form 1040NR, line 57	**41**	

Part VII — Additional Tax on Excess Contributions to Health Savings Accounts (HSAs). Complete this part if you, someone on your behalf, or your employer contributed more to your HSAs for 2018 than is allowable or you had an amount on line 49 of your 2017 Form 5329.

42	Enter the excess contributions from line 48 of your 2017 Form 5329. If zero, go to line 47 . . .	**42**	
43	If the contributions to your HSAs for 2018 are less than the maximum allowable contribution, see instructions. Otherwise, enter -0-	**43**	
44	2018 distributions from your HSAs from Form 8889, line 16	**44**	
45	Add lines 43 and 44	**45**	
46	Prior year excess contributions. Subtract line 45 from line 42. If zero or less, enter -0-	**46**	
47	Excess contributions for 2018 (see instructions)	**47**	
48	Total excess contributions. Add lines 46 and 47	**48**	
49	**Additional tax.** Enter 6% (0.06) of the **smaller** of line 48 **or** the value of your HSAs on December 31, 2018 (including 2018 contributions made in 2019). Include this amount on Schedule 4 (Form 1040), line 59, or Form 1040NR, line 57	**49**	

Part VIII — Additional Tax on Excess Contributions to an ABLE Account. Complete this part if contributions to your ABLE account for 2018 were more than is allowable.

50	Excess contributions for 2018 (see instructions)	**50**	
51	**Additional tax.** Enter 6% (0.06) of the **smaller** of line 50 **or** the value of your ABLE account on December 31, 2018. Include this amount on Schedule 4 (Form 1040), line 59, or Form 1040NR, line 57	**51**	

Part IX — Additional Tax on Excess Accumulation in Qualified Retirement Plans (Including IRAs). Complete this part if you did not receive the minimum required distribution from your qualified retirement plan.

52	Minimum required distribution for 2018 (see instructions)	**52**	
53	Amount actually distributed to you in 2018	**53**	
54	Subtract line 53 from line 52. If zero or less, enter -0-	**54**	
55	**Additional tax.** Enter 50% (0.50) of line 54. Include this amount on Schedule 4 (Form 1040), line 59, or Form 1040NR, line 57	**55**	

Sign Here Only if You Are Filing This Form by Itself and Not With Your Tax Return

Under penalties of perjury, I declare that I have examined this form, including accompanying attachments, and to the best of my knowledge and belief, it is true, correct, and complete. Declaration of preparer (other than taxpayer) is based on all information of which preparer has any knowledge.

▶ _____   ▶ _____
Your signature   Date

Paid Preparer Use Only	Print/Type preparer's name	Preparer's signature	Date	Check ☐ if self-employed	PTIN
	Firm's name ▶			Firm's EIN ▶	
	Firm's address ▶			Phone no.	

Form **5329** (2018)

20**18**

Instructions for Form 5329

Additional Taxes on Qualified Plans (Including IRAs) and Other Tax-Favored Accounts

 Department of the Treasury
Internal Revenue Service

Section references are to the Internal Revenue Code unless otherwise noted.

General Instructions

What's New

2018 Form 1040 redesigned. The 2018 Form 1040 has been redesigned and is supplemented with new Schedules 1 through 6. These additional schedules will be used as needed to complete more complex tax returns. References to Form 1040 and its related schedules have been revised accordingly in these instructions.

Reminder

The additional tax on early distributions doesn't apply to qualified 2017 disaster distributions. See the 2018 Form 8915B for more details.

> ⚠️ *At the time these instructions went to print, Congress was considering legislation that would provide additional tax relief for those affected by 2018 disasters. See IRS.gov/DisasterTaxRelief for information and updates.*

Future Developments

For the latest information about developments related to Form 5329 and its instructions, such as legislation enacted after they were published, go to *IRS.gov/Form5329*.

Purpose of Form

Use Form 5329 to report additional taxes on:
- IRAs,
- Other qualified retirement plans,
- Modified endowment contracts,
- Coverdell ESAs,
- QTPs,
- Archer MSAs,
- HSAs, or
- ABLE accounts.

Who Must File

You must file Form 5329 if any of the following apply, except you don't have to file Form 5329 to report a qualified 2017 disaster distribution.

- You received a distribution from a Roth IRA and either the amount on line 25c of Form 8606, Nondeductible IRAs, is more than zero, or the distribution includes a recapture amount subject to the 10% additional tax, or it's a qualified first-time homebuyer distribution (see *Distributions from Roth IRAs*, later).
- You received a distribution subject to the tax on early distributions from a qualified retirement plan (other than a Roth IRA). However, if distribution code 1 is correctly shown in box 7 of all your Forms 1099-R, and you owe the additional tax on each Form 1099-R, you don't have to file Form 5329. Instead, see the instructions for Schedule 4 (Form 1040), line 59, in the Instructions for Form 1040, or Form 1040NR, line 57, for how to report the 10% additional tax directly on that line.
- You received a distribution subject to the tax on early distributions from a qualified retirement plan (other than a Roth IRA), you meet an exception to the tax on early distributions from the list shown later, but box 7 of your Form 1099-R doesn't indicate an exception or the exception doesn't apply to the entire distribution.
- You received taxable distributions from Coverdell ESAs, QTPs, or ABLE accounts.
- The contributions for 2018 to your traditional IRAs, Roth IRAs, Coverdell ESAs, Archer MSAs, HSAs, or ABLE accounts exceed your maximum contribution limit, or you had a tax due from an excess contribution on line 17, 25, 33, 41, or 49 of your 2017 Form 5329.
- You didn't receive the minimum required distribution from your qualified retirement plan. This also includes trusts and estates that didn't receive this amount.

> 💡 *If you rolled over part or all of a distribution from a qualified retirement plan, the part rolled over isn't subject to the 10% additional tax on early distributions. See the instructions for Form 1040, lines 4a and 4b, or Form 1040NR, lines 17a and 17b, for how to report the rollover.*

When and Where To File

File Form 5329 with your 2018 Form 1040 or Form 1040NR by the due date, including extensions, of your Form 1040 or Form 1040NR.

If you don't have to file a 2018 income tax return, complete and file Form 5329 by itself at the time and place you would be required to file Form 1040 or Form 1040NR. If you file Form 5329 by itself, then it can't be filed electronically. Be sure to include your address on page 1 of the form and your signature and the date on page 2 of the form. Enclose, but don't attach, a check or money order payable to "United States Treasury" for any taxes due. Write your social security number and "2018 Form 5329" on the check. For information on other payment options, including credit or debit card payments, see the instructions for Form 1040 or Form 1040NR, or go to IRS.gov.

Prior tax years. If you are filing Form 5329 for a prior year, you must use the prior year's version of the form. If you don't have any other changes and haven't previously filed a federal income tax return for the prior year, file the prior year's version of Form 5329 by itself (discussed earlier). If you have other changes, file Form 5329 for the prior year with Form 1040X, Amended U.S. Individual Income Tax Return.

Definitions

Qualified retirement plan. A qualified retirement plan includes:
- A qualified pension, profit-sharing, or stock bonus plan (including a 401(k) plan);
- A tax-sheltered annuity contract;
- A qualified annuity plan; and
- An IRA.

Note. Modified endowment contracts aren't qualified retirement plans.

Traditional IRAs. For purposes of Form 5329, a traditional IRA is any IRA, including a simplified employee pension (SEP) IRA, other than a SIMPLE IRA or Roth IRA.

Early distribution. Generally, any distribution from your IRA, other

Cat. No. 13330R

qualified retirement plan, or modified endowment contract before you reach age 59½ is an early distribution.

Qualified retirement plan rollover. Generally, a rollover is a tax-free distribution of assets from one qualified retirement plan that is reinvested in another plan or the same plan. Generally, you must complete the rollover within 60 days of receiving the distribution. Any taxable amount not rolled over must be included in income and may be subject to the 10% additional tax on early distributions.

You can roll over (convert) amounts from a qualified retirement plan to a Roth IRA. Any amount rolled over to a Roth IRA is subject to the same rules for converting a traditional IRA to a Roth IRA. You must include in your gross income distributions from a qualified retirement plan that you would have had to include in income if you hadn't rolled them into a Roth IRA. The 10% additional tax on early distributions doesn't apply. For more information, see chapter 2 of Pub. 590-A.

Pursuant to Rev. Proc. 2016-47 in Internal Revenue Bulletin 2016-37, available at *IRS.gov/irb/ 2016-37_IRB#RP-2016–47*, you may make a written certification to a plan administrator or an IRA trustee that you missed the 60-day rollover contribution deadline because of one or more of the 11 reasons listed in Rev. Proc. 2016-47. See Rev. Proc. 2016-47 for information on how to self-certify for a waiver. Also see *Time Limit for Making a Rollover Contribution* under *Can You Move Retirement Plan Assets?* in Pub. 590-A for more information on ways to get a waiver of the 60-day rollover requirement.

Note. The following are effective January 1, 2018.
• If a plan loan offset is due to plan termination or severance from employment, you have until the due date, including extensions, to file your tax return for the tax year in which the offset occurs to roll over the plan loan offset amount.
• If a retirement account has been wrongfully levied by the IRS, the amount returned plus interest on such amount may be contributed to the account or to an individual retirement plan (other than an endowment contract) to which such a rollover contribution is permitted. You have until the due date, excluding extensions, for filing your tax return for the tax year in which the amount is returned, to make the contribution.

In-plan Roth rollover. If you are a participant in a 401(k), 403(b), or governmental 457(b) plan, your plan may permit you to roll over amounts from those plans to a designated Roth account within the same plan. The rollover of any untaxed amounts must be included in income. The 10% additional tax on early distributions doesn't apply. For more information, see *In-plan Roth rollovers* under *Rollovers* in Pub. 575.

Compensation. Compensation includes wages, salaries, tips, bonuses, and other pay you receive for services you perform. It also includes sales commissions, commissions on insurance premiums, and pay based on a percentage of profits. It includes net earnings from self-employment, but only for a trade or business in which your personal services are a material income-producing factor.

For IRAs, treat nontaxable combat pay and any differential wage payments, and all taxable alimony received under a decree of divorce or separate maintenance as compensation.

Compensation doesn't include any amounts received as a pension or annuity and doesn't include any amount received as deferred compensation.

Taxable compensation is your compensation that is included in gross income reduced by any deductions on Schedule 1 (Form 1040), lines 27 and 28, or Form 1040NR, lines 27 and 28, but not by any loss from self-employment.

ABLE rollover. For an ABLE account, a rollover means a contribution to an ABLE account of a designated beneficiary (or of an eligible individual who is a member of the family of the designated beneficiary) of all or a portion of an amount withdrawn from the designated beneficiary's ABLE account. The contribution must be made within 60 days of the withdrawal date; and, if the rollover is to the designated beneficiary's ABLE account, there must have been no rollover to an ABLE account of that beneficiary within the prior 12 months. An ABLE rollover doesn't include a contribution to an ABLE account of funds distributed from a QTP account.

Program-to-program transfer. For an ABLE account, a program-to-program transfer includes the direct transfer of the entire balance of an ABLE account into a second ABLE account if both accounts have the same designated beneficiary and the first

ABLE account is closed upon completion of the transfer. A program-to-program transfer also occurs when part or all of the balance in an ABLE account is transferred to the ABLE account of an eligible individual who is a member of the family of the former designated beneficiary, as long as no intervening distribution is made to the designated beneficiary.

Additional Information
See the following publications for more information about the items in these instructions.
• Pub. 560, Retirement Plans for Small Business.
• Pub. 575, Pension and Annuity Income.
• Pub. 590-A, Contributions to Individual Retirement Arrangements (IRAs).
• Pub. 590-B, Distributions from Individual Retirement Arrangements (IRAs).
• Pub. 721, Tax Guide to U.S. Civil Service Retirement Benefits.
• Pub. 969, Health Savings Accounts and Other Tax-Favored Health Plans.
• Pub. 970, Tax Benefits for Education.
• Pub. 976, Disaster Relief.

Specific Instructions

Joint returns. If both you and your spouse are required to file Form 5329, complete a separate form for each of you. Include the combined tax on Schedule 4 (Form 1040), line 59.

Amended returns. If you are filing an amended 2018 Form 5329, check the box at the top of page 1 of the form. Don't use the 2018 Form 5329 to amend your return for any other year. For information about amending a Form 5329 for a prior year, see *Prior tax years*, earlier.

Part I—Additional Tax on Early Distributions
In general, if you receive an early distribution (including an involuntary cashout) from an IRA, other qualified retirement plan, or modified endowment contract, the part of the distribution included in income generally is subject to the 10% additional tax. But see *Distributions from a designated Roth account* and *Distributions from Roth IRAs*, later.

The additional tax on early distributions doesn't apply to any of the following.

- A qualified 2017 disaster distribution. See the 2018 Form 8915B for more details.
- A qualified HSA funding distribution from an IRA (other than a SEP or SIMPLE IRA). See *Qualified HSA funding distribution* under *Health Savings Accounts* in Pub. 969 for details.
- A distribution from a traditional or SIMPLE IRA that was converted to a Roth IRA.
- A rollover from a qualified retirement plan to a Roth IRA.
- An in-plan Roth rollover.
- A distribution of certain excess IRA contributions (see the instructions for line 15, later, and the instructions for line 23, later).

Note. Any related IRA earnings withdrawn with excess IRA contributions are subject to the 10% additional tax on early distributions if you were under age 59½ at the time of the distribution.

- A distribution of excess deferrals. Excess deferrals include distributions of excess contributions from a qualified cash or deferred arrangement (section 401(k) plan), excess contributions from a tax-sheltered annuity (section 403(b) plan), excess contributions from a salary reduction SEP IRA, and excess contributions from a SIMPLE IRA.
- A distribution of excess aggregate contributions to meet nondiscrimination requirements for employee contributions and matching employer contributions.
- A distribution from an eligible governmental section 457 deferred compensation plan to the extent the distribution isn't attributable to an amount transferred from a qualified retirement plan.

See the instructions for line 2, later, for other distributions that aren't subject to the additional tax.

Line 1

Enter the amount of early distributions included in income that you received from:

- A qualified retirement plan, including earnings on withdrawn excess contributions to your IRAs included in income in 2018; or
- A modified endowment contract.

Certain prohibited transactions involving your IRA, such as borrowing from your IRA or pledging your IRA assets as security for a loan, are considered to be distributions and are generally subject to the additional tax on early distributions. See *Prohibited Transactions* under *What Acts Result in Penalties or Additional Taxes?* in Pub. 590-B for details.

Distributions from a designated Roth account. If you received an early distribution from your designated Roth account, include on line 1 the amount of the distribution that you must include in your income. You will find this amount in box 2a of your 2018 Form 1099-R. You also may need to include a recapture amount on line 1 if you have ever made an in-plan Roth rollover (discussed later).

TIP *If you never made an in-plan Roth rollover, you need to include on line 1 of this form only the amount from box 2a of your 2018 Form 1099-R reporting the early distribution.*

Recapture amount subject to the additional tax on early distributions. If you have ever made an in-plan Roth rollover and you received an early distribution for 2018, the recapture amount to include on line 1 is a portion of the amounts you rolled over.

The recapture amount that you must include on line 1 won't exceed the amount of your early distribution; and, for purposes of determining this recapture amount, you will allocate a rollover amount (or portion thereof) to an early distribution only once.

For more information about the recapture amount for early distributions from a designated Roth account, including how to figure it, see *Tax on Early Distributions* under *Special Additional Taxes* in Pub. 575.

Distributions from Roth IRAs. If you received an early distribution from your Roth IRAs, include on line 1 the part of the distribution that you must include in your income. You will find this amount on line 25c of your 2018 Form 8606. You also will need to include on line 1 the following amounts.

- A qualified first-time homebuyer distribution from line 20 of your 2018 Form 8606. Also include this amount on line 2 and enter exception number 09.
- Recapture amounts attributable to any conversions or rollovers to your Roth IRAs in 2014 through 2018. See *Recapture amount subject to the additional tax on early distributions* next.

TIP *If you didn't have a qualified first-time homebuyer distribution in 2018, and you didn't convert or roll over an amount to your Roth IRAs in 2014 through 2018, you only need to* include the amount from line 25c of your 2018 Form 8606 on line 1 of this form.

Recapture amount subject to the additional tax on early distributions. If you converted or rolled over an amount to your Roth IRAs in 2014 through 2018 and you received an early distribution for 2018, the recapture amount you must include on line 1 is the amount, if any, of the early distribution allocated to the taxable portion of your 2014 through 2018 conversions or rollovers.

Generally, an early distribution is allocated to your Roth IRA contributions first, then to your conversions and rollovers on a first-in, first-out basis. For each conversion or rollover, you must first allocate the early distribution to the portion that was subject to tax in the year of the conversion or rollover, and then to the portion that wasn't subject to tax. The recapture amount is the sum of the early distribution amounts that you allocate to these taxable portions of your conversions or rollovers.

The recapture amount that you must include on line 1 won't exceed the amount of your early distribution; and, for purposes of determining this recapture amount, you will allocate a contribution, conversion, or rollover amount (or portion thereof) to an early distribution only once.

For more information about the recapture amount for distributions from a Roth IRA, including how to figure it, see *Ordering Rules for Distributions* under *Are Distributions Taxable?* in chapter 2 of Pub. 590-B. Also, see *Example* next, which illustrates a situation where a taxpayer must include a recapture amount on line 1.

Example. You converted $20,000 from a traditional IRA to a Roth IRA in 2014 and converted $10,000 in 2015. Your 2014 Form 8606 had $5,000 on line 17 and $15,000 on line 18, and your 2015 Form 8606 had $3,000 on line 17 and $7,000 on line 18. You made Roth IRA contributions of $2,000 for 2014 and 2015. You didn't make any Roth IRA conversions or contributions for 2016 through 2018, or take any Roth IRA distributions before 2018.

On July 10, 2018, at age 53, you took a $33,000 distribution from your Roth IRA. Your 2018 Form 8606 shows $33,000 on line 19; $29,000 on line 23 ($33,000 minus $4,000 for your contributions on line 22); and $0 on line 25a ($29,000 minus your basis in conversions of $30,000).

First, $4,000 of the $33,000 is allocated to your 2018 Form 8606, line 22; then $15,000 to your 2014 Form 8606, line 18; $5,000 to your 2014 Form 8606, line 17; and $7,000 to your 2015 Form 8606, line 18. The remaining $2,000 is allocated to the $3,000 on your 2015 Form 8606, line 17. On line 1, enter $22,000 ($15,000 allocated to your 2014 Form 8606, line 18, plus the $7,000 that was allocated to your 2015 Form 8606, line 18).

If you take a Roth IRA distribution in 2019, the first $1,000 will be allocated to the $1,000 remaining from your 2015 Form 8606, line 17, and won't be subject to the additional tax on early distributions.

Additional information. For more details, see *Are Distributions Taxable?* in chapters 1 and 2 of Pub. 590-B.

Line 2

The additional tax on early distributions doesn't apply to the distributions described next. Enter on line 2 the amount that you can exclude. In the space provided, enter the applicable exception number (01–12). If more than one exception applies, enter 12.

Exceptions to the Additional Tax on Early Distributions

No. Exception

01 Qualified retirement plan distributions (doesn't apply to IRAs) you receive after separation from service when the separation from service occurs in or after the year you reach age 55 (age 50 for qualified public safety employees).

02 Distributions made as part of a series of substantially equal periodic payments (made at least annually) for your life (or life expectancy) or the joint lives (or joint life expectancies) of you and your designated beneficiary (if from an employer plan, payments must begin after separation from service).

03 Distributions due to total and permanent disability. You are considered disabled if you can furnish proof that you can't do any substantial gainful activity because of your physical or mental condition. A medical determination that your condition can be expected to result in death or to be of long, continued, and indefinite duration must be made.

04 Distributions due to death (doesn't apply to modified endowment contracts).

05 Qualified retirement plan distributions up to the amount you paid for unreimbursed medical expenses during the year **minus** 7.5% of your adjusted gross income (AGI) for the year.

06 Qualified retirement plan distributions made to an alternate payee under a qualified domestic relations order (doesn't apply to IRAs).

07 IRA distributions made to certain unemployed individuals for health insurance premiums.

08 IRA distributions made for qualified higher education expenses.

09 IRA distributions made for the purchase of a first home, up to $10,000.

10 Qualified retirement plan distributions made due to an IRS levy.

11 Qualified distributions to reservists while serving on active duty for at least 180 days.

12 Other (see *Other* next). Also, enter this code if more than one exception applies.

Other. The following exceptions also apply.

• Distributions incorrectly indicated as early distributions by code 1, J, or S in box 7 of Form 1099-R. Include on line 2 the amount you received when you were age 59½ or older.

• Distributions from a section 457 plan, which aren't from a rollover from a qualified retirement plan.

• Distributions from a plan maintained by an employer if:

1. You separated from service by March 1, 1986;

2. As of March 1, 1986, your entire interest was in pay status under a written election that provides a specific schedule for the distribution of your entire interest; and

3. The distribution is actually being made under the written election.

• Distributions that are dividends paid with respect to stock described in section 404(k).

• Distributions from annuity contracts to the extent that the distributions are allocable to the investment in the contract before August 14, 1982. For additional exceptions that apply to annuities, see *Tax on Early Distributions* under *Special Additional Taxes* in Pub. 575.

• Distributions that are phased retirement annuity payments made to federal employees. See Pub. 721 for more information on the phased retirement program.

• Permissible withdrawals under section 414(w).

Line 4

If any amount on line 3 was a distribution from a SIMPLE IRA received within 2 years from the date you first participated in the SIMPLE IRA plan, you must multiply that amount by 25% instead of 10%. These distributions are included in boxes 1 and 2a of Form 1099-R and are designated with code S in box 7.

Part II—Additional Tax on Certain Distributions From Education Accounts and ABLE Accounts

Line 5

Distributions from an ABLE account aren't included in income if made on or after the death of the designated beneficiary:

• To the estate of the designated beneficiary;

• To an heir or legatee of the designated beneficiary; or
• To pay outstanding obligations due for qualified disability expenses of the designated beneficiary, including a claim filed by a state under a state Medicaid plan.

Line 6

The additional tax doesn't apply to the distributions that are includible in income described next. Enter on line 6 the amount from line 5 that you can exclude.
• Distributions made due to the death or disability of the beneficiary.
• Distributions from an education account made on account of a tax-free scholarship, allowance, or payment described in section 25A(g)(2).
• Distributions from an education account made because of attendance by the beneficiary at a U.S. military academy. This exception applies only to the extent that the distribution doesn't exceed the costs of advanced education (as defined in title 10 of the U.S. Code) at the academy.
• Distributions from an education account included in income because you used the qualified education expenses to figure the American opportunity and lifetime learning credits.

Part III—Additional Tax on Excess Contributions to Traditional IRAs

If you contributed more for 2018 than is allowable or you had an amount on line 17 of your 2017 Form 5329, you may owe this tax. But you may be able to avoid the tax on any 2018 excess contributions (see the instructions for line 15, later).

Line 9

Enter the amount from line 16 of your 2017 Form 5329 only if the amount on line 17 of your 2017 Form 5329 is more than zero.

Line 10

Enter the difference, if any, of your contribution limit for traditional IRAs less your contributions to traditional IRAs and Roth IRAs for 2018.

If you aren't married filing jointly, your contribution limit for traditional IRAs is the smaller of your taxable compensation (defined earlier) or $5,500 ($6,500 if age 50 or older at the end of 2018). If you are married filing jointly, your contribution limit is generally $5,500 ($6,500 if age 50 or older at the end of 2018) and your spouse's contribution limit is $5,500 ($6,500 if

age 50 or older at the end of 2018). But if the combined taxable compensation for you and your spouse is less than $11,000 ($12,000 if one spouse is 50 or older at the end of 2018; $13,000 if both spouses are 50 or older at the end of 2018), see *How Much Can Be Contributed?* in Pub. 590-A for special rules.

Also include on line 11a or 11b of the IRA Deduction Worksheet—Schedule 1, Line 32, in the Instructions for Form 1040, or on line 11 of the IRA Deduction Worksheet—Line 32, in the Instructions for Form 1040NR, the smaller of:
• Form 5329, line 10; or
• The excess, if any, of Form 5329, line 9 over the sum of Form 5329, lines 11 and 12 (which you will complete next).

Line 11

Enter on line 11 any withdrawals from your traditional IRAs that are included in your income. Don't include any withdrawn contributions reported on line 12.

Line 12

Enter on line 12 any amounts included on line 9 that are excess contributions to your traditional IRAs for 1976 through 2016 that you had returned to you in 2018 and any 2017 excess contributions that you had returned to you in 2018 after the due date (including extensions) of your 2017 income tax return if:
• You didn't claim a deduction for the excess contributions,
• No traditional IRA deduction was allowable (without regard to the modified AGI limitation) for the excess contributions, and
• The total contributions to your traditional IRAs for the tax year for which the excess contributions were made weren't more than the amounts shown in the following table.

Year(s)	Contribution limit	Contribution limit if age 50 or older at the end of the year
2013 through 2017	$5,500	$6,500
2008 through 2012	$5,000	$6,000
2006 or 2007	$4,000	$5,000
2005	$4,000	$4,500
2002 through 2004	$3,000	$3,500
1997 through 2001	$2,000	—
before 1997	$2,250	—

If the excess contribution to your traditional IRA for the year included a rollover and the excess occurred because the information the plan was required to give you was incorrect, increase the contribution limit amount for the year shown in the table above by the amount of the excess that is due to the incorrect information.

If the total contributions for the year included employer contributions to a SEP, increase the contribution limit amount for the year shown in the table above by the smaller of the amount of the employer contributions or:

2017	$54,000
2015 or 2016	$53,000
2014	$52,000
2013	$51,000
2012	$50,000
2009, 2010, or 2011	$49,000
2008	$46,000
2007	$45,000
2006	$44,000
2005	$42,000
2004	$41,000
2002 or 2003	$40,000
2001	$35,000
before 2001	$30,000

Line 15

Enter the excess of your contributions to traditional IRAs for 2018 (unless withdrawn—discussed next) over your contribution limit for traditional IRAs. See the instructions for line 10, earlier, to figure your contribution limit for traditional IRAs. Any amount you contribute for the year in which you reach age 70½ or for a later year is an excess contribution because your contribution limit is zero. Don't include rollovers in figuring your excess contributions.

You can withdraw some or all of your excess contributions for 2018 and they will be treated as not having been contributed if:
• You make the withdrawal by the due date, including extensions, of your 2018 tax return;
• You don't claim a traditional IRA deduction for the withdrawn contributions; and
• You withdraw any earnings on the withdrawn contributions and include the earnings in gross income (see the Instructions for Form 8606 for details). Also, if you hadn't reached age 59½ at the time of the withdrawal, include the earnings as an early distribution on line 1 of Form 5329 for the year in which you report the earnings.

If you timely filed your return without withdrawing the excess contributions, you can still make the withdrawal no later than 6 months after the due date of your tax return, excluding extensions. If you do, file an amended return with "Filed pursuant to section 301.9100-2" written at the top. Report any related earnings for 2018 on the amended return and include an explanation of the withdrawal. Make any other necessary changes on the amended return (for example, if you reported the contributions as excess contributions on your original return, include an amended Form 5329 reflecting that the withdrawn contributions are no longer treated as having been contributed).

Part IV—Additional Tax on Excess Contributions to Roth IRAs

If you contributed more to your Roth IRA for 2018 than is allowable or you had an amount on line 25 of your 2017 Form 5329, you may owe this tax. But you may be able to avoid the tax on any 2018 excess contributions (see the instructions for line 23, later).

Line 18

Enter the amount from line 24 of your 2017 Form 5329 only if the amount on line 25 of your 2017 Form 5329 is more than zero.

Line 19

If you contributed less to your Roth IRAs for 2018 than your contribution limit for Roth IRAs, enter the difference. Your contribution limit for Roth IRAs is generally your contribution limit for traditional IRAs (see the instructions for line 10, earlier) reduced by the amount you contributed to traditional IRAs. But your contribution limit for Roth IRAs may be further reduced or eliminated if your modified AGI for Roth IRA purposes is over:
• $189,000 if married filing jointly or qualifying widow(er);
• $120,000 if single, head of household, or married filing separately and you didn't live with your spouse at any time in 2018; or
• $0 if married filing separately and you lived with your spouse at any time in 2018.

See *Can You Contribute to a Roth IRA?* in Pub. 590-A for details.

Line 20

Generally, enter the amount from Form 8606, line 19, plus any qualified distributions. But if you withdrew the entire balance of all of your Roth IRAs, don't enter less than the amount on Form 5329, line 18 (see *Example* next).

Example. You contributed $1,000 to a Roth IRA in 2016, your only contribution to Roth IRAs. In 2018, you discovered you weren't eligible to contribute to a Roth IRA in 2016. On September 7, 2018, you withdrew $800, the entire balance in the Roth IRA. You must file Form 5329 for 2016 and 2017 to pay the additional taxes for those years. When you complete Form 5329 for 2018, you enter $1,000 (not $800) on line 20, because you withdrew the entire balance.

Line 23

Enter the excess of your contributions to Roth IRAs for 2018 (unless withdrawn—discussed below) over your contribution limit for Roth IRAs. See the instructions for line 19, earlier, to figure your contribution limit for Roth IRAs.

Don't include rollovers in figuring your excess contributions.

You can withdraw some or all of your excess contributions for 2018 and they will be treated as not having been contributed if:
• You make the withdrawal by the due date, including extensions, of your 2018 tax return; and
• You withdraw any earnings on the withdrawn contributions and include the earnings in gross income (see the

Instructions for Form 8606 for details). Also, if you hadn't reached age 59½ at the time of the withdrawal, include the earnings as an early distribution on line 1 of Form 5329 for the year in which you report the earnings.

If you timely filed your return without withdrawing the excess contributions, you can still make the withdrawal no later than 6 months after the due date of your tax return, excluding extensions. If you do, file an amended return with "Filed pursuant to section 301.9100-2" written at the top. Report any related earnings for 2018 on the amended return and include an explanation of the withdrawal. Make any other necessary changes on the amended return (for example, if you reported the contributions as excess contributions on your original return, include an amended Form 5329 reflecting that the withdrawn contributions are no longer treated as having been contributed).

Part V—Additional Tax on Excess Contributions to Coverdell ESAs

If the contributions to your Coverdell ESAs for 2018 were more than is allowable or you had an amount on line 33 of your 2017 Form 5329, you may owe this tax. But you may be able to avoid the tax on any 2018 excess contributions (see the instructions for line 31, later).

Line 26

Enter the amount from line 32 of your 2017 Form 5329 only if the amount on line 33 of your 2017 Form 5329 is more than zero.

Line 27

Enter the excess, if any, of the maximum amount that can be contributed to your Coverdell ESAs for 2018 over the amount actually contributed for 2018. Your contribution limit is the smaller of $2,000 or the sum of the maximum amounts the contributor(s) to your Coverdell ESAs are allowed to contribute. The maximum contribution may be limited based on the contributor's modified AGI. See *Contributions* in chapter 7 of Pub. 970 for details.

Line 28

Enter your total distributions from Coverdell ESAs in 2018. Don't include rollovers or withdrawn excess contributions.

Line 31

Enter the excess of the contributions to your Coverdell ESAs for 2018 (unless withdrawn—discussed below) over your contribution limit for Coverdell ESAs. See the instructions for line 27, earlier, to figure your contribution limit for Coverdell ESAs.

Don't include rollovers in figuring your excess contributions.

You can withdraw some or all of the excess contributions for 2018 and they will be treated as not having been contributed if:
• You make the withdrawal before June 1, 2019; and
• You also withdraw any income earned on the withdrawn contributions and include the earnings in gross income for the year in which the contribution was made.

If you filed your return without withdrawing the excess contributions, you can still make the withdrawal, but it must be made before June 1, 2019. If you do, file an amended return. Report any related earnings for 2018 on the amended return and include an explanation of the withdrawal. Make any other necessary changes on the amended return (for example, if you reported the contributions as excess contributions on your original return, include an amended Form 5329 reflecting that the withdrawn contributions are no longer treated as having been contributed).

Part VI—Additional Tax on Excess Contributions to Archer MSAs

If you or your employer contributed more to your Archer MSA for 2018 than is allowable or you had an amount on line 41 of your 2017 Form 5329, you may owe this tax. But you may be able to avoid the tax on any 2018 excess contributions (see the instructions for line 39, later).

Line 34

Enter the amount from line 40 of your 2017 Form 5329 only if the amount on line 41 of your 2017 Form 5329 is more than zero.

Line 35

If contributions to your Archer MSAs for 2018 were less than your contribution limit for Archer MSAs, enter the difference on line 35. Your contribution limit for Archer MSAs is the smaller of line 3 or line 4 of Form 8853, Archer MSAs and Long-Term Care Insurance Contracts.

Also include on your 2018 Form 8853, line 5, the smaller of:
• Form 5329, line 35; or
• The excess, if any, of Form 5329, line 34, over Form 5329, line 36.

Line 39

Enter the excess of your contributions to your Archer MSA for 2018 from Form 8853, line 2 (unless withdrawn—discussed next), over your contribution limit (the smaller of line 3 or line 4 of Form 8853). Also include on line 39 any excess contributions your employer made. See the Instructions for Form 8853 for details.

You can withdraw some or all of the excess contributions for 2018 and they will be treated as not having been contributed if:
• You make the withdrawal by the due date, including extensions, of your 2018 tax return; and
• You withdraw any income earned on the withdrawn contributions and include the earnings in gross income for the year in which you receive the withdrawn contributions and earnings.

Include the withdrawn contributions and related earnings on Form 8853, lines 6a and 6b.

If you timely filed your return without withdrawing the excess contributions, you can still make the withdrawal no later than 6 months after the due date of your tax return, excluding extensions. If you do, file an amended return with "Filed pursuant to section 301.9100-2" written at the top. Report any related earnings for 2018 on the amended return and include an explanation of the withdrawal. Make any other necessary changes on the amended return (for example, if you reported the contributions as excess contributions on your original return, include an amended Form 5329 reflecting that the withdrawn contributions are no longer treated as having been contributed).

Part VII—Additional Tax on Excess Contributions to Health Savings Accounts (HSAs)

If you, someone on your behalf, or your employer contributed more to your HSAs for 2018 than is allowable or you had an amount on line 49 of your 2017 Form 5329, you may owe this tax. But you may be able to avoid the tax on any 2018 excess contributions (see the instructions for line 47 below).

Line 42

Enter the amount from line 48 of your 2017 Form 5329 only if the amount on line 49 of your 2017 Form 5329 is more than zero.

Line 43

If contributions to your HSAs for 2018 (line 2 of Form 8889, Health Savings Accounts (HSAs)) were less than your contribution limit for HSAs, enter the difference on line 43. Your contribution limit for HSAs is the amount on line 12 of Form 8889.

Also include on your 2018 Form 8889, line 13, the smaller of:
• Form 5329, line 43; or
• The excess, if any, of Form 5329, line 42, over Form 5329, line 44.

Line 47

Enter the excess of your contributions (including those made on your behalf) to your HSAs for 2018 from Form 8889, line 2 (unless withdrawn—discussed next), over your contribution limit (Form 8889, line 12). Also include on line 47 any excess contributions your employer made. See the Instructions for Form 8889 for details.

You can withdraw some or all of the excess contributions for 2018 and they will be treated as not having been contributed if:
• You make the withdrawal by the due date, including extensions, of your 2018 return; and
• You withdraw any income earned on the withdrawn contributions and include the earnings in gross income for the year in which you receive the withdrawn contributions and earnings.

Include the withdrawn contributions and related earnings on Form 8889, lines 14a and 14b.

If you timely filed your return without withdrawing the excess contributions, you can still make the withdrawal no later than 6 months after the due date of your tax return, excluding extensions. If you do, file an amended return with "Filed pursuant to section 301.9100-2" written at the top. Report any related earnings for 2018 on the amended return and include an explanation of the withdrawal. Make any other necessary changes on the amended return (for example, if you reported the contributions as excess contributions on your original return, include an amended Form 5329 reflecting that the withdrawn contributions are no longer treated as having been contributed).

Part VIII—Additional Tax on Excess Contributions to ABLE Accounts

If the contributions to your ABLE account for 2018 were more than is allowable, you may owe tax on the net income resulting from the excess contribution.

Line 50

Enter the excess, if any, of the contributions to your ABLE account for 2018 over the contribution limit. Total contributions (including contributions from a section 529 account) made to your ABLE account for 2018 may not exceed $15,000 plus, in the case of an employed designated beneficiary, the applicable amount under section 529A(b)(2)(B)(ii).

Don't include ABLE rollovers or program-to-program transfers in figuring your excess contributions.

You won't incur a tax on a contribution to your ABLE account that is in excess of the contribution limit if the qualified ABLE program returns the contribution, including all net income attributable to the contribution, to the person who made the contribution (the "contributor"), and the contributor receives the contribution on or before the due date (including extensions) for filing your federal income tax return. Any net income distributed from the excess contribution to the ABLE account is includible in the gross income of the contributor in the tax year in which the excess contribution was made.

If the contributor receives the contribution after you have filed your original tax return but before the due date (including extensions) for filing your return, you may file an amended return reflecting the return of the contribution to the contributor with "Filed pursuant to section 301.9100-2" written at the top. Make any necessary changes on the amended return. For example, if you reported the contribution as excess contributions on your original return, include an amended Form 5329 reflecting that the withdrawn contributions are no longer treated as having been contributed.

Part IX—Additional Tax on Excess Accumulation in Qualified Retirement Plans (Including IRAs)

You owe this tax if you don't receive the required minimum distribution from your qualified retirement plan, including an IRA or an eligible section 457 deferred compensation plan. The additional tax is 50% of the excess accumulation, which is the difference between the amount that was required to be distributed and the amount that was actually distributed. The tax is due for the tax year that includes the last day by which the minimum required distribution must be taken.

Line 52

IRA (other than a Roth IRA). You must start receiving distributions from your IRA by April 1 of the year following the year in which you reach age 70 1/2. At that time, you can receive your entire interest in the IRA or begin receiving periodic distributions. If you choose to receive periodic distributions, you must receive a minimum required distribution each year. You can figure the minimum required distribution by dividing the account balance of your IRAs (other than Roth IRAs) on December 31 of the year preceding the distribution by the applicable life expectancy. For applicable life expectancies, see *Figuring the Owner's Required Minimum Distribution* under *When Must You Withdraw Assets?* in Pub. 590-B.

If the trustee, custodian, or issuer of your IRA informs you of the minimum required distribution, you can use that amount.

If you have more than one IRA, you can take the minimum required distribution from any one or more of the IRAs (other than Roth IRAs).

For more details on the minimum distribution rules (including examples), see *When Must You Withdraw Assets?* in Pub. 590-B.

TIP *A qualified charitable distribution will count towards your required minimum distribution. See* Qualified charitable distributions *under* Are Distributions Taxable? *in chapter 1 of Pub. 590-B for more information.*

Trusts and estates. Include the amount of tax, if any, on Form 1041, Schedule G, line 7. Write "From Form 5329" and the amount of the tax to the left of the line 7 entry space.

Roth IRA. There are no minimum required distributions during the lifetime of the owner of a Roth IRA. Following the death of the Roth IRA owner, required distribution rules apply to the beneficiary. See *Must You Withdraw or Use Assets?* in Pub. 590-B for details.

Qualified retirement plans (other than IRAs) and eligible section 457 deferred compensation plans. In general, you must begin receiving distributions from your plan no later than April 1 following the later of (a) the year in which you reach age 70 1/2, or (b) the year in which you retire.

Exception. If you owned more than 5% of the employer maintaining the plan, you must begin receiving distributions no later than April 1 of the year following the year in which you reach age 70 1/2, regardless of when you retire.

Your plan administrator should figure the amount that must be distributed each year.

Waiver of tax. The IRS can waive part or all of this tax if you can show that any shortfall in the amount of distributions was due to reasonable error and you are taking reasonable steps to remedy the shortfall. If you believe you qualify for this relief, attach a statement of explanation and file Form 5329 as follows.

1. Complete lines 52 and 53 as instructed.

2. Enter "RC" and the amount you want waived in parentheses on the dotted line next to line 54. Subtract this amount from the total shortfall you figured without regard to the waiver, and enter the result on line 54.

3. Complete line 55 as instructed. You must pay any tax due that is reported on line 55.

The IRS will review the information you provide and decide whether to grant your request for a waiver.

Privacy Act and Paperwork Reduction Act Notice. We ask for the information on this form to carry out the Internal Revenue laws of the United States. We need this information to ensure that you are complying with these laws and to allow us to figure and collect the right amount of tax. You are required to give us this information if you made certain contributions or received certain distributions from qualified plans, including IRAs, and other tax-favored accounts. Our legal right to ask for the information requested on this form is sections 6001, 6011, 6012(a), and 6109 and their regulations. If you do not provide this information, or you provide incomplete or false information, you may be subject to penalties.

You are not required to provide the information requested on a form that is subject to the Paperwork Reduction Act unless the form displays a valid OMB control number. Books or records relating to a form or its instructions must be retained as long as their contents may become material in the administration of any Internal Revenue law. Generally, tax returns and return information are confidential, as required by section 6103. However, we may give this information to the Department of Justice for civil and criminal litigation, and to cities, states, the District of Columbia, and U.S. commonwealths and possessions to carry out their tax laws. We may also disclose this information to other countries under a tax treaty, to federal and state agencies to enforce federal nontax criminal laws, or to federal law enforcement and intelligence agencies to combat terrorism.

The average time and expenses required to complete and file this form will vary depending on individual circumstances. For the estimated averages, see the instructions for your income tax return.

If you have suggestions for making this form simpler, we would be happy to hear from you. See the instructions for your income tax return.

Form **5330** (Rev. December 2013) Department of the Treasury Internal Revenue Service	**Return of Excise Taxes Related to Employee Benefit Plans** (Under sections 4965, 4971, 4972, 4973(a)(3), 4975, 4976, 4977, 4978, 4979, 4979A, 4980, and 4980F of the Internal Revenue Code) ▶ Information about Form 5330 and its instructions is at *www.irs.gov/form5330*.	OMB No. 1545-0575

Filer tax year beginning , **and ending** ,

A Name of filer (see instructions)	B Filer's identifying number (Enter either the EIN or SSN, but not both. See instructions.)
Number, street, and room or suite no. (If a P.O. box or foreign address, see instructions.)	Employer identification number (EIN)
City or town, state or province, country, and ZIP or foreign postal code	Social security number (SSN)
C Name of plan	E Plan sponsor's EIN
D Name and address of plan sponsor	F Plan year ending (MM/DD/YYYY)
H If this is an **amended return,** check here . . . . ▶ ☐	G Plan number

---

Part I **Taxes.** You can only complete one section of Part I for each Form 5330 filed (see instructions).

Section A. Taxes that are reported by the last day of the 7th month after the end of the tax year of the employer (or other person who must file the return)

FOR IRS USE ONLY

1	Section 4972 tax on nondeductible contributions to qualified plans (from Schedule A, line 12)	161	**1**
2	Section 4973(a)(3) tax on excess contributions to section 403(b)(7)(A) custodial accounts (from Schedule B, line 12)	164	**2**
3a	Section 4975(a) tax on prohibited transactions (from Schedule C, line 3)	159	**3a**
b	Section 4975(b) tax on failure to correct prohibited transactions	224	**3b**
4	Section 4976 tax on disqualified benefits for funded welfare plans	200	**4**
5a	Section 4978 tax on ESOP dispositions	209	**5a**
b	The tax on line 5a is a result of the application of: ☐ Sec. 664(g) ☐ Sec. 1042		**5b**
6	Section 4979A tax on certain prohibited allocations of qualified ESOP securities or ownership of synthetic equity	203	**6**
7	**Total Section A taxes.** Add lines 1 through 6. Enter here and on Part II, line 17 . . . ▶		**7**

Section B. Taxes that are reported by the last day of the 7th month after the end of the employer's tax year or 8¹/₂ months after the last day of the plan year that ends within the filer's tax year

8a	Section 4971(a) tax on failure to meet minimum funding standards (from Schedule D, line 2) . .	163	**8a**
b	Section 4971(b) tax for failure to correct minimum funding standards	225	**8b**
9a	Section 4971(f)(1) tax on failure to pay liquidity shortfall (from Schedule E, line 4)	226	**9a**
b	Section 4971(f)(2) tax for failure to correct liquidity shortfall	227	**9b**
10a	Section 4971(g)(2) tax on failure to comply with a funding improvement or rehabilitation plan (see instructions)	450	**10a**
b	Section 4971(g)(3) tax on failure to meet requirements for plans in endangered or critical status (from Schedule F, line 1c)	451	**10b**
c	Section 4971(g)(4) tax on failure to adopt rehabilitation plan (from Schedule F, line 2d) . .	452	**10c**

Section B1. Tax that is reported by the last day of the 7th month after the end of the calendar year in which the excess fringe benefits were paid to the employer's employees

11	Section 4977 tax on excess fringe benefits (from Schedule G, line 4)	201	**11**
12	**Total Section B taxes.** Add lines 8a through 11. Enter here and on Part II, line 17 . . . ▶		**12**

Section C. Tax that is reported by the last day of the 15th month after the end of the plan year

13	Section 4979 tax on excess contributions to certain plans (from Schedule H, line 2). Enter here and on Part II, line 17	205	**13**

For Privacy Act and Paperwork Reduction Act Notice, see instructions. Cat. No. 11870M Form **5330** (Rev. 12-2013)

Form 5330 (Rev. 12-2013)   Page **2**

	Name of Filer:	Filer's identifying number:		

Section D. Tax that is reported by the last day of the month following the month in which the reversion occurred

14	Section 4980 tax on reversion of qualified plan assets to an employer (from Schedule I, line 3). Enter here and on Part II, line 17 . . . . ▶	204	**14**	

Section E. Tax that is reported by the last day of the month following the month in which the failure occurred

15	Section 4980F tax on failure to provide notice of significant reduction in future accruals (from Schedule J, line 5). Enter here and on Part II, line 17 . . . . ▶	228	**15**	

Section F. Taxes reported on or before the 15th day of the 5th month following the close of the entity manager's taxable year during which the plan became a party to a prohibited tax shelter transaction

16	Section 4965 tax on prohibited tax shelter transactions for entity managers (from Schedule K, line 2). Enter here and on Part II, line 17 . . . . ▶	237	**16**	

Part II	**Tax Due**

17	Enter the amount from Part I, line 7, 12, 13, 14, 15, or 16 (whichever is applicable)	**17**	
18	Enter amount of tax paid with Form 5558 or any other tax paid prior to filing this return	**18**	
19	**Tax due.** Subtract line 18 from line 17. If the result is greater than zero, enter here, and attach check or money order payable to "United States Treasury." Write your name, identifying number, plan number, and "Form 5330, Section(s) " on your payment . . . . ▶	**19**	

Sign Here	Under penalties of perjury, I declare that I have examined this return, including accompanying schedules and statements, and to the best of my knowledge and belief, it is true, correct, and complete. Declaration of preparer (other than taxpayer) is based on all information of which preparer has any knowledge.			
	▶ Your Signature	▶ Telephone number	▶ Date	

Paid Preparer Use Only	Print/Type preparer's name	Preparer's signature	Date	Check ☐ if self-employed	PTIN
	Firm's name ▶			Firm's EIN ▶	
	Firm's address ▶			Phone no.	

Form **5330** (Rev. 12-2013)

Form 5330 (Rev. 12-2013)   Page **3**

Name of Filer: Filer's identifying number:

Schedule A. Tax on Nondeductible Employer Contributions to Qualified Employer Plans (Section 4972)
Reported by the last day of the 7th month after the end of the tax year of the employer (or other person who must file the return)

1	Total contributions for your tax year to your qualified employer plan (under section 401(a), 403(a), 408(k), or 408(p))	**1**	
2	Amount allowable as a deduction under section 404	**2**	
3	Subtract line 2 from line 1	**3**	
4	Enter amount of any prior year nondeductible contributions made for years beginning after 12/31/86 . . . . **4**		
5	Amount of any prior year nondeductible contributions for years beginning after 12/31/86 returned to you in this tax year for any prior tax year . . **5**		
6	Subtract line 5 from line 4 . . . . **6**		
7	Amount of line 6 carried forward and deductible in this tax year . . . **7**		
8	Subtract line 7 from line 6	**8**	
9	Tentative taxable excess contributions. Add lines 3 and 8	**9**	
10	Nondeductible section 4972(c)(6) or (7) contributions exempt from excise tax	**10**	
11	Taxable excess contributions. Subtract line 10 from line 9	**11**	
12	Multiply line 11 by 10%. Enter here and on Part I, line 1 . . . . ▶	**12**	

Schedule B. Tax on Excess Contributions to Section 403(b)(7)(A) Custodial Accounts (Section 4973(a)(3))
Reported by the last day of the 7th month after the end of the tax year of the employer (or other person who must file the return)

1	Total amount contributed for current year less rollovers (see instructions)	**1**	
2	Amount excludable from gross income under section 403(b) (see instructions)	**2**	
3	Current year excess contributions. Subtract line 2 from line 1. If zero or less, enter -0- . . .	**3**	
4	Prior year excess contributions not previously eliminated. If zero, go to line 8	**4**	
5	Contribution credit. If line 2 is more than line 1, enter the excess; otherwise, enter -0-.	**5**	
6	Total of all prior years' distributions out of the account included in your gross income under section 72(e) and not previously used to reduce excess contributions	**6**	
7	Adjusted prior years' excess contributions. Subtract the total of lines 5 and 6 from line 4 . .	**7**	
8	Taxable excess contributions. Add lines 3 and 7	**8**	
9	Multiply line 8 by 6%	**9**	
10	Enter the value of your account as of the last day of the year	**10**	
11	Multiply line 10 by 6%	**11**	
12	**Excess contributions tax.** Enter the lesser of line 9 or line 11 here and on Part I, line 2 . . ▶	**12**	

Form **5330** (Rev. 12-2013)

Form 5330 (Rev. 12-2013)   Page **4**

Name of Filer: Filer's identifying number:

Schedule C. Tax on Prohibited Transactions (Section 4975) *(see instructions)* **Reported by the last day of the 7th month after the end of the tax year of the employer (or other person who must file the return)**

1   Is the excise tax a result of a prohibited transaction that was (box "a" or box "b" must be checked):
   a ☐ discrete   **b** ☐ other than discrete (a lease or a loan)

2   Complete the table below to disclose the prohibited transactions and figure the initial tax (see instructions)

(a) Transaction number	(b) Date of transaction (see instructions)	(c) Description of prohibited transaction	(d) Amount involved in prohibited transaction (see instructions)	(e) Initial tax on prohibited transaction (multiply each transaction in column (d) by the appropriate rate (see instructions))
(i)				
(ii)				
(iii)				
(iv)				
(v)				
(vi)				
(vii)				
(viii)				
(ix)				
(x)				
(xi)				
(xii)				

3   Add amounts in column (e); enter here and on Part I, line 3a . . . . ▶

4   Have you corrected all of the prohibited transactions that you are reporting on this return? If "Yes," complete Schedule C, line 5, on the next page. If "No," attach statement (see instructions) . . . ▶ ☐ **Yes**   ☐ **No**

Form **5330** (Rev. 12-2013)

Form 5330 (Rev. 12-2013)   Page **5**

Name of Filer: Filer's identifying number:

Schedule C. Tax on Prohibited Transactions (Section 4975) Reported by the last day of the 7th month after the end of the tax year of the employer (or other person who must file the return) *(continued)*

5   Complete the table below, if applicable, of other participating disqualified persons and description of correction (see instructions).

(a) Item no. from line 2	(b) Name and address of disqualified person	(c) EIN or SSN	(d) Date of correction	(e) Description of correction

Schedule D. Tax on Failure to Meet Minimum Funding Standards (Section 4971(a)) Reported by the last day of the 7th month after the end of the employer's tax year or 8¹/₂ months after the last day of the plan year that ends within the filer's tax year

1	Aggregate unpaid required contributions (accumulated funding deficiency for multiemployer plans) (see instructions) . . . . ▶	**1**	
2	Multiply line 1 by 10% (5% for multiemployer plans). Enter here and on Part I, line 8a . . . . ▶	**2**	

Form **5330** (Rev. 12-2013)

Form 5330 (Rev. 12-2013)   Page **6**

Name of Filer: Filer's identifying number:

Schedule E. Tax on Failure to Pay Liquidity Shortfall (Section 4971(f)(1)) Reported by the last day of the 7th month after the end of the employer's tax year or 8^{1}/$_{2}$ months after the last day of the plan year that ends within the filer's tax year

		(a) 1st Quarter	(b) 2nd Quarter	(c) 3rd Quarter	(d) 4th Quarter	(e) Total Add cols. a-d for line 3
1	Amount of shortfall	1				
2	Shortfall paid by the due date	2				
3	Net shortfall amount . . .	3				
4	Multiply line 3, column (e), by 10%. Enter here and on Part I, line 9a . . . . ▶	4				

Schedule F. Tax on Multiemployer Plans in Endangered or Critical Status (Section 4971(g)(3), 4971(g)(4)) Reported by the last day of the 7th month after the end of the employer's tax year or 8^{1}/$_{2}$ months after the last day of the plan year that ends within the filer's tax year

1	Section 4971(g)(3) tax on failure to meet requirements for plans in endangered or critical status . .	1	
a	Enter the amount of contributions necessary to meet the applicable benchmarks or requirements .	1a	
b	Enter the amount of the accumulated funding deficiency	1b	
c	Enter the greater of line 1a or line 1b, here and on Part I, line 10b . . . . ▶	1c	
2	Section 4971(g)(4) tax on failure to adopt rehabilitation plan	2	
a	Enter the amount of the excise tax on the accumulated funding deficiency under section 4971(a)(2) from Schedule D, line 2	2a	
b	Enter the number of days during the tax year which are included in the period beginning on the first day of the 240 day period and ending on the day the rehabilitation plan is adopted ▶ _____	2b	
c	Multiply line 2b by $1,100	2c	
d	Enter the greater of line 2a or line 2c, here and on Part I, line 10c . . . . ▶	2d	

Schedule G. Tax on Excess Fringe Benefits (Section 4977) Reported by the last day of the 7th month after the end of the calendar year in which the excess fringe benefits were paid to the employer's employees

1	Did you make an election to be taxed under section 4977? . . . . ☐ Yes ☐ No		
2	If "Yes," enter the calendar year (YYYY) in which the excess fringe benefits were paid ▶		
3	If line 1 is "Yes," enter the excess fringe benefits on this line (see instructions)	3	
4	Enter 30% of line 3 here and on Part I, line 11 . . . . ▶	4	

Schedule H. Tax on Excess Contributions to Certain Plans (Section 4979) Reported by the last day of the 15th month after the end of the plan year

1	Enter the amount of an excess contribution under a cash or deferred arrangement that is part of a plan qualified under section 401(a), 403(a), 403(b), 408(k), or 501(c)(18) or excess aggregate contributions .	1	
2	Multiply line 1 by 10% and enter here and on Part I, line 13 . . . . ▶	2	

Schedule I. Tax on Reversion of Qualified Plan Assets to an Employer (Section 4980) Reported by the last day of the month following the month in which the reversion occurred

1	Date reversion occurred . . . . ▶ MM _____ DD _____ YY _____		
2a	Employer reversion amount _____ **b** Excise tax rate _____		
3	Multiply line 2a by line 2b and enter the amount here and on Part I, line 14 . . . . . . ▶	3	
4	Explain below why you qualify for a rate other than 50%:		

_____

Schedule J. Tax on Failure to Provide Notice of Significant Reduction in Future Accruals (Section 4980F) Reported by the last day of the month following the month in which the failure occurred

1	Enter the number of applicable individuals who were not provided ERISA section 204(h) notice ▶ _____	1	
2	Enter the effective date of the amendment . . . . . ▶ MM _____ DD _____ YY _____	2	
3	Enter the number of days in the noncompliance period ▶ _____	3	
4	Enter the total number of failures to provide ERISA section 204(h) notice (see instructions) . .	4	
5	Multiply line 4 by $100. Enter here and on Part I, line 15 . . . . ▶	5	
6	Provide a brief description of the failure, and of the correction, if any		

_____

Schedule K. Tax on Prohibited Tax Shelter Transactions (Section 4965) Reported on or before the 15th day of the 5th month following the close of the entity manager's tax year during which the plan became a party to a prohibited tax shelter transaction

1	Enter the number of prohibited tax shelter transactions you caused the same plan to be a party to ▶ _____	1	
2	Multiply line 1 by $20,000. Enter the result here and on Part I, line 16 . . . . ▶	2	

Form **5330** (Rev. 12-2013)

Instructions for Form 5330

Department of the Treasury
Internal Revenue Service

(Rev. December 2013)

Return of Excise Taxes Related to Employee Benefit Plans

Section references are to the Internal Revenue Code unless otherwise noted.

Future developments. For the latest information about developments related to Form 5330 and its instructions, such as legislation enacted after they were published, go to *www.irs.gov/form5330*.

General Instructions

Purpose of Form

File Form 5330 to report the tax on:
* A prohibited tax shelter transaction (section 4965(a)(2));
* A minimum funding deficiency (section 4971(a) and (b));
* A failure to pay liquidity shortfall (section 4971(f));
* A failure to comply with a funding improvement or rehabilitation plan (section 4971(g)(2));
* A failure to meet requirements for plans in endangered or critical status (section 4971(g)(3));
* A failure to adopt rehabilitation plan (section 4971(g)(4));
* Nondeductible contributions to qualified plans (section 4972);
* Excess contributions to a section 403(b)(7)(A) custodial account (section 4973(a)(3));
* A prohibited transaction (section 4975);
* A disqualified benefit provided by funded welfare plans (section 4976);
* Excess fringe benefits (section 4977);
* Certain employee stock ownership plan (ESOP) dispositions (section 4978);
* Excess contributions to plans with cash or deferred arrangements (section 4979);
* Certain prohibited allocations of qualified securities by an ESOP (section 4979A);
* Reversions of qualified plan assets to employers (section 4980);
* A failure of an applicable plan reducing future benefit accruals to satisfy notice requirements (section 4980F).

Who Must File

A Form 5330 must be filed by any of the following.

1. A plan entity manager of a tax-exempt entity who approves, or otherwise causes the entity to be party to, a prohibited tax shelter transaction during the tax year and knows or has reason to know the transaction is a prohibited tax shelter transaction under section 4965(a)(2).

2. An employer liable for the tax under section 4971 for failure to meet the minimum funding standards under section 412.

3. An employer liable for the tax under section 4971(f) for a failure to meet the liquidity requirement of section 430(j) (or section 412(m)(5) as it existed prior to amendment by the Pension Protection Act of 2006 (PPA '06)), for plans with delayed effective dates under PPA '06.

4. An employer with respect to a multiemployer plan liable for the tax under section 4971(g)(2) for failure to comply with a funding improvement or rehabilitation plan under section 432.

5. An employer with respect to a multiemployer plan liable for the tax under section 4971(g)(3) for failure to meet the requirements for plans in endangered or critical status under section 432.

6. A multiemployer plan sponsor liable for the tax under section 4971(g)(4) for failure to adopt a rehabilitation plan within the time required under section 432.

7. An employer liable for the tax under section 4972 for nondeductible contributions to qualified plans.

8. An individual liable for the tax under section 4973(a)(3) because an excess contribution to a section 403(b)(7)(A) custodial account was made for them and that excess has not been eliminated, as specified in sections 4973(c)(2)(A) and (B).

9. A disqualified person liable for the tax under section 4975 for participating in a prohibited transaction (other than a fiduciary acting only as such), or an individual or his or her beneficiary who engages in a prohibited transaction with respect to his or her individual retirement account, unless section 408(e)(2)(A) or section 408(e)(4) applies, for each tax year or part of a tax year in the taxable period applicable to such prohibited transaction.

10. An employer liable for the tax under section 4976 for maintaining a funded welfare benefit plan that provides a disqualified benefit during any tax year.

11. An employer who pays excess fringe benefits and has elected to be taxed under section 4977 on such payments.

12. An employer or worker-owned cooperative, as defined in section 1042(c)(2), that maintains an employee stock ownership plan (ESOP) that disposes of the qualified securities, as defined in section 1042(c)(1), within the specified 3-year period (see section 4978).

13. An employer liable for the tax under section 4979 on excess contributions to plans with a cash or deferred arrangement, etc.

14. An employer or worker-owned cooperative that made the written statement described in section 664(g)(1)(E) or 1042(b)(3)(B) and made an allocation prohibited under section 409(n) of qualified securities of an ESOP taxable under section 4979A; or an employer or worker-owned cooperative who made an allocation of S corporation stock of an ESOP prohibited under section 409(p) taxable under section 4979A.

15. An employer who receives an employer reversion from a deferred compensation plan taxable under section 4980.

16. An employer or multiemployer plan liable for the tax under section 4980F for failure to give notice of a significant reduction in the rate of future benefit accrual.

A Form 5330 and tax payment is required for any of the following.
* Each year any of the following under *Who Must File*, earlier, apply: (1), (2), (3), (5), (6), (7), (8), (9), (10), (11), (12), (13), (14), or (16).
* Each failure of an employer to make the required contribution to a multiemployer plan, as required by a funding improvement or rehabilitation plan under section 432.

Cat. No. 11871X

- A reversion of plan assets from a qualified plan taxable under section 4980.
- Each year or part of a year in the taxable period in which a prohibited transaction occurs under section 4975. See the instructions for Schedule C, line 2, columns (d) and (e), for a definition of "taxable period."

When To File

File one Form 5330 to report all excise taxes with the same filing due date. However, if the taxes are from separate plans, file separate forms for each plan.

Generally, filing Form 5330 starts the statute of limitations running only with respect to the particular excise tax(es) reported on that Form 5330. However, statutes of limitations with respect to the prohibited transaction excise tax(es) are based on the filing of the applicable Form 5500, Annual Return/Report of Employee Benefit Plan.

Use Table 1 to determine the due date of Form 5330.

Extension. File Form 5558, Application for Extension of Time to File Certain Employee Plan Returns, to request an extension of time to file. If approved, you may be granted an extension of up to 6 months after the normal due date of Form 5330.

 Form 5558 does not extend the time to pay your taxes. See the instructions for Form 5558.

Where To File

 File Form 5330 at the following address:

> Department of the Treasury
> Internal Revenue Service Center
> Ogden, UT 84201

Private delivery services. You can use certain private delivery services designated by the IRS to meet the "timely mailing as timely filing/paying" rule for tax returns and payments. These private delivery services include only the following:

- DHL Express (DHL): DHL Same Day Service.
- Federal Express (FedEx): FedEx Priority Overnight, FedEx Standard Overnight, FedEx 2Day, FedEx International Priority, and FedEx International First.
- United Parcel Service (UPS): UPS Next Day Air, UPS Next Day Air Saver, UPS 2nd Day Air, UPS 2nd Day Air

A.M., UPS Worldwide Express Plus, and UPS Worldwide Express.

The private delivery service can tell you how to get written proof of the mailing date.

 Private delivery services cannot deliver items to P.O. boxes. You must use the U.S. Postal Service to mail any item to an IRS P.O. box address.

Table 1. Excise Tax Due Dates

IF the taxes are due under section . . .	THEN file Form 5330 by the . . .
4965	15th day of the 5th month following the close of the entity manager's tax year during which the tax-exempt entity becomes a party to the transaction.
4971	last day of the 7th month after the end of the employer's tax year or $8^1\!2$ months after the last day of the plan year that ends with or within the filer's tax year.
4971(f)	last day of the 7th month after the end of the employer's tax year or $8^1\!2$ months after the last day of the plan year that ends with or within the filer's tax year.
4971(g)(2)	last day of the 7th month after the end of the employer's tax year or $8^1\!2$ months after the last day of the plan year that ends with or within the filer's tax year.
4971(g)(3)	last day of the 7th month after the end of the employer's tax year or $8^1\!2$ months after the last day of the plan year that ends with or within the filer's tax year.
4971(g)(4)	last day of the 7th month after the end of the employer's tax year or $8^1\!2$ months after the last day of the plan year that ends with or within the filer's tax year.
4972	last day of the 7th month after the end of the tax year of the employer or other person who must file this return.
4973(a)(3)	last day of the 7th month after the end of the tax year of the individual who must file this return.
4975	last day of the 7th month after the end of the tax year of the employer or other person who must file this return.
4976	last day of the 7th month after the end of the tax year of the employer or other person who must file this return.
4977	last day of the 7th month after the end of the calendar year in which the excess fringe benefits were paid to your employees.
4978	last day of the 7th month after the end of the tax year of the employer or other person who must file this return.
4979	last day of the 15th month after the close of the plan year to which the excess contributions or excess aggregate contributions relate.
4979A	last day of the 7th month after the end of the tax year of the employer or other person who must file this return.
4980	last day of the month following the month in which the reversion occurred.
4980F	last day of the month following the month in which the failure occurred.

If the filing due date falls on a Saturday, Sunday, or legal holiday, the return may be filed on the next business day.

Interest and Penalties

Interest. Interest is charged on taxes not paid by the due date even if an extension of time to file is granted. Interest is also charged on penalties imposed from the due date, including extensions, to the date of payment for failure to file, negligence, fraud, gross valuation overstatements, and substantial understatements of tax. The interest rate is determined under section 6621.

Penalty for late filing of return. If you do not file a return by the due date, including extensions, you may have to pay a penalty of 5% of the unpaid tax for each month or part of a month the return is late, up to a maximum of 25% of the unpaid tax. The minimum penalty for a return that is more than 60 days late is the smaller of the tax due or $100. The penalty will not be imposed if you can show that the failure to file on time was due to reasonable cause. If you file late, you must attach a statement to Form 5330 explaining the reasonable cause.

Penalty for late payment of tax. If you do not pay the tax when due, you may have to pay a penalty of ½ of 1% of the unpaid tax for each month or part of a month the tax is not paid, up to a maximum of 25% of the unpaid tax. The penalty will not be imposed if you can show that the failure to pay on time was due to reasonable cause.

Interest and penalties for late filing and late payment will be billed separately after the return is filed.

Claim for Refund or Credit/Amended Return

File an amended Form 5330 for any of the following.
- To claim a refund of overpaid taxes reportable on Form 5330.
- To receive a credit for overpaid taxes.
- To report additional taxes due within the same tax year of the filer if those taxes have the same due date as those previously reported. Check the box in item H of the Entity Section and report the correct amount of taxes on Schedule A through K, as appropriate, and on Part I, lines 1 through 16. See the instructions for Part II, lines 17 through 19.

If you file an amended return to claim a refund or credit, the claim must state in detail the reasons for claiming the refund. In order for the IRS to promptly consider your claim, you must provide the appropriate supporting evidence. See Regulations section 301.6402-2 for more details.

Specific Instructions

Filer tax year. Enter the tax year of the employer, entity, or individual on whom the tax is imposed by using the plan year beginning and ending dates entered in Part I of Form 5500 or by using the tax year of the business return filed.

Item A. Name and address of filer. Enter the name and address of the employer, individual, or other entity who is liable for the tax.

Include the suite, room, or other unit numbers after the street number. If the post office does not deliver mail to the street address and you have a P.O. box, show the box number instead of the street address.

If the plan has a foreign address, enter the information in the following order: city or town, state or province, country, and ZIP or foreign postal code. Follow the country's practice for entering the postal code. Do not abbreviate the country name.

Item B. Filer's identifying number. Enter the filer's identifying number in the appropriate section. The filer's identifying number is either the filer's employer identification number (EIN) or the filer's social security number (SSN), but not both. The identifying number of an individual, other than a sole proprietor with an EIN, is his or her social security number. The identifying number for all other filers is their EIN. The EIN is the nine-digit number assigned to the plan sponsor/employer, entity, or individual on whom the tax is imposed.

Item C. Name of plan. Enter the formal name of the plan, name of the plan sponsor, or name of the insurance company or financial institution of the direct filing entity (DFE). In the case of a group insurance arrangement (GIA), enter the name of the trust or other entity that holds the insurance contract. In the case of a master trust investment account (MTIA), enter the name of the sponsoring employers.

If the plan covers only the employees of one employer, enter the employer's name or enough information to identify the plan. This should be the same name indicated on the Form 5500 series return/report if that form is required to be filed for the plan.

Item D. Name and address of plan sponsor. The term "plan sponsor" means:

1. The employer, for an employee benefit plan established or maintained by a single employer;

2. The employee organization, in the case of a plan of an employee organization;

3. The association, committee, joint board of trustees, or other similar group of representatives of the parties who establish or maintain the plan, if the plan is established or maintained jointly by one or more employers and one or more employee organizations, or by two or more employers.

Include the suite, room, or other unit numbers after the street number. If the post office does not deliver mail to the street address and you have a P.O. box, show the box number instead of the street address.

If the plan has a foreign address, enter the information in the following order: city or town, state or province, and country. Follow the country's practice for entering the postal code. Do not abbreviate the country name.

Item E. Plan sponsor's EIN. Enter the nine-digit EIN assigned to the plan sponsor. This should be the same number used to file the Form 5500 series return/report.

Item F. Plan year ending. "Plan year" means the calendar or fiscal year on which the records of the plan are kept. Enter eight digits in month/date/year order. This number assists the IRS in properly identifying the plan and time period for which the Form 5330 is being filed. For example, a plan year ending March 31, 2007, should be shown as 03/31/2007.

Item G. Plan number. Enter the three-digit number that the employer or plan administrator assigned to the plan. This three-digit number is used with the EIN entered on line B and is used by the IRS, the Department of Labor, and the Pension Benefit Guaranty Corporation as a unique 12-digit number to identify the plan.

 If the plan number is not provided, this will cause a delay in processing your return.

Item H. Amended return. If you are filing an amended Form 5330, check the box on this line, and see the instructions for Part II, lines 17 through 19. Also see *Claim for Refund or Credit/Amended Return*, earlier.

Filer's signature. To reduce the possibility of correspondence and penalties, please sign and date the form. Also enter a daytime phone number where you can be reached.

Preparer's signature. Anyone who prepares your return and does not charge you should not sign your return. For example, a regular full-time employee or your business partner who prepares the return should not sign.

Generally, anyone who is paid to prepare the return must sign the return in the space provided and fill in the *Paid*

Preparer's Use Only area. See section 7701(a)(36)(B) for exceptions.

In addition to signing and completing the required information, the paid preparer must give a copy of the completed return to the taxpayer.

Note. A paid preparer may sign original or amended returns by rubber stamp, mechanical device, or computer software program.

Part I. Taxes

Line 4. Enter the total amount of the disqualified benefit under section 4976. Section 4976 imposes an excise tax on employers who maintain a funded welfare benefit plan that provides a disqualified benefit during any tax year. The tax is 100% of the disqualified benefit.

Generally, a *disqualified benefit* is any of the following.
* Any post-retirement medical benefit or life insurance benefit provided for a key employee unless the benefit is provided from a separate account established for the key employee under section 419A(d).
* Any post-retirement medical benefit or life insurance benefit unless the plan meets the nondiscrimination requirements of section 505(b) for those benefits.
* Any portion of the fund that reverts to the benefit of the employer.

Lines 5a and 5b. Section 4978 imposes an excise tax on a sale or transfer of securities acquired in a sale or qualified gratuitous transfer to which section 1042 or section 664(g) applied, respectively, if the sale or transfer takes place within 3 years after the date of the acquisition of qualified securities, as defined in section 1042(c)(1) or a section 664(g) transfer.

The tax is 10% of the amount realized on the disposition of the qualified securities if an ESOP or eligible worker-owned cooperative, as defined in section 1042(c)(2), disposes of the qualified securities within the 3-year period described above, and either of the following applies:
* The total number of shares held by that plan or cooperative after the disposition is less than the total number of employer securities held immediately after the sale, or
* Except to the extent provided in regulations, the value of qualified securities held by the plan or cooperative after the disposition is less than 30% of the total value of all

employer securities as of the disposition (60% of the total value of all employer securities in the case of any qualified employer securities acquired in a qualified gratuitous transfer to which section 664(g) applied).

See section 4978(b)(2) for the limitation on the amount of tax.

The section 4978 tax must be paid by the employer or the eligible worker-owned cooperative that made the written statement described in section 1042(b)(3)(B) on dispositions that occurred during their tax year.

The section 4978 tax does not apply to a distribution of qualified securities or sale of such securities if any of the following occurs.
* The death of the employee.
* The retirement of the employee after the employee has reached age 59½.
* The disability of the employee (within the meaning of section 72(m)(7)).
* The separation of the employee from service for any period that results in a 1-year break in service, as defined in section 411(a)(6)(A).

For purposes of section 4978, an exchange of qualified securities in a reorganization described in section 368(a)(1) for stock of another corporation will not be treated as a disposition.

For section 4978 excise taxes, the amount entered in Part I, line 5a is the amount realized on the disposition of qualified securities, multiplied by 10%. Also check the appropriate box on line 5b.

Line 6. Section 4979A imposes a 50% excise tax on allocated amounts involved in any of the following.

1. A prohibited allocation of qualified securities by any ESOP or eligible worker-owned cooperative.

2. A prohibited allocation described in section 664(g)(5)(A). Section 664(g)(5)(A) prohibits any portion of the assets of the ESOP attributable to securities acquired by the plan in a qualified gratuitous transfer to be allocated to the account of:

a. Any person related to the decedent within the meaning of section 267(b) or a member of the decedent's family within the meaning of section 2032A(e)(2), or

b. Any person who, at the time of the allocation or at any time during the 1-year period ending on the date of acquisition of qualified employer securities by the plan, is a 5%

shareholder of the employer maintaining the plan.

3. The accrual or allocation of S corporation shares in an ESOP during a nonallocation year constituting a prohibited allocation under section 409(p).

4. A synthetic equity owned by a disqualified person in any nonallocation year.

Prohibited allocations for ESOP or worker-owned cooperative. For purposes of items (1) and (2) above, a "prohibited allocation of qualified securities by any ESOP or eligible worker-owned cooperative" is any allocation of qualified securities acquired in a nonrecognition-of-gain sale under section 1042, which violates section 409(n), and any benefit that accrues to any person in violation of section 409(n).

Under section 409(n), an ESOP or worker-owned cooperative cannot allow any portion of assets attributable to employer securities acquired in a section 1042 sale to accrue or be allocated, directly or indirectly, to the taxpayer, or any person related to the taxpayer, involved in the transaction during the nonallocation period. For purposes of section 409(n), "relationship to the taxpayer" is defined under section 267(b).

The nonallocation period is the period beginning on the date the qualified securities are sold and ending on the later of:
* 10 years after the date of sale, or
* The date on which the final payment is made if acquisition indebtedness was incurred at the time of sale.

The employer sponsoring the plan or the eligible worker-owned cooperative is responsible for paying the tax.

Generally, the prohibited allocation rules for securities in an S corporation are effective for plan years beginning after December 31, 2004; however, these rules are effective for plan years ending after March 14, 2001, if:
* *The ESOP was established after March 14, 2001; or*
* *The ESOP was established on or before March 14, 2001, and the employer maintaining the plan was **not** an S corporation.*

Prohibited allocations of securities in an S corporation. For purposes of items (3) and (4), under *Line 6*, earlier, the excise tax on these transactions under section 4979A is

50% of the amount involved. The amount involved includes the following.

1. The value of any synthetic equity owned by a disqualified person in any nonallocation year. "Synthetic equity" means any stock option, warrant, restricted stock, deferred issuance stock right, or similar interest or right that gives the holder the right to acquire or receive stock of the S corporation in the future. Synthetic equity may also include a stock appreciation right, phantom stock unit, or similar right to a future cash payment based on the value of the stock or appreciation; and nonqualified deferred compensation as described in Regulations section 1.409(p)-1(f)(2)(iv). The value of a synthetic equity is the value of the shares on which the synthetic equity is based or the present value of the nonqualified deferred compensation.

2. The value of any S corporation shares in an ESOP accruing during a nonallocation year or allocated directly or indirectly under the ESOP or any other plan of the employer qualified under section 401(a) for the benefit of a disqualified person. For additional information, see Regulations section 1.409(p)-1(b)(2).

3. The total value of all deemed-owned shares of all disqualified persons.

For this purpose, a "nonallocation year" means a plan year where the ESOP, at any time during the year, holds employer securities in an S corporation, and disqualified persons own at least:
• 50% of the number of outstanding shares of the S corporation (including deemed-owned ESOP shares), or
• 50% of the aggregate number of outstanding shares of stock (including deemed-owned ESOP shares) and synthetic equity in the S corporation.

For purposes of determining a nonallocation year, the attribution rules of section 318(a) will apply; however, the option rule of section 318(a)(4) will not apply. Additionally, the attribution rules defining family member are modified to include the individual's:
• Spouse,
• Ancestor or lineal descendant of the individual or the individual's spouse, and
• A brother or sister of the individual or of the individual's spouse and any lineal descendant of the brother or sister.

A spouse of an individual legally separated from an individual under a decree of divorce or separate maintenance is not treated as the individual's spouse.

An individual is a disqualified person if:
• The total number of shares owned by the person and the members of the person's family, as defined in section 409(p)(4)(D), is at least 20% of the deemed-owned shares, as defined in section 409(p)(4)(C), in the S corporation; or
• The person owns at least 10% of the deemed-owned shares, as defined in section 409(p)(4)(C), in the S corporation.

⚠️ **CAUTION** *Under section 409(p)(7), the Secretary of the Treasury may, through regulations or other guidance of general applicability, provide that a nonallocation year occurs in any case in which the principal purpose of the ownership structure of an S corporation constitutes an avoidance or evasion of section 409(p). See Regulations section 1.408(p)-1.*

For section 4979A excise taxes, the amount entered in Part I, line 6, is 50% of the amount involved in the prohibited allocations described in items (1) through (4), earlier, under *Line 6*.

Line 10a. Under section 4971(g)(2), each employer who contributes to a multiemployer plan and fails to comply with a funding improvement or rehabilitation plan will be liable for an excise tax for each failure to make a required contribution within the time frame under such plan. Enter the amount of each contribution the employer failed to make in a timely manner.

A "funding improvement plan" is a plan which consists of the actions, including options or a range of options to be proposed to the bargaining parties, formulated to provide, based on reasonably anticipated experience and reasonable actuarial assumptions, for the attainment of the following requirements by the plan during the funding improvement period.

1. The plan's funded percentage as of the close of the funding improvement period equals or exceeds a percentage equal to the sum of:
a. The percentage as of the beginning of the funding improvement period, plus
b. 33% of the difference between 100% and the percentage as of the beginning of the funding improvement period (or 20% of the difference if the plan is in seriously endangered status).

2. No accumulated funding deficiency for any plan year during the funding improvement period, taking into account any extension of amortization period under section 431(d).

A "rehabilitation plan" is a plan which consists of actions, including options or a range of options to be proposed to the bargaining parties, formulated to enable the plan to cease to be in critical status by the end of the rehabilitation period.

All or part of this excise tax may be waived under section 4971(g)(5).

Line 16. If a tax-exempt entity manager approves or otherwise causes the entity to be a party to a prohibited tax shelter transaction during the year and knows or has reason to know that the transaction is a prohibited tax shelter transaction, the entity manager must pay an excise tax under section 4965(b)(2).

For purposes of section 4965, plan entities are:
• Qualified pension, profit-sharing, and stock bonus plans described in section 401(a);
• Annuity plans described in section 403(a);
• Annuity contracts described in section 403(b);
• Qualified tuition programs described in section 529;
• Retirement plans maintained by a governmental employer described in section 457(b);
• Individual retirement accounts within the meaning of section 408(a);
• Individual retirement annuities within the meaning of section 408(b);
• Archer medical savings accounts (MSAs) within the meaning of section 220(d);
• Coverdell education savings accounts described in section 530; and
• Health savings accounts within the meaning of section 223(d).

An *entity manager* is the person who approves or otherwise causes the entity to be a party to a prohibited tax shelter transaction.

The excise tax under section 4965(a)(2) is $20,000 for each approval or other act causing the organization to be a party to a prohibited tax shelter transaction.

A "prohibited tax shelter transaction" is any listed transaction and any prohibited reportable transaction, as defined below.

1. A "listed transaction" is a reportable transaction that is the same as, or substantially similar to, a

transaction specifically identified by the Secretary as a tax avoidance transaction for purposes of section 6011.

2. A "prohibited reportable transaction" is:

a. Any confidential transaction within the meaning of Regulations section 1.6011-4(b)(3), or

b. Any transaction with contractual protection within the meaning of Regulations section 1.6011-4(b)(4).

Part II. Tax Due

If you are filing an amended Form 5330 and you paid taxes with your original return and those taxes have the same due date as those previously reported, check the box in item H and enter the tax reported on your original return in the entry space for line 18. If you file Form 5330 for a claim for refund or credit, show the amount of overreported tax in parentheses on line 19. Otherwise, show the amount of additional tax due on line 19 and include the payment with the amended Form 5330.

Lines 17–19. Make your check or money order payable to the "United States Treasury" for the full amount due. Attach the payment to your return. Write your name, identifying number, plan number, and "Form 5330, Section ____" on your payment.

File at the address shown under *Where To File*, earlier.

Schedule A. Tax on Nondeductible Employer Contributions to Qualified Employer Plans (Section 4972)

Section 4972. Section 4972 imposes an excise tax on employers who make nondeductible contributions to their qualified plans. The excise tax is equal to 10% of the nondeductible contributions in the plan as of the end of the employer's tax year.

A "qualified employer plan" for purposes of this section means any plan qualified under section 401(a), any annuity plan qualified under section 403(a), and any simplified employee pension plan qualified under section 408(k) or any simple retirement account under section 408(p). The term qualified plan does not include certain governmental plans and certain plans maintained by tax-exempt organizations.

For purposes of section 4972, "nondeductible contributions" for the employer's current tax year are the sum of:

1. The excess (if any) of the employer's contribution for the tax year less the amount allowable as a deduction under section 404 for that year, and

2. The total amount of the employer's contributions for each preceding tax year that was not allowable as a deduction under section 404 for such preceding year, reduced by the sum of:

a. The portion of that amount available for return under the applicable qualification rules and actually returned to the employer prior to the close of the current tax year, and

b. The portion of such amount that became deductible for a preceding tax year or for the current tax year.

Although pre-1987 nondeductible contributions are not subject to this excise tax, they are taken into account to determine the extent to which post-1986 contributions are deductible. See section 4972 and Pub. 560, Retirement Plans for Small Business, for details.

Defined benefit plans exception. For purposes of determining the amount of nondeductible contributions subject to the 10% excise tax, the employer may elect not to include any contributions to a defined benefit plan except, in the case of a multiemployer plan, to the extent those contributions exceed the full-funding limitation (as defined in section 431(c)(6)). This election applies to terminated and ongoing plans. An employer making this election cannot also benefit from the exceptions for terminating plans and for certain contributions to defined contribution plans under section 4972(c)(6). When determining the amount of nondeductible contributions, the deductible limits under section 404(a)(7) must be applied first to contributions to defined contribution plans and then to contributions to defined benefit plans.

Defined contribution plans exception. In determining the amount of nondeductible contributions subject to the 10% excise tax, do not include any of the following.
- Employer contributions to one or more defined contribution plans which are nondeductible solely because of section 404(a)(7) that do not exceed the

matching contributions described in section 401(m)(4)(A).
- Contributions to a SIMPLE 401(k) or a SIMPLE IRA considered nondeductible because they are not made in connection with the employer's trade or business. However, this provision pertaining to SIMPLEs does not apply to contributions made on behalf of the employer or the employer's family.

For purposes of this exception, the combined plan deduction limits are first applied to contributions to the defined benefit plan and then to the defined contribution plan.

Restorative payments to a defined contribution plan are not considered nondeductible contributions if the payments are made to restore some or all of the plan's losses due to an action (or a failure to act) that creates a reasonable risk of liability for breach of fiduciary duty. Amounts paid in excess of the loss are not considered restorative payments.

For these purposes, multiemployer plans are not taken into consideration in applying the overall limit on deductions where there is a combination of defined benefit and defined contribution plans.

Schedule B. Tax on Excess Contributions to Section 403(b)(7)(A) Custodial Accounts (Section 4973(a)(3))

Section 4973(a) imposes a 6% excise tax on excess contributions to section 403(b)(7)(A) custodial accounts at the close of the tax year. The tax is paid by the individual account holder.

Line 1. Enter total current year contributions, less any rollover contributions described in sections 403(b)(8) or 408(d)(3)(A).

Line 2. Enter the amount excludable under section 415(c) (limit on annual additions).

TIP *To determine the amount excludable for a specific year, see Pub. 571, Tax-Sheltered Annuity Plans (403(b) Plans), for that year.*

The limit on annual additions under section 415(c)(1)(A) is subject to cost-of-living adjustments as described in section 415(d). The dollar limit for a calendar year, as adjusted annually, is published during the fourth quarter of the prior calendar year in the Internal Revenue Bulletin.

Schedule C. Tax on Prohibited Transactions (Section 4975)

Section 4975. Section 4975 imposes an excise tax on a disqualified person who engages in a prohibited transaction with the plan.

Plan. For purposes of this section, the term "plan" means any of the following.
- A trust described in section 401(a) that forms part of a plan.
- A plan described in section 403(a) that is exempt from tax under section 501(a).
- An individual retirement account described in section 408(a).
- An individual retirement annuity described in section 408(b).
- An Archer MSA described in section 220(d).
- A Coverdell education savings account described in section 530.
- A Health Savings Account described in section 223(d).
- A trust described in section 501(c)(22).

⚠️ **CAUTION** *If the IRS determined at any time that your plan was a plan as defined above, it will always remain subject to the excise tax on prohibited transactions under section 4975. This also applies to the tax on minimum funding deficiencies under section 4971.*

Disqualified person. A "disqualified person" is a person who is any of the following.

1. A fiduciary.

2. A person providing services to the plan.

3. An employer, any of whose employees are covered by the plan.

4. An employee organization, any of whose members are covered by the plan.

5. A direct or indirect owner of 50% or more of:

a. The combined voting power of all classes of stock entitled to vote, or the total value of shares of all classes of stock of a corporation;

b. The capital interest or the profits interest of a partnership; or

c. The beneficial interest of a trust or unincorporated enterprise in (a), (b), or (c), which is an employer or an employee organization described in (3) or (4) above. A limited liability company should be treated as a corporation or a partnership, depending on how the organization is treated for federal tax purposes.

6. A member of the family of any individual described in (1), (2), (3), or (5). A "member of a family" is the spouse, ancestor, lineal descendant, and any spouse of a lineal descendant.

7. A corporation, partnership, or trust or estate of which (or in which) any direct or indirect owner holds 50% or more of the interest described in (5a), (5b), or (5c) of such entity. For this purpose, the beneficial interest of the trust or estate is owned, directly or indirectly, or held by persons described in (1) through (5).

8. An officer, director (or an individual having powers or responsibilities similar to those of officers or directors), a 10% or more shareholder or highly compensated employee (earning 10% or more of the yearly wages of an employer) of a person described in (3), (4), (5), or (7).

9. A 10% or more (in capital or profits) partner or joint venturer of a person described in (3), (4), (5), or (7).

10. Any disqualified person, as described in (1) through (9) above, who is a disqualified person with respect to any plan to which a section 501(c)(22) trust applies, that is permitted to make payments under section 4223 of the Employee Retirement Income Security Act (ERISA).

Prohibited transaction. A *prohibited transaction* is any direct or indirect:

1. Sale or exchange, or leasing of any property between a plan and a disqualified person; or a transfer of real or personal property by a disqualified person to a plan where the property is subject to a mortgage or similar lien placed on the property by the disqualified person within 10 years prior to the transfer, or the property transferred is subject to a mortgage or similar lien which the plan assumes;

2. Lending of money or other extension of credit between a plan and a disqualified person;

3. Furnishing of goods, services, or facilities between a plan and a disqualified person;

4. Transfer to, or use by or for the benefit of, a disqualified person of income or assets of a plan;

5. Act by a disqualified person who is a fiduciary whereby he or she deals with the income or assets of a plan in his or her own interest or account; or

6. Receipt of any consideration for his or her own personal account by any disqualified person who is a fiduciary from any party dealing with the plan connected with a transaction involving the income or assets of the plan.

Exemptions. See sections 4975(d), 4975(f)(6)(B)(ii), and 4975(f)(6)(B)(iii) for specific exemptions to prohibited transactions. Also see section 4975(c)(2) for certain other transactions or classes of transactions that may become exempt.

Line 1. Check the box that best characterizes the prohibited transaction for which an excise tax is being paid. A prohibited transaction is *discrete* unless it is of an ongoing nature. Transactions involving the use of money (loans, etc.) or other property (rent, etc.) are of an ongoing nature and will be treated as a new prohibited transaction on the first day of each succeeding tax year or part of a tax year that is within the taxable period.

Line 2, Column (b). List the date of all prohibited transactions that took place in connection with a particular plan during the current tax year. Also, list the date of all prohibited transactions that took place in prior years unless either the transaction was corrected in a prior tax year or the section 4975(a) tax was assessed in the prior tax year. A disqualified person who engages in a prohibited transaction must file a separate Form 5330 to report the excise tax due under section 4975 for each tax year.

Line 2, Columns (d) and (e). The "amount involved in a prohibited transaction" means the greater of the amount of money and the fair market value (FMV) of the other property given, or the amount of money and the FMV of the other property received. However, for services described in sections 4975(d)(2) and (10), the amount involved only applies to excess compensation. For purposes of section 4975(a), FMV must be determined as of the date on which the prohibited transaction occurs. If the use of money or other property is involved, the amount involved is the greater of the amount paid for the use or the FMV of the use for the period for which the money or other property is used. In addition, transactions involving the use of money or other property will be treated as giving rise to a prohibited transaction occurring on the date of the actual transaction, plus a new prohibited transaction on the first day of each

Figure 1. Example for the calendar 2006 plan year used when filing for the 2006 tax year

Schedule C. Tax on Prohibited Transactions (Section 4975) (see instructions) **Reported by the last day of the 7th month after the end of the tax year of the employer (or other person who must file the return)**

(a) Transaction number	(b) Date of transaction (see instructions)	(c) Description of prohibited transaction	(d) Amount involved in prohibited transaction (see instructions)	(e) Initial tax on prohibited transaction (multiply each transaction in column (d) by the appropriate rate (see instructions))
(i)	7-1-06	Loan	$6,000	$900
(ii)				
(iii)				
3 Add amounts in column (e). Enter here and on Part I, line 3a . . . . ▶				$900

succeeding tax year or portion of a succeeding tax year which is within the taxable period. The "taxable period" for this purpose is the period of time beginning with the date of the prohibited transaction and ending with the earliest of:

1. The date the correction is completed,

2. The date of the mailing of a notice of deficiency, or

3. The date on which the tax under section 4975(a) is assessed.

See the instructions for Schedule C, under *Additional tax for failure to correct the prohibited transaction (section 4975(b))*, for the definition of "correction."

⚠ **CAUTION** *Temporary Regulations section 141.4975-13 states that, until final regulations are written under section 4975(f), the definitions of* amount involved *and* correction *found in Regulations section 53.4941(e)-1 will apply.*

Failure to transmit participant contributions. For purposes of calculating the excise tax on a prohibited transaction where there is a failure to transmit participant contributions (elective deferrals) or amounts that would have otherwise been payable to the participant in cash, the amount involved is based on interest on those elective deferrals. See Rev. Rul. 2006-38.

Column (e). The initial tax on a prohibited transaction is 15% of the amount involved in each prohibited transaction for each year or part of a year in the taxable period. Multiply the amount in column (d) by 15%.

Example. The example of a prohibited transaction below does not cover all types of prohibited transactions. For more examples, see Regulations section 53.4941(e)-1(b)(4).

A disqualified person borrows money from a plan in a prohibited transaction under section 4975. The FMV of the use of the money and the actual interest on the loan is $1,000 per month (the actual interest is paid in this example). The loan was made on July 1, 2006 (date of transaction) and repaid on December 31, 2007 (date of correction). The disqualified person's tax year is the calendar year. On July 31, 2008, the disqualified person files a delinquent Form 5330 for the 2006 plan year (which in this case is the calendar year) and a timely Form 5330 for the 2007 plan year (which in this case is the calendar year). No notice of deficiency with respect to the tax imposed by section 4975(a) has been mailed to the disqualified person and no assessment of such excise tax has been made by the IRS before the time the disqualified person filed the Forms 5330.

Each prohibited transaction has its own separate taxable period that begins on the date the prohibited transaction occurred or is deemed to occur and ends on the date of the correction. The taxable period that begins on the date the loan occurs runs from July 1, 2006 (date of loan) through December 31, 2007 (date of correction). When a loan is a prohibited transaction, the loan is treated as giving rise to a prohibited transaction on the date the transaction occurs, and an additional prohibited transaction on the first day of each succeeding tax year (or portion of a tax year) within the taxable period that begins on the date the loan occurs. Therefore, in this example, there are two prohibited transactions, the first occurring on July 1, 2006, and ending on December 31, 2006, and the second occurring on January 1, 2007, and ending on December 31, 2007.

Section 4975(a) imposes a 15% excise tax on the amount involved for each tax year or part thereof in the taxable period of each prohibited transaction.

The Form 5330 for the year ending December 31, 2006: The amount involved to be reported on the Form 5330, Schedule C, line 2, column (d), for the 2006 plan year, is $6,000 (6 months x $1,000). The tax due is $900 ($6,000 x 15%). (See *Figure 1*.) (Any interest and penalties imposed for the delinquent filing of Form 5330 and the delinquent payment of the excise tax for 2006 will be billed separately to the disqualified person.)

The Form 5330 for the year ending December 31, 2007: The excise tax to be reported on the 2007 Form 5330 would include both the prohibited transaction of July 1, 2006, with an amount involved of $6,000, resulting in a tax due of $900 ($6,000 x 15%), and the second prohibited transaction of January 1, 2007, with an amount involved of $12,000 (12 months x $1,000), resulting in a tax due of $1,800 ($12,000 x 15%). (See *Figure 2*.) The taxable period for the second prohibited transaction runs from January 1, 2007, through December 31, 2007 (date of correction). Because there are two prohibited transactions with taxable periods running during 2007, the section 4975(a) tax is due for the 2007 tax year for both prohibited transactions.

TIP *When a loan from a qualified plan that is a prohibited transaction spans successive tax years, constituting multiple prohibited transactions, and during those years the first tier prohibited transaction excise tax rate changes, the first tier excise tax liability for each prohibited transaction is the sum of the products resulting from multiplying the amount involved for each year in the taxable period for that prohibited transaction by the excise tax rate in effect at the beginning of that taxable*

Figure 2. Example for the calendar 2007 plan year used when filing for the 2007 tax year

Schedule C. Tax on Prohibited Transactions (Section 4975) (see instructions) **Reported by the last day of the 7th month after the end of the tax year of the employer (or other person who must file the return)**

(a) Transaction number	(b) Date of transaction (see instructions)	(c) Description of prohibited transaction	(d) Amount involved in prohibited transaction (see instructions)	(e) Initial tax on prohibited transaction (multiply each transaction in column (d) by the appropriate rate (see instructions))
(i)	7-1-06	Loan	$6,000	$900
(ii)	1-1-07	Loan	$12,000	$1,800
(iii)				
3 Add amounts in column (e). Enter here and on Part I, line 3a . . . . ▶				$2,700

period. *For more information, see Rev. Rul. 2002-43, 2002-32 I.R.B. 85 at www.irs.gov/pub/irs-irbs/irb02-28.pdf. Unlike the previous example, the example in Rev. Rul. 2002-43 contains unpaid interest.*

Additional tax for failure to correct the prohibited transaction (section 4975(b)). To avoid liability for additional taxes and penalties, and in some cases further initial taxes, a correction must be made within the taxable period. The term "correction" is defined as undoing the prohibited transaction to the extent possible, but in any case placing the plan in a financial position not worse than that in which it would be if the disqualified person were acting under the highest fiduciary standards.

If the prohibited transaction is not corrected within the taxable period, an additional tax equal to 100% of the amount involved will be imposed under section 4975(b). Any disqualified person who participated in the prohibited transaction (other than a fiduciary acting only as such) must pay this tax imposed by section 4975(b). Report the additional tax in Part I, Section A, line 3b.

Line 4. Check "No" if there has not been a correction of all of the prohibited transactions by the end of the tax year for which this Form 5330 is being filed. Attach a statement indicating when the correction has been or will be made.

Line 5. If more than one disqualified person participated in the same prohibited transaction, list on this schedule the name, address, and SSN or EIN of each disqualified person, other than the disqualified person who files this return.

For all transactions complete columns (a), (b), and (c). If the transaction has been corrected, complete columns (a) through (e). If additional space is needed, you may attach a statement fully explaining the correction and identifying persons involved in the prohibited transaction.

Prohibited transactions and investment advice. The prohibited transaction rules of section 4975(c) will not apply to any transaction in connection with investment advice, if the investment advice provided by a fiduciary adviser is provided under an eligible investment advice arrangement.

For this purpose an "eligible investment advice arrangement" is an arrangement which either:
• Provides that any fees, including any commission or other compensation, received by the fiduciary adviser for investment advice or with respect to the sale, holding, or acquisition of any security or other property for the investment of plan assets do not vary depending on the basis of any investment option selected; or
• Uses a computer model under an investment advice program, described in section 4975(f)(8)(C), in connection with investment advice provided by a fiduciary adviser to a participant or beneficiary.
Additionally, the eligible investment advice arrangement must meet the provisions of section 4975(f)(8)(D), (E), (F), (G), (H), and (I).

For purposes of the statutory exemption on investment advice, a "fiduciary adviser" is defined in section 4975(f)(8)(J).

Correcting certain prohibited transactions. Generally, if a disqualified person enters into a direct or indirect prohibited transaction, listed in (1) through (4) below, in connection with the acquisition, holding, or disposition of certain securities or commodities, and the transaction is corrected within the correction period, it will not be treated as a prohibited transaction and no tax will be assessed.

1. Sale or exchange, or leasing of any property between a plan and a disqualified person.

2. Lending of money or other extension of credit between a plan and a disqualified person.

3. Furnishing of goods, services, or facilities between a plan and a disqualified person.

4. Transfer to, or use by or for the benefit of, a disqualified person of income or assets of a plan.

However, if at the time the transaction was entered into, the disqualified person knew or had reason to know that the transaction was prohibited, the transaction would be subject to the tax on prohibited transactions.

For purposes of section 4975(d)(23) the term "correct" means to:
• Undo the transaction to the extent possible and in all cases to make good to the plan or affected account any losses resulting from the transaction, and
• Restore to the plan or affected account any profits made through the use of assets of the plan.

The "correction period" is the 14-day period beginning on the date on which the disqualified person discovers or reasonably should have discovered that the transaction constitutes a prohibited transaction.

Schedule D. Tax on Failure to Meet Minimum Funding Standards (Section 4971(a))

In the case of a single-employer plan, section 4971(a) imposes a 10% tax on the aggregate unpaid minimum required contributions for all plan years remaining unpaid as of the end of any plan year. In the case of a multiemployer plan, section 4971(a) imposes a 5% tax on the amount of the accumulated funding deficiency determined as of the end of the plan year.

If a plan fails to meet the funding requirements under section 412, the employer and all controlled group members will be subject to excise taxes under section 4971(a) and (b).

Except in the case of a multiemployer plan, all members of a controlled group are jointly and severally liable for this tax. A "controlled group" in this case means a controlled group of corporations under section 414(b), a group of trades or businesses under common control under section 414(c), an affiliated service group under section 414(m), and any other group treated as a single employer under section 414(o).

 If the IRS determined at any time that your plan was a plan as defined as Schedule C, it will always remain subject to the excise tax on failure to meet minimum funding standards.

Line 1. Enter the amount (if any) of the aggregate unpaid minimum required contributions (or in the case of a multiemployer plan, an accumulated funding deficiency as defined in section 431(a) (or section 418B if a multiemployer plan in reorganization).

Line 2. Multiply line 1 by the applicable tax rate shown below and enter the result.
• 10% for plans other than multiemployer plans.
• 5% for all multiemployer plans.

Additional tax for failure to correct. For single-employer plans, when an initial tax is imposed under section 4971(a) on any unpaid minimum required contribution and the unpaid minimum required contribution remains unpaid as of the close of the taxable period, an additional tax of 100% of the amount that remains unpaid is imposed under section 4971(b).

For multiemployer plans, when an initial tax is imposed under section 4971(a)(2) on an accumulated funding deficiency and the accumulated funding deficiency is not corrected within the taxable period, an additional tax equal to 100% of the accumulated funding deficiency, to the extent not corrected, is imposed under section 4971(b).

For this purpose, the "taxable period" is the period beginning with the end of the plan year where there is an unpaid minimum required contribution or an

accumulated funding deficiency and ending on the earlier of:
• The date the notice of deficiency for the section 4971(a) excise tax is mailed, or
• The date the section 4971(a) excise tax is assessed.

Report the tax for failure to correct the unpaid minimum required contribution or the accumulated funding deficiency in Part I, Section B, line 8b.

Special rule for certain single-employer defined benefit plans. Single-employer defined benefit plans to which section 430 does not yet apply (because of a delayed effective date under the Pension Protection Act of 2006) should follow the instructions for multiemployer plans.

Schedule E. Tax on Failure to Pay Liquidity Shortfall (Section 4971(f)(1))

If your plan has a liquidity shortfall for which an excise tax under section 4971(f)(1) is imposed for any quarter of the plan year, complete lines 1 through 4.

Line 1. Enter the amount of the liquidity shortfall(s) for each quarter of the plan year.

Line 2. Enter the amount of any contributions made to the plan by the due date of the required quarterly installment(s) that partially corrected the liquidity shortfall(s) reported on line 1.

Line 3. Enter the net amount of the liquidity shortfall (subtract line 2 from line 1).

Additional tax for failure to correct liquidity shortfall. If the plan has a liquidity shortfall as of the close of any quarter and as of the close of the following 4 quarters, an additional tax will be imposed under section 4971(f)(2) equal to the amount on which tax was imposed by section 4971(f)(1) for such quarter. Report the additional tax in Part I, Section B, line 9b.

Schedule F. Tax on Multiemployer Plans in Endangered or Critical Status (Sections 4971(g)(3) & 4971(g)(4))

For years beginning after 2007, section 4971(g) imposes an excise tax on employers who contribute to multiemployer plans for failure to comply with a funding improvement or rehabilitation plan, failure to meet

requirements for plans in endangered or critical status, or failure to adopt a rehabilitation plan. See the instructions for line 10a, earlier.

Line 1. Under section 4971(g)(3), a multiemployer plan that is in seriously endangered status when it fails to meet its applicable benchmarks by the end of the funding improvement period will be treated as having an accumulated funding deficiency for the last plan year in such period and each succeeding year until the funding benchmarks are met.

Similarly, a plan that is in critical status and either fails to meet the requirements of section 432 by the end of the rehabilitation period, or has received certification under section 432(b)(3)(A)(ii) for 3 consecutive plan years that the plan is not making the scheduled progress in meeting its requirements under the rehabilitation plan, will be treated as having an accumulated funding deficiency for the last plan year in such period and each succeeding plan year until the funding requirements are met.

In both cases, the accumulated funding deficiency is an amount equal to the greater of the amount of the contributions necessary to meet the benchmarks or requirements, or the amount of the accumulated funding deficiency without regard to this rule. The existence of an accumulated funding deficiency triggers the initial 5% excise tax under section 4971(a).

A plan is in "endangered status" if either of the following occurs.
• The plan's actuary timely certifies that the plan is not in critical status for that plan year and at the beginning of that plan year the plan's funded percentage for the plan year is less than 80%.
• The plan has an accumulated funding deficiency for the plan year or is projected to have such an accumulated funding deficiency for any of the 6 succeeding plan years, taking into account any extension of amortization periods under section 431(d).

A plan is in "critical status" if it is determined by the multiemployer plan's actuary that one of the four formulas in section 432(b)(2) is met for the applicable plan year.

All or part of this excise tax may be waived due to reasonable cause.

Line 2. Under section 4971(g)(4), the plan sponsor of a multiemployer plan in critical status, as defined above, will be liable for an excise tax for failure to adopt a rehabilitation plan within the

time prescribed under section 432. The tax is equal to the greater of:
• The amount of tax imposed under section 4971(a)(2); or
• An amount equal to $1,100, multiplied by the number of days in the tax year which are included in the period that begins on the first day of the 240-day period that a multiemployer plan has to adopt a rehabilitation plan once it has entered critical status and that ends on the day that the rehabilitation plan is adopted.

Liability for this tax is imposed on each plan sponsor. This excise tax may not be waived.

Schedule G. Tax on Excess Fringe Benefits (Section 4977)

If you made an election to be taxed under section 4977 to continue your nontaxable fringe benefit policy that was in existence on or after January 1, 1984, check "Yes" on line 1 and complete lines 2 through 4.

Line 3. Excess fringe benefits are calculated by subtracting 1% of the aggregate compensation paid by you to your employees during the calendar year that was includable in their gross income from the aggregate value of the nontaxable fringe benefits under sections 132(a)(1) and (2).

Schedule H. Tax on Excess Contributions To Certain Plans (Section 4979)

Any employer who maintains a plan described in section 401(a), 403(a), 403(b), 408(k), or 501(c)(18) may be subject to an excise tax on excess aggregate contributions made on behalf of highly compensated employees. The employer may also be subject to an excise tax on excess contributions to a cash or deferred arrangement connected with the plan.

The tax is on the excess contributions and the excess aggregate contributions made to or on behalf of the highly compensated employees as defined in section 414(q).

A "highly compensated employee" generally is an employee who:

1. Was a 5-percent owner at any time during the year or the preceding year, or

2. For the preceding year had compensation from the employer in excess of a dollar amount for the year

($105,000 for 2008) and, if the employer so elects, was in the top-paid group for the preceding year.

An employee is in the "top-paid group" for any year if the employee is in the group consisting of the top 20% of employees when ranked on the basis of compensation paid. An employee (who is not a 5% owner) who has compensation in excess of $105,000 is not a highly compensated employee if the employer elects the top-paid group limitation and the employee is not a member of the top-paid group.

The excess contributions subject to the section 4979 excise tax are equal to the amount by which employer contributions actually paid over to the trust exceed the employer contributions that could have been made without violating the special nondiscrimination requirements of section 401(k)(3) or section 408(k)(6) in the instance of certain SEPs.

The excess aggregate contributions subject to the section 4979 excise tax are equal to the amount by which the aggregate matching contributions of the employer and the employee contributions (and any qualified nonelective contribution or elective contribution taken into account in computing the contribution percentage under section 401(m)) actually made on behalf of the highly compensated employees for each plan year exceed the maximum amount of contributions permitted in the contribution percentage computation under section 401(m)(2)(A).

However, there is no excise tax liability if the excess contributions or the excess aggregate contributions and any income earned on the contributions are distributed (or, if forfeitable, forfeited) to the participants for whom the excess contributions were made within 2½ months after the end of the plan year.

Schedule I. Tax on Reversion of Qualified Plan Assets to an Employer (Section 4980)

Section 4980 imposes an excise tax on an employer reversion of qualified plan assets to an employer. Generally, the tax is 20% of the amount of the employer reversion. The excise tax rate increases to 50% if the employer does not establish or maintain a qualified replacement plan following the plan termination or provide certain pro-rata benefit increases in connection with the plan termination. See section

4980(d)(1)(A) or (B) for more information.

An "employer reversion" is the amount of cash and the FMV of property received, directly or indirectly, by an employer from a qualified plan. For exceptions to this definition, see section 4980(c)(2)(B) and section 4980(c)(3).

A "qualified plan" is:
• Any plan meeting the requirements of section 401(a) or 403(a), other than a plan maintained by an employer if that employer has at all times been exempt from federal income tax; or
• A governmental plan within the meaning of section 414(d).

Terminated defined benefit plan. If a defined benefit plan is terminated, and an amount in excess of 25% of the maximum amount otherwise available for reversion is transferred from the terminating defined benefit plan to a defined contribution plan, the amount transferred is not treated as an employer reversion for purposes of section 4980. However, the amount the employer receives is subject to the 20% excise tax. For additional information, see Rev. Rul. 2003-85, 2003-32 I.R.B. 291 at *www.irs.gov/irb/2003-32_IRB/ar11.html*.

Lines 1–4. Enter the date of reversion on line 1. Enter the reversion amount on line 2a and the applicable excise tax rate on line 2b. If you use a tax percentage other than 50% on line 2b, explain on line 4 why you qualify to use a rate other than 50%.

Schedule J. Tax on Failure to Provide Notice of Significant Reduction in Future Accruals (Section 4980F)

Section 204(h) notice. Section 4980F imposes an excise tax on an employer (or, in the case of a multiemployer plan, the plan) for failure to give section 204(h) notice of plan amendments that provide for a significant reduction in the rate of future benefit accrual or the elimination or significant reduction of an early retirement benefit or retirement-type subsidy. The tax is $100 per day per each applicable individual and each employee organization representing participants who are applicable individuals for each day of the noncompliance period. This notice is called a "section 204(h) notice" because section 204(h) of ERISA has parallel notice requirements.

An "applicable individual" is a participant in the plan, or an alternate payee of a participant under a qualified domestic relations order, whose rate of future benefit accrual (or early retirement benefit or retirement-type subsidy) under the plan may reasonably be expected to be significantly reduced by a plan amendment. (For plan years beginning after December 31, 2007, the requirement to give 204(h) notice was extended to an employer who has an obligation to contribute to a multiemployer plan.)

Whether a participant, alternate payee, or an employer (as described in the above paragraph) is an applicable individual is determined on a typical business day that is reasonably approximate to the time the section 204(h) notice is provided (or on the latest date for providing section 204(h) notice, if earlier), based on all relevant facts and circumstances. For more information in determining whether an individual is a participant or alternate payee, see Regulations section 54.4980F-1, Q&A 10.

The "noncompliance period" is the period beginning on the date the failure first occurs and ending on the date the notice of failure is provided or the failure is corrected.

Exceptions. The section 4980F excise tax will not be imposed for a failure during any period in which the following occurs.

1. Any person subject to liability for the tax did not know that the failure existed and exercised reasonable diligence to meet the notice requirement. A person is considered to have exercised reasonable diligence but did not know the failure existed only if:

a. The responsible person exercised reasonable diligence in attempting to deliver section 204(h) notice to applicable individuals by the latest date permitted; or

b. At the latest date permitted for delivery of section 204(h) notice, the person reasonably believed that section 204(h) notice was actually delivered to each applicable individual by that date.

2. Any person subject to liability for the tax exercised reasonable diligence to meet the notice requirement and corrects the failure within 30 days after the employer (or other person responsible for the tax) knew, or exercising reasonable diligence would have known, that the failure existed.

Generally, section 204(h) notice must be provided at least 45 days before the effective date of the section 204(h) amendment. For exceptions to this rule, see Regulations section 54.4980F-1, Q&A 9.

If the person subject to liability for the excise tax exercised reasonable diligence to meet the notice requirement, the total excise tax imposed during a tax year of the employer will not exceed $500,000. Furthermore, in the case of a failure due to reasonable cause and not to willful neglect, the Secretary of the Treasury is authorized to waive the excise tax to the extent that the payment of the tax would be excessive relative to the failure involved. See Rev. Proc. 2013-4, 2013-1 I.R.B. 123, as revised by subsequent documents, available at *www.irs.gov/irb/2013-01_IRB/ar09.html*, for procedures to follow in applying for a waiver of part or all of the excise tax due to reasonable cause.

Line 4. A *failure* occurs on any day that any applicable individual is not provided section 204(h) notice.

Example. There are 1,000 applicable individuals (AI). The plan administrator fails to give section 204(h) notice to 100 AIs for 60 days, and to 50 of those AIs for an additional 30 days. In this case there are 7,500 failures ((100 AI x 60 days) + (50 AI x 30 days) = 7,500).

Schedule K. Tax on Prohibited Tax Shelter Transactions (Section 4965)

Section 4965 provides that an entity manager of a tax-exempt organization may be subject to an excise tax on prohibited tax shelter transactions under section 4965. In the case of a plan entity, an *entity manager* is any person who approves or otherwise causes the tax-exempt entity to be a party to a prohibited tax shelter transaction. The excise tax is $20,000 and is assessed for each approval or other act causing the organization to be a party to the prohibited tax shelter transaction.

Privacy Act and Paperwork Reduction Act Notice. We ask for the information on this form to carry out the Internal Revenue laws of the United States. This form is required to be filed under sections 4965, 4971, 4972, 4973, 4975, 4976, 4977, 4978, 4979, 4979A, 4980, and 4980F of the Internal

Revenue Code. Section 6109 requires you to provide your identifying number. If you fail to provide this information in a timely manner, you may be liable for penalties and interest. Routine uses of this information include giving it to the Department of Justice for civil and criminal litigation, and cities, states, and the District of Columbia for use in administering their tax laws. We may also disclose this information to federal and state or local agencies to enforce federal nontax criminal laws and to combat terrorism.

You are not required to provide the information requested on a form that is subject to the Paperwork Reduction Act unless the form displays a valid OMB control number. Books or records relating to a form or its instructions must be retained as long as their contents may become material in the administration of any Internal Revenue law. Generally, tax returns and return information are confidential, as required by section 6103.

The time needed to complete and file this form will vary depending on individual circumstances. The estimated average time is:

Recordkeeping. . .	30 hr., 22 min.
Learning about the law or the form	15 hr., 45 min.
Preparing and sending the form to the IRS	18 hr., 08 min.

If you have suggestions for making this form simpler, we would be happy to hear from you. You can send us comments from *www.irs.gov/ formspubs*. Click on "More Information" and then on "Comment on Tax Forms and Publications." Or you can also send your comments to the Internal Revenue Service, Tax Forms and Publications Division, 1111 Constitution Ave. NW, IR-6526, Washington, DC 20224. Do not send the tax form to this address. Instead, see *Where To File*, earlier.

Although we cannot respond individually to each comment received, we do appreciate your feedback and will consider your comments as we revise our tax forms and instructions.

Index

2828 ☐ VOID ☐ CORRECTED

TRUSTEE'S or ISSUER'S name, street address, city or town, state or province, country, and ZIP or foreign postal code	**1** IRA contributions (other than amounts in boxes 2–4, 8–10, 13a, and 14a) $	OMB No. 1545-0747 20**19** Form **5498**	**IRA Contribution Information**
	2 Rollover contributions $		
	3 Roth IRA conversion amount $	**4** Recharacterized contributions $	**Copy A**
TRUSTEE'S or ISSUER'S TIN PARTICIPANT'S TIN	**5** FMV of account $	**6** Life insurance cost included in box 1 $	**For Internal Revenue Service Center** File with Form 1096.
PARTICIPANT'S name	**7** IRA ☐ SEP ☐ SIMPLE ☐ Roth IRA ☐		
	8 SEP contributions $	**9** SIMPLE contributions $	**For Privacy Act and Paperwork Reduction Act Notice, see the 2019 General Instructions for Certain Information Returns.**
Street address (including apt. no.)	**10** Roth IRA contributions $	**11** Check if RMD for 2020 ☐	
	12a RMD date	**12b** RMD amount $	
City or town, state or province, country, and ZIP or foreign postal code	**13a** Postponed/late contrib. $	**13b** Year **13c** Code	
	14a Repayments $	**14b** Code	
Account number (see instructions)	**15a** FMV of certain specified assets $	**15b** Code(s)	

Form **5498**   Cat. No. 50010C   www.irs.gov/Form5498   Department of the Treasury - Internal Revenue Service

Do Not Cut or Separate Forms on This Page — Do Not Cut or Separate Forms on This Page

Form 8606

Department of the Treasury
Internal Revenue Service (99)

Nondeductible IRAs

▶ Go to *www.irs.gov/Form8606* for instructions and the latest information.

▶ Attach to 2018 Form 1040 or 2018 Form 1040NR.

OMB No. 1545-0074

2018

Attachment
Sequence No. **48**

Name. If married, file a separate form for each spouse required to file 2018 Form 8606. See instructions.

Your social security number

Fill in Your Address Only if You Are Filing This Form by Itself and Not With Your Tax Return

Home address (number and street, or P.O. box if mail is not delivered to your home)

Apt. no.

City, town or post office, state, and ZIP code. If you have a foreign address, also complete the spaces below (see instructions).

If this is an amended return, check here ▶ ☐

Foreign country name

Foreign province/state/county

Foreign postal code

Part I **Nondeductible Contributions to Traditional IRAs and Distributions From Traditional, SEP, and SIMPLE IRAs**

Complete this part only if one or more of the following apply.

- You made nondeductible contributions to a traditional IRA for 2018.
- You took distributions from a traditional, SEP, or SIMPLE IRA in 2018 **and** you made nondeductible contributions to a traditional IRA in 2018 or an earlier year. For this purpose, a distribution does not include a rollover (other than a repayment of a qualified 2017 disaster distribution (see 2018 Form 8915B)), qualified charitable distribution, one-time distribution to fund an HSA, conversion, recharacterization, or return of certain contributions.
- You converted part, but not all, of your traditional, SEP, and SIMPLE IRAs to Roth IRAs in 2018 **and** you made nondeductible contributions to a traditional IRA in 2018 or an earlier year.

1	Enter your nondeductible contributions to traditional IRAs for 2018, including those made for 2018 from January 1, 2019, through April 15, 2019. See instructions	**1**
2	Enter your total basis in traditional IRAs. See instructions	**2**
3	Add lines 1 and 2	**3**

In 2018, did you take a distribution from traditional, SEP, or SIMPLE IRAs, or make a Roth IRA conversion?

No ▶ Enter the amount from line 3 on line 14. Do not complete the rest of Part I.

Yes ▶ Go to line 4.

4	Enter those contributions included on line 1 that were made from January 1, 2019, through April 15, 2019	**4**
5	Subtract line 4 from line 3	**5**
6	Enter the value of **all** your traditional, SEP, and SIMPLE IRAs as of December 31, 2018, plus any outstanding rollovers. Subtract any repayments of qualified 2017 disaster distributions (see 2018 Form 8915B). If the result is zero or less, enter -0-. See instructions	**6**
7	Enter your distributions from traditional, SEP, and SIMPLE IRAs in 2018. **Do not** include rollovers (other than repayments of qualified 2017 disaster distributions (see 2018 Form 8915B)), qualified charitable distributions, a one-time distribution to fund an HSA, conversions to a Roth IRA, certain returned contributions, or recharacterizations of traditional IRA contributions (see instructions)	**7**
8	Enter the net amount you converted from traditional, SEP, and SIMPLE IRAs to Roth IRAs in 2018. Also enter this amount on line 16	**8**
9	Add lines 6, 7, and 8	**9**
10	Divide line 5 by line 9. Enter the result as a decimal rounded to at least 3 places. If the result is 1.000 or more, enter "1.000"	**10** × .
11	Multiply line 8 by line 10. This is the nontaxable portion of the amount you converted to Roth IRAs. Also enter this amount on line 17	**11**
12	Multiply line 7 by line 10. This is the nontaxable portion of your distributions that you did not convert to a Roth IRA	**12**
13	Add lines 11 and 12. This is the nontaxable portion of all your distributions	**13**
14	Subtract line 13 from line 3. This is **your total basis in traditional IRAs for 2018 and earlier years**	**14**
15a	Subtract line 12 from line 7	**15a**
b	Enter the amount on line 15a attributable to qualified 2017 disaster distributions from 2018 Form 8915B (see instructions). Also, enter this amount on 2018 Form 8915B, line 22	**15b**
c	**Taxable amount.** Subtract line 15b from line 15a. If more than zero, also include this amount on 2018 Form 1040, line 4b; or 2018 Form 1040NR, line 17b	**15c**

Note: You may be subject to an additional 10% tax on the amount on line 15c if you were under age 59½ at the time of the distribution. See instructions.

For Privacy Act and Paperwork Reduction Act Notice, see separate instructions.

Cat. No. 63966F

Form **8606** (2018)

Form 8606 (2018)   Page **2**

Part II | **2018 Conversions From Traditional, SEP, or SIMPLE IRAs to Roth IRAs**

Complete this part if you converted part or all of your traditional, SEP, and SIMPLE IRAs to a Roth IRA in 2018.

16	If you completed Part I, enter the amount from line 8. Otherwise, enter the net amount you converted from traditional, SEP, and SIMPLE IRAs to Roth IRAs in 2018.	**16**	
17	If you completed Part I, enter the amount from line 11. Otherwise, enter your basis in the amount on line 16 (see instructions)	**17**	
18	**Taxable amount.** Subtract line 17 from line 16. If more than zero, also include this amount on 2018 Form 1040, line 4b; or 2018 Form 1040NR, line 17b	**18**	

Part III | **Distributions From Roth IRAs**

Complete this part only if you took a distribution from a Roth IRA in 2018. For this purpose, a distribution does not include a rollover (other than a repayment of a qualified 2017 disaster distribution (see 2018 Form 8915B)), qualified charitable distribution, one-time distribution to fund an HSA, recharacterization, or return of certain contributions (see instructions).

19	Enter your total nonqualified distributions from Roth IRAs in 2018, including any qualified first-time homebuyer distributions, and any qualified 2017 disaster distributions (see instructions). Also see 2018 Form 8915B	**19**	
20	Qualified first-time homebuyer expenses (see instructions). **Do not** enter more than $10,000 . .	**20**	
21	Subtract line 20 from line 19. If zero or less, enter -0-	**21**	
22	Enter your basis in Roth IRA contributions (see instructions). If line 21 is zero, **stop here**	**22**	
23	Subtract line 22 from line 21. If zero or less, enter -0- and skip lines 24 and 25. If more than zero, you may be subject to an additional tax (see instructions)	**23**	
24	Enter your basis in conversions from traditional, SEP, and SIMPLE IRAs and rollovers from qualified retirement plans to a Roth IRA. See instructions	**24**	
25a	Subtract line 24 from line 23. If zero or less, enter -0- and skip lines 25b and 25c	**25a**	
b	Enter the amount on line 25a attributable to qualified 2017 disaster distributions from 2018 Form 8915B (see instructions). Also, enter this amount on 2018 Form 8915B, line 23	**25b**	
c	**Taxable amount.** Subtract line 25b from line 25a. If more than zero, also include this amount on 2018 Form 1040, line 4b; or 2018 Form 1040NR, line 17b	**25c**	

Sign Here Only if You Are Filing This Form by Itself and Not With Your Tax Return

Under penalties of perjury, I declare that I have examined this form, including accompanying attachments, and to the best of my knowledge and belief, it is true, correct, and complete. Declaration of preparer (other than taxpayer) is based on all information of which preparer has any knowledge.

▶ Your signature   ▶ Date

Paid Preparer Use Only	Print/Type preparer's name	Preparer's signature	Date	Check ☐ if self-employed	PTIN
	Firm's name ▶			Firm's EIN ▶	
	Firm's address ▶			Phone no.	

Form **8606** (2018)

20**18**

Instructions for Form 8606

Nondeductible IRAs

Department of the Treasury
Internal Revenue Service

Section references are to the Internal Revenue Code unless otherwise noted.

General Instructions

Future Developments

For the latest information about developments related to 2018 Form 8606 and its instructions, such as legislation enacted after they were published, go to *IRS.gov/Form8606*.

What's New

Form 1040A has been retired. Form 1040A is not in use for years after 2017. All references to the form have been removed or explained.

Modified AGI limit for Roth IRA contributions increased. You can contribute to a Roth IRA for 2018 only if your 2018 modified adjusted gross income (AGI) for Roth IRA purposes is less than:
• $199,000 if married filing jointly or qualifying widow(er);
• $135,000 if single, head of household, or married filing separately and you didn't live with your spouse at any time in 2018; or
• $10,000 if married filing separately and you lived with your spouse at any time in 2018.
See *Roth IRAs*, later.

Due date for contributions. The due date for making contributions for 2018 to your IRA for most people is Monday, April 15, 2019. If you live in Maine or Massachusetts, you have until Wednesday, April 17, 2019, because of the Patriots Day holiday in those states and the Emancipation Day holiday in the District of Columbia.

 At the time this publication went to print, Congress was considering legislation that would do the following.

1. Provide additional tax relief for those affected by certain 2018 disasters.

2. Extend certain tax benefits that expired at the end of 2017 and that currently can't be claimed on your 2018 tax return.

3. Change certain other tax provisions.

To learn whether this legislation was enacted resulting in changes that affect your 2018 tax return, go to IRS.gov/ Extenders and IRS.gov/FormsUpdates.

Reminder

No recharacterizations of conversions made in 2018 or later. A conversion of a traditional IRA to a Roth IRA, and a rollover from any other eligible retirement plan to a Roth IRA, made after December 31, 2017, cannot be recharacterized as having been made to a traditional IRA. For more information, see *Recharacterizations*, later.

Purpose of Form

Use Form 8606 to report:
• Nondeductible contributions you made to traditional IRAs;
• Distributions from traditional, SEP, or SIMPLE IRAs, if you have ever made nondeductible contributions to traditional IRAs;
• Conversions from traditional, SEP, or SIMPLE IRAs to Roth IRAs; and
• Distributions from Roth IRAs.

Additional information. For more details on IRAs, see Pub. 590-A, Contributions to Individual Retirement Arrangements (IRAs); and Pub. 590-B, Distributions from Individual Retirement Arrangements (IRAs).

 If you received distributions from a traditional, SEP, or SIMPLE IRA in 2018 and you have never made nondeductible contributions (including nontaxable amounts you rolled over from a qualified retirement plan) to traditional IRAs, don't report the distributions on 2018 Form 8606. Instead, see the instructions for Form 1040, lines 4a and 4b; or Form 1040NR, lines 17a and 17b. Also, to find out if any of your contributions to traditional, SEP, or SIMPLE IRAs are deductible, see the instructions for Schedule 1 (Form 1040), line 32; or Form 1040NR, line 32.

Who Must File

File Form 8606 if any of the following apply.
• You made nondeductible contributions to a traditional IRA for 2018, including a repayment of a qualified reservist distribution.
• You received distributions from a traditional, SEP, or SIMPLE IRA in 2018 and your basis in traditional IRAs is more than zero. For this purpose, a distribution doesn't include a distribution that is rolled over (other than a repayment of a qualified 2017 disaster distribution (see 2018 Form 8915B)), qualified charitable distribution, one-time distribution to fund an HSA, conversion, recharacterization, or return of certain contributions.
• You converted an amount from a traditional, SEP, or SIMPLE IRA to a Roth IRA in 2018.
• You received distributions from a Roth IRA in 2018 (other than a rollover, recharacterization, or return of certain contributions—see the instructions for Part III, later).
• You received a distribution from an inherited traditional IRA that has a basis, or you received a distribution from an inherited Roth IRA that wasn't a qualified distribution. You may need to file more than one Form 8606. See *IRA with basis* under *What if You Inherit an IRA?* in Pub. 590-B for more information.

Note. If you recharacterized a 2018 Roth IRA contribution as a traditional IRA contribution, or vice versa, treat the contribution as having been made to the second IRA, not the first IRA. See *Recharacterizations*, later.

TIP *You don't have to file Form 8606 solely to report regular contributions to Roth IRAs. But see* What Records Must I Keep, *later.*

When and Where To File

File 2018 Form 8606 with your **2018** Form 1040 or 1040NR by the due date, including extensions, of your return.

If you aren't required to file an income tax return but are required to file Form 8606, sign Form 8606 and send it to the IRS at the same time and place

Cat. No. 25399E

you would otherwise file Form 1040 or 1040NR. Be sure to include your address on page 1 of the form and your signature and the date on page 2 of the form.

Definitions

Deemed IRAs

A qualified employer plan (retirement plan) can maintain a separate account or annuity under the plan (a deemed IRA) to receive voluntary employee contributions. If in 2018 you had a deemed IRA, use the rules for either a traditional IRA or a Roth IRA depending on which type it was. See Pub. 590-A for more details.

Traditional IRAs

For purposes of Form 8606, a traditional IRA is an individual retirement account or an individual retirement annuity other than a SEP, SIMPLE, or Roth IRA.

Contributions. An overall contribution limit applies to traditional IRAs and Roth IRAs. See *Overall Contribution Limit for Traditional and Roth IRAs*, later. Contributions to a traditional IRA may be fully deductible, partially deductible, or completely nondeductible.

Basis. Your basis in traditional, SEP, and SIMPLE IRAs is the total of all your nondeductible contributions and nontaxable amounts included in rollovers made to these IRAs minus the total of all your nontaxable distributions, adjusted if necessary (see the instructions for *line 2*, later).

 Keep track of your basis to figure the nontaxable part of your future distributions.

SEP IRAs

A simplified employee pension (SEP) is an employer-sponsored plan under which an employer can make contributions to traditional IRAs for its employees. If you make contributions to that IRA (excluding employer contributions you make if you are self-employed), they are treated as contributions to a traditional IRA and may be deductible or nondeductible. SEP IRA distributions are reported in the same manner as traditional IRA distributions.

SIMPLE IRAs

A SIMPLE IRA plan is a tax-favored retirement plan that certain small employers (including self-employed

individuals) can set up for the benefit of their employees. Your participation in your employer's SIMPLE IRA plan doesn't prevent you from making contributions to a traditional or Roth IRA.

Roth IRAs

A Roth IRA is similar to a traditional IRA, but has the following features.
• Contributions are never deductible.
• Contributions can be made after the owner reaches age 70½.
• No minimum distributions are required during the Roth IRA owner's lifetime.
• Qualified distributions aren't includible in income.

Qualified distribution. Generally, a qualified distribution is any distribution from your Roth IRA that meets the following requirements.

1. It is made after the 5-year period beginning with the first year for which a contribution was made to a Roth IRA (including a conversion or a rollover from a qualified retirement plan) set up for your benefit, and

2. The distribution is made:

a. On or after the date you reach age 59½,

b. After your death,

c. Due to your disability, or

d. For qualified first-time homebuyer expenses.

Contributions. You can contribute to a Roth IRA for 2018 only if your 2018 modified AGI for Roth IRA purposes is less than:
• $199,000 if married filing jointly or qualifying widow(er);
• $135,000 if single, head of household, or if married filing separately and you didn't live with your spouse at any time in 2018; or
• $10,000 if married filing separately and you lived with your spouse at any time in 2018.

Use the Maximum Roth IRA Contribution Worksheet to figure the maximum amount you can contribute to a Roth IRA for 2018. If you are married filing jointly, complete the worksheet separately for you and your spouse.

 If you contributed too much to your Roth IRA, see Recharacterizations, *later.*

Modified AGI for Roth IRA purposes. First, figure your AGI (Form 1040, line 7; or Form 1040NR, line 35). Then, refigure it by:

1. Subtracting the following.

a. Roth IRA conversions included on Form 1040, line 4b; or Form 1040NR, line 17b.

b. Roth IRA rollovers from qualified retirement plans included on Form 1040, line 4b; or Form 1040NR, line 17b.

2. Adding the following.

a. IRA deduction from Schedule 1 (Form 1040), line 32; or Form 1040NR, line 32.

b. Student loan interest deduction from Schedule 1 (Form 1040), line 33; or Form 1040NR, line 33.

c. Domestic production activities deduction included on Schedule 1 (Form 1040), line 36; or Form 1040NR, line 34.

Note. For 2018, the DPAD deduction is only for certain taxpayers who have a DPAD from fiscal-year pass-through entities.

d. Exclusion of interest from Form 8815, Exclusion of Interest From Series EE and I U.S. Savings Bonds Issued After 1989.

e. Exclusion of employer-provided adoption benefits from Form 8839, Qualified Adoption Expenses.

f. Foreign earned income exclusion from Form 2555, Foreign Earned Income; or Form 2555-EZ, Foreign Earned Income Exclusion.

g. Foreign housing exclusion or deduction from Form 2555.

 At the time these instructions went to print, the deduction for qualified tuition and fees had expired. To find out if legislation extended this deduction, go to IRS.gov/ Extenders.

 When figuring modified AGI for Roth IRA purposes, you may have to refigure items based on modified AGI, such as taxable social security benefits and passive activity losses allowed under the special allowance for rental real estate activities. See Can You Contribute to a Roth IRA? in Pub. 590-A for details.

Distributions. See the instructions for Part III, later.

Maximum Roth IRA Contribution Worksheet

Keep for Your Records

Caution: *If married filing jointly and the combined taxable compensation (defined below) for you and your spouse is less than $11,000 ($12,000 if one spouse is 50 or older at the end of 2018; $13,000 if both spouses are 50 or older at the end of 2018),* **don't** *use this worksheet. Instead, see Pub. 590-A for special rules.*

1. If married filing jointly, enter $5,500 ($6,500 if age 50 or older at the end of 2018). All others, enter the **smaller** of $5,500 ($6,500 if age 50 or older at the end of 2018) or your taxable compensation (defined below) .... **1.** _____

2. Enter your total contributions to traditional IRAs for 2018 .... **2.** _____

3. Subtract line 2 from line 1 .... **3.** _____

4. Enter: $199,000 if married filing jointly or qualifying widow(er); $10,000 if married filing separately and you lived with your spouse at any time in 2018. All others, enter $135,000 .... **4.** _____

5. Enter your modified AGI for Roth IRA purposes (discussed earlier) .... **5.** _____

6. Subtract line 5 from line 4. If zero or less, **stop here**; you may not contribute to a Roth IRA for 2018. See *Recharacterizations* below if you made Roth IRA contributions for 2018 .... **6.** _____

7. If line 4 above is $135,000, enter $15,000; otherwise, enter $10,000. If line 6 is more than or equal to line 7, skip lines 8 and 9 and enter the amount from line 3 on line 10 .... **7.** _____

8. Divide line 6 by line 7 and enter the result as a decimal (rounded to at least 3 places) .... **8.** _____

9. Multiply line 1 by line 8. If the result isn't a multiple of $10, increase it to the next multiple of $10 (for example, increase $490.30 to $500). Enter the result, but not less than $200 .... **9.** _____

10. **Maximum 2018 Roth IRA Contribution.** Enter the **smaller** of line 3 or line 9. See *Recharacterizations* below if you contributed more than this amount to Roth IRAs for 2018 .... **10.** _____

Overall Contribution Limit for Traditional and Roth IRAs

If you aren't married filing jointly, your limit on contributions to traditional and Roth IRAs is generally the smaller of $5,500 ($6,500 if age 50 or older at the end of 2018) or your taxable compensation (defined below).

If you are married filing jointly, your contribution limit is generally $5,500 ($6,500 if age 50 or older at the end of 2018) and your spouse's contribution limit is $5,500 ($6,500 if age 50 or older at the end of 2018) as well. But if the combined taxable compensation of both you and your spouse is less than $11,000 ($12,000 if one spouse is 50 or older at the end of 2018; $13,000 if both spouses are 50 or older at the end of 2018), see *Kay Bailey Hutchison Spousal IRA Limit* in Pub. 590-A for special rules.

This limit doesn't apply to employer contributions to a SEP or SIMPLE IRA.

Note. Rollovers, Roth IRA conversions, Roth IRA rollovers from qualified retirement plans and repayments of qualified 2017 disaster distributions (see Form 8915B and its instructions), and qualified reservist distributions don't affect your contribution limit.

⚠️ *The amount you can contribute to a Roth IRA also may be* **CAUTION** *limited by your modified AGI (see* Contributions, *earlier, and the* Maximum Roth IRA Contribution Worksheet*).*

Taxable compensation. Taxable compensation includes the following.
• Wages, salaries, tips, etc. If you received a distribution from a nonqualified deferred compensation plan or nongovernmental section 457 plan that is included in Form W-2, box 1, or in Form 1099-MISC, box 7, don't include that distribution in taxable compensation. The distribution should be shown in (a) Form W-2, box 11; (b) Form W-2, box 12, with code Z; or (c) Form 1099-MISC, box 15b. If it isn't, contact your employer for the amount of the distribution.
• Nontaxable combat pay if you were a member of the U.S. Armed Forces.

• Self-employment income. If you are self-employed (a sole proprietor or a partner), taxable compensation is your net earnings from your trade or business (provided your personal services are a material income-producing factor) reduced by your deduction for contributions made on your behalf to retirement plans and the deductible part of your self-employment tax.
• Alimony and separate maintenance.

See *What Is Compensation?* under *Who Can Open a Traditional IRA?* in chapter 1 of Pub. 590-A for details.

Recharacterizations

Generally, you can recharacterize (correct) an IRA contribution by making a trustee-to-trustee transfer from one IRA to another type of IRA. Trustee-to-trustee transfers are made directly between financial institutions or within the same financial institution. You generally must make the transfer by the due date of your return (including extensions) and reflect it on your return. However, if you timely filed your return without making the transfer, you can make the transfer within 6 months of the due date of your return, excluding extensions. If necessary, file an amended return reflecting the transfer (see *Amending Form 8606*, later). Write "Filed pursuant to section 301.9100-2" on the amended return.

No recharacterizations of conversions made in 2018 or later. A conversion of a traditional IRA to a Roth IRA, and a rollover from any other eligible retirement plan to a Roth IRA, made in tax years beginning after December 31, 2017, cannot be recharacterized as having been made to a traditional IRA.

Reporting recharacterizations. Treat any recharacterized IRA contribution as though the amount of the contribution was originally contributed to the second IRA, not the first IRA. For the recharacterization, you must transfer the amount of the original contribution plus any related earnings or less any related loss. In most cases, your IRA trustee or custodian figures the amount of the related earnings you must transfer. If you need to figure the related earnings, see *How Do You Recharacterize a Contribution?* in chapter 1 of Pub. 590-A. Treat any earnings or loss that occurred in the first IRA as having occurred in the second IRA. You can't deduct any loss that occurred while the funds were in the first IRA. Also, you can't take a deduction for a contribution to a traditional IRA if you later recharacterize the amount. The following discussion explains how to report the two different types of recharacterizations, including the statement that you must attach to your return explaining the recharacterization.

1. You made a contribution to a traditional IRA and later recharacterized part or all of it in a trustee-to-trustee transfer to a Roth IRA. If you recharacterized only part of the contribution, report the nondeductible traditional IRA portion of the remaining contribution, if any, on Form 8606, Part I. If you recharacterized the entire contribution, don't report the contribution on Form 8606. In either case, attach a statement to your return explaining the recharacterization. If the recharacterization occurred in 2018, include the amount transferred from the traditional IRA on Form 1040, line 4a; or Form 1040NR, line 17a. If the recharacterization occurred in 2019, report the amount transferred only in the attached statement, and not on your 2018 or 2019 tax return.

Example. You are single, covered by an employer retirement plan, and you contributed $4,000 to a new traditional IRA on May 27, 2018. On February 24, 2019, you determine that your 2018 modified AGI will limit your traditional IRA deduction to $1,000. The value of your traditional IRA on that date is $4,400. You decide to recharacterize $3,000 of the traditional IRA contribution as a Roth IRA contribution, and have $3,300 ($3,000 contribution plus $300 related earnings) transferred from your traditional IRA to a Roth IRA in a trustee-to-trustee transfer. You deduct the $1,000 traditional IRA contribution on Form 1040. You don't file Form 8606. You attach a statement to your return explaining the recharacterization. The statement indicates that you contributed $4,000 to a traditional IRA on May 27, 2018; recharacterized $3,000 of that contribution on February 24, 2018, by transferring $3,000 plus $300 of related earnings from your traditional IRA to a Roth IRA in a trustee-to-trustee transfer; and deducted the remaining traditional IRA contribution of $1,000 on Form 1040. You don't report the $3,300 distribution from your traditional IRA on your 2018 Form 1040 because the distribution occurred in 2019. You don't report the distribution on your 2019 Form 1040 because the recharacterization related to 2018 and was explained in an attachment to your 2018 return.

2. You made a contribution to a Roth IRA and later recharacterized part or all of it in a trustee-to-trustee transfer to a traditional IRA. Report the nondeductible traditional IRA portion of the recharacterized contribution, if any, on Form 8606, Part I. Don't report the Roth IRA contribution (whether or not you recharacterized all or part of it) on Form 8606. Attach a statement to your return explaining the recharacterization. If the recharacterization occurred in 2018, include the amount transferred from the Roth IRA on Form 1040, line 4a; or Form 1040NR, line 17a. If the recharacterization occurred in 2019, report the amount transferred only in the attached statement, and not on your 2018 or 2019 tax return.

Example. You are single, covered by an employer retirement plan, and you contributed $4,000 to a new Roth IRA on June 16, 2018. On December 29, 2018, you determine that your 2018 modified AGI will allow a full traditional IRA deduction. You decide to recharacterize the Roth IRA contribution as a traditional IRA contribution and have $4,200, the balance in the Roth

IRA account ($4,000 contribution plus $200 related earnings), transferred from your Roth IRA to a traditional IRA in a trustee-to-trustee transfer. You deduct the $4,000 traditional IRA contribution on Form 1040. You don't file Form 8606. You attach a statement to your return explaining the recharacterization. The statement indicates that you contributed $4,000 to a new Roth IRA on June 16, 2018; recharacterized that contribution on December 29, 2018, by transferring $4,200, the balance in the Roth IRA, to a traditional IRA in a trustee-to-trustee transfer; and deducted the traditional IRA contribution of $4,000 on Form 1040. You include the $4,200 distribution from your Roth IRA on your 2018 Form 1040, line 4a.

Return of IRA Contributions

If, in 2018, you made traditional IRA contributions or Roth IRA contributions for 2018 and you had those contributions returned to you with any related earnings (or minus any loss) by the due date (including extensions) of your 2018 tax return, the returned contributions are treated as if they were never contributed. Don't report the contribution or distribution on Form 8606 or take a deduction for the contribution. However, you must include the amount of the distribution of the returned contributions you made in 2018 and any related earnings on your 2018 Form 1040, line 4a; or Form 1040NR, line 17a. Also include the related earnings on your 2018 Form 1040, line 4b; or Form 1040NR, line 17b. Attach a statement explaining the distribution. See Pub. 590-B to determine whether you can deduct any loss that occurred. Also, if you were under age 59½ at the time of a distribution with related earnings, you generally are subject to the additional 10% tax on early distributions (see Form 5329, Additional Taxes on Qualified Plans (Including IRAs) and Other Tax-Favored Accounts).

If you timely filed your 2018 tax return without withdrawing a contribution that you made in 2018, you can still have the contribution returned to you within 6 months of the due date of your 2018 tax return, excluding extensions. If you do, file an amended return with "Filed pursuant to section 301.9100-2" written at the top. Report any related earnings on the amended return and include an explanation of the withdrawn contribution. Make any other necessary changes on the amended return (for example, if you reported the contributions as excess contributions on your original return, include an amended Form 5329 reflecting that the withdrawn contributions are no longer treated as having been contributed.

In most cases, the related earnings that you must withdraw are figured by your IRA trustee or custodian. If you need to figure the related earnings on IRA contributions that were returned to you, see *Contributions Returned Before Due Date of Return* in chapter 1 of Pub. 590-A. If you made a contribution or distribution while the IRA held the returned contribution, see Pub. 590-A.

If you made a contribution for 2017 and you had it returned to you in 2018 as described above, don't report the distribution on your 2018 tax return. Instead, report it on your 2017 original or amended return in the manner described above.

Example. On May 28, 2018, you contributed $4,000 to your traditional IRA that has basis. The value of the IRA was $18,000 prior to the contribution. On December 29, 2018, when you are age 57 and the value of the IRA is $23,600, you realize you can't make the entire contribution because your taxable compensation for the year will be only $3,000. You decide to have $1,000 of the contribution returned to you and withdraw $1,073 from your IRA ($1,000 contribution plus $73 earnings). You didn't make any other withdrawals or contributions. You don't file Form 8606. You deduct the $3,000 remaining contribution on Form 1040. You include $1,073 on Form 1040, line 4a, and $73 on line 4b. You attach a statement to your tax return explaining the distribution. Because you properly removed the excess contribution with the related earnings by the due date of your tax return, you aren't subject to the additional 6% tax on excess contributions, reported on Form 5329. However, because you were under age 59½ at the time of the distribution, the $73 of earnings is subject to the additional 10% tax on early distributions. You include $7.30 on Schedule 4 (Form 1040), line 59.

Return of Excess Traditional IRA Contributions

The return (distribution) in 2018 of excess traditional IRA contributions for years prior to 2018 isn't taxable if all three of the following apply.

1. The distribution was made after the due date, including extensions, of your tax return for the year for which the contribution was made (if the distribution was made earlier, see *Return of IRA Contributions*, earlier).

2. No deduction was allowable (without regard to the modified AGI limitation) or taken for the excess contributions.

3. The total contributions (excluding rollovers) to your traditional and SEP IRAs for the year for which the excess contributions were made didn't exceed the amounts shown in the following table.

Year(s)	Contribution limit	Contribution limit if age 50 or older at the end of the year
2013 through 2017	$5,500	$6,500
2008 through 2012	$5,000	$6,000
2006 or 2007	$4,000	$5,000
2005	$4,000	$4,500
2002 through 2004	$3,000	$3,500
1997 through 2001	$2,000	—
before 1997	$2,250	—

If the excess contribution to your traditional IRA for the year included a rollover and the excess occurred because the information the plan was required to give you was incorrect, increase the contribution limit amount for the year shown in the table above by the amount of the excess that is due to the incorrect information.

If the total contributions for the year included employer contributions to a SEP IRA, increase the contribution limit amount for the year shown in the table above by the smaller of the amount of the employer contributions or:

2017	$54,000
2015 or 2016	$53,000
2014	$52,000
2013	$51,000
2012	$50,000
2009, 2010, or 2011	$49,000
2008	$46,000
2007	$45,000
2006	$44,000
2005	$42,000
2004	$41,000
2002 or 2003	$40,000
2001	$35,000
before 2001	$30,000

Include the total amount distributed on Form 1040, line 4a; or Form 1040NR, line 17a; and attach a statement to your return explaining the distribution. See *Example*, later.

If you meet these conditions and are otherwise required to file Form 8606:
• Don't take into account the amount of the withdrawn contributions in figuring line 2 (for 2018 or for any later year), and
• Don't include the amount of the withdrawn contributions on line 7.

Example. You are single, you retired in 2015, and you had no taxable compensation after 2015. However, you made traditional IRA contributions (that you didn't deduct) of $3,000 in 2016 and $4,000 in 2017. In November 2018, a tax practitioner informed you that you had made excess contributions for those years because you had no taxable compensation. You withdrew the $7,000 and filed amended returns for 2016 and 2017 reflecting the additional 6% tax on excess contributions on Form 5329. You include the $7,000 distribution on your 2018 Form 1040, line 4a, enter -0- on line 4b, and attach a statement to your return explaining the distribution, including the fact that you filed amended returns for 2016 and 2017, and paid the additional 6% tax on the excess contributions for those years. The statement indicates that the distribution isn't taxable because (a) it was made after the due dates of your 2016 and 2017 tax returns, including extensions; (b) your total IRA contributions for each year didn't exceed $5,500 ($6,500 if age 50 or older at the end of that year); and (c) you didn't take a deduction for the contributions, and no deduction was allowable because you didn't have any taxable compensation for those years. The statement also indicates that the distribution reduced your excess contributions to -0-, as reflected on your 2018 Form 5329. Don't file Form 8606 for 2018. If you are required to file Form 8606 in a year after 2018, don't include the $7,000 you withdrew in 2018 on line 2.

Amending Form 8606

Generally, after you file your return, you can change a nondeductible contribution to a traditional IRA to a deductible contribution or vice versa if you make the change within the time limit for filing Form 1040X, Amended U.S. Individual Income Tax Return (see *When To File* in the Form 1040X instructions). You also may be able to make a recharacterization (discussed earlier). If necessary, complete a new Form 8606 showing the revised information and file it with Form 1040X.

Penalty for Not Filing

If you are required to file Form 8606 to report a nondeductible contribution to a traditional IRA for 2018, but don't do so, you must pay a $50 penalty, unless you can show reasonable cause.

Overstatement Penalty

If you overstate your nondeductible contributions, you must pay a $100 penalty, unless you can show reasonable cause.

What Records Must I Keep?

To verify the nontaxable part of distributions from your IRAs, including Roth IRAs, keep a copy of the following forms and records until all distributions are made.
• Page 1 of Forms 1040 (or Forms 1040A, 1040NR, or 1040-T) filed for each year you made a nondeductible contribution to a traditional IRA.
• Forms 8606 and any supporting statements, attachments, and worksheets for all applicable years.
• Forms 5498, IRA Contribution Information, or similar statements you received each year showing contributions you made to a traditional IRA or Roth IRA.
• Forms 5498 or similar statements you received showing the value of your traditional IRAs for each year you received a distribution.

• Forms 1099-R or W-2P you received for each year you received a distribution.

Note. Forms 1040-T, 1040A, and W-2P are forms that were used in prior years.

Specific Instructions

Name and social security number (SSN). If you file a joint return, enter only the name and SSN of the spouse whose information is being reported on Form 8606.

More than one Form 8606 required. If both you and your spouse are required to file Form 8606, file a separate Form 8606 for each of you. If you are required to file Form 8606 for IRAs inherited from more than one decedent, file a separate Form 8606 for the IRA from each decedent.

Part I—Nondeductible Contributions to Traditional IRAs and Distributions From Traditional, SEP, and SIMPLE IRAs

Line 1

If you used the IRA Deduction Worksheet in the Form 1040 or 1040NR instructions, subtract line 12 of the worksheet (or the amount you chose to deduct on Schedule 1 (Form 1040), line 32; or Form 1040NR, line 32, if less) from the smaller of line 10 or line 11 of the worksheet. Enter the result on line 1 of Form 8606. You can't deduct the amount included on line 1.

If you used the worksheet Figuring Your Reduced IRA Deduction for 2018 in Pub. 590-A, enter on line 1 of Form 8606 any nondeductible contributions from the appropriate lines of that worksheet.

If you didn't have any deductible contributions, you can make nondeductible contributions up to your contribution limit (see *Overall Contribution Limit for Traditional and Roth IRAs*, earlier). Enter on line 1 of Form 8606 your nondeductible contributions.

Include on line 1 any repayment of a qualified reservist distribution.

Don't include on line 1 contributions that you had returned to you with the related earnings (or less any loss). See *Return of IRA Contributions*, earlier.

Line 2

Generally, if this is the first year you are required to file Form 8606, enter -0-. Otherwise, use the Total Basis Chart to find the amount to enter on line 2.

However, you may need to enter an amount that is more than -0- (even if this is the first year you are required to file Form 8606) or increase or decrease the amount from the chart if your basis changed because of any of the following.
• You had a return of excess traditional IRA contributions (see *Return of Excess Traditional IRA Contributions*, earlier).
• Incident to divorce, you transferred or received part or all of a traditional IRA (see the last bulleted item under *Line 7*, later).
• You rolled over any nontaxable portion of your qualified retirement plan to a traditional, SEP, or SIMPLE IRA that wasn't previously reported on Form 8606, line 2. Include the nontaxable portion on line 2.

Line 4

If you made contributions to traditional IRAs for 2018 in 2018 and 2019 and you have both deductible and nondeductible contributions, you can choose to treat the contributions made in 2018 as nondeductible contributions and then as deductible contributions, or vice versa.

Example. You made contributions for 2018 of $2,000 in May 2018 and $2,000 in January 2019, of which $3,000 are deductible and $1,000 are nondeductible. You choose $1,000 of your contribution in 2018 to be nondeductible. You enter the $1,000 on line 1, but not line 4, and it becomes part of your basis for 2018.

Although the contributions to traditional IRAs for 2018 that you made from January 1, 2019, through April 15, 2019 (April 17, 2019, if you live in Maine or Massachusetts), can be treated as nondeductible, they aren't included in figuring the nontaxable part of any distributions you received in 2018.

Line 6

Enter the total value of all your traditional, SEP, and SIMPLE IRAs as of December 31, 2018, plus any outstanding rollovers. A statement should be sent to you by January 31, 2019, showing the value of each IRA on December 31, 2018. However, if you recharacterized any amounts originally contributed, enter on line 6 the total value, taking into account all recharacterizations of those amounts, including recharacterizations made after December 31, 2018.

For purposes of line 6, a rollover is a tax-free distribution from one traditional, SEP, or SIMPLE IRA that is contributed to another traditional, SEP, or SIMPLE IRA. The rollover must be completed within 60 days after receiving the distribution from the first IRA. An outstanding rollover is generally the amount of any distribution received in 2018 after November 1, 2018, that was rolled over in 2019, but within the 60-day rollover period. A rollover between a SIMPLE IRA and a qualified retirement plan or an IRA (other than a SIMPLE IRA) can only take place after your first 2 years of participation in the SIMPLE IRA. See Pub. 590-A for more details.

Pursuant to Rev. Proc. 2016-47 in Internal Revenue Bulletin 2016-37, available at *IRS.gov/irb/ 2016-37_IRB#RP-2016-47*, you may make a written certification to a plan administrator or an IRA trustee that you missed the 60-day rollover contribution deadline because of one or more of the 11 reasons listed in Rev. Proc. 2016-47. See Rev. Proc. 2016-47 for information on how to self-certify for a waiver. Also see *Time Limit for Making a Rollover Contribution* under *Can You Move Retirement Plan Assets?* in Pub. 590-A for more information on ways to get a waiver of the 60-day rollover requirement.

Note. Don't include an outstanding rollover from a traditional, SEP, or SIMPLE IRA to a qualified retirement plan.

Repayments in 2018 of qualified 2017 disaster distributions.

The amount you would otherwise enter on line 6 should be reduced by the total amount of qualified 2017 disaster distribution repayments that were made in 2018 for qualified 2017 disaster distributions made in 2018. Do not reduce line 6 by qualified 2017 disaster distribution repayments that were made in 2018 for qualified 2017 disaster distributions made in 2017.

Example. You received a $30,000 qualified 2017 disaster distribution on January 1, 2018 from your traditional IRA. On November 25, 2018, you made a repayment of $10,000 to your traditional IRA. The value of all of your traditional, SEP, and SIMPLE IRAs as of December 31, 2018, was $50,000. You had no outstanding rollovers. You would enter $40,000 ($50,000 minus $10,000 repayment) on line 6.

Total Basis Chart

IF the last Form 8606 you filed was for . . .	THEN enter on line 2 . . .
A year after 2000 and before 2018	The amount from line 14 of that Form 8606
A year after 1992 and before 2001	The amount from line 12 of that Form 8606
A year after 1988 and before 1993	The amount from line 14 of that Form 8606
1988	The total of the amounts on lines 7 and 16 of that Form 8606
1987	The total of the amounts on lines 4 and 13 of that Form 8606

Instructions for Form 8606 (2018)

Line 7

⚠️ **CAUTION** *If you received a distribution in 2018 from a traditional, SEP, or SIMPLE IRA, and you also made contributions for 2018 to a traditional IRA that may not be fully deductible because of the income limits, you must make a special computation before completing the rest of this form. For details, including how to complete Form 8606, see* Are Distributions Taxable? *in chapter 1 of Pub. 590-B.*

Don't include any of the following on line 7.
- Distributions that you converted to a Roth IRA.
- Recharacterizations of traditional IRA contributions to Roth IRA contributions.
- Distributions you rolled over to another traditional, SEP, or SIMPLE IRA (whether or not the distribution is an outstanding rollover included on line 6).
- Distributions you rolled over to a qualified retirement plan.
- A one-time distribution to fund an HSA. For details, see Pub. 969, Health Savings Accounts and Other Tax-Favored Health Plans.
- Distributions that are treated as a return of contributions under *Return of IRA Contributions*, earlier.
- Qualified charitable distributions (QCDs). For details, see *Are Distributions Taxable?* in chapter 1 of Pub. 590-B.
- Distributions that are treated as a return of excess contributions under *Return of Excess Traditional IRA Contributions*, earlier.
- Distributions that are incident to divorce. The transfer of part or all of your traditional, SEP, or SIMPLE IRA to your spouse under a divorce or separation agreement isn't taxable to you or your spouse. If this transfer results in a change in the basis of the traditional IRA of either spouse, both spouses must file Form 8606 and show the increase or decrease in the amount of basis on line 2. Attach a statement explaining this adjustment. Include in the statement the character of the amounts in the traditional IRA, such as the amount attributable to nondeductible contributions. Also, include the name and social security number of the other spouse.

⚠️ **CAUTION** *Qualified 2017 disaster distribution. Be sure to include on line 7 all qualified 2017 disaster distributions made in 2018, even if they were later repaid.*

Line 8

If, in 2018, you converted any amounts from traditional, SEP, or SIMPLE IRAs to a Roth IRA, enter on line 8 the net amount you converted.

Line 15b

If all your distributions are qualified 2017 disaster distributions, enter the amount from line 15a on line 15b. If you have distributions unrelated to qualified disasters, as well as qualified 2017 disaster distributions, you will need to multiply the amount on line 15a by a fraction. The numerator of the fraction is the total of your qualified 2017 disaster distributions and the denominator is the amount from Form 8606, line 7.

Example. On June 1, 2018, you received a qualified 2017 hurricane disaster distribution from your traditional IRA in the amount of $100,000. The limit for the qualified 2017 hurricane disaster distributions is $100,000. You had losses as a result of Hurricane Harvey. You had no other losses from disasters in 2017. Later in 2018, you received a $50,000 distribution from your traditional IRA (that you did not roll over). You reported $100,000 on 2018 Form 8915B. You had no other distributions in 2018. You will report total distributions of $150,000 on Form 8606, line 7. You then will complete lines 8 through 14 as instructed. Form 8606, line 15a, shows an amount of $120,000. You will enter $80,000 ($120,000 x $100,000/$150,000) on line 15b. You also will enter $80,000 on 2018 Form 8915B, line 22.

Line 15c

If you were under age 59½ at the time you received distributions from your traditional, SEP, or SIMPLE IRA, there generally is an additional 10% tax on the portion of the distribution that is included in income (25% for a distribution from a SIMPLE IRA during the first 2 years of your participation in the plan). See the instructions for Schedule 4 (Form 1040), line 59; or the instructions for Form 1040NR, line 57; and also the Instructions for Form 5329.

Part II—2018 Conversions From Traditional, SEP, or SIMPLE IRAs to Roth IRAs

Complete Part II if you converted part or all of your traditional, SEP, or SIMPLE IRAs to a Roth IRA in 2018.

Line 16

If you didn't complete line 8, see the instructions for that line. Then, enter on line 16 the amount you would have entered on line 8 had you completed it.

Line 17

If you didn't complete line 11, enter on line 17 the amount from line 2 (or the amount you would have entered on line 2 if you had completed that line) plus any contributions included on line 1 that you made before the conversion.

Line 18

If your entry on line 18 is zero or less, don't include the result on Form 1040, line 4b; or Form 1040NR, line 17b. Include the full amount of the distribution on Form 1040, line 4a; or Form 1040NR, line 17a.

Part III—Distributions From Roth IRAs

Complete Part III to figure the taxable part, if any, of your 2018 Roth IRA distributions.

Line 19

Don't include on line 19 any of the following.
- Distributions that you rolled over, including distributions made in 2018 and rolled over after December 31, 2018 (outstanding rollovers).
- Recharacterizations.
- Distributions that are a return of contributions under *Return of IRA Contributions*, earlier.
- Distributions made on or after age 59½ if you made a contribution (including a conversion or a rollover from a qualified retirement plan) for any year from 1998 through 2013.
- A one-time distribution to fund an HSA. For details, see Pub. 969.
- Qualified charitable distributions (QCDs). For details, see *Are Distributions Taxable?* in chapter 1 of Pub. 590-B.
- Distributions made upon death or due to disability if a contribution was made (including a conversion or a rollover from a qualified retirement plan) for any year from 1998 through 2013.
- Distributions that are incident to divorce. The transfer of part or all of your Roth IRA to your spouse under a divorce or separation agreement isn't taxable to you or your spouse.

Qualified 2017 disaster distributions Be sure to include on line 19 all qualified 2017 disaster distributions made in 2018, even if they were later repaid, unless they fall under the 4th or 7th bullet above.

If, after considering the items above, you don't have an amount to enter on line 19, don't complete Part III; your Roth IRA distribution(s) isn't taxable. Instead, include your total Roth IRA distribution(s) on Form 1040, line 4a; or Form 1040NR, line 17a.

Line 20

If you had a qualified first-time homebuyer distribution from your Roth IRA and you made a contribution (including a conversion or a rollover from a qualified retirement plan) to a Roth IRA for any year from 1998 through 2013, enter the amount of your qualified expenses on line 20, but don't enter more than $10,000 reduced by the total of all your prior qualified first-time homebuyer distributions. For details, see *Are Distributions Taxable?* in chapter 2 of Pub. 590-B.

Line 22

Figure the amount to enter on line 22 as follows.
• If you didn't take a Roth IRA distribution before 2018 (other than an amount rolled over or recharacterized or a returned contribution), enter on line 22 the total of all your regular contributions to Roth IRAs for 1998 through 2018 (excluding rollovers from other Roth IRAs and any contributions that you had returned to you), adjusted for any recharacterizations.
• If you did take such a distribution before 2018, see the Basis in Regular Roth IRA Contributions Worksheet to figure the amount to enter.
• Increase the amount on line 22 by any amount rolled in from a designated Roth account that is treated as investment in the contract.
• Increase or decrease the amount on line 22 by any basis in regular contributions received or transferred incident to divorce. Also attach a statement similar to the one explained in the last bulleted item under *Line 7*, earlier.
• Increase the amount on line 22 by the amounts received as a military gratuity or SGLI payment that was rolled over to your Roth IRA.
• Increase the amount on line 22 by any amount received as qualified settlement income in connection with the Exxon Valdez litigation and rolled over to your Roth IRA.
• Increase the amount on line 22 by any "airline payments" you received as a result of your employment with an airline that you rolled over to your Roth IRA. However, don't include the amounts attributable to airline payments that you transferred from a Roth IRA to a traditional IRA because of the FAA Modernization and Reform Act of 2012.

Line 23

Generally, there is an additional 10% tax on 2018 distributions from a Roth IRA that are shown on line 23. The additional tax is figured on Form 5329, Part I. See the Instructions for Form 5329, line 1, for details and exceptions.

Line 24

Figure the amount to enter on line 24 as follows.
• If you have never made a Roth IRA conversion or rolled over an amount from a qualified retirement plan to a Roth IRA, enter -0- on line 24.
• If you took a Roth IRA distribution (other than an amount rolled over or recharacterized or a returned contribution) before 2018 in excess of your basis in regular Roth IRA contributions, see the Basis in Roth IRA Conversions and Rollovers From Qualified Retirement Plans to Roth IRAs chart to figure the amount to enter on line 24.
• If you didn't take such a distribution before 2018, enter on line 24 the total of all your conversions to Roth IRAs. These amounts are shown on line 14c of your 1998, 1999, and 2000 Forms 8606 and line 16 of your 2001 through 2018 Forms 8606. Also include on line 24 any amounts rolled over from a qualified retirement plan to a Roth IRA for 2008, 2009, and 2011 to 2018 reported on your Form 1040, Form 1040A, or Form 1040NR, and line 21 of your 2010 Form 8606. Don't include amounts rolled in from a designated Roth account since these amounts are included on line 22.
• Increase or decrease the amount on line 24 by any basis in conversions to Roth IRAs and amounts rolled over from a qualified retirement plan to a Roth IRA received or transferred incident to divorce. Also attach a statement similar to the one explained in the last bulleted item under *Line 7*, earlier.

Line 25b

If all your distributions are qualified 2017 disaster distributions, enter the amount from line 25a on line 25b. If you have distributions unrelated to qualified disasters, as well as qualified 2017 disaster distributions, you will need to multiply the amount on line 25a by a fraction. The numerator of the fraction is the total of your qualified 2017 disaster distributions and the denominator is the amount from Form 8606, line 21.

Example. On June 1, 2018, you received a qualified 2017 hurricane disaster distribution from your Roth IRA in the amount of $100,000. The limit for

the qualified 2017 hurricane disaster distributions is $100,000. You had losses as a result of Hurricane Harvey. You had no other losses from disasters in 2017. Later in 2018, you received a $50,000 distribution from your Roth IRA (that you did not roll over). You reported $100,000 on 2018 Form 8915B. You had no other distributions in 2018. You will report total distributions of $150,000 on Form 8606, line 19. You then will complete lines 22 through 24 as instructed. Form 8606, line 25a, shows an amount of $120,000. You will enter $80,000 ($120,000 x $100,000/$150,000) on line 25b. You also will enter $80,000 on 2018 Form 8915B, line 23.

Privacy Act and Paperwork Reduction Act Notice

We ask for the information on this form to carry out the Internal Revenue laws of the United States. We need this information to ensure that you are complying with these laws and to allow us to figure and collect the right amount of tax. You are required to give us this information if you made certain contributions or received certain distributions from qualified plans, including IRAs and other tax-favored accounts. Our legal right to ask for the information requested on this form is sections 6001, 6011, 6012(a), and 6109 and their regulations. If you do not provide this information, or you provide incomplete or false information, you may be subject to penalties.

You are not required to provide the information requested on a form that is subject to the Paperwork Reduction Act unless the form displays a valid OMB control number. Books or records relating to a form or its instructions must be retained as long as their contents may become material in the administration of any Internal Revenue law. Generally, tax returns and return information are confidential, as required by section 6103. However, we may give the information to the Department of Justice for civil and criminal litigation, and to cities, states, the District of Columbia, and U.S. commonwealths and possessions to carry out their tax laws. We may also disclose this information to other countries under a tax treaty, to federal and state agencies to enforce federal nontax criminal laws, or to federal law enforcement and intelligence agencies to combat terrorism.

The average time and expenses required to complete and file this form will vary depending on individual circumstances. For the estimated averages, see the instructions for your income tax return.

If you have suggestions for making this form simpler, we would be happy to hear from you. See the instructions for your income tax return.

Basis in Regular Roth IRA Contributions Worksheet—Line 22

Keep for Your Records

Before you begin: You will need your Form 8606 for the most recent year prior to 2018 when you received a distribution.

Note. Don't complete this worksheet if you never received a distribution from your Roth IRAs prior to 2018.

1. Enter the most recent year prior to 2018 you reported distributions on Form 8606 (for example, 2 0 1 4) .... **1.** _ _ _ _

2. Enter your basis in Roth IRA contributions reported on Form 8606 for the year entered on line 1 (see Table 1) .... **2.** _____

3. Enter your Roth IRA distributions* reported on Form 8606 for the year entered on line 1 (see Table 2) .... **3.** _____

4. Subtract line 3 from line 2. Enter zero if the resulting amount is zero or less .... **4.** _____

5. Enter the total of all your regular contributions** to Roth IRAs after the year entered on line 1 .... **5.** _____

6. Add lines 4 and 5. Enter this amount on your 2018 Form 8606, line 22 .... **6.** _____

*Excluding rollovers, recharacterizations, and contributions that you had returned to you.
**Excluding rollovers, conversions, and any contributions that you had returned to you.

Table 1 for Line 2 above

IF the year entered on Line 1 was	THEN enter on Line 2 the amount from the following line ......
2017, 2016, 2015, 2014, 2013, 2012, 2011, 2009, 2008, 2007, 2006, 2005, and 2004	Form 8606, line 22
2010	Form 8606, line 29
2003, 2002, 2001	Form 8606, line 20
2000 and 1999	Form 8606, line 18d
1998	Form 8606, line 19c

Table 2 for Line 3 above

IF the year entered on Line 1 was	THEN enter on Line 3 the amount from the following line ......
2017, 2016, 2015, 2014, 2013, 2012, 2011, 2009, 2008, 2007, 2006, 2005, 2004, 2003, 2002, and 2001	Form 8606, line 19
2010	Form 8606, line 26
2000 and 1999	Form 8606, line 17
1998	Form 8606, line 18

Instructions for Form 8606 (2018)

Basis in Roth IRA Conversions and Rollovers From Qualified Retirement Plans to Roth IRAs—Line 24

IF the most recent year prior to 2018 in which you had a distribution[1] in excess of your basis in contributions was	THEN enter on Form 8606, line 24, this amount	PLUS the sum of the amounts on the following lines . . . .
2017 (your 2017 Form 8606, line 22, was less than line 19 of that Form 8606)	The excess, if any, of your 2017 Form 8606, line 24, over line 23[2] of that Form 8606.	Line 16 of your 2018 Form 8606 and certain rollovers [3] reported on your 2018 tax return.
2016 (your 2016 Form 8606, line 22, was less than line 19 of that Form 8606)	The excess, if any, of your 2016 Form 8606, line 24, over line 23[2] of that Form 8606.	Line 16 of your 2017 and 2018 Forms 8606 and certain rollovers[3] reported on your 2017 and 2018 tax returns.
2015 (your 2015 Form 8606, line 22, was less than line 19 of that Form 8606)	The excess, if any, of your 2015 Form 8606, line 24, over line 23[2] of that Form 8606.	Line 16 of your 2016 through 2018 Forms 8606 and certain rollovers[3] reported on your 2016 through 2018 tax returns.
2014 (your 2014 Form 8606, line 22, was less than line 19 of that Form 8606)	The excess, if any, of your 2014 Form 8606, line 24, over line 23[2] of that Form 8606.	Line 16 of your 2015 through 2018 Forms 8606 and certain rollovers[3] reported on your 2015 through 2018 tax returns.
2013 (your 2013 Form 8606, line 22, was less than line 19 of that Form 8606)	The excess, if any, of your 2013 Form 8606, line 24, over line 23[2] of that Form 8606.	Line 16 of your 2014 through 2018 Forms 8606 and certain rollovers[3] reported on your 2014 through 2018 tax returns.
2012 (your 2012 Form 8606, line 22, was less than line 19 of that Form 8606)	The excess, if any, of your 2012 Form 8606, line 24, over line 23[2] of that Form 8606.	Line 16 of your 2013 through 2018 Forms 8606 and certain rollovers[3] reported on your 2013 through 2018 tax returns.
2011 (your 2011 Form 8606, line 22, was less than line 19 of that Form 8606)	The excess, if any, of your 2011 Form 8606, line 24, over line 23[2] of that Form 8606.	Line 16 of your 2012 through 2018 Forms 8606 and certain rollovers[3] reported on your 2012 through 2018 tax returns.
2010 (your 2010 Form 8606, line 29, was less than line 26 of that Form 8606)	The excess, if any, of your 2010 Form 8606, line 31, over line 30 of that Form 8606 (refigure line 30 without taking into account any amount entered on Form 8606, line 27).	Line 16 of your 2011 through 2018 Forms 8606 and certain rollovers[3] reported on your 2011 through 2018 tax returns, **OR** Line 16 of your 2011 through 2018 Forms 8606; lines 16 and 21 of your 2010 Form 8606[4] if you didn't check the boxes on line 19 or 24 of your 2010 Form 8606; and certain rollovers[3] reported on your 2011 through 2018 tax returns.
2009 (your 2009 Form 8606, line 22, was less than line 19 of that Form 8606)	The excess, if any, of your 2009 Form 8606, line 24, over line 23[2] of that Form 8606.	Line 16 of your 2010 through 2018 Forms 8606; line 21 of your 2010 Form 8606[4]; and certain rollovers[3] reported on your 2011 through 2018 tax returns.
2008 (your 2008 Form 8606, line 22, was less than line 19 of that Form 8606)	The excess, if any, of your 2008 Form 8606, line 24, over line 23[2] of that Form 8606.	Line 16 of your 2009 through 2018 Forms 8606; line 21 of your 2010 Form 8606[4]; and certain rollovers[3] reported on your 2009 and 2011 through 2018 tax returns.
2007 (your 2007 Form 8606, line 22, was less than line 19 of that Form 8606)	The excess, if any, of your 2007 Form 8606, line 24, over line 23[2] of that Form 8606.	Line 16 of your 2008 through 2018 Forms 8606; line 21 of your 2010 Form 8606[4]; and certain rollovers[3] reported on your 2008, 2009, and 2011 through 2018 tax returns.
2006 (your 2006 Form 8606, line 22, was less than line 19 of that Form 8606)	The excess, if any, of your 2006 Form 8606, line 24, over line 23[2] of that Form 8606.	Line 16 of your 2007 through 2018 Forms 8606; line 21 of your 2010 Form 8606[4]; and certain rollovers[3] reported on your 2008, 2009, and 2011 through 2018 tax returns.

1. Excluding rollovers, recharacterizations, and contributions that you had returned to you.

2. Refigure line 23 without taking into account any amount entered on Form 8606, line 20.

3. Amounts rolled over from qualified retirement plans to Roth IRAs from your Form 1040, line 4a; or Form 1040NR, line 17a.

4. Don't include any in-plan Roth rollovers entered on line 21.

Continued on next page.

Basis in Roth IRA Conversions and Rollovers From Qualified Retirement Plans to Roth IRAs—Line 24 (*continued*)

IF the most recent year prior to 2018 in which you had a distribution[1] in excess of your basis in contributions was . . .	THEN enter on Form 8606, line 24, this amount	PLUS the sum of the amounts on the following lines . . . .
2005 (your 2005 Form 8606, line 22, was less than line 19 of that Form 8606)	The excess, if any, of your 2005 Form 8606, line 24, over line 23[2] of that Form 8606.	Line 16 of your 2006 through 2018 Forms 8606; line 21 of your 2010 Form 8606[4]; and certain rollovers[3] reported on your 2008, 2009, and 2011 through 2018 tax returns.
2004 (your 2004 Form 8606, line 22, was less than line 19 of that Form 8606)	The excess, if any, of your 2004 Form 8606, line 24, over line 23[2] of that Form 8606.	Line 16 of your 2005 through 2018 Forms 8606; line 21 of your 2010 Form 8606[4]; and certain rollovers[3] reported on your 2008, 2009, and 2011 through 2018 tax returns.
2003 (you had an amount on your 2003 Form 8606, line 21)	The excess, if any, of your 2003 Form 8606, line 22, over line 21 of that Form 8606.	Line 16 of your 2004 through 2018 Forms 8606; line 21 of your 2010 Form 8606[4]; and certain rollovers[3] reported on your 2008, 2009, and 2011 through 2018 tax returns.
2002 (you had an amount on your 2002 Form 8606, line 21)	The excess, if any, of your 2002 Form 8606, line 22, over line 21 of that Form 8606.	Line 16 of your 2003 through 2018 Forms 8606; line 21 of your 2010 Form 8606[4]; and certain rollovers[3] reported on your 2008, 2009, and 2011 through 2018 tax returns.
2001 (you had an amount on your 2001 Form 8606, line 21)	The excess, if any, of your 2001 Form 8606, line 22, over line 21 of that Form 8606.	Line 16 of your 2002 through 2018 Forms 8606; line 21 of your 2010 Form 8606[4]; and certain rollovers[3] reported on your 2008, 2009, and 2011 through 2018 tax returns.
2000 (you had an amount on your 2000 Form 8606, line 19)	The excess, if any, of your 2000 Form 8606, line 25, over line 19 of that Form 8606.	Line 16 of your 2001 through 2018 Forms 8606; line 21 of your 2010 Form 8606[4]; and certain rollovers[3] reported on your 2008, 2009, and 2011 through 2018 tax returns.
1999 (you had an amount on your 1999 Form 8606, line 19)	The excess, if any, of your 1999 Form 8606, line 25, over line 19 of that Form 8606.	Line 14c of your 2000 Form 8606; line 16 of your 2001 through 2018 Forms 8606; line 21 of your 2010 Form 8606[4]; and certain rollovers[3] reported on your 2008, 2009, and 2011 through 2018 tax returns.
1998 (you had an amount on your 1998 Form 8606, line 20)	The excess, if any, of your 1998 Form 8606, line 14c, over line 20 of that Form 8606.	Line 14c of your 1999 and 2000 Forms 8606; line 16 of your 2001 through 2018 Forms 8606; line 21 of your 2010 Form 8606[4]; and certain rollovers[3] reported on your 2008, 2009, and 2011 through 2018 tax returns.
Didn't have such a distribution in excess of your basis in contributions	The amount from your 2018 Form 8606, line 16	Line 14c of your 1998 through 2000 Forms 8606; line 16 of your 2001 through 2017 Forms 8606; line 21 of your 2010 Form 8606[4]; and certain rollovers[3] reported on your 2008, 2009, and 2011 through 2018 tax returns.

1. Excluding rollovers, recharacterizations, and contributions that you had returned to you.

2. Refigure line 23 without taking into account any amount entered on Form 8606, line 20.

3. Amounts rolled over from qualified retirement plans to Roth IRAs from your Form 1040, line 16a for 2017 and earlier returns (lines 4a for 2018 tax returns); Form 1040A, line 12a (Form 1040A was retired for 2018); or Form 1040NR, line 17a.

4. Don't include any in-plan Roth rollovers entered on line 21.

Revenue Ruling 2002-62

Part I

Section 72.—Annuities; Certain Proceeds of Endowment and Life Insurance Contracts

SECTION 1. PURPOSE AND BACKGROUND

.01 The purpose of this revenue ruling is to modify the provisions of Q&A-12 of Notice 89-25, 1989-1 C.B. 662, which provides guidance on what constitutes a series of substantially equal periodic payments within the meaning of 72(t)(2)(A)(iv) of the Internal Revenue Code from an individual account under a qualified retirement plan. Section 72(t) provides for an additional income tax on early withdrawals from qualified retirement plans (as defined in 4974(c)). Section 4974(c) provides, in part, that the term "qualified retirement plan" means (1) a plan described in 401 (including a trust exempt from tax under 501(a)), (2) an annuity plan described in 403(a), (3) a tax-sheltered annuity arrangement described in 403(b), (4) an individual retirement account described in 408(a), or (5) an individual retirement annuity described in 408(b).

.02 (a) Section 72(t)(1) provides that if an employee or IRA owner receives any amount from a qualified retirement plan before attaining age 59½, the employee's or IRA owner's income tax is increased by an amount equal to 10-percent of the amount that is includible in the gross income unless one of the exceptions in 72(t)(2) applies.

(b) Section 72(t)(2)(A)(iv) provides, in part, that if distributions are part of a series of substantially equal periodic payments (not less frequently than annually) made for the life (or life expectancy) of the employee or the joint lives (or joint life expectancy) of the employee and beneficiary, the tax described in 72(t)

Revenue Ruling 2002-62 (continued)

(1) will not be applicable. Pursuant to 72(t)(5), in the case of distributions from an IRA, the IRA owner is substituted for the employee for purposes of applying this exception.

(c) Section 72(t)(4) provides that if the series of substantially equal periodic payments that is otherwise excepted from the 10-percent tax is subsequently modified (other than by reason of death or disability) within a 5-year period beginning on the date of the first payment, or, if later, age 59½, the exception to the 10-percent tax does not apply, and the taxpayer's tax for the year of modification shall be increased by an amount which, but for the exception, would have been imposed, plus interest for the deferral period.

(d) Q&A-12 of Notice 89-25 sets forth three methods for determining whether payments to individuals from their IRAs or, if they have separated from service, from their qualified retirement plans, constitute a series of substantially equal periodic payments for purposes of 72(t)(2)(A)(iv).

(e) Final Income Tax Regulations that were published in the April 17, 2002, issue of the Federal Register under 401(a)(9) provide new life expectancy tables for determining required minimum distributions.

SECTION 2. METHODS

.01 General rule. Payments are considered to be substantially equal periodic payments within the meaning of 72(t)(2)(A)(iv) if they are made in accordance with one of the three calculations described in paragraphs (a) – (c) of this subsection (which is comprised of the three methods described in Q&A-12 of Notice 89-25).

Revenue Ruling 2002-62 (continued)

(a) The required minimum distribution method. The annual payment for each year is determined by dividing the account balance for that year by the number from the chosen life expectancy table for that year. Under this method, the account balance, the number from the chosen life expectancy table and the resulting annual payments are redetermined for each year. If this method is chosen, there will not be deemed to be a modification in the series of substantially equal periodic payments, even if the amount of payments changes from year to year, provided there is not a change to another method of determining the payments.

(b) The fixed amortization method. The annual payment for each year is determined by amortizing in level amounts the account balance over a specified number of years determined using the chosen life expectancy table and the chosen interest rate. Under this method, the account balance, the number from the chosen life expectancy table and the resulting annual payment are determined once for the first distribution year and the annual payment is the same amount in each succeeding year.

(c) The fixed annuitization method. The annual payment for each year is determined by dividing the account balance by an annuity factor that is the present value of an annuity of $1 per year beginning at the taxpayer's age and continuing for the life of the taxpayer (or the joint lives of the individual and beneficiary). The annuity factor is derived using the mortality table ... and using the chosen interest rate. Under this method,

Revenue Ruling 2002-62 (continued)

the account balance, the annuity factor, the chosen interest rate and the resulting annual payment are determined once for the first distribution year and the annual payment is the same amount in each succeeding year.

.02 Other rules. The following rules apply for purposes of this section.

(a) Life expectancy tables. The life expectancy tables that can be used to determine distribution periods are: (1) the uniform lifetime table in Appendix A*, or (2) the single life expectancy table in 1.401(a)(9)-9, Q&A-1 of the Income Tax Regulations* or (3) the joint and last survivor table in 1.401(a)(9)-9, Q&A-3*. The number that is used for a distribution year is the number shown from the table for the employee's (or IRA owner's) age on his or her birthday in that year.

If the joint and survivor table is being used, the age of the beneficiary on the beneficiary's birthday in the year is also used. In the case of the required minimum distribution method, the same life expectancy table that is used for the first distribution year must be used in each following year. Thus, if the taxpayer uses the single life expectancy table for the required minimum distribution method in the first distribution year, the same table must be used in subsequent distribution years.

(b) Beneficiary under joint tables. If the joint life and last survivor table in 1.401(a)(9)-9, Q&A-3, is used, the survivor must be the actual beneficiary of the employee with respect to the account for the year of the distribution. If there is more than one

* You can find these tables in Appendix B of this book.

Revenue Ruling 2002-62 (continued)

beneficiary, the identity and age of the beneficiary used for purposes of each of the methods described in section 2.01 are determined under the rules for determining the designated beneficiary for purposes of 401(a)(9). The beneficiary is determined for a year as of January 1 of the year, without regard to changes in the beneficiary in that year or beneficiary determinations in prior years. For example, if a taxpayer starts distributions from an IRA in 2003 at age 50 and a 25-year-old and 55-year-old are beneficiaries on January 1, the 55-year-old is the designated beneficiary and the number for the taxpayer from the joint and last survivor tables (age 50 and age 55) would be 38.3, even though later in 2003 the 55-year-old is eliminated as a beneficiary. However, if that beneficiary is eliminated or dies in 2003, under the required minimum distribution method, that individual would not be taken into account in future years. If, in any year there is no beneficiary, the single life expectancy table is used for that year.

(c) Interest rates. The interest rate that may be used is any interest rate that is not more than 120 percent of the federal mid-term rate (determined in accordance with 1274(d) for either of the two months immediately preceding the month in which the distribution begins). The revenue rulings that contain the 1274(d) federal mid-term rates may be found at www.irs.gov/tax_regs/fedrates.html.

(d) Account balance. The account balance that is used to determine payments must be determined in a reasonable manner based on the facts and circumstances. For

Revenue Ruling 2002-62 (continued)

example, for an IRA with daily valuations that made its first distribution on July 15, 2003, it would be reasonable to determine the yearly account balance when using the required minimum distribution method based on the value of the IRA from December 31, 2002 to July 15, 2003. For subsequent years, under the required minimum distribution method, it would be reasonable to use the value either on the December 31 of the prior year or on a date within a reasonable period before that year's distribution.

(e) Changes to account balance. Under all three methods, substantially equal periodic payments are calculated with respect to an account balance as of the first valuation date selected in paragraph (d) above. Thus, a modification to the series of payments will occur if,

after such date, there is (i) any addition to the account balance other than gains or losses, (ii) any nontaxable transfer of a portion of the account balance to another retirement plan, or (iii) a rollover by the taxpayer of the amount received resulting in such amount not being taxable.

.03 Special rules. The special rules described below may be applicable.

(a) Complete depletion of assets. If, as a result of following an acceptable method of determining substantially equal periodic payments, an individual's assets in an individual account plan or an IRA are exhausted, the individual will not be subject to additional income tax under 72(t)(1) as a result of not receiving substantially equal periodic payments and the resulting cessation of payments will not be treated as a modification of the series of payments.

Revenue Ruling 2002-62 (continued)

(b) One-time change to required minimum distribution method. An individual who begins distributions in a year using either the fixed amortization method or the fixed annuitization method may in any subsequent year switch to the required minimum distribution method to determine the payment for the year of the switch and all subsequent years and the change in method will not be treated as a modification within the meaning of 72(t)(4). Once a change is made under this paragraph, the required minimum distribution method must be followed in all subsequent years. Any subsequent change will be a modification for purposes of 72(t)(4).

SECTION 3. EFFECTIVE DATE AND TRANSITIONAL RULES

The guidance in this revenue ruling replaces the guidance in Q&A-12 of Notice 89-25 for any series of payments commencing on or after January 1, 2003, and may be used for distributions commencing in 2002. If a series of payments commenced in a year prior to 2003 that satisfied 72(t)(2)(A)(iv), the method of calculating the payments in the series is permitted to be changed at any time to the required minimum distribution method described in section 2.01(a) of this guidance, including use of a different life expectancy table.

SECTION 4. EFFECT ON OTHER DOCUMENTS

Q&A-12 of Notice 89-25 is modified.

SECTION 5. REQUEST FOR COMMENTS

The Service and Treasury invite comments with respect to the guidance provided in this revenue ruling. Comments should reference Rev. Rul. 2002-62. Comments may be submitted to CC:ITA:RU (Rev. Rul. 2002-62), room 5226, Internal Revenue Service, POB 7604 Ben Franklin Station, Washington, DC 20044.

Revenue Ruling 2002-62 (continued)

Comments may be hand delivered between the hours of 8:30 a.m. and 5 p.m. Monday to Friday to: CC:ITA:RU (Rev. Rul. 2002-62), Courier's Desk, Internal Revenue Service, 1111 Constitution Avenue NW, Washington, DC. Alternatively, comments may be submitted via the Internet at Notice.Comments@irscounsel. treas.gov. All comments will be available for public inspection and copying.

Drafting Information

The principal author of this revenue ruling is Michael Rubin of the Employee Plans, Tax Exempt and Government Entities Division. For further information regarding this revenue ruling, please contact Mr. Rubin at 1-202-283-9888 (not a toll-free number).

Life Expectancy Tables

Table I: Single Life Expectancy

Age	Divisor	Age	Divisor	Age	Divisor	Age	Divisor
0	82.4	29	54.3	58	27.0	87	6.7
1	81.6	30	53.3	59	26.1	88	6.3
2	80.6	31	52.4	60	25.2	89	5.9
3	79.7	32	51.4	61	24.4	90	5.5
4	78.7	33	50.4	62	23.5	91	5.2
5	77.7	34	49.4	63	22.7	92	4.9
6	76.7	35	48.5	64	21.8	93	4.6
7	75.8	36	47.5	65	21.0	94	4.3
8	74.8	37	46.5	66	20.2	95	4.1
9	73.8	38	45.6	67	19.4	96	3.8
10	72.8	39	44.6	68	18.6	97	3.6
11	71.8	40	43.6	69	17.8	98	3.4
12	70.8	41	42.7	70	17.0	99	3.1
13	69.9	42	41.7	71	16.3	100	2.9
14	68.9	43	40.7	72	15.5	101	2.7
15	67.9	44	39.8	73	14.8	102	2.5
16	66.9	45	38.8	74	14.1	103	2.3
17	66.0	46	37.9	75	13.4	104	2.1
18	65.0	47	37.0	76	12.7	105	1.9
19	64.0	48	36.0	77	12.1	106	1.7
20	63.0	49	35.1	78	11.4	107	1.5
21	62.1	50	34.2	79	10.8	108	1.4
22	61.1	51	33.3	80	10.2	109	1.2
23	60.1	52	32.3	81	9.7	110	1.1
24	59.1	53	31.4	82	9.1	111+	1.0
25	58.2	54	30.5	83	8.6		
26	57.2	55	29.6	84	8.1		
27	56.2	56	28.7	85	7.6		
28	55.3	57	27.9	86	7.1		

Table II: Joint Life and Last Survivor Expectancy

AGES	30	31	32	33	34	35	36	37	38	39
30	60.2	59.7	59.2	58.8	58.4	58.0	57.6	57.3	57.0	56.7
31	59.7	59.2	58.7	58.2	57.8	57.4	57.0	56.6	56.3	56.0
32	59.2	58.7	58.2	57.7	57.2	56.8	56.4	56.0	55.6	55.3
33	58.8	58.2	57.7	57.2	56.7	56.2	55.8	55.4	55.0	54.7
34	58.4	57.8	57.2	56.7	56.2	55.7	55.3	54.8	54.4	54.0
35	58.0	57.4	56.8	56.2	55.7	55.2	54.7	54.3	53.8	53.4
36	57.6	57.0	56.4	55.8	55.3	54.7	54.2	53.7	53.3	52.8
37	57.3	56.6	56.0	55.4	54.8	54.3	53.7	53.2	52.7	52.3
38	57.0	56.3	55.6	55.0	54.4	53.8	53.3	52.7	52.2	51.7
39	56.7	56.0	55.3	54.7	54.0	53.4	52.8	52.3	51.7	51.2
40	56.4	55.7	55.0	54.3	53.7	53.0	52.4	51.8	51.3	50.8
41	56.1	55.4	54.7	54.0	53.3	52.7	52.0	51.4	50.9	50.3
42	55.9	55.2	54.4	53.7	53.0	52.3	51.7	51.1	50.4	49.9
43	55.7	54.9	54.2	53.4	52.7	52.0	51.3	50.7	50.1	49.5
44	55.5	54.7	53.9	53.2	52.4	51.7	51.0	50.4	49.7	49.1
45	55.3	54.5	53.7	52.9	52.2	51.5	50.7	50.0	49.4	48.7
46	55.1	54.3	53.5	52.7	52.0	51.2	50.5	49.8	49.1	48.4
47	55.0	54.1	53.3	52.5	51.7	51.0	50.2	49.5	48.8	48.1
48	54.8	54.0	53.2	52.3	51.5	50.8	50.0	49.2	48.5	47.8
49	54.7	53.8	53.0	52.2	51.4	50.6	49.8	49.0	48.2	47.5
50	54.6	53.7	52.9	52.0	51.2	50.4	49.6	48.8	48.0	47.3
51	54.5	53.6	52.7	51.9	51.0	50.2	49.4	48.6	47.8	47.0
52	54.4	53.5	52.6	51.7	50.9	50.0	49.2	48.4	47.6	46.8
53	54.3	53.4	52.5	51.6	50.8	49.9	49.1	48.2	47.4	46.6
54	54.2	53.3	52.4	51.5	50.6	49.8	48.9	48.1	47.2	46.4
55	54.1	53.2	52.3	51.4	50.5	49.7	48.8	47.9	47.1	46.3
56	54.0	53.1	52.2	51.3	50.4	49.5	48.7	47.8	47.0	46.1
57	54.0	53.0	52.1	51.2	50.3	49.4	48.6	47.7	46.8	46.0
58	53.9	53.0	52.1	51.2	50.3	49.4	48.5	47.6	46.7	45.8
59	53.8	52.9	52.0	51.1	50.2	49.3	48.4	47.5	46.6	45.7

Table II: Joint Life and Last Survivor Expectancy (continued)

AGES	30	31	32	33	34	35	36	37	38	39
60	53.8	52.9	51.9	51.0	50.1	49.2	48.3	47.4	46.5	45.6
61	53.8	52.8	51.9	51.0	50.0	49.1	48.2	47.3	46.4	45.5
62	53.7	52.8	51.8	50.9	50.0	49.1	48.1	47.2	46.3	45.4
63	53.7	52.7	51.8	50.9	49.9	49.0	48.1	47.2	46.3	45.3
64	53.6	52.7	51.8	50.8	49.9	48.9	48.0	47.1	46.2	45.3
65	53.6	52.7	51.7	50.8	49.8	48.9	48.0	47.0	46.1	45.2
66	53.6	52.6	51.7	50.7	49.8	48.9	47.9	47.0	46.1	45.1
67	53.6	52.6	51.7	50.7	49.8	48.8	47.9	46.9	46.0	45.1
68	53.5	52.6	51.6	50.7	49.7	48.8	47.8	46.9	46.0	45.0
69	53.5	52.6	51.6	50.6	49.7	48.7	47.8	46.9	45.9	45.0
70	53.5	52.5	51.6	50.6	49.7	48.7	47.8	46.8	45.9	44.9
71	53.5	52.5	51.6	50.6	49.6	48.7	47.7	46.8	45.9	44.9
72	53.5	52.5	51.5	50.6	49.6	48.7	47.7	46.8	45.8	44.9
73	53.4	52.5	51.5	50.6	49.6	48.6	47.7	46.7	45.8	44.8
74	53.4	52.5	51.5	50.5	49.6	48.6	47.7	46.7	45.8	44.8
75	53.4	52.5	51.5	50.5	49.6	48.6	47.7	46.7	45.7	44.8
76	53.4	52.4	51.5	50.5	49.6	48.6	47.6	46.7	45.7	44.8
77	53.4	52.4	51.5	50.5	49.5	48.6	47.6	46.7	45.7	44.8
78	53.4	52.4	51.5	50.5	49.5	48.6	47.6	46.6	45.7	44.7
79	53.4	52.4	51.5	50.5	49.5	48.6	47.6	46.6	45.7	44.7
80	53.4	52.4	51.4	50.5	49.5	48.5	47.6	46.6	45.7	44.7
81	53.4	52.4	51.4	50.5	49.5	48.5	47.6	46.6	45.7	44.7
82	53.4	52.4	51.4	50.5	49.5	48.5	47.6	46.6	45.6	44.7
83	53.4	52.4	51.4	50.5	49.5	48.5	47.6	46.6	45.6	44.7
84	53.4	52.4	51.4	50.5	49.5	48.5	47.6	46.6	45.6	44.7
85	53.3	52.4	51.4	50.4	49.5	48.5	47.5	46.6	45.6	44.7
86	53.3	52.4	51.4	50.4	49.5	48.5	47.5	46.6	45.6	44.6
87	53.3	52.4	51.4	50.4	49.5	48.5	47.5	46.6	45.6	44.6
88	53.3	52.4	51.4	50.4	49.5	48.5	47.5	46.6	45.6	44.6
89	53.3	52.4	51.4	50.4	49.5	48.5	47.5	46.6	45.6	44.6

AGES	30	31	32	33	34	35	36	37	38	39

Table II: Joint Life and Last Survivor Expectancy (continued)

AGES	30	31	32	33	34	35	36	37	38	39
90	53.3	52.4	51.4	50.4	49.5	48.5	47.5	46.6	45.6	44.6
91	53.3	52.4	51.4	50.4	49.5	48.5	47.5	46.6	45.6	44.6
92	53.3	52.4	51.4	50.4	49.5	48.5	47.5	46.6	45.6	44.6
93	53.3	52.4	51.4	50.4	49.5	48.5	47.5	46.6	45.6	44.6
94	53.3	52.4	51.4	50.4	49.5	48.5	47.5	46.6	45.6	44.6
95	53.3	52.4	51.4	50.4	49.5	48.5	47.5	46.5	45.6	44.6
96	53.3	52.4	51.4	50.4	49.5	48.5	47.5	46.5	45.6	44.6
97	53.3	52.4	51.4	50.4	49.5	48.5	47.5	46.5	45.6	44.6
98	53.3	52.4	51.4	50.4	49.5	48.5	47.5	46.5	45.6	44.6
99	53.3	52.4	51.4	50.4	49.5	48.5	47.5	46.5	45.6	44.6
100	53.3	52.4	51.4	50.4	49.5	48.5	47.5	46.5	45.6	44.6
101	53.3	52.4	51.4	50.4	49.5	48.5	47.5	46.5	45.6	44.6
102	53.3	52.4	51.4	50.4	49.5	48.5	47.5	46.5	45.6	44.6
103	53.3	52.4	51.4	50.4	49.5	48.5	47.5	46.5	45.6	44.6
104	53.3	52.4	51.4	50.4	49.5	48.5	47.5	46.5	45.6	44.6
105	53.3	52.4	51.4	50.4	49.4	48.5	47.5	46.5	45.6	44.6
106	53.3	52.4	51.4	50.4	49.4	48.5	47.5	46.5	45.6	44.6
107	53.3	52.4	51.4	50.4	49.4	48.5	47.5	46.5	45.6	44.6
108	53.3	52.4	51.4	50.4	49.4	48.5	47.5	46.5	45.6	44.6
109	53.3	52.4	51.4	50.4	49.4	48.5	47.5	46.5	45.6	44.6
110	53.3	52.4	51.4	50.4	49.4	48.5	47.5	46.5	45.6	44.6
111	53.3	52.4	51.4	50.4	49.4	48.5	47.5	46.5	45.6	44.6
112	53.3	52.4	51.4	50.4	49.4	48.5	47.5	46.5	45.6	44.6
113	53.3	52.4	51.4	50.4	49.4	48.5	47.5	46.5	45.6	44.6
114	53.3	52.4	51.4	50.4	49.4	48.5	47.5	46.5	45.6	44.6
115+	53.3	52.4	51.4	50.4	49.4	48.5	47.5	46.5	45.6	44.6

Table II: Joint Life and Last Survivor Expectancy (continued)									
AGES	40	41	42	43	44	45	46	47	48	49
40	50.2	49.8	49.3	48.9	48.5	48.1	47.7	47.4	47.1	46.8
41	49.8	49.3	48.8	48.3	47.9	47.5	47.1	46.7	46.4	46.1
42	49.3	48.8	48.3	47.8	47.3	46.9	46.5	46.1	45.8	45.4
43	48.9	48.3	47.8	47.3	46.8	46.3	45.9	45.5	45.1	44.8
44	48.5	47.9	47.3	46.8	46.3	45.8	45.4	44.9	44.5	44.2
45	48.1	47.5	46.9	46.3	45.8	45.3	44.8	44.4	44.0	43.6
46	47.7	47.1	46.5	45.9	45.4	44.8	44.3	43.9	43.4	43.0
47	47.4	46.7	46.1	45.5	44.9	44.4	43.9	43.4	42.9	42.4
48	47.1	46.4	45.8	45.1	44.5	44.0	43.4	42.9	42.4	41.9
49	46.8	46.1	45.4	44.8	44.2	43.6	43.0	42.4	41.9	41.4
50	46.5	45.8	45.1	44.4	43.8	43.2	42.6	42.0	41.5	40.9
51	46.3	45.5	44.8	44.1	43.5	42.8	42.2	41.6	41.0	40.5
52	46.0	45.3	44.6	43.8	43.2	42.5	41.8	41.2	40.6	40.1
53	45.8	45.1	44.3	43.6	42.9	42.2	41.5	40.9	40.3	39.7
54	45.6	44.8	44.1	43.3	42.6	41.9	41.2	40.5	39.9	39.3
55	45.5	44.7	43.9	43.1	42.4	41.6	40.9	40.2	39.6	38.9
56	45.3	44.5	43.7	42.9	42.1	41.4	40.7	40.0	39.3	38.6
57	45.1	44.3	43.5	42.7	41.9	41.2	40.4	39.7	39.0	38.3
58	45.0	44.2	43.3	42.5	41.7	40.9	40.2	39.4	38.7	38.0
59	44.9	44.0	43.2	42.4	41.5	40.7	40.0	39.2	38.5	37.8
60	44.7	43.9	43.0	42.2	41.4	40.6	39.8	39.0	38.2	37.5
61	44.6	43.8	42.9	42.1	41.2	40.4	39.6	38.8	38.0	37.3
62	44.5	43.7	42.8	41.9	41.1	40.3	39.4	38.6	37.8	37.1
63	44.5	43.6	42.7	41.8	41.0	40.1	39.3	38.5	37.7	36.9
64	44.4	43.5	42.6	41.7	40.8	40.0	39.2	38.3	37.5	36.7
65	44.3	43.4	42.5	41.6	40.7	39.9	39.0	38.2	37.4	36.6
66	44.2	43.3	42.4	41.5	40.6	39.8	38.9	38.1	37.2	36.4
67	44.2	43.3	42.3	41.4	40.6	39.7	38.8	38.0	37.1	36.3
68	44.1	43.2	42.3	41.4	40.5	39.6	38.7	37.9	37.0	36.2
69	44.1	43.1	42.2	41.3	40.4	39.5	38.6	37.8	36.9	36.0

Table II: Joint Life and Last Survivor Expectancy (continued)

AGES	40	41	42	43	44	45	46	47	48	49
70	44.0	43.1	42.2	41.3	40.3	39.4	38.6	37.7	36.8	35.9
71	44.0	43.0	42.1	41.2	40.3	39.4	38.5	37.6	36.7	35.9
72	43.9	43.0	42.1	41.1	40.2	39.3	38.4	37.5	36.6	35.8
73	43.9	43.0	42.0	41.1	40.2	39.3	38.4	37.5	36.6	35.7
74	43.9	42.9	42.0	41.1	40.1	39.2	38.3	37.4	36.5	35.6
75	43.8	42.9	42.0	41.0	40.1	39.2	38.3	37.4	36.5	35.6
76	43.8	42.9	41.9	41.0	40.1	39.1	38.2	37.3	36.4	35.5
77	43.8	42.9	41.9	41.0	40.0	39.1	38.2	37.3	36.4	35.5
78	43.8	42.8	41.9	40.9	40.0	39.1	38.2	37.2	36.3	35.4
79	43.8	42.8	41.9	40.9	40.0	39.1	38.1	37.2	36.3	35.4
80	43.7	42.8	41.8	40.9	40.0	39.0	38.1	37.2	36.3	35.4
81	43.7	42.8	41.8	40.9	39.9	39.0	38.1	37.2	36.2	35.3
82	43.7	42.8	41.8	40.9	39.9	39.0	38.1	37.1	36.2	35.3
83	43.7	42.8	41.8	40.9	39.9	39.0	38.0	37.1	36.2	35.3
84	43.7	42.7	41.8	40.8	39.9	39.0	38.0	37.1	36.2	35.3
85	43.7	42.7	41.8	40.8	39.9	38.9	38.0	37.1	36.2	35.2
86	43.7	42.7	41.8	40.8	39.9	38.9	38.0	37.1	36.1	35.2
87	43.7	42.7	41.8	40.8	39.9	38.9	38.0	37.0	36.1	35.2
88	43.7	42.7	41.8	40.8	39.9	38.9	38.0	37.0	36.1	35.2
89	43.7	42.7	41.7	40.8	39.8	38.9	38.0	37.0	36.1	35.2
90	43.7	42.7	41.7	40.8	39.8	38.9	38.0	37.0	36.1	35.2
91	43.7	42.7	41.7	40.8	39.8	38.9	37.9	37.0	36.1	35.2
92	43.7	42.7	41.7	40.8	39.8	38.9	37.9	37.0	36.1	35.1
93	43.7	42.7	41.7	40.8	39.8	38.9	37.9	37.0	36.1	35.1
94	43.7	42.7	41.7	40.8	39.8	38.9	37.9	37.0	36.1	35.1
95	43.6	42.7	41.7	40.8	39.8	38.9	37.9	37.0	36.1	35.1
96	43.6	42.7	41.7	40.8	39.8	38.9	37.9	37.0	36.1	35.1
97	43.6	42.7	41.7	40.8	39.8	38.9	37.9	37.0	36.1	35.1
98	43.6	42.7	41.7	40.8	39.8	38.9	37.9	37.0	36.0	35.1
99	43.6	42.7	41.7	40.8	39.8	38.9	37.9	37.0	36.0	35.1

AGES	40	41	42	43	44	45	46	47	48	49
100	43.6	42.7	41.7	40.8	39.8	38.9	37.9	37.0	36.0	35.1
101	43.6	42.7	41.7	40.8	39.8	38.9	37.9	37.0	36.0	35.1
102	43.6	42.7	41.7	40.8	39.8	38.9	37.9	37.0	36.0	35.1
103	43.6	42.7	41.7	40.8	39.8	38.9	37.9	37.0	36.0	35.1
104	43.6	42.7	41.7	40.8	39.8	38.8	37.9	37.0	36.0	35.1
105	43.6	42.7	41.7	40.8	39.8	38.8	37.9	37.0	36.0	35.1
106	43.6	42.7	41.7	40.8	39.8	38.8	37.9	37.0	36.0	35.1
107	43.6	42.7	41.7	40.8	39.8	38.8	37.9	37.0	36.0	35.1
108	43.6	42.7	41.7	40.8	39.8	38.8	37.9	37.0	36.0	35.1
109	43.6	42.7	41.7	40.7	39.8	38.8	37.9	37.0	36.0	35.1
110	43.6	42.7	41.7	40.7	39.8	38.8	37.9	37.0	36.0	35.1
111	43.6	42.7	41.7	40.7	39.8	38.8	37.9	37.0	36.0	35.1
112	43.6	42.7	41.7	40.7	39.8	38.8	37.9	37.0	36.0	35.1
113	43.6	42.7	41.7	40.7	39.8	38.8	37.9	37.0	36.0	35.1
114	43.6	42.7	41.7	40.7	39.8	38.8	37.9	37.0	36.0	35.1
115+	43.6	42.7	41.7	40.7	39.8	38.8	37.9	37.0	36.0	35.1

Table II: Joint Life and Last Survivor Expectancy (continued)

Table II: Joint Life and Last Survivor Expectancy (continued)

AGES	50	51	52	53	54	55	56	57	58	59
50	40.4	40.0	39.5	39.1	38.7	38.3	38.0	37.6	37.3	37.1
51	40.0	39.5	39.0	38.5	38.1	37.7	37.4	37.0	36.7	36.4
52	39.5	39.0	38.5	38.0	37.6	37.2	36.8	36.4	36.0	35.7
53	39.1	38.5	38.0	37.5	37.1	36.6	36.2	35.8	35.4	35.1
54	38.7	38.1	37.6	37.1	36.6	36.1	35.7	35.2	34.8	34.5
55	38.3	37.7	37.2	36.6	36.1	35.6	35.1	34.7	34.3	33.9
56	38.0	37.4	36.8	36.2	35.7	35.1	34.7	34.2	33.7	33.3
57	37.6	37.0	36.4	35.8	35.2	34.7	34.2	33.7	33.2	32.8
58	37.3	36.7	36.0	35.4	34.8	34.3	33.7	33.2	32.8	32.3
59	37.1	36.4	35.7	35.1	34.5	33.9	33.3	32.8	32.3	31.8
60	36.8	36.1	35.4	34.8	34.1	33.5	32.9	32.4	31.9	31.3
61	36.6	35.8	35.1	34.5	33.8	33.2	32.6	32.0	31.4	30.9
62	36.3	35.6	34.9	34.2	33.5	32.9	32.2	31.6	31.1	30.5
63	36.1	35.4	34.6	33.9	33.2	32.6	31.9	31.3	30.7	30.1
64	35.9	35.2	34.4	33.7	33.0	32.3	31.6	31.0	30.4	29.8
65	35.8	35.0	34.2	33.5	32.7	32.0	31.4	30.7	30.0	29.4
66	35.6	34.8	34.0	33.3	32.5	31.8	31.1	30.4	29.8	29.1
67	35.5	34.7	33.9	33.1	32.3	31.6	30.9	30.2	29.5	28.8
68	35.3	34.5	33.7	32.9	32.1	31.4	30.7	29.9	29.2	28.6
69	35.2	34.4	33.6	32.8	32.0	31.2	30.5	29.7	29.0	28.3
70	35.1	34.3	33.4	32.6	31.8	31.1	30.3	29.5	28.8	28.1
71	35.0	34.2	33.3	32.5	31.7	30.9	30.1	29.4	28.6	27.9
72	34.9	34.1	33.2	32.4	31.6	30.8	30.0	29.2	28.4	27.7
73	34.8	34.0	33.1	32.3	31.5	30.6	29.8	29.1	28.3	27.5
74	34.8	33.9	33.0	32.2	31.4	30.5	29.7	28.9	28.1	27.4
75	34.7	33.8	33.0	32.1	31.3	30.4	29.6	28.8	28.0	27.2
76	34.6	33.8	32.9	32.0	31.2	30.3	29.5	28.7	27.9	27.1
77	34.6	33.7	32.8	32.0	31.1	30.3	29.4	28.6	27.8	27.0
78	34.5	33.6	32.8	31.9	31.0	30.2	29.3	28.5	27.7	26.9
79	34.5	33.6	32.7	31.8	31.0	30.1	29.3	28.4	27.6	26.8

Table II: Joint Life and Last Survivor Expectancy (continued)

AGES	50	51	52	53	54	55	56	57	58	59
80	34.5	33.6	32.7	31.8	30.9	30.1	29.2	28.4	27.5	26.7
81	34.4	33.5	32.6	31.8	30.9	30.0	29.2	28.3	27.5	26.6
82	34.4	33.5	32.6	31.7	30.8	30.0	29.1	28.3	27.4	26.6
83	34.4	33.5	32.6	31.7	30.8	29.9	29.1	28.2	27.4	26.5
84	34.3	33.4	32.5	31.7	30.8	29.9	29.0	28.2	27.3	26.5
85	34.3	33.4	32.5	31.6	30.7	29.9	29.0	28.1	27.3	26.4
86	34.3	33.4	32.5	31.6	30.7	29.8	29.0	28.1	27.2	26.4
87	34.3	33.4	32.5	31.6	30.7	29.8	28.9	28.1	27.2	26.4
88	34.3	33.4	32.5	31.6	30.7	29.8	28.9	28.0	27.2	26.3
89	34.3	33.3	32.4	31.5	30.7	29.8	28.9	28.0	27.2	26.3
90	34.2	33.3	32.4	31.5	30.6	29.8	28.9	28.0	27.1	26.3
91	34.2	33.3	32.4	31.5	30.6	29.7	28.9	28.0	27.1	26.3
92	34.2	33.3	32.4	31.5	30.6	29.7	28.8	28.0	27.1	26.2
93	34.2	33.3	32.4	31.5	30.6	29.7	28.8	28.0	27.1	26.2
94	34.2	33.3	32.4	31.5	30.6	29.7	28.8	27.9	27.1	26.2
95	34.2	33.3	32.4	31.5	30.6	29.7	28.8	27.9	27.1	26.2
96	34.2	33.3	32.4	31.5	30.6	29.7	28.8	27.9	27.0	26.2
97	34.2	33.3	32.4	31.5	30.6	29.7	28.8	27.9	27.0	26.2
98	34.2	33.3	32.4	31.5	30.6	29.7	28.8	27.9	27.0	26.2
99	34.2	33.3	32.4	31.5	30.6	29.7	28.8	27.9	27.0	26.2
100	34.2	33.3	32.4	31.5	30.6	29.7	28.8	27.9	27.0	26.1
101	34.2	33.3	32.4	31.5	30.6	29.7	28.8	27.9	27.0	26.1
102	34.2	33.3	32.4	31.4	30.5	29.7	28.8	27.9	27.0	26.1
103	34.2	33.3	32.4	31.4	30.5	29.7	28.8	27.9	27.0	26.1
104	34.2	33.3	32.4	31.4	30.5	29.6	28.8	27.9	27.0	26.1
105	34.2	33.3	32.3	31.4	30.5	29.6	28.8	27.9	27.0	26.1
106	34.2	33.3	32.3	31.4	30.5	29.6	28.8	27.9	27.0	26.1
107	34.2	33.3	32.3	31.4	30.5	29.6	28.8	27.9	27.0	26.1
108	34.2	33.3	32.3	31.4	30.5	29.6	28.8	27.9	27.0	26.1
109	34.2	33.3	32.3	31.4	30.5	29.6	28.7	27.9	27.0	26.1

Table II: Joint Life and Last Survivor Expectancy (continued)									
AGES	50	51	52	53	54	55	56	57	58	59
110	34.2	33.3	32.3	31.4	30.5	29.6	28.7	27.9	27.0	26.1
111	34.2	33.3	32.3	31.4	30.5	29.6	28.7	27.9	27.0	26.1
112	34.2	33.3	32.3	31.4	30.5	29.6	28.7	27.9	27.0	26.1
113	34.2	33.3	32.3	31.4	30.5	29.6	28.7	27.9	27.0	26.1
114	34.2	33.3	32.3	31.4	30.5	29.6	28.7	27.9	27.0	26.1
115+	34.2	33.3	32.3	31.4	30.5	29.6	28.7	27.9	27.0	26.1

Table II: Joint Life and Last Survivor Expectancy (continued)

AGES	60	61	62	63	64	65	66	67	68	69
60	30.9	30.4	30.0	29.6	29.2	28.8	28.5	28.2	27.9	27.6
61	30.4	29.9	29.5	29.0	28.6	28.3	27.9	27.6	27.3	27.0
62	30.0	29.5	29.0	28.5	28.1	27.7	27.3	27.0	26.7	26.4
63	29.6	29.0	28.5	28.1	27.6	27.2	26.8	26.4	26.1	25.7
64	29.2	28.6	28.1	27.6	27.1	26.7	26.3	25.9	25.5	25.2
65	28.8	28.3	27.7	27.2	26.7	26.2	25.8	25.4	25.0	24.6
66	28.5	27.9	27.3	26.8	26.3	25.8	25.3	24.9	24.5	24.1
67	28.2	27.6	27.0	26.4	25.9	25.4	24.9	24.4	24.0	23.6
68	27.9	27.3	26.7	26.1	25.5	25.0	24.5	24.0	23.5	23.1
69	27.6	27.0	26.4	25.7	25.2	24.6	24.1	23.6	23.1	22.6
70	27.4	26.7	26.1	25.4	24.8	24.3	23.7	23.2	22.7	22.2
71	27.2	26.5	25.8	25.2	24.5	23.9	23.4	22.8	22.3	21.8
72	27.0	26.3	25.6	24.9	24.3	23.7	23.1	22.5	22.0	21.4
73	26.8	26.1	25.4	24.7	24.0	23.4	22.8	22.2	21.6	21.1
74	26.6	25.9	25.2	24.5	23.8	23.1	22.5	21.9	21.3	20.8
75	26.5	25.7	25.0	24.3	23.6	22.9	22.3	21.6	21.0	20.5
76	26.3	25.6	24.8	24.1	23.4	22.7	22.0	21.4	20.8	20.2
77	26.2	25.4	24.7	23.9	23.2	22.5	21.8	21.2	20.6	19.9
78	26.1	25.3	24.6	23.8	23.1	22.4	21.7	21.0	20.3	19.7
79	26.0	25.2	24.4	23.7	22.9	22.2	21.5	20.8	20.1	19.5
80	25.9	25.1	24.3	23.6	22.8	22.1	21.3	20.6	20.0	19.3
81	25.8	25.0	24.2	23.4	22.7	21.9	21.2	20.5	19.8	19.1
82	25.8	24.9	24.1	23.4	22.6	21.8	21.1	20.4	19.7	19.0
83	25.7	24.9	24.1	23.3	22.5	21.7	21.0	20.2	19.5	18.8
84	25.6	24.8	24.0	23.2	22.4	21.6	20.9	20.1	19.4	18.7
85	25.6	24.8	23.9	23.1	22.3	21.6	20.8	20.1	19.3	18.6
86	25.5	24.7	23.9	23.1	22.3	21.5	20.7	20.0	19.2	18.5
87	25.5	24.7	23.8	23.0	22.2	21.4	20.7	19.9	19.2	18.4
88	25.5	24.6	23.8	23.0	22.2	21.4	20.6	19.8	19.1	18.3
89	25.4	24.6	23.8	22.9	22.1	21.3	20.5	19.8	19.0	18.3

Table II: Joint Life and Last Survivor Expectancy (continued)

AGES	60	61	62	63	64	65	66	67	68	69
90	25.4	24.6	23.7	22.9	22.1	21.3	20.5	19.7	19.0	18.2
91	25.4	24.5	23.7	22.9	22.1	21.3	20.5	19.7	18.9	18.2
92	25.4	24.5	23.7	22.9	22.0	21.2	20.4	19.6	18.9	18.1
93	25.4	24.5	23.7	22.8	22.0	21.2	20.4	19.6	18.8	18.1
94	25.3	24.5	23.6	22.8	22.0	21.2	20.4	19.6	18.8	18.0
95	25.3	24.5	23.6	22.8	22.0	21.1	20.3	19.6	18.8	18.0
96	25.3	24.5	23.6	22.8	21.9	21.1	20.3	19.5	18.8	18.0
97	25.3	24.5	23.6	22.8	21.9	21.1	20.3	19.5	18.7	18.0
98	25.3	24.4	23.6	22.8	21.9	21.1	20.3	19.5	18.7	17.9
99	25.3	24.4	23.6	22.7	21.9	21.1	20.3	19.5	18.7	17.9
100	25.3	24.4	23.6	22.7	21.9	21.1	20.3	19.5	18.7	17.9
101	25.3	24.4	23.6	22.7	21.9	21.1	20.2	19.4	18.7	17.9
102	25.3	24.4	23.6	22.7	21.9	21.1	20.2	19.4	18.6	17.9
103	25.3	24.4	23.6	22.7	21.9	21.0	20.2	19.4	18.6	17.9
104	25.3	24.4	23.5	22.7	21.9	21.0	20.2	19.4	18.6	17.8
105	25.3	24.4	23.5	22.7	21.9	21.0	20.2	19.4	18.6	17.8
106	25.3	24.4	23.5	22.7	21.9	21.0	20.2	19.4	18.6	17.8
107	25.2	24.4	23.5	22.7	21.8	21.0	20.2	19.4	18.6	17.8
108	25.2	24.4	23.5	22.7	21.8	21.0	20.2	19.4	18.6	17.8
109	25.2	24.4	23.5	22.7	21.8	21.0	20.2	19.4	18.6	17.8
110	25.2	24.4	23.5	22.7	21.8	21.0	20.2	19.4	18.6	17.8
111	25.2	24.4	23.5	22.7	21.8	21.0	20.2	19.4	18.6	17.8
112	25.2	24.4	23.5	22.7	21.8	21.0	20.2	19.4	18.6	17.8
113	25.2	24.4	23.5	22.7	21.8	21.0	20.2	19.4	18.6	17.8
114	25.2	24.4	23.5	22.7	21.8	21.0	20.2	19.4	18.6	17.8
115+	25.2	24.4	23.5	22.7	21.8	21.0	20.2	19.4	18.6	17.8

Table II: Joint Life and Last Survivor Expectancy (continued)

AGES	70	71	72	73	74	75	76	77	78	79
70	21.8	21.3	20.9	20.6	20.2	19.9	19.6	19.4	19.1	18.9
71	21.3	20.9	20.5	20.1	19.7	19.4	19.1	18.8	18.5	18.3
72	20.9	20.5	20.0	19.6	19.3	18.9	18.6	18.3	18.0	17.7
73	20.6	20.1	19.6	19.2	18.8	18.4	18.1	17.8	17.5	17.2
74	20.2	19.7	19.3	18.8	18.4	18.0	17.6	17.3	17.0	16.7
75	19.9	19.4	18.9	18.4	18.0	17.6	17.2	16.8	16.5	16.2
76	19.6	19.1	18.6	18.1	17.6	17.2	16.8	16.4	16.0	15.7
77	19.4	18.8	18.3	17.8	17.3	16.8	16.4	16.0	15.6	15.3
78	19.1	18.5	18.0	17.5	17.0	16.5	16.0	15.6	15.2	14.9
79	18.9	18.3	17.7	17.2	16.7	16.2	15.7	15.3	14.9	14.5
80	18.7	18.1	17.5	16.9	16.4	15.9	15.4	15.0	14.5	14.1
81	18.5	17.9	17.3	16.7	16.2	15.6	15.1	14.7	14.2	13.8
82	18.3	17.7	17.1	16.5	15.9	15.4	14.9	14.4	13.9	13.5
83	18.2	17.5	16.9	16.3	15.7	15.2	14.7	14.2	13.7	13.2
84	18.0	17.4	16.7	16.1	15.5	15.0	14.4	13.9	13.4	13.0
85	17.9	17.3	16.6	16.0	15.4	14.8	14.3	13.7	13.2	12.8
86	17.8	17.1	16.5	15.8	15.2	14.6	14.1	13.5	13.0	12.5
87	17.7	17.0	16.4	15.7	15.1	14.5	13.9	13.4	12.9	12.4
88	17.6	16.9	16.3	15.6	15.0	14.4	13.8	13.2	12.7	12.2
89	17.6	16.9	16.2	15.5	14.9	14.3	13.7	13.1	12.6	12.0
90	17.5	16.8	16.1	15.4	14.8	14.2	13.6	13.0	12.4	11.9
91	17.4	16.7	16.0	15.4	14.7	14.1	13.5	12.9	12.3	11.8
92	17.4	16.7	16.0	15.3	14.6	14.0	13.4	12.8	12.2	11.7
93	17.3	16.6	15.9	15.2	14.6	13.9	13.3	12.7	12.1	11.6
94	17.3	16.6	15.9	15.2	14.5	13.9	13.2	12.6	12.0	11.5
95	17.3	16.5	15.8	15.1	14.5	13.8	13.2	12.6	12.0	11.4
96	17.2	16.5	15.8	15.1	14.4	13.8	13.1	12.5	11.9	11.3
97	17.2	16.5	15.8	15.1	14.4	13.7	13.1	12.5	11.9	11.3
98	17.2	16.4	15.7	15.0	14.3	13.7	13.0	12.4	11.8	11.2
99	17.2	16.4	15.7	15.0	14.3	13.6	13.0	12.4	11.8	11.2

AGES	70	71	72	73	74	75	76	77	78	79
Table II: Joint Life and Last Survivor Expectancy (continued)										
100	17.1	16.4	15.7	15.0	14.3	13.6	12.9	12.3	11.7	11.1
101	17.1	16.4	15.6	14.9	14.2	13.6	12.9	12.3	11.7	11.1
102	17.1	16.4	15.6	14.9	14.2	13.5	12.9	12.2	11.6	11.0
103	17.1	16.3	15.6	14.9	14.2	13.5	12.9	12.2	11.6	11.0
104	17.1	16.3	15.6	14.9	14.2	13.5	12.8	12.2	11.6	11.0
105	17.1	16.3	15.6	14.9	14.2	13.5	12.8	12.2	11.5	10.9
106	17.1	16.3	15.6	14.8	14.1	13.5	12.8	12.2	11.5	10.9
107	17.0	16.3	15.6	14.8	14.1	13.4	12.8	12.1	11.5	10.9
108	17.0	16.3	15.5	14.8	14.1	13.4	12.8	12.1	11.5	10.9
109	17.0	16.3	15.5	14.8	14.1	13.4	12.8	12.1	11.5	10.9
110	17.0	16.3	15.5	14.8	14.1	13.4	12.7	12.1	11.5	10.9
111	17.0	16.3	15.5	14.8	14.1	13.4	12.7	12.1	11.5	10.8
112	17.0	16.3	15.5	14.8	14.1	13.4	12.7	12.1	11.5	10.8
113	17.0	16.3	15.5	14.8	14.1	13.4	12.7	12.1	11.4	10.8
114	17.0	16.3	15.5	14.8	14.1	13.4	12.7	12.1	11.4	10.8
115+	17.0	16.3	15.5	14.8	14.1	13.4	12.7	12.1	11.4	10.8

Table II: Joint Life and Last Survivor Expectancy (continued)

AGES	80	81	82	83	84	85	86	87	88	89
80	13.8	13.4	13.1	12.8	12.6	12.3	12.1	11.9	11.7	11.5
81	13.4	13.1	12.7	12.4	12.2	11.9	11.7	11.4	11.3	11.1
82	13.1	12.7	12.4	12.1	11.8	11.5	11.3	11.0	10.8	10.6
83	12.8	12.4	12.1	11.7	11.4	11.1	10.9	10.6	10.4	10.2
84	12.6	12.2	11.8	11.4	11.1	10.8	10.5	10.3	10.1	9.9
85	12.3	11.9	11.5	11.1	10.8	10.5	10.2	9.9	9.7	9.5
86	12.1	11.7	11.3	10.9	10.5	10.2	9.9	9.6	9.4	9.2
87	11.9	11.4	11.0	10.6	10.3	9.9	9.6	9.4	9.1	8.9
88	11.7	11.3	10.8	10.4	10.1	9.7	9.4	9.1	8.8	8.6
89	11.5	11.1	10.6	10.2	9.9	9.5	9.2	8.9	8.6	8.3
90	11.4	10.9	10.5	10.1	9.7	9.3	9.0	8.6	8.3	8.1
91	11.3	10.8	10.3	9.9	9.5	9.1	8.8	8.4	8.1	7.9
92	11.2	10.7	10.2	9.8	9.3	9.0	8.6	8.3	8.0	7.7
93	11.1	10.6	10.1	9.6	9.2	8.8	8.5	8.1	7.8	7.5
94	11.0	10.5	10.0	9.5	9.1	8.7	8.3	8.0	7.6	7.3
95	10.9	10.4	9.9	9.4	9.0	8.6	8.2	7.8	7.5	7.2
96	10.8	10.3	9.8	9.3	8.9	8.5	8.1	7.7	7.4	7.1
97	10.7	10.2	9.7	9.2	8.8	8.4	8.0	7.6	7.3	6.9
98	10.7	10.1	9.6	9.2	8.7	8.3	7.9	7.5	7.1	6.8
99	10.6	10.1	9.6	9.1	8.6	8.2	7.8	7.4	7.0	6.7
100	10.6	10.0	9.5	9.0	8.5	8.1	7.7	7.3	6.9	6.6
101	10.5	10.0	9.4	9.0	8.5	8.0	7.6	7.2	6.9	6.5
102	10.5	9.9	9.4	8.9	8.4	8.0	7.5	7.1	6.8	6.4
103	10.4	9.9	9.4	8.8	8.4	7.9	7.5	7.1	6.7	6.3
104	10.4	9.8	9.3	8.8	8.3	7.9	7.4	7.0	6.6	6.3
105	10.4	9.8	9.3	8.8	8.3	7.8	7.4	7.0	6.6	6.2
106	10.3	9.8	9.2	8.7	8.2	7.8	7.3	6.9	6.5	6.2
107	10.3	9.8	9.2	8.7	8.2	7.7	7.3	6.9	6.5	6.1
108	10.3	9.7	9.2	8.7	8.2	7.7	7.3	6.8	6.4	6.1
109	10.3	9.7	9.2	8.7	8.2	7.7	7.2	6.8	6.4	6.0

AGES	80	81	82	83	84	85	86	87	88	89
110	10.3	9.7	9.2	8.6	8.1	7.7	7.2	6.8	6.4	6.0
111	10.3	9.7	9.1	8.6	8.1	7.6	7.2	6.8	6.3	6.0
112	10.2	9.7	9.1	8.6	8.1	7.6	7.2	6.7	6.3	5.9
113	10.2	9.7	9.1	8.6	8.1	7.6	7.2	6.7	6.3	5.9
114	10.2	9.7	9.1	8.6	8.1	7.6	7.1	6.7	6.3	5.9
115+	10.2	9.7	9.1	8.6	8.1	7.6	7.1	6.7	6.3	5.9

Table II: Joint Life and Last Survivor Expectancy (continued)

AGES	90	91	92	93	94	95	96	97	98	99
90	7.8	7.6	7.4	7.2	7.1	6.9	6.8	6.6	6.5	6.4
91	7.6	7.4	7.2	7.0	6.8	6.7	6.5	6.4	6.3	6.1
92	7.4	7.2	7.0	6.8	6.6	6.4	6.3	6.1	6.0	5.9
93	7.2	7.0	6.8	6.6	6.4	6.2	6.1	5.9	5.8	5.6
94	7.1	6.8	6.6	6.4	6.2	6.0	5.9	5.7	5.6	5.4
95	6.9	6.7	6.4	6.2	6.0	5.8	5.7	5.5	5.4	5.2
96	6.8	6.5	6.3	6.1	5.9	5.7	5.5	5.3	5.2	5.0
97	6.6	6.4	6.1	5.9	5.7	5.5	5.3	5.2	5.0	4.9
98	6.5	6.3	6.0	5.8	5.6	5.4	5.2	5.0	4.8	4.7
99	6.4	6.1	5.9	5.6	5.4	5.2	5.0	4.9	4.7	4.5
100	6.3	6.0	5.8	5.5	5.3	5.1	4.9	4.7	4.5	4.4
101	6.2	5.9	5.6	5.4	5.2	5.0	4.8	4.6	4.4	4.2
102	6.1	5.8	5.5	5.3	5.1	4.8	4.6	4.4	4.3	4.1
103	6.0	5.7	5.4	5.2	5.0	4.7	4.5	4.3	4.1	4.0
104	5.9	5.6	5.4	5.1	4.9	4.6	4.4	4.2	4.0	3.8
105	5.9	5.6	5.3	5.0	4.8	4.5	4.3	4.1	3.9	3.7
106	5.8	5.5	5.2	4.9	4.7	4.5	4.2	4.0	3.8	3.6
107	5.8	5.4	5.1	4.9	4.6	4.4	4.2	3.9	3.7	3.5
108	5.7	5.4	5.1	4.8	4.6	4.3	4.1	3.9	3.7	3.5
109	5.7	5.3	5.0	4.8	4.5	4.3	4.0	3.8	3.6	3.4
110	5.6	5.3	5.0	4.7	4.5	4.2	4.0	3.8	3.5	3.3
111	5.6	5.3	5.0	4.7	4.4	4.2	3.9	3.7	3.5	3.3
112	5.6	5.3	4.9	4.7	4.4	4.1	3.9	3.7	3.5	3.2
113	5.6	5.2	4.9	4.6	4.4	4.1	3.9	3.6	3.4	3.2
114	5.6	5.2	4.9	4.6	4.3	4.1	3.9	3.6	3.4	3.2
115+	5.5	5.2	4.9	4.6	4.3	4.1	3.8	3.6	3.4	3.1

Table II: Joint Life and Last Survivor Expectancy (continued)

Table II: Joint Life and Last Survivor Expectancy (continued)									
AGES	**100**	**101**	**102**	**103**	**104**	**105**	**106**	**107**	**108**	**109**
100	4.2	4.1	3.9	3.8	3.7	3.5	3.4	3.3	3.3	3.2
101	4.1	3.9	3.7	3.6	3.5	3.4	3.2	3.1	3.1	3.0
102	3.9	3.7	3.6	3.4	3.3	3.2	3.1	3.0	2.9	2.8
103	3.8	3.6	3.4	3.3	3.2	3.0	2.9	2.8	2.7	2.6
104	3.7	3.5	3.3	3.2	3.0	2.9	2.7	2.6	2.5	2.4
105	3.5	3.4	3.2	3.0	2.9	2.7	2.6	2.5	2.4	2.3
106	3.4	3.2	3.1	2.9	2.7	2.6	2.4	2.3	2.2	2.1
107	3.3	3.1	3.0	2.8	2.6	2.5	2.3	2.2	2.1	2.0
108	3.3	3.1	2.9	2.7	2.5	2.4	2.2	2.1	1.9	1.8
109	3.2	3.0	2.8	2.6	2.4	2.3	2.1	2.0	1.8	1.7
110	3.1	2.9	2.7	2.5	2.3	2.2	2.0	1.9	1.7	1.6
111	3.1	2.9	2.7	2.5	2.3	2.1	1.9	1.8	1.6	1.5
112	3.0	2.8	2.6	2.4	2.2	2.0	1.9	1.7	1.5	1.4
113	3.0	2.8	2.6	2.4	2.2	2.0	1.8	1.6	1.5	1.3
114	3.0	2.7	2.5	2.3	2.1	1.9	1.8	1.6	1.4	1.3
115+	2.9	2.7	2.5	2.3	2.1	1.9	1.7	1.5	1.4	1.2

Table II: Joint Life and Last Survivor Expectancy (continued)						
AGES	110	111	112	113	114	115+
110	1.5	1.4	1.3	1.2	1.1	1.1
111	1.4	1.2	1.1	1.1	1.0	1.0
112	1.3	1.1	1.0	1.0	1.0	1.0
113	1.2	1.1	1.0	1.0	1.0	1.0
114	1.1	1.0	1.0	1.0	1.0	1.0
115+	1.1	1.0	1.0	1.0	1.0	1.0

Table III: Uniform Lifetime Table					
Age	Applicable Divisor	Age	Applicable Divisor	Age	Applicable Divisor
70	27.4	86	14.1	101	5.9
71	26.5	87	13.4	102	5.5
72	25.6	88	12.7	103	5.2
73	24.7	89	12.0	104	4.9
74	23.8	90	11.4	105	4.5
75	22.9	91	10.8	106	4.2
76	22.0	92	10.2	107	3.9
77	21.2	93	9.6	108	3.7
78	20.3	94	9.1	109	3.4
79	19.5	95	8.6	110	3.1
80	18.7	96	8.1	111	2.9
81	17.9	97	7.6	112	2.6
82	17.1	98	7.1	113	2.4
83	16.3	99	6.7	114	2.1
84	15.5	100	6.3	115+	1.9
85	14.8				

Table IV: Survivor Benefit Limits			
Excess of Employee's Age Over Beneficiary's Age	**Applicable Percentage**	**Excess of Employee's Age Over Beneficiary's Age**	**Applicable Percentage**
10 years or less	100%	28	62%
11	96%	29	61%
12	93%	30	60%
13	90%	31	59%
14	87%	32	59%
15	84%	33	58%
16	82%	34	57%
17	79%	35	56%
18	77%	36	56%
19	75%	37	55%
20	73%	38	55%
21	72%	39	54%
22	70%	40	54%
23	68%	41	53%
24	67%	42	53%
25	66%	43	53%
26	64%	44 and greater	52%
27	63%		

Index

T

On Nolo.com you'll also find:

Books & Software

Nolo publishes hundreds of great books and software programs for consumers and business owners. Order a copy, or download an ebook version instantly, at Nolo.com.

Online Forms

You can quickly and easily make a will or living trust, form an LLC or corporation, apply for a provisional patent, or make hundreds of other forms—online.

Free Legal Information

Thousands of articles answer common questions about everyday legal issues, including wills, bankruptcy, small business formation, divorce, patents, employment, and much more.

Plain-English Legal Dictionary

Stumped by jargon? Look it up in America's most up-to-date source for definitions of legal terms, free at Nolo.com.

Lawyer Directory

Nolo's consumer-friendly lawyer directory provides in-depth profiles of lawyers all over America. You'll find information you need to choose the right lawyer.

RET14